T0304005

Government, SMEs and Entrepreneurship Development

Government, SMEs and Entrepreneurship Development

Policy, Practice and Challenges

Edited by
ROBERT A. BLACKBURN
and
MICHAEL T. SCHAPER

Routledge
Taylor & Francis Group

LONDON AND NEW YORK

First published 2012 by Gower Publishing

2 Park Square, Milton Park, Abingdon, Oxon OX14 4RN
711 Third Avenue, New York, NY 10017, USA

Routledge is an imprint of the Taylor & Francis Group, an informa business

First issued in paperback 2016

Gower Applied Business Research
Our programme provides leaders, practitioners, scholars and researchers with thought provoking, cutting edge books that combine conceptual insights, interdisciplinary rigour and practical relevance in key areas of business and management.

British Library Cataloguing in Publication Data
 Government, SMEs and entrepreneurship development : policy,

   practice and challenges.
   1. Small business--Growth. 2. Small business--Government
   policy. 3. New business enterprises--Government policy.
   4. Industrial promotion.
   I. Blackburn, Robert A., 1957- II. Schaper, Michael, professor.
   354.2'799-dc23

   ISBN 978-1-4094-3035-3 (hbk)
   ISBN 978-1-138-24825-0 (pbk)

Library of Congress Cataloging-in-Publication Data
Government, SMEs and entrepreneurship development : policy, practice and challenges / [edited] by Robert A. Blackburn and Michael T. Schaper.
     p. cm.
  Includes bibliographical references and index.
  ISBN 978-1-4094-3035-3 (hbk.)
  1. Small business--Government policy. 2.
Entrepreneurship--Government policy. I. Blackburn, Robert A., 1957- II.
Schaper, Michael, professor.
  HD2341.G59 2012
  338.6'42--dc23
                                                                  2012019044

Contents

List of Figures

List of Tables

Acknowledgements

This book is the result of the support, ideas and contribution of a number of people. We would like to thank our colleagues and friends who have all helped in the process of producing this volume, and to especially acknowledge the contribution of all the authors. Over the course of several months they have worked with us to develop their ideas, have responded to our suggestions for editorial changes with good grace and patience, and have produced excellent chapters that form the backbone of the book.

A heartfelt thanks also goes to our partners, Helen Young and Nadine White for their patience, assistance and occasional editorial suggestion.

We also wish to thank Gower, and particularly Martin West, for the commissioning of the book and providing advice and support during its production.

Finally, we would like to thank Valerie Thorne for her invaluable administrative support and advice, which has been crucial in the production of the book.

Robert A Blackburn, Kingston-upon-Thames, UK
Michael T Schaper, Canberra, Australia

About the Editors

Robert A Blackburn is a Professor and Director of Research, Faculty of Business and Law; and Director of the Small Business Research Centre, Kingston University in the UK. He is also Editor-in-Chief of the *International Small Business Journal*. He is interested in sociological and economic analyses of entrepreneurship and small firms. His publications include *Small Business and Entrepreneurship, 5 Volume Major Work* (Sage, 2008) (ed. with C. Brush); *Researching the Small Enterprise* (Sage, 2001) (with co-author J. Curran); and *Intellectual Property and Innovation Management in Small Firms* (ed. Routledge, 2003). He has undertaken research for private and public sector organisations including governments across the world, the OECD and the European Commission. He was appointed as an 'expert' for the European Commission's *Economic and Social Committee on the Entrepreneurship Green Paper* and *Action Plan*. His latest research involves understanding the role of community organisations in developing small firms, and the role of trust in SMEs' external relations. He has recently been appointed as Special Advisor to the House of Lords SME Export Committee. In 2011, Robert received the Queen's Award for Enterprise Promotion. r.blackburn@kingston.ac.uk

Michael T Schaper is currently the deputy chairman (small business) of the Australian Competition & Consumer Commission, and is also an Adjunct Professor with Curtin Business School, Curtin University, in Western Australia. Michael has held a number of positions within government, including roles as inaugural Small Business Commissioner for the Australian Capital Territory and chairman of the Small and Micro-Business Advisory Council of the ACT, as well as having served as a policy adviser to state and federal Ministers. Michael is a past president of the Small Enterprise Association of Australia and New Zealand, and a previous director of the International Council for Small Business, as well as having held professorial appointments at a number of Australian universities. michael.schaper@gmail.com

About the Contributors

Norin Arshed is a Researcher in the Marketing Department at the University of Strathclyde. Prior to this she completed her PhD at the Hunter Centre for Entrepreneurship also at the University of Strathclyde. She has professional experience both in the public and private sectors as well as an understanding of the SME sector. Her research interest lies in the field of enterprise policy, with institutional theory underpinning her research. Her thesis concentrates on how enterprise policy is formulated in the UK. It investigates the role and contribution from those closely linked to the formulation process, also examining how enterprise policy is implemented and how enterprise policy is perceived and experienced by its users. norin.arshed@strath.ac.uk

Robert J Bennett is Emeritus Professor of Geography at the University of Cambridge and a Senior Associate at the Judge Business School. He has previously held positions at UCL, LSE and Berkeley. Author of many books and research papers, he is widely known for his research on small firms, external business advice and their interrelation with the agents of local economic development – Business Links, Chambers of Commerce and local government. He has been an advisor to various organisations in the public and private sectors, including Parliamentary Committees. rjb7@cam.ac.uk

Mahamadou Biga-Diambeidou is Associate Professor of Entrepreneurship at ICN Business School in France. He is also Visiting Research Fellow at Australian Centre for Entrepreneurship Research, QUT Business School, Australia, and Associate Researcher at the Center for Research in Entrepreneurial Change and Innovative Strategies, Louvain School of Management at Université catholique de Louvain in Belgium, where he also took his PhD. His main research focuses on the early growth and development of new ventures. His work has evoked interest from organisations such as the OECD Working Party on Entrepreneurship Indicators. His work has been published in book, book chapters and journals such as *Journal of Small Business and Enterprise Development*, *International Journal of Service Technology and Management*, *Canadian Journal of Regional Sciences*, *Gestion 2000*. mahamadou.biga@icn-groupe.fr

Richard Blundel is a Senior Lecturer in Enterprise Development at the Open University Business School, UK. He edits the *Quarterly Survey of Small Business in Britain* and is co-author (with Nigel Lockett) of *Exploring Entrepreneurship: Practices and Perspectives* (Oxford University Press, 2011). He is also a board member of the Institute of Small Business and Entrepreneurship (ISBE), chair of ISBE's 'Social, Environmental and Ethical Enterprise' conference track, and a deputy chair of the Social and Sustainable Enterprise Network. His research interests are in the fields of organisation studies and entrepreneurship, with a focus on growth processes, innovation, sustainability and artisanal firms. He has published in journals such as *Entrepreneurship & Regional Development, Enterprise & Society, Journal of Small Business Management, and Industry & Innovation.* richard.blundel@open.ac.uk

Ron Botham was previously Professor of Entrepreneurship and Regional Development at the University of Glasgow, Scotland from 1999 to 2009. Before joining the university, he spent 15 years in a variety of research and strategy posts in the Scottish Development Agency/Scottish Enterprise with responsibility for, inter alia, industrial clusters, commercialising science, and technology and entrepreneurship. He is currently an independent consultant and visiting professor at the University of Strathclyde's Hunter Centre for Entrepreneurship. He has a BSc and MSc from the London School of Economics and a PhD from Reading University. rbotham@rbotham.karoo.co.uk

Simon Bridge has been involved in formulating, delivering and/or assessing enterprise policy for over 25 years, most recently as an enterprise and economic development consultant and before that as the Enterprise Director of a small business agency. He is also now a Visiting Professor at the University of Ulster. Much of his varied experience and learning is reflected in his books: *Rethinking Enterprise Policy: Can Failure Trigger New Understanding?* (Palgrave Macmillan, 2010) and (co-written with Ken O'Neill and others) *Understanding Enterprise, Entrepreneurship and Small Business* (Palgrave Macmillan, 2009) and *Understanding the Social Economy and the Third Sector* (Palgrave Macmillan, 2009). simonbridge@btconnect.com

Ross Brown is a Senior Researcher at Scottish Enterprise. His main research interests lie in the areas of entrepreneurship, innovation, business internationalisation and regional development. His current research interests are concerned with high growth entrepreneurship, the growth of new technology-based firms, MNE subsidiary development and public policy. A key aspect of his work is to explore the effects of entrepreneurship on regional development.

He has published extensively in these areas in journals such as *Regional Studies*, *European Business Review*, *European Planning Studies*, *Small Business Economics*, *Local Economy* and in various international business books. He has also acted as an expert adviser in these areas to the OECD, European Commission and government agencies in Europe and North America. Ross.Brown@scotent.co.uk

Jenny Buchan is a Senior Lecturer in business law at the Australian School of Business, University of New South Wales, Sydney, Australia. Prior to becoming an academic in 2002 she worked for 19 years as a commercial lawyer in private practice in New Zealand and Australia. Jenny co-chaired the International Society of Franchising's annual conference in Sydney in 2010, and is a member of the Australian Competition and Consumer Commission's Franchising Consultative Committee. Jenny teaches franchise law and contract law. Her research interests are franchise law and its intersection with consumer protection and insolvency law. jm.buchan@unsw.edu.au

Sara Carter OBE is Professor and Head of Department for the Hunter Centre for Entrepreneurship and Associate Dean, Strathclyde Business School in Scotland, as well as a Visiting Professor at Nordland Research Institute, Norway. She has undertaken many studies of entrepreneurship and the small business sector, funded by research councils and national and international development agencies. Sara was a member of the UK Government Women's Enterprise Task Force from 2007–2009, and an Erskine Visiting Fellow at the University of Canterbury, in Christchurch, New Zealand in 2010. sara.carter@strath.ac.uk

Paul Cowie is currently a PhD Student in the School of Architecture, Planning and Landscape at Newcastle University in the UK. The subject of his research is the impact of in-migrant networks on the rural economy, particularly in relation to the knowledge economy. As part of the PhD Paul undertook an internship with the UK's Department for Business, Innovation and Skills. The purpose of the internship was to investigate the possibility of developing a real-time evaluation framework which could be used to continuously evaluate BIS's policy programmes. Prior to embarking on the PhD, Paul spent 12 years working as a commercial development lawyer, mainly dealing with large regeneration projects acting on behalf of local government and regional development agencies. p.j.cowie@newcastle.ac.uk

Juan S Federico is a Researcher and Lecturer in the Institute of Industry at the Universidad Nacional de General Sarmiento, Argentina. He is also a member of the Entrepreneurial Development Program (PRODEM) at the same university. Juan is a PhD candidate at the Department of Business Economics of the Universtat Autonoma de Barcelona, Spain. His main research interests are new venture growth, strategy, entrepreneurial policies and international entrepreneurship. jfederic@ungs.edu.ar

Thomas Fell is a Research Assistant for Strategic Economic Solutions, a private economic consultancy based in Canberra, Australia; his work includes survey design and analysis, undertaking interviews and consultations, and preparing local and regional economic overviews. He has an Honours degree in natural resource management from the University of New England (Australia) and has worked in the areas of environmental policy and human resources with the Australian Government Department of Agriculture, Fisheries and Forestry. He has also completed a Bachelor of Music at the Australian National University. twjfell@gmail.com

Charles Harvie is presently an Associate Professor and Head of the School of Economics at the University of Wollongong, Australia. In addition to this, he is also the Director of his School's Centre for Small Business and Regional Research which he established in 2000. Charles has over 120 publications in the form of journal articles, books and book chapters. His research interests are in entrepreneurialism, SMEs and economic growth, measuring SME technical efficiency, energy and economic development and economic transition in China and Vietnam. He has published his research in journals such as *Applied Economics*, *Australian Economic Papers*, *Energy Economics*, *International Journal of Social Economics* and the *Journal of Policy Modelling*. He has also authored and edited books on SMEs in East Asia and on the Chinese, Korean and Vietnamese economies. charvie@uow.edu.au

Kim Houghton established his firm Strategic Economic Solutions in 1997 to help Australian regional communities understand and prosper from economic changes happening around them. Under Kim's leadership the company has undertaken many practical and research projects on issues affecting regional economic growth. The company has also created innovative programmes to help small businesses directly – including the Springboard Business Development programme. Kim previously worked at the Australian National University in Pacific economic relations, and in the Australian Government's Department of the Prime Minister and Cabinet. Kim has a PhD in economics from the Australian National University and a BSc from the University of Tasmania. kim@economicsolutions.com.au

Tanya Jurado has been closely involved in research into SMEs through her work at the New Zealand Centre for SME Research at Massey University. She has collaborated on a number of SME-related research projects including management capability, management development, SME internationalisation and business sustainability. Tanya was also part of the research team that analysed high-growth SMEs for the OECD's Working Party on SMEs and Entrepreneurship, and has published her research on SMEs in a number of journals and conference proceedings. At present Tanya lives in Brussels where she is currently completing her PhD (through Massey University) on the evolution of New Zealand SME policy. t.r.Jurado@massey.ac.nz

Hugo D Kantis is Professor in the Institute of Industry at the Universidad Nacional de General Sarmiento, Argentina. He is also Director of the Master's Course in Industrial Economics and Development and the Entrepreneurial Development Program (PRODEM) at the same university. Hugo is also a consultant for national and international organisms. His main research interests are entrepreneurship, new venture growth, entrepreneurial policies, SMEs and strategy. He has authored several books and articles focused on entrepreneurship in Latin America and is a member of the editorial board of journals such as *Venture Capital*, the *International Small Business Journal* and *Journal of Small Business Management*. hkantis@fibertel.com.ar

Phillip Kemp is the Executive Director of Business Foundations, Western Australia's largest non-government business development organisation and business incubator organisation; he is also the chairman of Australia's peak body for business incubation, Business Innovation and Incubation Australia. Phillip has qualifications in small business facilitation, company management and agricultural science, and is recognised as an industry expert in the field of small business development. He has previously published papers on SME and micro-enterprise development issues, with particular reference to international best practice in business incubation operation and the provision of SME and micro-enterprise business support services. phil@businessfoundationsinc.com.au

Rita Klapper has more than a decade's practical experience of entrepreneurship and business networks, holding research and teaching posts on several continents. These have included roles as Associate Professor for Strategy & Entrepreneurship at Rouen Business School, France, and more recently as Visiting Senior Research Fellow at Haaga Helia, University of Applied Sciences in Helsinki and Visiting Professor at both the Helsinki School of Economics and the Nagoya University of Business & Commerce in Japan. Her PhD focused on the role of social capital in French entrepreneurial networks at the pre-organisation stage. Rita's research interests now focus on all aspects of entrepreneurship, in particular entrepreneurial networks, social capital, international entrepreneurship and innovative pedagogy for entrepreneurship. Rita has worked with companies such as Mitsubishi Electric (Germany), Panasonic (Japan), Centaur (France) and Nutriset (France). rkl@rouenbs.fr

Arto Henrikki Lahti has written ten textbooks and about 50 research reports/articles, with a major focus on the Schumpeterian dynamics of the global economy. Arto has conducted strategy analyses for more than 300 firms across the EU countries and is a board member in 30 SMEs. He was previously also chairman of the Finnish Association for Business Administration in the 1990s. He was a presidential candidate for Finland in 2006. arto.lahti@aalto.fi

Jonathan G Lashley is a Fellow at the Sir Arthur Lewis Institute of Social and Economic Studies (SALISES) of the University of the West Indies, Cave Hill Campus, Barbados. His research interests relate directly to social and economic development policy in the Caribbean, and he has published academic studies in the areas of enterprise development, entrepreneurship and microfinance. His research is focused on policy formulation in a context that addresses the particular idiosyncrasies of the small states of the Caribbean, especially as they approach 50 years of independence. jonathan.lashley@cavehill.uwi.edu

Viet Le is currently a lecturer in Entrepreneurship in the Faculty of Business and Enterprise, Swinburne University of Technology, Melbourne, Australia. His research interests include entrepreneurship development, SMEs, enterprise performance in efficiency and productivity, small firm exports and innovation. He has lectured on new venture development and management, business innovation, and the economics of small and medium-sized enterprises. clle@swin.edu.au

Fergus Lyon is Professor of Enterprise and Organisations in the Centre for Enterprise and Economic Development Research at Middlesex University, UK. His research interests include social enterprise, trust and co-operation between enterprises, enterprise behaviour in public services and business support. He is leading a five-year programme of research on social enterprise as part of the Third Sector Research Centre, a project funded by the Economic and Social Research Council and the UK Office of Civil Society. Previously he has carried out research in Ghana, Nigeria, India, Pakistan and Nepal. He is also a founder and director of a social enterprise preschool. f.lyon@mdx.ac.uk

Colin Mason is currently Professor of Entrepreneurship in the Hunter Centre for Entrepreneurship at the University of Strathclyde in Glasgow, Scotland. In autumn 2012 he will be taking up a new post at the University of Glasgow. His research focuses on entrepreneurship and regional development with a particular emphasis on access to finance. Colin has written extensively on business angel investing and has been closely involved with government and private sector initiatives to promote the business angel market, both in the UK and elsewhere. He is the founding editor of the journal *Venture Capital: An International Journal of Entrepreneurial Finance* (published by Taylor and Francis Ltd) and Consulting Editor of the *International Small Business Journal* (Sage). colin.mason@strath.ac.uk

Claire Massey is Head of the School of Management at Massey University (New Zealand) and also Professor of Enterprise Development. She was formerly Director of the New Zealand Centre for SME Research. Claire has published extensively on the topic of SMEs, with a particular interest in government policy. Claire is a past president of the Small Enterprise Association of Australia and New Zealand and former senior vice-president of the International Council for Small Business. c.l.massey@massey.ac.nz

Andrew Maville has front-line experience as a pre-start business adviser with TEDCO, a Local Enterprise Agency (LEA) in the north east of England. He previously worked for another LEA, Project North East, and has written on small business issues as a researcher, author and editor for the publisher Cobweb Information Ltd. His interest in practical economic development interventions, underpinned by an MA in Regional Development, comes from having worked within small businesses and their support organisations since 1988. It particularly stems from researching 20 years of interventions in SMEs for a DTI publication whilst working at Durham University Business School in 1992. He writes here in a personal capacity. a.maville@dunelm.org.uk

Tui McKeown is a senior lecturer in the Department of Management within the Faculty of Business and Economics at Monash University, Australia.Her research focuses on an active examination of the changing world of self-employment in general, and on independent contracting in particular. A key philosophy informing this research is the desire to explore, debate and share ideas that develop a broader understanding of what constitutes work and how work 'fits' with the changing social, political and legal contexts of the twenty-first century. Tui.McKeown@monash.edu

Adrian Monaghan is a Lecturer in Strategy and Corporate Social Responsibility and a member of the Centre for Enterprise and Innovation Research at the University of Salford, UK. His research focuses on the contribution that the grassroots can make to transitions towards sustainability. This interest follows on from his doctoral research, which examined successive transitions in the UK body disposal system. The transitions framework was used to interpret current challenges faced in the UK and to develop policy recommendations to support future sustainable innovations in the system. This research coincided with his previous role as manager of the ESRC Sustainable Technologies Programme, whose aim was to promote social science insights into the processes and practices of innovation for sustainability. a.monaghan@salford.ac.uk

Ken O'Neill is Professor Emeritus at the University of Ulster, a former President of the International Council for Small Business, on the Steering Committee of the International Small Business Congress, and a former President of the UK's Institute for Small Business and Entrepreneurship. For much of his career Ken has been developing and delivering programmes for SME owners, managers and advisers. In 2005, he became the first person to receive The Queen's Award for Enterprise Promotion – Lifetime Achievement Award. His publications (co-written with Simon Bridge and others) include *Understanding Enterprise, Entrepreneurship and Small Business* (Palgrave Macmillan, 2009) and *Understanding the Social Economy and the Third Sector* (Palgrave Macmillan, 2009). k.oneill1@ntlworld.com

Ken Phillips is co-founder and Executive Director of the Independent Contractors of Australia. Amongst his many activities, Ken has published extensively on independent contractor issues and directs research on related commercial and competition issues. His strongest interest is management issues and the development of internal and external relationship building for organisations. Within this framework he promotes the concept of 'markets in the firm'. Ken is known for approaching issues from outside normal perspectives and is frequently sought out for media comment. Ken was ICA's representative at the 2003 and 2006 International Labour Organisation debate on the 'scope of employment relationships.' The ILO outcomes formed the conceptual basis for Australia's *Independent Contractors Act*. He is also the author of *Independence and the Death of Employment.* kenmargp@net2000.com.au

Leandro Sepulveda is a Senior Researcher at the Centre for Enterprise and Economic Development Research at Middlesex University, UK. He has over 15 years experience in policy-oriented research, specialising in enterprise and economic development. His work in the UK has been commissioned by Treasury, the Department for Business, Innovation and Skills (BIS), the Office for Civil Society, and the Economic and Social Research Council (ESRC). He has also worked in Latin America as an external consultant for ECLAC-United Nations. Leandro has authored a number of reports and book chapters, and published journal articles in *Entrepreneurship & Regional Development*, *Environment and Planning A*, *Local Economy*, *Policy & Politics* and *Regional Studies*. L.Sepulveda@mdx.ac.uk

Christine Thomas is a Senior Research Fellow in the Faculty of Mathematics, Computing and Technology at the Open University, UK and chair of the Integrated Waste Systems research group. Her research is on policy and social aspects of sustainable waste and resource management with a focus on understanding and influencing consumer and organisational pro-environmental behaviours, particularly in waste avoidance and recycling, and often working closely with a wide range of stakeholders including practitioners in the public and community sectors. c.i.thomas@open.ac.uk

Paul Toulson is an Associate Professor of HRM in the College of Business at Massey University, New Zealand. He has held various academic and professional appointments, is a Life Fellow of the Human Resources Institute of New Zealand (HRINZ), and an Associate Fellow of the New Zealand Psychological Society (NZPsS). Prior to his university career, Paul held roles in industrial organisational psychology and personnel management in the public sector. p.toulson@massey.ac.nz

David Tweed is Associate Pro Vice-Chancellor in the College of Business, at Massey University, Auckland, New Zealand. His research interests include entrepreneurship, small business and policy. He has 20 years experience delivering senior-level courses for Massey University's Executive MBA programme and has taught postgraduate courses in China. His PhD looked at business performance measurement and business failure using data collected from 1,500 small enterprises. d.m.tweed@massey.ac.nz

Paull Weber is a lecturer in entrepreneurship and small business in the School of Management, Curtin University in Western Australia. He is also deputy chair of Business Foundations, a business incubator and business advisory service provider, a member of the Australian Competition and Consumer Commission's Small Business Consultative Committee. His journal publications, book chapters and book authorship focus on entrepreneurship, small business and tourism. His current research activities and interests are understanding the prevalence and scope of scams committed against SMEs, benchmarking of SMEs, lifestyle entrepreneurship and mature-age entrepreneurship. p.weber@curtin.edu.au

Lei Ye is completing a PhD at Massey University, New Zealand, on SME policy in China. Her PhD was inspired through her master's research project, which examined SME family business in China. Her research interests include Chinese SMEs, Chinese culture and its impact on management, and the impact of government policies on SMEs in mainland China. l.ye1@massey.ac.nz

Foreword

by Mark Prisk MP

The British Government is striving to make the UK the best place in the world to start and grow a business. This will help us achieve balanced and sustainable economic recovery now, and prosperity in the future. The changing economic environment represents a real opportunity for business. Helping new firms to start and existing ones to grow will transform the economy, and create the thousands of jobs needed for the future. Start-ups and small firms are right at the very heart of the Government's economic plan. That is why the Government has already sought to get to grips with regulatory burdens and have scrapped planned regulations, with the aim of providing additional support to micro-businesses and start-ups. In addition, policy interventions have been implemented to provide additional finance to SMEs, to provide them with the ability to invest in new products and services, to drive innovation, ultimately fostering economic growth.

Entrepreneurs also need to access business information and advice quickly and easily. An improved website is providing online business help and information, tailored for each user. On the advice side, businesses repeatedly tell us that the guidance they value most comes from those with real, hands-on experience of enterprise. So we have launched a national mentoring network which allows those with a business, or thinking of starting a business, to receive useful, practical advice from people who have done it and succeeded before.

Robert Blackburn and Michael Schaper have brought together an important new volume of work that is significant in scope and depth. This book provides fascinating reading for those interested in designing, implementing and analysing policy programmes focused on entrepreneurship and small business development. The contributors share with us the differing contexts within which small business policy operates and the experiences and challenges faced by policymakers across the globe.

I am very pleased to endorse this book. It provides us with a great opportunity to learn from the experiences of others in this critical area of policy development, and help us implement successful policies for the future.

Mark Prisk MP
Minister of State for Business and Enterprise
Department for Business, Innovation and Skills, UK

Foreword

by Senator the Hon. Nick Sherry

Effective policy in the fields of small business development, enterprise and entrepreneurship development is no easy task.

Over the last 30 years, governments across the world have increasingly turned their mind to the issue. What can the many different levels of government – local, state/provincial, national, regional and global – do to encourage the growth of new enterprises, and the development of existing ones? What are the most effective programmes, and why? How do we ensure that public spending is allocated efficiently, and achieves meaningful results?

These are the questions that Robert Blackburn and Michael Schaper have turned to in this new book, and it gives me great pleasure to provide these introductory comments. They have compiled a set of chapters which will provide a great deal of useful background and reflection for future policymakers, as well as public servants and other delivery agents working in these fields. The many different authors who have contributed to the volume have provided a wide-ranging set of perspectives on the topic – from historical profiles of past experience in SME and enterprise development, to critical analysis of some of the key policy instruments being used today, and on to different means of measuring and evaluating our work in this area.

Along the way, they have produced a series of reflections that will assist everyone working in this area. They discuss what works and what doesn't, what programmes are genuinely new and innovative, and which ones have already been replicated in the past. Some of the readings will provide direct, practical advice to policy and programme delivery agents, whilst others throw up challenging questions that encourage us to keep working on improving the quality and capacity of our service mechanisms. Overall, they have produced a volume that will be a major contribution to our understanding and work in this area.

Senator the Hon. Nick Sherry
Minister for Small Business, Commonwealth of Australia 2010–2011
Parliament House, Canberra

1

Introduction

Robert A Blackburn and Michael T Schaper

Small and medium-sized enterprises (SMEs) are now recognised by researchers, analysts and policymakers as central to economies across the world, through their contributions to wealth creation, income generation, output and employment (OECD 2011). In particular, the underlying entrepreneurial activity behind SMEs has been increasingly recognised as a major driving force for innovation and economic growth in all economies (Audretsch and Thurik 2001). As a result the success, or otherwise, of SMEs and entrepreneurship has become increasingly important to governments and public administrators. Yet it also gives rise to a critical question: what policies can governments adopt to foster such activity? This, in turn, raises other questions: What can policymakers learn from the experiences of other countries? What interventions seem to work, and which are of more limited utility? And how does one assess the evidence on the effectiveness of such policies?

Hence the need for this book. It is designed to be a means of sharing the experiences of practitioners, academics and analysts from a number of regions in the world, in relation to the strategies that different governments, agencies and communities have adopted to support SMEs and entrepreneurship. The contributors have attempted to examine a number of issues, including the rationales for intervention, the policy tools and instruments used to promote SMEs, the outcomes of policy initiatives, and the methods of policy evaluation. The key audiences for the book include those in organisations seeking to formulate and deliver policies seeking to promote entrepreneurship and SMEs, together with students, researchers and analysts of policy development.

A book entitled *Government, SMEs and Entrepreneurship Development: Policy, Practice and Challenges* could be encyclopaedic in length but we do not purport to cover all the issues, or provide solutions to all of the challenges facing policymakers seeking to develop SMEs and entrepreneurship. There has been an increasing number of books attempting to pull together broad general strands of the debate on policy intervention for SMEs and entrepreneurship so far (see, for example, Audretsch, Grilo and Thurik 2009, Lundström and Stevenson 2005, Smallbone 2010, Welter and Smallbone 2011) and academic journals have also devoted special issues to the subject (for example, Minniti 2008, Robson, Wijbenga and Parker 2009). We do not simply wish to extend this academic library. Instead, the focus is very much on the issues, experiences and practical tools that can help policymakers, elected officials and administrators convert ideas into effective SME policy interventions.

The Problem of Policy Intervention and Rationale for the Book

A book on SMEs, entrepreneurship and public policy touches on a variety of underlying issues that require addressing before improvements to the arsenal of policy interventions can be suggested. For example, a key weakness in the literature is that the world-views of owner–managers are often overlooked (Gibb 2000) and this may lead to policy failure, or unforseen effects (Parker 2007). Most SME owner–managers and entrepreneurs strive for independence and are often antithetical to government interventions: '… at best, the attitude of many SME owners to government are somewhat ambivalent' (Bannock 2005: 63). Yet, given the significance and potential of SMEs to economic development (Audretsch et al. 2009, van Praag and Versloot 2007, Wennekers and Thurik 1999), most governments across the world have sought to cultivate, develop and support entrepreneurial activities through a growing panoply of interventions. How effective these interventions are is open to question (see, for example, Curran and Storey 2002, Norrman and Bager-Sjögren 2010, OECD 2008). In some cases, interventions miss the point through being poorly conceived, fail for lack of take-up, or are sometimes overly complex to administer (see Bennett 2008; Greene, Mole and Storey 2008). Indeed, it may be fair to argue that there are too many initiatives for SMEs and entrepreneurship and what we need is fewer interventions but ones that have much higher impact.

An analysis of public policy for SMEs and entrepreneurship reveals a number of common problems. First, there appears to be a *gap* between the research evidence and policy interventions. Even in regions of the world where policymakers and researchers have ostensibly well-developed links, such as in the UK (Blackburn and Smallbone 2008), critiques of policy abound. Thus, a central key criticism of SME and entrepreneurship policies is that of re-inventing the wheel, or a poor accumulation and sharing of knowledge and experience (for example, Dennis 2005: 227). Second, and linked to this, is a *lack of sufficient evidence* to make informed and reliable evaluations of interventions (for example, Storey 2008), thus making it difficult to develop policies based on systematic analyses of previous interventions. Third, there is often a *communication barrier* between those parties interested in policy: policymakers, academics and practitioners do not appear to effectively share their knowledge or experience with each other. Nor does the lacuna between policy and research appear to be closing. Whether or not the problem is a result of poorly focused academic research, as claimed by many policymakers, or the inability of policymakers to listen, as claimed by academics, is unclear. Shergold, for example, has bemoaned the gap between public policy needs and the ability of researchers and academics to meet those needs. He argues (2011: 3) that '…a wealth of valuable academic research is failing to find a practical use in public policy…' and that many academics could not clearly explain how policy works, its practical implications, or spell out what real-world reforms or changes their research has identified as being most useful. On the other hand, some researchers have pointed out the inability of policymakers to take radical actions based on research evidence (Curran and Storey 2002). Whatever the problems surrounding evaluating the precise effects of interventions, public policy for SMEs and entrepreneurship presents numerous challenges for government administrations around the world. By sharing experiences, better utilising the evidence base and developing appropriate evaluation tools, public agencies can hopefully formulate more effective interventions to enhance the performance of SMEs and entrepreneurship activities.

The analyses in the following chapters are designed to help those interested in policy development for SMEs and who want to learn from others. Some of the major SME policy development methods are examined: what they are, how they work, and the success (or otherwise) of such interventions in different nations. How do we ensure SME development is effective, and that it is evaluated in a meaningful way? Some practical implementation issues for government, SME policymakers, small business assistance organisations and researchers are also discussed. Whilst it would be wrong to suggest that policymakers have all the solutions to help stimulate an enterprise culture, or help business owners and their enterprises overcome all their challenges, we should not be complacent regarding this highly significant component of economy and society. Hence, policy development, design, implementation and evaluation should be subject to ongoing scrutiny and improvement and we regard this book as part of what should be an ongoing process.

Public Policy for SMEs and Entrepreneurship: The Historical Context

In seeking to raise our understanding of public policy for SMEs and entrepreneurship, it is important to set the chapters in this book within a broader historical context. This can help interested parties understand the ways in which policy has developed, its key ingredients and diverse interest groups, as well the ability of initiatives to achieve their objectives.

Public policy focusing on the promotion of SMEs and entrepreneurship is a relatively new field compared with wider fiscal, monetary, competition or industrial policies. But it nevertheless does have a substantial track record and is no longer in its infancy. Once regarded as peripheral to the economy, the significance of SMEs and entrepreneurship has now been promoted to one of key importance in the economic and community development strategies of many nations – and this has led to a substantial growth in the range of assistance programmes (for example, Audretsch 2011, Welter and Smallbone 2011, Stevenson and Lundström 2001) as well as the development of evaluation techniques (for example, Storey 2000). Such interventions are many and varied, and include the development of specific dedicated government agencies and/ or statutory authorities with a brief to promote SMEs and entrepreneurship; the establishment of business advisory services; the creation of statutory Small Business Commissioners and ombudsmen for the sector; targeted finance initiatives, soft loans, export finance and dedicated venture capital schemes; training and education schemes designed to foster enterprise, or to give prospective and new entrepreneurs sufficient business skills; particular programmes to support targeted groups in the population; and the development of an infrastructure conducive for SME and entrepreneurship promotion, such as broadband access and business incubators.

Although the experiences of policy development for SMEs and entrepreneurship vary across different economies, some general patterns can be identified. The evolution of public policy for SMEs and entrepreneurship usually demonstrates an initial period of arrested development followed by incremental additions with periodic boosts of activity. The early initiatives for small firms tended to focus on addressing financial issues: gap filling or helping firms overcome specific crises. In the UK the MacMillan report in the early 1930s identified a lack of sufficient long-term capital for SMEs – the so called 'MacMillan Gap' (MacMillan Report 1931); and in the USA the Small Business Administration, established in 1953, tended to focus on loan assistance to small firms (Hart 2003, Stevenson and Lundström 2001). Despite such developments, in the post-Second World War period small firms were increasingly regarded as an anachronism by academics and policymakers – part of a by-gone age – and industrial policy in some leading economies actively encouraged mergers and acquisitions in an attempt to stimulate growth and become major global players (Levicki 1984). Such polices were also often underpinned with analysis from academics who espoused the virtues of large organisations in terms of their economies of scale, technological superiority, systematic planning and marketing capabilities (for example, Galbraith 1967). Even Schumpeter (1976), often cited as a supporter of entrepreneurship, placed large corporations centre stage in the innovation process in his so-called Mark II theory of innovation.

By the early 1970s, however, new thinking and evidence was emerging regarding the contribution and significance of small firms to economies which provided a catalyst for public policy (see Stevenson and Lundström 2001: Ch 2). For example, the Bolton Report (Bolton 1971) in the UK noted a decline in the economic contribution of small firms after the Second World War and recommended the need for a dedicated small firm advisory service, due to market failures in advice and support provision. Many analysts identify this as the starting point for small business policy in the UK. Similarly, in Australia the federal government commissioned the Wiltshire Inquiry (1971) which led to the first attempts to establish advisory services, skills training and financial support for small firms. In addition to this increased awareness amongst politicians of the role of small firms in their economies, academics were also now beginning to emphasise their significance. The report by Birch (1979), which identified the employment contribution of small firms in the USA, provided a further boost to those designing the policies and institutions to promote SMEs worldwide. Public policy for SMEs thrived during the latter part of the twentieth century throughout the developed economies, and much of this development was based on the combination of a growing research base and a political will amongst governments seeking to promote entrepreneurship and small firms in their economies.

This book has a dual focus on both small firms and entrepreneurship. Although SME policy initially focused on addressing supply side gaps, or market failures (such as in the provision of advice, finance, premises and training for small firms), with time this has evolved into the promotion of entrepreneurship through a wider range of policy areas. The term 'entrepreneurship' has also become increasingly used in political discourse and policy initiatives. This is not just a matter of fashion or rhetoric, but most probably a reflection of the increased recognition of entrepreneurs and enterprising behaviour to every economy and society. In other words, the new forms of entrepreneurship policies are not merely modernising small business policies. Instead, they are attempts to embed policies seeking to affect levels of entrepreneurship in the economy throughout all policy areas, rather than just focusing on small business-specific initiatives (Audretsch and Thurik 2001). This is one of the reasons for the broad title for this book, spanning both SME development and entrepreneurship.

In recent years, there have also been a number of overt attempts to bridge the academic-policy divide mentioned earlier. Most of the major entrepreneurship and SME conferences now have a policy track, illustrating an increased level of awareness in this topic amongst the research community. The International Council for Small Business, for example, now holds an annual 'public policy day' as part of its world conference. Similarly, the annual conferences of the UK's Institute for Small Business and Entrepreneurship, the European-based Research in Entrepreneurship and the US Association for Small Business and Entrepreneurship all hold policy roundtables and paper tracks on public policy at their annual conferences.

Structure of the Book and Main Themes of the Chapters

This book is divided into three main sections with 19 main chapters. The chapters are a result of a selection process from over 30 abstracts and were extensively reviewed by the editors. Each chapter is written by experts in their field and draw upon primary and secondary evidence from a number of countries, providing a breadth and depth of experience on issues surrounding policy development.

In Part One, we present eight chapters that demonstrate the experience of policy development in different countries. These countries span the Northern and Southern Hemispheres, developing and developed economies, and those that have experienced free market capitalism as well as formerly planned economies. In Part Two, the practical tools to foster development are examined. This section contains seven chapters showing a breadth of experiences and mechanisms to promote small firms and entrepreneurship, ranging from business incubators through to social enterprise support policies. Finally, Part Three focuses on the perennial challenge of assessment and evaluation of policies and programmes. It examines the logical link between programme goals and outcomes, explores some of the mechanisms used to perform such assessments, and discusses the challenges that evaluators face in their work.

What overall picture can be drawn of SME and entrepreneurship policy and what lessons can be learnt in relation to policy, practices and challenges? A number of key themes can be drawn from across the book, although we would encourage readers to refer to specific chapters to understand the detailed analysis upon which these are based.

SME development policy is still dynamic and expanding. The various chapters provide a history of the development of policy interventions in specific domains, and demonstrate the variety of ways in which they are delivered and evaluated. Whilst not claiming representativeness, it is evident that this policy field is undergoing constant change. These changes include the specific policy objectives, and the target audience for interventions, as well as extension of the geographical scope for intervention. It is also clear that the objectives of some areas of development and provision have been easier to achieve than others, whilst some are enduring and others are more fleeting. For example, several authors note a shift in language and emphasis by policymakers away from SME start-ups towards a focus on entrepreneurship and growth (for example, Chapter 3), as well as on new areas such as social enterprise (Chapter 15).

The population of SMEs is complex and diverse; interventions need to be sensitive to this in order to raise their effectiveness. Although the terms 'SME' and 'entrepreneurship' are now mainstream, these terms are meaningless to many people running a business. People also start, run and exit from their business for a variety of reasons. Their ambitions and capabilities vary, and the types of policy that will be of practical help to them must also be varied. In this book we present a number of examples of this diversity, such as the self-employed (Chapter 11), social enterprises (Chapter 15) and franchisees (Chapter 16). Sometimes there is more than one set of policy tools that can be used to achieve a desired outcome, as the case of small firm sustainability programmes shows (Chapter 12). As these contributions point out, policies need to appreciate this diversity and focus on the specific characteristics of such business owners, their motivations and self-definitions, otherwise they will miss the mark and be rendered ineffective.

Policy objectives for SMEs and entrepreneurship often pursue similar goals across the world but its development frequently takes different routes. Many of the chapters, especially those in Part One, show a broad similarity of policy objectives in different countries. Governments in various nations often have a common focus on objectives such as encouraging new firm formation, the provision of financial assistance, policies for entrepreneurship education, incubator promotion, technology-related initiatives and reductions in regulation (see, for example, Chapter 4). With time, it also appears that policies have evolved beyond merely filling supply side gaps (such as problems with access to finance) and have instead come to focus on normative changes, such as developing an enterprise culture, or encouraging entrepreneurship amongst younger people (see Chapter 18). Despite these common aims, however, the timing and routes to achieving these objectives are shown to be heavily contingent on a country's historical, legal, economic and political milieu. For example, in formerly planned economies such as Vietnam (Chapter 7), a key emphasis in early development of policy has been on reductions in regulation. This has implications for sharing and transfer of experiences of SME and entrepreneurship promotion: not all policy approaches will work equally well in all countries.

Not everyone conceives of, or defines, 'small business' and 'entrepreneurship' in the same way. Although most definitions utilise employment numbers, accompanied by financial indicators such as assets and turnover, the thresholds can vary between different jurisdictions. For example, most European Union (EU) member states have adopted the same definitions of micro, small and medium-sized enterprises, with SMEs as a whole having a size of between 1–249 employees (Chapter 9; Commission of the European Communities 2003), whilst other countries such as China adopt an upper size threshold of up to 500 people in certain industries (Chapter 8). This creates challenges for those seeking to analyse the development of SMEs over time, and impedes comparative analyses. On a more conceptual level, different definitions of entrepreneurship also abound between nations (see Chapter 6) which can confuse policy audiences, although policymakers themselves are beginning to recognise and make strides to define the construct for practical audiences (OECD 2011). Certainly, definitional clarity is required if the evidence base is to be more informative for policymakers looking to share experiences. This places responsibility on both the producers as well as the users of the evidence base and requires better communication across different jurisdictions.

Policies can make a difference, but it takes time and refinements for them to be effective. Whilst it would intuitively appear obvious that a policy intervention designed to stimulate change will have an effect on SMEs and entrepreneurship, the evidence in these chapters suggest that such change is not always obvious, automatic or rapid. The business environment is complex and, as has been argued elsewhere, individual small-scale change programmes can often have little effect when macro-economic conditions dominate performance (Storey 2008). However, the contributors to this book show that developing an effective intervention can take a number of iterations and in the early days a strategy may fail. For example, attempts to introduce a business birth rate strategy in Scotland (Chapter 2) struggled to meet the original policy objectives, and this lead to subsequent fundamental changes in the targets and forms of delivery. Of course, the effects of some policies (such as the deregulation of a previously heavily regulated economy) can have an immediate impact, as exemplified by Vietnam (Chapter 7), but this tends to occur in environments where entrepreneurship has previously been held back by government ideology and institutions. It has to be recognised that policy formulation is an iterative process rather than a single shot, and this iterative process can take time to have effects.

Interventions seeking to develop an enterprise 'culture' are one of the most challenging areas to affect impact. Two recent themes in the development of SME and entrepreneurship policy have been attempts to stimulate an enterprise culture, and to open up entrepreneurship to different groups in society. The evidence suggests that such wholesale cultural interventions are difficult to implement and can often founder. The examples drawn from France (Chapter 9) and the Caribbean (Chapter 6) illustrate such problems: in each case, a number of challenges exist, ranging from the education system through to the risk-averse nature of much of the population. Similar problems can occur in most economies, especially where there has been a strong corporatist influence in the educational system and labour market.

Policymaking is often more ad-hoc and subjective than many people realise; it is not necessarily objective or rational. Although the evidence base and general level of knowledge about SMEs and entrepreneurship has grown substantially, how this feeds into policy developments is unclear. The actual policy process making appears unsystematic and subject to short-term demand by governments and their civil servants. Evidence from the UK (Chapter 5) exemplifies the ways in which the policymaking process is subject to a number of factors that affect policy outcomes. Textbook treatments, such as the ROAMEF Cycle (Rationale, Objectives, Appraisal, Monitoring, Evaluation and Feedback), appear far from reality. Related to this is the notion of mission creep leading to ill-focused objectives. Evidence from the Caribbean (Chapter 6) demonstrates the inappropriate use of SME policies as a 'cure-all' for economy and society and the downside of 'mission creep'. In reality, support programmes and the general policy environment is frequently affected by the political will of governments and the need of politicians to try and meet their election campaign or manifesto pledges. Certainly, there are numerous chapters that clearly show shifts in policies for SMEs over time. In some cases these appear to be based on, and justified by, research evidence; however, the message to come across from these chapters is that short-term switches and changes to existing policies should be undertaken with care and need to be customer focused.

In seeking to deliver interventions, policymakers need to work with localised institutions whilst avoiding overcrowding the marketplace. A common theme in many nations covered in this book is that of working with existing support providers to deliver initiatives, rather than creating new or government-based organisations. Initiatives that are developed and delivered with localised agencies usually tend to have the client audience in mind and can be cost effective (Chapters 13 and 14). However, other routes to reaching SMEs are also worth considering. For example, business incubators can be one way of assisting SMEs, and can be especially effective if they are focused on a specific dimension that aligns itself with incubator tenants (Chapter 10). Such approaches also have the advantage of overcoming the 'culture clash' (Gibb 2000) that often exists between government civil servants and owner managers (Chapter 19). Conversely, care should be taken regarding the encouragement of local agencies, in order to avoid an unnecessary proliferation of agencies and a subsequent confusion in the marketplace (Chapter 8).

Effective evaluation is critical to effective policy development. One of the holy grails of SME and entrepreneurship policy development is the development and implementation of appropriate evaluation tools. The various authors in Part Three all demonstrate the need for robust evidence as a basis for sound evaluation. They also argue the need to collect this whilst an initiative is ongoing – in 'real time' – and then to feed the results back into the policymaking process (Chapter 17). They also confirm what has previously been mentioned in the literature: that policy objectives continue too often to be vague; that measuring so-called additionality is highly problematic; finding control groups is challenging; evaluation methods tend to be ex-post; and the outcomes of evaluations are not adequately aired. However, the chapters also provide examples of the tools that may be employed to make evaluation more effective (especially Chapters 18 and 20). Lessons may also be learnt from other fields of intervention outside conventional business models. Evaluation and monitoring provides a crucible for policymakers and academics to come together and share knowledge and expertise. It is important that we treat interventions and the assumptions upon which these are based more critically (Chapter 19). There may be a key role for academics in this process because of their relative independence from the political process, their ability to assimilate a diverse literature base and feed this into new policy ideas, as well as their skills in evaluation techniques.

Conclusion: A Work in Progress

This introduction has sought to provide an overview of the themes that follow in the successive chapters of this book. Overall – as the above discussion indicates – there is no one 'silver bullet' or magical policy solution that will always work, or is readily transferable from one situation to another. Different programmes, methods of delivery and tools of evaluation can have different effects in different contexts. This book does not purport to identify quick solutions or universal fixes to the challenge of effective policy. What it does seek to do, though, is to contribute to the development of effective SME and entrepreneurship policy by presenting new evidence and highlighting the challenges for policy development and practice as experienced in different countries. In doing so, it is hoped that the book will stimulate debate and encourage a fuller exchange of ideas between policymakers, practitioners and academics, with the ultimate goal of a more creative policy environment.

It is important that policymakers draw upon the latest evidence available when developing initiatives for SMEs. It is also important that academics and those contributing to the evidence base make available their results in an accessible way to policymakers. This is already underway through dialogues between policymakers, analysts and academics, but much more needs to be undertaken if the efficacy of interventions is to be strengthened and we are to avoid the mistakes of the past. The following chapters in this book seek to add to this dialogue and hence contribute to the development of more effective interventions.

References

Audretsch, D. 2011. Entrepreneurship Policy, in _World Encyclopedia of Entrepreneurship_, edited by L-P Dana. Cheltenham and Northampton MA: Edward Elgar, 111–121.

Audretsch, D.B., Grilo, I. and Thurik, A.R. 2009. _Handbook of Research on Entrepreneurship Policy_. Cheltenham and Northampton MA: Edward Elgar.

Audretsch, D.B. and Thurik, A.R. 2001. What's new about the new economy? Sources of growth in the managed and entrepreneurial economies. _Industrial and Corporate Change_, 10(1) 267–315.

Bannock, G. 2005. _The Economics and Management of Small Businesses_. Oxford and New York: Routledge.

Bennett, R. 2008. SME policy support in Britain since the 1990s: what have we learnt? _Environment and Planning C: Government and Policy_, 26(2), 375–397.

Birch, D.L. 1979. _The Job Generation Process_. Cambridge MA: MIT Program on Neighborhood and Regional Change.

Blackburn, R. and Smallbone, D. 2008. Researching small firms and entrepreneurship in the UK: Developments and distinctiveness. _Entrepreneurship Theory and Practice_, 32(2), 267–288.

Bolton, J.E. 1971. _Small Firms: Report of the Committee of Inquiry on Small Firms_, Cmnd 4811. London: HMSO.

Commission of the European Communities 2003. The New SME Definition: User Guide and Model Declaration. _Commission Recommendation 2003/361/ EC, OJ L124, 20.5.2003_, Brussels: Commission of the European Communities.

Curran, J. and Storey, D.J. 2002. Small business policy in the United Kingdom: the inheritance of the Small Business Service and implications for its future effectiveness. *Environment and Planning C: Government and Policy*, 20(2), 163–177.

Dennis, W.J. Jr. 2005. Entrepreneurship, small business and public policy levers. *Journal of Small Business Management*, 29(2), 149–162.

Galbraith, J.K. 1967. *The New Industrial State*. Princeton NJ: Princeton University Press.

Gibb, A.A. 2000. SME policy, academic research and the growth of ignorance: mythical concepts, myths, assumptions, rituals and confusions. *International Small Business Journal*, 18(3), 13–35.

Greene, F.J., Mole, K.F. and Storey, D.J. 2008. *Three Decades of Enterprise Culture: Entrepreneurship, Economic Regeneration and Public Policy*, London: Palgrave.

Hart, D.M. 2003. *The Emergence of Entrepreneurship Policy, Governance, Start-ups, and Growth in the U.S. Knowledge Economy*. Cambridge: Cambridge University Press.

Levicki, C. 1984. *Small Business Theory and Policy*. Beckenham: Croom Helm.

Lundström, A. and Stevenson, L.A. 2005. *Entrepreneurship Policy: Theory and Practice*, ISEN International Studies in Entrepreneurship. New York: Springer.

MacMillan Report 1931. *Committee on Finance and Industry*, Report, Cmnd. 3897. London: HSMO.

Minniti, M. 2008. The role of government policy on rntrepreneurial activity: productive, unproductive, or destrcutive? *Entrepreneurship Theory and Practice*, 32(5), 779–790.

Norrman, C. and Bager-Sjögren, L. 2010. Entrepreneurship policy to support new innovative ventures: Is it effective? *International Small Business Journal*, 28(6), 602–619.

Organisation for Economic Co-operation and Development (OECD) 2008. *OECD Framework for the Evaluation of SME and Entrepreneurship Policies and Programmes*. Paris: Organization for Economic Co-operation and Development Publishing.

Organisation for Economic Co-operation and Development (OECD) 2011. *Entrepreneurship at a Glance 2011*. Paris: Organization for Economic Co-operation and Development Publishing.

Parker, S. 2007. Policymakers Beware!, in *Handbook of Research on Entrepreneurship Policy*, edited by D.B Audretsch et al. Cheltenham and Northampton, MA: Edward Elgar, 54–63.

Robson, P.J.A., Wijbenga, F. and Parker, S.C. 2009. Entrepreneurship and policy: challenges and directions for future research. *International Small Business Journal*, 27(5), 531–535.

Schumpeter, J. 1976. *Capitalism, Socialism and Democracy*. London: George Allen and Unwin.

Shergold, P. 2011. Seen but not heard. *Australian Literary Review*, 6(4), 3–4.

Smallbone, D. 2010. *Entrepreneurship and Public Policy Volumes I and II*. Cheltenham and Northampton, MA: Edward Elgar.

Stevenson, L. and Lundström, A. 2001. *Entrepreneurship Policy for the Future: Volume 3. Patterns and Trends in Entrepreneurship/SME Policy and Practice in Ten Economies*. Stockholm: Swedish Foundation for Small Business Research.

Storey, D.J. 2000. Six Steps to Heaven: Evaluating the Impact of Public Policies to Support Small Businesses in Developed Economies, in *Handbook of Entrepreneurship*, edited by D.L. Sexton and H. Landstrom. Oxford: Blackwell, 176–193.

Storey, D.J. 2008. *Entrepreneurship and SME Policy*. Lyon: World Entrepreneurship Forum.

van Praag, C.M. and Versloot, P.H. 2007. What is the value of entrepreneurship? A review of recent research. *Small Business Economics*, 29(4), 351–382.

Welter, F. and Smallbone, D. 2011. *Handbook of Research on Entrepreneurship Policies in Central and Eastern Europe*. Cheltenham and Northampton, MA: Edward Elgar.

Wennekers, S. and Thurik, R. 1999. Linking entrepreneurship and economic growth. *Small Business Economics*, 13(1), 27–55.

Wiltshire Inquiry 1971. *Report of the Committee on Small Business, June*. Canberra: Department of Trade and Industry, Commonwealth of Australia.

PART ONE
Global Experiences in Policy Development

2

The Evolution of Enterprise Policy in Scotland

Ross Brown and Colin Mason[1]

Chapter Summary

Scotland is often seen as being at the forefront of policy innovation in the realm of enterprise policy. This chapter assesses the policy rationale and framework conditions for changes in enterprise policies in Scotland. There are several dimensions to these changes. First, Scotland has undergone a major policy shift away from the attraction of inward investment towards the development of a more endogenously-based economic development strategy. Second, at the turn of the century enterprise policy underwent a major strategic re-orientation from a focus on creating new business start-ups towards a much narrower focus on developing the pipeline of high potential start-ups. More recently, the promotion of high-growth firms (HGF) has moved to the centre stage of enterprise policy in Scotland. Using the country as a contextual backdrop, the chapter provides useful insights for other regional economies embarking on the design (or redesign) of their enterprise policies.

Introduction

Scotland is a small country with a population of just over five million inhabitants. It has been a constituent part of the UK ever since the Acts of Union in 1706 (England) and 1707 (Scotland) brought the two Kingdoms together. However, following the establishment of the Scottish Parliament in 1999, Scotland is

---

1   The authors are grateful to Ron Botham, Martin Hughes, Charlie Woods and the book editors for their helpful comments on earlier versions of this chapter. They would also like to thank Geraldine Brown for her assistance in producing Figure 2.1.

now governed jointly under a system of shared sovereignty between the UK and Scottish Parliament. Under this system, the Scottish Parliament has responsibility to legislate over 'devolved matters' such as health, education and economic development while the UK Parliament has responsibility for 'reserved matters' such as defence, foreign policy and employment law. The Scottish Executive was established in 1999 as the executive arm of the devolved government of Scotland. In 2007, following the Scottish Parliamentary election, the term 'Executive' was changed to 'Government' by the Scottish National Party administration.

SMEs dominate the Scottish economy. At present there are 294,525 SMEs (0–249 employees) in Scotland which represent 99.2 per cent of all enterprises and account for 52.9 per cent of all employment (Scottish Government 2010). While SMEs are numerically dominant, larger firms account for the majority of turnover and employment in Scotland. As of March 2010, there were only 2,260 large businesses employing more than 250 employees. Large businesses account for 47 per cent of employment and 62.6 per cent of turnover in Scotland (Scottish Government 2010). Exports from Scotland are strongly dominated by five main sectors: food and drink, chemicals, business services, electrical and instrument engineering and mechanical engineering. Together these sectors account for over half of Scotland's exports (Scottish Government 2010).

This chapter outlines and assesses the evolution of enterprise policy in Scotland. It begins by outlining the dominant trends in post-war industrial policy. It then examines the shift in emphasis during the 1990s towards a focus on business start-ups and then examines how, at the beginning of the twenty-first century, it changed to a focus on high-growth start-ups. The penultimate section examines how enterprise policy has now become strongly focused on the promotion of rapidly growing firms. (The major changes in policy emphasis are illustrated in Figure 2.1.) The chapter ends with some brief conclusions and reflections.

From Home-Grown Ships to Foreign-Owned Chips

Industrial and enterprise policies in Scotland have shifted significantly over the twentieth century. During the first half of the last century, traditional industries such as coal mining, shipbuilding and heavy engineering dominated the Scottish economy. However, during the post-war period a combination of industrialisation in emerging economies and the decline of defence-related procurement severely affected these industries, resulting in major restructuring and job loss (Devine 1999). UK regional policy sought to mitigate

Policy Emphasis

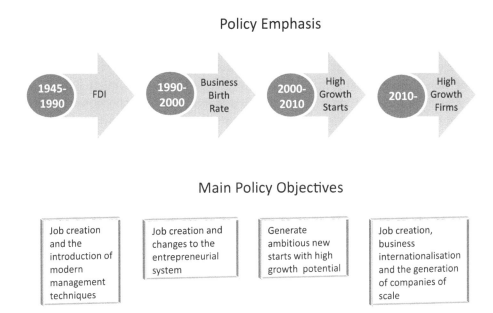

Main Policy Objectives

| Job creation and the introduction of modern management techniques | Job creation and changes to the entrepreneurial system | Generate ambitious new starts with high growth potential | Job creation, business internationalisation and the generation of companies of scale |

Figure 2.1   Key enterprise policy changes in Scotland, 1945–2010

this de-industrialisation process by attracting so-called 'sunrise industries' to economically lagging regions such as Scotland. Sectors such as chemicals, electrical engineering, electronics and car production were actively sought to replace the declining 'sunset' industries (SCDI 1961). Therefore, from 1945 until the early 1990s the primary mechanism for revitalising the Scottish economy was viewed as the attraction of inward investment (Dimitratos, Liouka, Ross and Young 2009). Conversely, SMEs were not viewed as a key area of public policy during this time.

While most of the early inward investment in these emerging industries was driven by British firms such as Rolls Royce and Ferranti, from the late 1940s and 1950s onwards the most important investors were foreign-owned (mostly US) multinational enterprises such as NCR, Polaroid and IBM which opened in 1946, 1950 and 1951 respectively (Brown 2002). By establishing large-scale manufacturing operations in Scotland, these firms were able to access the growing European marketplace, an abundant source of well-qualified English-speaking employees, and an attractive package of regional incentives. In purely volume terms the policy appeared to work very successfully: for example, between 1945 and 1969 the number of US firms operating in Scotland grew from just six to 124 (Dimitratos et al. 2009). Growing especially fast in the 1960s and 1970s, the Scottish share of inward investment into the UK was more than 35 per cent (Halkier 2006). As well as the attraction of new employment, these

US companies were also viewed as a conduit for bringing modern management techniques to the British economy (Dunning 1958).

Despite burgeoning levels of investment, academic observers began to question this externally-driven model of economic development. John Firn (1975), in his seminal contribution, claimed that Scotland had become a 'branch plant economy' and the centrality of foreign direct investment (FDI) began to be increasingly questioned in Scotland as the problems with this exogenous economic development strategy started to become apparent (Brown 2002). First, increasingly critical appraisals noted the weak supplier linkages, low innovation levels, mature products and truncated management structures of many foreign-owned manufacturing plants (Clarke and Beaney 1993, Turok, 1993). Second, closures started to occur amongst some foreign-owned plants, especially in the electronics sector, as their products matured and they became less cost competitive. Third, Scotland started to lose its competitiveness for FDI amid heightening global competition for 'greenfield' FDI projects from lower-cost regions in Europe and subsequently further afield (Brown and Raines 2000). Policymakers in Scotland therefore began to look elsewhere for policy prescriptions and the 'birth, growth and development rates of indigenous business began to take centre stage (Hood and Paterson 2002: 237).

Enterprise Policy During the 1990s: Trying to Grow Your Own

After nearly four decades of policy which strongly focused on the attraction of inward investment, public policy in Scotland underwent a major re-orientation in favour of a focus on 'growing its own'. This recognition of the importance of new business start-ups was very much in line with UK policy which, from the early 1980s under the administration of Margaret Thatcher, had made the promotion of new enterprises a central plank of economic policy (Storey 1994). In Scotland the principal body responsible for implementing enterprise policy became Scottish Enterprise, which is now also the main economic development agency in Scotland. It was formed following the merger of the Scottish Development Agency and the Training Agency and started operations on 1 April 1991. Scottish Enterprise is directly funded by the Scottish Government and has a staff of around 1,000 employees who are based at its Glasgow headquarters and 12 regional offices located across Scotland.

During the 1990s Scottish Enterprise started to pay an increasing amount of attention to the role of new business start-ups in promoting economic growth. One of the key catalysts behind this transition in policy focus was Crawford Beveridge, a Scot, who had been attracted back from Silicon Valley where he had been working in a senior position in the electronics industry to become the organisation's new chief executive. One of his initial observations on his return was the low level of business start-up activity in Scotland. This resulted in the Business Birth Rate Enquiry (Scottish Enterprise 1993), a major piece of investigative research by Scottish Enterprise which had a highly significant impact on public policy in Scotland.

The key contributions of the inquiry were to highlight the economic importance of new business births for regional development and quantify the relative underperformance of Scotland compared to other parts of the UK in terms of business start-ups and growth. The work showed that new starts accounted for some 125,000 jobs during the 1980s in Scotland, a much larger number than that produced by inward investment or the expansion of larger enterprises (Hood and Paterson 2002). The inquiry ultimately led to the development of the Business Birth Rate Strategy (BBRS) which was launched in 1993 (Scottish Enterprise 1993). According to the strategy, 'addressing the problems of Scotland's business birth rate will be as much a fundamental part of Scottish Enterprise's work as inward investment, company development, trade development or skills training' (Scottish Enterprise 1993: 21). The primary aim of the BBRS was the extremely ambitious objective of raising the business birth rate in Scotland to that of the UK level by the late 1990s. Achieving this goal would require the birth rate per capita in Scotland to increase by 3.5 times its historic growth rate (Hood and Paterson 2002).

The strategy had six main priorities:

1. unlocking the potential for setting up businesses;
2. improving the environment for entrepreneurs;
3. improving access to finance;
4. widening the entrepreneurial base (particularly amongst women and ethnic minorities);
5. increasing start-ups in key sectors; and
6. increasing the number of fast-growing new starts.

The implementation of the strategy was supported with an annual expenditure of approximately £20 million per annum – approximately 4 per cent of the entire expenditure of Scottish Enterprise (Fraser of Allander 2001). It comprised a variety of initiatives, including: personal enterprise shows to encourage more people to consider starting a business; enterprise education initiatives in schools and universities; new business network groups; the establishment of LINC Scotland to promote business angels; and access to advisory services. Scottish Enterprise also invested a considerable amount of human and financial resources into the development of the BBRS. However, it is important to note that the promotion of new business start-ups was already being pursued through various initiatives in Scotland prior to the launch of the BBRS. What the BBRS did was to unify and consolidate these initiatives and helped place the development of new business births at the heart of Scotland's economic development strategy (Scottish Enterprise 1993). Importantly, it also sought to generate 'buy-in' from other external parties in Scotland such as universities, local authorities and various business organisations.

In 2001, Scottish Enterprise commissioned an independent review of the BBRS to judge the effectiveness of this approach towards enterprise promotion (Fraser of Allander 2001). Its main conclusion – which influenced the future direction of policy in Scotland – was that the BBRS had failed to achieve its main objective of raising the business birth rate to the average level within the UK. The study concluded that many of the activities undertaken as part of the strategy, such as enterprise education initiatives, would only bring improvements to the business birth rate over a much longer period of time than that covered by the strategy (that is, the 1990s). However, not all the review's findings were negative. For example, it reported that the environment for new business starts had improved significantly in Scotland in areas such as support networks, funding and education, and noted that that there had been signs of a small increase in the business birth rate (Fraser of Allander 2001). But it concluded that a good deal more was needed in areas such as support to rapid growth firms, business counselling and standardisation of multiple schemes of business support.

Thus, while Scottish Enterprise achieved acclaim for highlighting the importance of the business birth rate (Hood and Paterson 2002), it was nevertheless seen as a strategy that largely failed (van Stel and Storey 2004). Because of the highly ambitious nature of the BBRS it became progressively evident that the targets within the strategy were unachievable (Fraser of Allander 2001). Throughout the 1990s the Scottish business birth rate remained lower than the UK average (Hood and Paterson 2002). Indeed, Crawford Beveridge acknowledged that to close this 'enterprise gap' more time would be required and that it would take 40 or 50 years to make such a fundamental transformation happen in Scotland (Haney 2001). At this time, the academic literature was also increasingly questioning whether the focus on raising business births as a whole was the most appropriate objective. Various studies showed that simply encouraging more and more people to start their own businesses did not automatically lead to job creation or economic growth (van Stel and Storey 2004). Prompted by the perceived failure of the BBRS and the emerging evidence base showing the lack of impact made by most new start-ups, public policy embarked on a change of direction.

A New Enterprise Policy for a New Century: Quality not Quantity

By the turn of the twenty-first century it became increasingly apparent that the goals of the BBRS needed to be fundamentally re-examined. The independent review of the strategy had questioned the validity of the 'volume' nature of the BBRS and its associated high opportunity cost (Fraser of Allander 2001). The review highlighted the fact that a focus on high-growth starts might be a more appropriate strategic emphasis. However, in contrast to the policy of stimulating new business starts as a whole, a policy focusing specifically on high-growth starts would inevitably encounter the difficulties associated with 'picking winners' (Fraser of Allander 2001: 67). According to the review, the greater risks associated with starting a high-tech company together with their greater orientation to wider external markets, means there is a higher probability of policy having an impact by supporting these types of firms. Implicit within this policy change was the assumption that it was high technology firms that would be the primary generators of high-growth starts.

In line with this new evidence, the Scottish Government launched a new economic strategy in 2001. This placed new starts with the greatest growth potential at the centre of Scottish enterprise policy (Scottish Executive 2001). A number of issues are important to highlight in connection with the new strategic direction undertaken. First, the most explicit objective was the need to focus on high-growth new starts on the grounds that they would eventually become larger, more established-sized 'companies of scale'. Second, although the core thread of the BBRS continued to be at the centre of the new approach, the 'volume' support for new starts was to be undertaken in new ways through call centre-type support and the provision of web-based tools for new entrepreneurs. Third, the focus on high-potential start-ups was firmly embedded in Scottish Enterprise's cluster policies which were being devised during the late 1990s and early 2000s. Finally, during the mid-1990s a major piece of research had highlighted the potential for greater commercialisation of academic research in Scotland (Scottish Enterprise and The Royal Society of Edinburgh 1996). Therefore, Scottish universities were accorded a key place in this new strategy as a potential source of new technology-based spin-offs.

The creation of a new High Growth Start-Up Unit within Scottish Enterprise was at the heart of the new policy emphasis on supporting businesses with the greatest growth potential. The main focus of the Unit was to help firms with their business plans, help to obtain venture capital, access grants and assistance with intellectual property (IP) protection. The Unit was specifically designed to offer support which drew on mentors who had 'first hand' knowledge of growing businesses themselves. It explicitly viewed high-tech firms as the principal source of high-growth entrepreneurship within the Scottish economy. A key source of these new high-tech start-ups was considered to be spin-offs from Scotland's research intensive universities (Targeting Innovation 2008).

Owing to the large degree of risk associated with these new high-tech firms, quite often the main sources of funding was from equity investors rather than traditional financial institutions such as banks. Therefore, another key component of this new policy emphasis was the development of new investment support policies by Scottish Enterprise. During the 2000s, Scottish Enterprise developed a suite of investment products to help support high-growth start-ups, such as the Scottish Seed Fund, Scottish Co-Investment Fund and the Scottish Venture Fund. The Scottish Seed Fund, launched in 2006, was designed to assist fund early-stage new businesses with funding of between £20,000–£100,000 to help develop new products, enter new markets and to increase employment. The provision of this kind of risk capital funding was seen as critical to help enable these new businesses to set up and grow.

In common with many advanced countries (OECD 2010), innovation support has become central to policies to promote high-growth entrepreneurship in Scotland. Indeed, there has been a major confluence during the last decade between entrepreneurship and innovation policy (Mason and Brown 2011). For example, in Scotland a raft of innovation-related policy initiatives have been launched in order to aid the development of new, high potential, technology-based firms, including new assistance mechanisms such as the Proof of Concept programme, Enterprise Fellowships and Intermediate Technology Institutes. Whereas previous forms of innovation policy in Scotland largely supported R&D projects in existing companies, these new forms of innovation support were targeted towards assisting with the development of new IP generation in very early stage or embryonic firms.

The experience of implementing the strategy revealed a number of problems when attempting to increase the number of new high-tech, high-growth start-ups. First, by focusing strongly on developing new technology-based firms, policymakers became overly preoccupied by the technological merits of different firms and not with their inherent growth capabilities. As a consequence, support was concentrated in a small number of high-tech sectors, such as digital media and life sciences. Second, by focusing on new high-tech firms, emphasis has strongly been on support for university spin-offs.

However, increasing evidence has emerged that these firms tend to experience little turnover or employment growth and generally remain small (Targeting Innovation 2008). Finally, the emergent evidence base surrounding firm growth reveals that these firms emerge from a very wide variety of different sectors and are not particularly associated with high-tech firms (Mason, Bishop and Robinson 2009). Therefore, policymakers may have been culpable of looking in the wrong places when trying to identify potential sources of rapidly growing firms (Mason and Brown 2011).

The highly problematic issue of predicting which new starts will grow is well recognised within the academic literature (Freel 1998, Parker 2007). However, it was only belatedly recognised by policymakers in Scotland that predicting which new starts had the greatest growth potential was fraught with difficulties (Brown, Gordon and Wilson 2008). Accordingly, at the start of the new decade, observers were increasingly calling for newer forms of support to help advance the important objective of promoting rapidly growing firms (Brown and Mason 2012).

An Enterprise Policy for the Future: Doing More with Less

By 2010, Scotland's enterprise policy had begun to shift away from early stage high-tech firms towards a stronger focus on firms experiencing rapid growth. This policy interest in HGFs was provoked by a growing body of empirical evidence which showed the substantial benefits economies derive from these firms (Henrekson and Johansson 2010). For example, according to recent research, HGFs account for as much as half of all new private-sector employment generated in UK firms (Anyadike-Danes, Bonner, Hart and Mason 2009). These firms also generate a number of positive externalities for regional economies in terms of raising productivity, increasing exports, generating knowledge spillovers and creating supplier linkages (Mason et al. 2009). On account of these positive characteristics, a large number of academic observers (Anyadike-Danes et al. 2009, Shane 2009, Brown and Mason 2012) and public policy organisations (Levy, Lee and Peate 2011) began to call for greater policy support to aid the creation and development of HGFs in the UK.

Despite these calls for a policy shift, policymakers and academics knew very little about HGFs, their development impacts and how best to support them. In order to gain a deeper understanding of the nature of rapidly growing enterprises in Scotland, a major piece of investigative research on HGFs was commissioned by Scottish Enterprise (Mason and Brown 2010). This work suggested that there are certain distinctive characteristics of Scottish HGFs compared to those examined elsewhere. Most of these firms were sizeable, well-established enterprises, and the vast majority were more than ten years old. A significant proportion had their origins in existing businesses which had undergone a major business transformation such as management buy-outs. HGFs were found in almost all sectors of the economy and not particularly concentrated in high-tech sectors of the economy. Interestingly, a large number were externally-owned firms, especially in sectors such as food and drink where acquisition has driven up the levels of foreign ownership (Brown 2011). They typically have innovative business models involving close relationships with their customers or end-users, partnering and recurring revenue streams. Most have significant international sales, with some exemplifying the 'born global' phenomenon (McDougall, Oviatt and Shane 1994).

The rationale for introducing new initiatives to help produce more HGFs undoubtedly has certain attractions for policymakers. First, because of the severity of the economic downturn suffered by the global economy during the late 2000s, the level of financial resources for strategic industrial intervention has significantly diminished in recent years and will do so for the foreseeable future. Therefore, it seems sensible for economic development bodies to focus their resources where they can have the largest economic impact. Second, enterprise support bodies, such as Scottish Enterprise, have already stated that they intend to 'focus our support on those companies who can make the greatest contribution to the Scottish economy' (Scottish Enterprise 2011: 3). By working intensively with a smaller number of high-potential companies, public policy can, arguably, have a greater impact on the economy than by trying to assist companies irrespective of their growth capabilities (Mole, Hart, Roper, and Saal 2011).

Scotland is perhaps ahead of many countries in terms of its existing support mechanisms for promoting HGFs (Brown and Mason 2012), with a number of features in its current system of enterprise support that help spur business growth. For example, Scottish Enterprise operates a system of account management with businesses with high-growth potential. Under this system an ongoing relationship is built between around 100 Scottish Enterprise account managers and 2,000 Scottish firms (Scottish Enterprise 2011). This enables the development agency to obtain a deep insight into a company's growth challenges whilst also providing a conduit to channel other forms of support on offer from Scottish Enterprise, such as innovation support, capital grants and business internationalisation assistance.

Scottish Enterprise has also developed more bespoke forms of support for HGFs. A good example of this type of customised support is the assistance offered through the Companies of Scale programme operated by Scottish Enterprise. This programme offers a small number of rapidly growing firms the opportunity to form a very close interactive relationship with Scottish

Enterprise as well as close networking with other high-growth businesses (see Brown and Mason 2012). It is often this kind of strategic relationship with business support agencies which firms appreciate the most, rather than more traditional forms of 'transactional' assistance such as grants and tax credits (Mason and Brown 2011). However, owing to the relatively formative nature of these types of high-growth programmes, there is still a lack of evaluation evidence examining their effectiveness (OECD 2010).

Conclusion

This chapter has highlighted the ways in which enterprise policy has evolved in Scotland. Four concluding observations can be made. First, while the various types of enterprise policy have been presented as being characteristic of different discrete time periods, the reality is that these policy objectives have often overlapped over different time periods. For example, although much less prominence is accorded to FDI in recent years, it is still seen as a key policy objective for the Scottish Government (Scottish Government 2007). Second, as others have noted elsewhere (Gertler 2010), local institutions in Scotland, such as Scottish Enterprise, were founded to play a key role in shaping the entrepreneurial system within regional economies. Some have noted that a region's 'institutional thickness' is important because it can 'underpin and stimulate a diffused entrepreneurship – a recognized set of codes of conduct, supports, and practices which certain individuals can dip into with relative ease' (Amin and Thrift 1994: 15). Third, while the appropriateness (or otherwise) of the current focus on HGFs in Scotland remains an open question, it appears that for this policy emphasis to be effectively deployed, a substantial recalibration of current enterprise policy instruments will be required (Brown and Mason 2012). Finally, despite demonstrating considerable innovation in the realm of enterprise policy, Scotland continues to underperform the UK as a whole on a number of different economic variables (such as gross domestic product (GDP) per capita, employment, business birth rates and innovation levels). This suggests that policy panaceas to cure structural economic problems remain as elusive as ever.

References

Amin, A. and Thrift, N. 1994. Living in the Global, in *Globalization, Institutions, and Regional Development in Europe*, edited by A. Amin and N Thrift. Oxford: Oxford University Press, 1–22.

Anyadike-Danes, M, Bonner, K. and Hart, M. (2009) Measuring Business Growth: High-Growth firms and their contribution to employment in the UK, Research Report for NESTA. Download from:http://www.nesta.org.uk/publications/reports/assets/features/measuring_business_growth. Accessed: 23 April 201

Brown, R. 2002. The Future of ICT Industries in Scotland: Towards a Post-branch Plant Economy? in *Scotland in a Global Economy: The 2020 Vision*, edited by N. Hood et al. Basingstoke: Palgrave Macmillan, 130–148.

Brown, R. 2011. The Determinants of High Growth Entrepreneurship in the Scottish Food and Drink Cluster, in *The Handbook of Research on Entrepreneurship in Agriculture and Rural Development*, edited by G. Alsos et al. Cheltenham: Edward Elgar, 131–146.

Brown, R., Gordon, J. and Wilson, D. 2008. *An Interim Review of the Intermediate Technology Institutes*. Glasgow: Scottish Enterprise.

Brown, R. and Mason, C. 2012. Raising the batting average: re-orientating regional industrial policy to generate more high growth firms, *Local Economy*, 27(1), 33–49.

Brown, R. and Raines, P. 2000. The Changing Nature of Foreign Investment Policy in Europe: From Promotion to Management, in *Regions, Globalization, and the Knowledge-Based Economy*, edited by J. Dunning. Oxford: Oxford University Press, 435–458.

Clarke, T. and Beaney, P. 1993. Between autonomy and dependence: corporate strategy, plant status and local agglomeration in the Scottish electronics industry. *Environment and Planning A*, 25(2), 213–232.

Devine, T. 1999. *Scottish Nation, 1700–2000*. London: The Penguin Press.

Dimitratos, P., Liouka, I., Ross, D. and Young, S. 2009. The multinational enterprise and subsidiary evolution: Scotland since 1945. *Business History*, 51(3), 401–425.

Dunning J. 1958. *American Investment in British Manufacturing Industry*. London: Allen and Unwin.

Firn, J. 1975. External control and regional development: the case of Scotland. *Environment and Planning A*, 7(4), 393–414.

Fraser of Allander 2001. *Promoting Business Start-ups: A New Strategic Formula*, Report for Scottish Enterprise, Glasgow.

Freel, M. 1998. Policy, prediction and growth: picking start-up winners? *Journal of Small Business and Enterprise Development*, 5(1), 19–32.

Gertler, M. 2010. Rules of the game: the place of institutions in regional economic change. *Regional Studies*, 44(1), 1–15.

Halkier, H. 2006. *Institutions, Discourse and Regional Development: The Scottish Development Agency and the Politics of Regional Policy*. Brussels: Peter Lang.

Haney, C. 2001. Beveridge admits he got it wrong on birth rate strategy, *Business AM*, 19 February 01.

Henrekson, M. and Johansson, D. 2010. Gazelles as job creators: a survey and interpretation of the evidence. *Small Business Economics*, 35(2), 227–244.

Hood, N. and Paterson, C. 2002. The Growth and Development of New Firms, in *Scotland in a Global Economy: The 2020 Vision*, edited by N Hood et al. Basingstoke: Palgrave Macmillan, 237–257.

Levy, C., Lee, N. and Peate, A. 2011. *Ready, Steady, Grow? How the Government can Support the Development of More High Growth Firms*, a joint Cities 2020 and Knowledge Economy Programme Report, London: The Work Foundation.

Mason, G., Bishop, K. and Robinson, C. 2009. *Business Growth and Innovation; The Wider Impact of Rapidly Growing Firms in UK City-Region. s*. London: NESTA. [Online] Available at: http://www.niesr.ac.uk/pdf/190509_94959. pdf. Accessed: 12 May 2011

Mason, C. and Brown, R. 2010. *High Growth Firms in Scotland*, Final Report for Scottish Enterprise, Glasgow. [Online] Available at: http://www. scottish-enterprise.com/News/2010/11/High-growth-firms-could-be-key-to-economic-success.aspx. Accessed: 5 May 2011

Mason, C. and Brown, R. 2011. Creating good public policy to support high growth firms, *Small Business Economics*, DOI 10.1007/s11187-011-9369-9

McDougall, P., Oviatt, B. and Shane, S. 1994. Explaining the formation of international new ventures: The limits of theories of international business research. *Journal of Business Venturing*, 9(6), 469–487.

Mole, K., Hart, M., Roper, S. and Saal, D. 2011. Broader or deeper? Exploring the most effective intervention profile for public small business support. *Environment and Planning A*, 43(1), 87–105.

Organisation for Economic Cooperation and Development (OECD) 2010. *High-Growth Enterprises: What Governments Can do to Make a Difference*, OECD Studies on SMEs and Entrepreneurship. Paris: OECD.

Parker, S.C. 2007. Policymakers Beware!, in *Handbook of Research on Entrepreneurship Policy*, edited by D. Audretsch, I Grilo and A Thurik. Cheltenham: Edward Elgar, 54–63.

Scottish Council Development and Industry 1961. *Inquiry into the Scottish Economy, 1960–61*, Toothill Report. Glasgow: Scottish Council Development and Industry.

Scottish Enterprise 1993. *Improving the Business Birth Rate: A Strategy for Scotland*. Glasgow: Scottish Enterprise.

Scottish Enterprise 2011. *Scottish Enterprise Business Plan 2011/14*, (Glasgow: Scottish Enterprise). [Online] Available at: http://www.scottishenterprise. com/News/ 2011/03/Business-Plan-launched.aspx. Accessed: 15 May 2011

Scottish Enterprise and Royal Society of Edinburgh 1996. *Technology Ventures; Commercialising Scotland's Science Base*. Glasgow: Scottish Enterprise.

Scottish Executive 2001. *A Smart, Successful Scotland: Ambitions for the Enterprise Networks*. Edinburgh: Scottish Executive.

Scottish Government 2007. *The Government Economic Strategy*. Edinburgh: The Scottish Government. [Online] Available at: http://www.scotland.gov.uk/ Publications/2007/11/12115041/0

Scottish Government 2010. *Scottish Corporate Sector Statistics 2010*. Edinburgh: The Scottish Government. [Online] Available at: http://www.scotland.gov. uk/Resource/ Doc/982/0106216.pdf

Shane, S. 2009. Why encouraging more people to become entrepreneurs is bad public policy. *Small Business Econ*omics, 33(2), 141–149.

Storey, D. J. 1994. *Understanding the Small Business Sector*. London: Routledge.

Targeting Innovation 2008. *Scottish University Spin-Off Study*. Glasgow: Targeting Innovation.

Turok, I. 1993. Inward investment and local linkages: how deeply embedded is Silicon Glen? *Regional Studies*, 27(5), 401–417.

van Stel, A.J. and Storey, D.J. 2004. The link between firm births and job creation: is there a Upas Tree effect? *Regional Studies* 38(8), 893–909.

3

SME Policy Development in New Zealand 1978–2008

Tanya Jurado and Claire Massey

Chapter Summary

SMEs play a significant role in the New Zealand economy. Yet until recently, New Zealand policymakers and researchers have focused primarily on big business and no research has comprehensively examined the development of SME policy. This chapter outlines the development of SME policy in New Zealand during the period 1978 to 2008. It identifies three dominant development phases (protectionism; market forces and reform; consolidation), examines changes in the broader environment and considers the range of influences and relevant policy instruments that were used to support small businesses and/or entrepreneurs.

Introduction

SMEs play a significant part in the New Zealand economy, but they have not always received the attention from policymakers that they deserve, and have only recently been identified as a sector in their own right. Until a decade ago SMEs were, at best, seen as a vehicle to alleviate social and economic problems (for instance, unemployment). More recently the focus has shifted, and today SMEs are seen as a vehicle of a different type, that is, as a way of driving behavioural changes such as increasing innovation and productivity. This chapter identifies the key factors that have helped to shape New Zealand SME policy in the period under consideration (1978 to 2008) and outlines the shift in thinking over this time.

In the early years of the period under review, government support for SMEs took place in the context of the prevailing economic wisdom of the time. 'Big business' was regarded as the growth engine of the economy, with SME policy an incidental by-product. However, by 2008, policymakers were designing SME-specific policy informed by calls from domestic researchers (for example, Devlin 1984, Bollard 1988, Massey 2006). This emerging thinking was congruent with international research on the benefits of having stand-alone policy supporting SMEs and/or entrepreneurship (for example, Storey 1994, 2005, Dennis 2005, Audretsch, Grilo and Thurik 2007, Minniti 2008). The review period has been grouped into three phases: the first spans the years 1978 to 1984 where SME policy was developed against a backdrop of an overall protectionist economic policy (Easton 1997); the second covers 1984 to 1999, a period where New Zealand underwent radical economic reform based primarily on neoliberal economic principles (Bertram 2009); whilst the final phase (1999–2008) is characterised by a 'third way' that sought to gradually adjust many of the economic reforms undertaken in the previous phase (Chatterjee, Conway, Dalziel, Eichbaum, Harris, Philpott and Shaw 1999).

Background

New Zealand is a constitutional monarchy with one legislative house, and has a population of 4.4 million. The majority of New Zealanders are of European descent, with significantly smaller populations of indigenous Māori, Asians and Pacific Islanders. The economy has a large primary sector and a sizeable industry and service sectors. New Zealand is characterised by the small size of its domestic market and the attendant challenges of exporting from a remote geographical base. While there is no formal definition of an SME, in 1999 the Ministry of Economic Development (MED) adopted the practice of identifying SMEs as firms that employ fewer than 20 employees (MED 1999). Applying this definition to the most recent data available provides a profile of a sector where 97 per cent of all enterprises employed 19 or fewer people and accounted for 30 per cent of employment (MED 2010).

1978–1984: Protectionism and Regional Development

The period 1978–1984 was characterised by high levels of inflation, stagnant growth and rising unemployment. The Government's response to global developments such as the UK joining the EEC in 1973 and the oil shocks of the

1970s was to insulate the economy, and invest in so-called 'Think Big' initiatives – so named because of the perception that they would enable the country to become independent of larger economies. Key areas of the economy, such as agriculture, were also heavily subsidised and import licensing, price and wage controls, tariffs and tax incentives were introduced or increased (Easton 1997).

This period could be considered to be the dawn of SME policy development in New Zealand. International public investigations into the role of small businesses in the economy (the Bolton Report (1971) in the UK and the Wiltshire Report (1971) in Australia) and the activities of the US Small Business Agency had already begun the process of highlighting the merits of SMEs to policymakers. These reports influenced thinking in New Zealand, and contributed to the establishment of the New Zealand Small Business Agency (SBA) in 1978 and to the emerging regional employment policy, which relied heavily on SMEs. However, while SMEs were seen to have a role to play, policymakers continued to operate on the premise that economic growth was only possible when driven by large enterprises.

Prevailing characteristics of this period were the protectionist measures which afforded all businesses the luxury of not having to compete directly with external competitors, with consequent detrimental effects on the way businesses in New Zealand were run (Bollard and Jackson 1992). Two key policies impacted on SMEs during this time: regional policy and export diversification, as a consequence of the 1983 Closer Economic Relations (CER) free-trade agreement with Australia.

The economic development of the regions became a priority and represented a substantial proportion of all public funding for business assistance (Massey and Jurado 2005), most of it channelled through the Development Finance Corporation (DFC). The SBA began operating in 1978 as a branch of the DFC, with an ambit to: encourage cooperation and coordination between government and non-government organizations (NGOs) engaged in assisting SMEs; collaborate with existing organisations in developing programmes of financial, technical and management assistance to SMEs; provide advisory and other services for SMEs; and provide guarantees for loans (Devlin and Le Heron 1977). To meet these objectives, the SBA engaged communities in the delivery of small business assistance and continued to provide these services until 1987. Amongst those who owned or managed SMEs this activity served to reinforce their expectations that government should afford them protection from competition. There was limited interest in improving competitiveness through the development of managerial or marketing skills. Indeed, for most of this period, the prevailing view of advisors was that there was already enough assistance available for businesses in terms of advisory services and assistance (Le Heron 1979). Consequently any form of targeted assistance was not a priority (Haines 1991).

Near the end of the period, policymakers began to consider SMEs as a vehicle for employment. Following trends in the United Kingdom, where so-called 'enterprise policies' were designed to encourage the unemployed to become self-employed (Storey 1994), and the influential US-based study by David Birch (1979) into the employment generation role of small business, local researchers and advisors advocated the employment potential of New Zealand SMEs (Devlin 1984, Bollard 1988).

At the same time policymakers became concerned with the diversification of exports, the expansion of the manufacturing sector and the need to 'pick winners' (Easton 1997). The range of assistance schemes available to small firms was largely financial, including grants, loans, tax incentives, export incentives, regional development assistance, and assistance in the development of technology (Massey and Jurado 2005). With tariff walls to shield domestic firms from competition, this meant that there were few incentives for SMEs to consider exporting as a way of addressing scale-related difficulties. Towards the end of this period, however, CER exposed New Zealand firms to more competition in Australia, and signalled the beginning of a change in attitude among SMEs towards 'how business was done' (Baker 2008). For some business commentators, the opening of the New Zealand market to competition with Australian firms exposed serious deficiencies in managerial and general business practices (Jones 1992, Bollard and Jackson 1992).

In sum, during this phase, Government policy focused on protection from competition, the provision of financial assistance, regional development opportunities, and a largely-indiscriminate programme of assistance to the limited number of export-oriented enterprises. However, the opening of open trade with Australia was beginning to change the way policymakers and firms thought about SMEs.

1984–1999: Market Forces and Reform

By 1984, the New Zealand economy was over-regulated, with a heavily subsidised agricultural sector, soaring unemployment, high levels of inflation, and economic stagnation (Easton 1997). In a series of rapid moves, the currency was floated, banks deregulated, farming subsidies were removed and industry assistance and import protections were reduced (Bollard 2005). A casualty of the reforms was the SBA which was disestablished on the grounds that the level playing field of the reforms meant that small businesses needed no greater support than large. SME policy became focused on enhancing managerial competencies, while regional policy emphasised greater regional and local partnerships to encourage SME growth. The contribution of SMEs to community employment led to important policy developments. Finally, a concerted policy to support high-growth SMEs consolidated a tiered approach to SME policy, as a way to encourage export competitiveness.

The underlying government philosophy of this era was that the market should regulate the economy and businesses should operate in a market environment with limited government intervention (Easton 1997). Commentators reflected that 'the general aim of industrial deregulation has been to eliminate [under performing managers] by forcing firms to actively compete, with only the best surviving' (Campbell, Bollard and Savage 1989: 4). A similar view guided decisions on the government agencies delivering business assistance. Although this phase saw an overall reduction in government intervention (such as the closure of the SBA), there was interest in assisting where market failures were clear and identifiable (for example, in areas of poor managerial competence), and later to ease unemployment. The increase in competition and the focus on export opportunities continued to influence SME policy over this period.

The new social and economic environment generated by the extensive reforms served to further highlight a 'failure of management' in New Zealand businesses (Jones 1992). Policymakers emphasised the importance of developing managerial capabilities (Bollard 2005), influenced by management theory such as Porter's 'five forces' on competition and 'total quality management' theory (Knuckey, Johnston, Campbell-Hunt, Carlaw, Corbett and Massey 1999). Notwithstanding this emerging emphasis, the primary focus remained on providing SMEs with generic business assistance through locally run regional development boards.

The speed of economic reforms, combined with the 1987 share market crash left many sectors in New Zealand vulnerable and unemployment rates were high. Government had to re-consider its role in the SME sector, especially in the regions. There were growing concerns that too few firms had embraced the free market environment in which they operated, and that business assistance was under-utilised because of information asymmetries (Harper 1994).

By 1987 the SBA was disestablished but its advisory functions were taken over by the Business Development Boards (BDBs), which were established by the Ministry of Commerce (later Ministry of Economic Development) in 1990 to enable SMEs to contribute to regional development. BDBs carried out various functions similar to those of the Business Enterprise Centres in the UK. These functions included the administration of various grants such as the Business Development Investigation Grants to fund new business opportunities; the

Expert Assistance Grant Scheme to access management consultants; and the Enterprise Growth Development Scheme to assist with export-related costs (Austin, Fox and Hamilton 1996). BDBs also oversaw the Business Development Programme, which aimed to provide businesses with information, capability improvement services and fostered regional cooperation (Austin et al. 1996). A proliferation of consultants and the lack of evidence that the BDBs were effective led to their being dismantled in 1998.

Another development of this period was the increasing focus on assisting disadvantaged minority groups and alleviating areas of high unemployment. The Enterprise Assistance Programme was a multi-agency programme that focused on fostering enterprise in Māori, Pacific Islanders and women, as well as fostering local employment, and assisting business through the Business Development Programme and the Technology for Business Growth scheme (Nyamori and Lawrence 1997). Other measures to address unemployment were developed by the Department of Labour, for example a range of local initiatives administered by the Community Employment Development Unit and the Local Employment and Enterprise Development Scheme. These measured continued the regional policy focus on local initiatives to foster growth (Perry 1991). The Government's drive to generate employment in both existing SMEs and new firms caused researchers at the time to call for 'a comprehensive small business policy' (Tweed and Cameron 1991: 55), while others expressed doubts that employment policies would result in economic growth (Perry 1991).

In the mid-1990s, the provision of business assistance changed from being based on one-off grants to the provision of ongoing assistance based on existing business strengths and skills. However, the applications for these grants did not increase at the anticipated rate and the Government commissioned a study to identify the reasons for this. The findings identified a lack of management competence, low growth ambition and a preference by owner–managers to remain in control of their business (Austin et al. 1996). In effect, this study challenged the assumptions of policymakers about the needs and expectations of SME owner–managers, in particular regarding growth.

Government approaches to SME business assistance over the period 1984–1999 were founded on SMEs becoming significant contributors to wider economic growth, yet not all SMEs were able to contribute to this objective. The Government responded by developing a multi-tiered SME policy, with 'high-growth' SMEs receiving more targeted funding than the bulk of SMEs with low growth ambitions, characterised as the 'champagne glass' approach to SME support (Massey 2006). This involved assistance for businesses where the high-growth, exporting SMEs (the so-called 'champagne bubbles') were supported by Trade New Zealand with the remaining growth-oriented firms ('those in the glass') being supported by the Ministry of Commerce. The rest of the firms ('those in the stem') were left to be supported by the Community Employment Group. This meant that Government policy was increasingly focused on more glamorous companies (as implied by the champagne metaphor). As a consequence, SMEs suffered from lower levels of engagement by Government.

By 1999 SME policy was firmly positioned as an important component of economic policy, despite the fact that only a small portion of the SME sector was made up of high-growth firms (HGFs). Furthermore, there was an awareness of the failure of some policies to deliver, despite having been initially successful. This experience helped shape and inform approaches in the period 1999–2008.

1999–2008: Post-Reform Consolidation

The economic reforms of the late 1980s resulted in the rise of a service industry that challenged a long-standing dependency on commodity exports (Bertram 2009). New Zealand's move in this regard reflected what was happening in other Organisation for Economic and Co-operation and Development (OECD) countries, as well as the economic theories that identified the growth potential of the 'knowledge economy' (Gibb 1999). The end of 1999 saw the election of a centre-left Labour Party administration which continued to hold office until 2008, and which proceeded to consolidate the economic reforms implemented since 1984. It also targeted underperforming and underrepresented sectors of society (such as Māori, Pacific Islanders, women and young entrepreneurs) by increasing assistance to these groups.

Government assistance increasingly focused on building capability in owner–managers, and developing entrepreneurship, alongside regional development and continued export diversification. Internationally, SMEs were receiving more attention, assisted by the launch of the OECD *Bologna Charter on SME Policies* in 2000. In New Zealand this recognition was reflected in the range of policies used to assist SMEs and in the establishment of the Small Business Advisory Group, which consisted of SME owners and provided independent policy ideas to Ministers. Policymakers also sought advice by actively seeking input from national and international researchers, industry representatives and other stakeholders, as exemplified by the Business Capability Partnership. There were also mounting calls for SME policy to encourage growth at the firm level, by focusing on firm and industry factors with a parallel decrease in attention on regional factors (Bollard 2005).

Government interest in entrepreneurship increased, as manifest by the thinking encapsulated in the 1999 publication *Bright Future*.[1] The backbone of this policy was to articulate the link between entrepreneurship, growth and innovation, reflecting national (Harper 1992) and international research in these areas (Gibb 1999). The main objectives for SME policy included skills enhancement, improving research and development (R&D), increasing access to capital, and fostering innovation and creative industries. This policy actively targeted growth-oriented entrepreneurial firms (NZ Government 1999).

SME policy focus shifted from being predominantly firm-based and advancing generic business assistance, to building the capabilities of individual managers and encouraging innovation. A Government report called the small business sector 'complex' and appealed for more research into firm size determinants and into what constitutes a 'successful firm' (Morrison 1999). The visibility of SMEs in the economic policy arena increased with the launch of the Growth and Innovation Framework (GIF) in 2002[2] and was reinforced with the establishment of the portfolio of Minister for Small Business in 2001, albeit in a position outside of cabinet.

Policy instruments were also refined to target start-ups and high-technology industries. Through Technology New Zealand three schemes were run to increase the uptake of R&D: Technology for Business Growth, Technology Industry Fellowships and Smart Start. Research on 'best practice' continued to identify management capability as an area where government needed to provide leadership.[3] One response was the introduction of a R&D tax credit (Ministry of Research Science and Technology 2007).[4]

The 2003 merger of Industry New Zealand and Trade New Zealand to form New Zealand Trade & Enterprise (NZTE) aimed to develop competitive advantage by encouraging professionalism amongst SMEs in their business development and business processes (NZ Government 2003). NZTE provided Enterprise Awards and also managed the BIZ programme, established in 1998 to assess business needs and deliver training seminars, one-on-one mentoring, and networking opportunities (Massey, Lewis and Tweed 2003). Meanwhile, the MED contracted agencies (including NGOs) to deliver advice and assistance to firms. Exports were also encouraged because external competition was thought to help businesses increase productivity levels (MED 2006) and to this end 2007

---

1   Although this report was produced by the National (conservative) administration, the Labour Government which succeeded it also adopted the main recommendations.

2   The GIF evolved into the Economic Transformation Agenda, and then became the Economic Growth Agenda.

3   For a study on business practices at the time see Knuckey, Leung-Wai and Meskill (1999).

4   Although the Government scrapped this tax credit in 2009, it recently established the new Ministry of Science and Innovation.

was designated 'Export Year' in an effort to encourage businesses to engage in the global economy (NZ Government 2007).

By 2008, the MED had refined its approach to policy development, announcing its intent to tailor policies according to different SME needs. Policies were grouped into three areas: foundation policies (those that provide a stable operating environment, including macroeconomic policy, regulation, property rights, tax, education, entrepreneurship, infrastructure and immigration); generic policies focusing on building capability and improving the business environment; and finally targeted and tailored policies including the Enterprising Partnerships Fund, the Revamped Growth Services Fund and TechNZ (Wigglesworth 2009). Simultaneously, the Government introduced a new regional development policy, namely the Enterprising Partnerships Fund. Its focus was commercially driven regional projects to generate economic benefits through partnerships between business, industry, local governments and education, training and research organisations. Unlike previous regional policies, the overall aim was to develop and implement strategies that would improve the business environment and increase the number of internationally competitive firms (MED 2006).

Public assistance was also directed towards the development of business capability in areas such as entrepreneurship education and sustainability, examples being the Young Enterprise Scheme provided in schools countrywide (Lewis and Massey 2003) and the Eco-Verification programme which sought to encourage sustainable business practices (MED 2008).

Finally, New Zealand SME policy development saw government agencies more proactively engaging with researchers, SME business practitioners and industry associations. The Workplace Productivity Working Group sought to improve productivity through the encouragement of collaboration between government, industry, firms and unions; the Business Capability Partnership, a private–public partnership established in 2004, sought to enhance business and management capability by focusing on policies to help grow competitive firms (Massey and Ingley 2007); and the establishment of the Small Business Advisory Group created a forum where SME owner–managers could voice concerns (such as those over the cost of compliance) to the Minister for Small Business.

Conclusion

In the course of the past 30 years there have been many debates as to how to approach business assistance for SMEs. After several decades researching the SME sector, Storey (2008) concluded 'macro' policies (that is, demand management, immigration policy, competition policy, tax and benefit regime and regulation) are more effective than 'micro' policies (training, business advice, enterprise education and/or access to finance programmes). Since 1984, the New Zealand approach has focused primarily on 'macro' policies that affected and reformed the SME operating environment. Modest government involvement in 'micro' policies, particularly during the post-1999 period of reform consolidation, left provision of these primarily to NGOs.

As part of broader economic policy frameworks to advance an innovative and internationalised economy, SMEs were encouraged to export and to play a significant role in regional development. Successful provision of an 'enabling environment' is reflected in the routine high ranking of New Zealand in international ease of doing business surveys.[5] Yet, as low productivity rates show, these policies do not imply overall economic success. Partial success means that today the Government continues to plays an important role in the 'micro' aspects of SME policy such as provision of business and management capability support to firms to facilitate increases in productivity, exporting and global competitiveness.

Overall the Government has shifted SME policy emphasis away from firm-based initiatives toward development of business and management capability. One of the changes that influenced policymaking relates to SME owners' expectations of government assistance. Pre-1984 public policies afforded SMEs with protection from external competition and with some financial assistance. Policymakers considered SMEs to be a largely homogeneous sector, and business assistance programmes were not targeted. In the middle period expectations of SME owner–managers were re-shaped within the context of economic reforms. The Government's role was re-defined to enable firms to adapt to changing circumstances, leading to a multi-agency approach to enterprise development, in particular in the area of self-employment, and to concerted efforts to support high-growth SMEs. As government intervention became more measured private and local partnerships took an increasing role in providing business assistance. The facilitation of this 'enabling environment' continued in the most recent phase (1999–2008) of consolidation. Public policy centred on promoting awareness of good business practices, export assistance and encouraging R&D and innovation. SME policy had become a recognised and distinct part of economic policy, thanks largely to the emerging research

---

5   For example, New Zealand ranked third for ease of doing business and first for ease of starting a business in International Finance Corporation/ The World Bank Group (2010). *Doing Business 2011 New Zealand: Making a Difference for Entrepreneurs* [Online] Available at: http://www. doingbusiness.org/~/media/FPDKM/Doing%20Business/Documents/Profiles/Country/DB11/ NZL.pdf [accessed: 15 June 2011].

field of entrepreneurship. Accordingly, in 2008 New Zealand SME policy was directed at enhancing management and business capability, particularly in areas such as innovation, as a key driver of firm growth.

This analysis provides policymakers with the historical context in which to consider the development of government policy for SMEs in a small OECD economy since 1978. The analysis underscores the need for policymakers to be aware of, and take into account, external economic events and to better understand international policy trends in the formulation of appropriate policy responses. Salient elements include macro-economic reforms in New Zealand, and the increasing international focus on SME policy. It is also important to note the value of engaging stakeholders, both business and academic, in the development of SME policy, as has been shown with the approach to management and business capability. Given the importance of SMEs to economic growth internationally, this 'bigger picture' of the environment in which New Zealand SME policy is developed and applied may carry important lessons and indeed help inform policymaking elsewhere.

References

Audretsch, D.B., Grilo, I. and Thurik, A.R. 2007. Explaining Entrepreneurship and the Role of Policy: A Framework, in *Handbook of Research on Entrepreneurship Policy*, edited by D. B. Audretsch et al. Cheltenham: Edward Elgar, 1–17.

Austin, J.T., Fox, M.A and Hamilton, R.T. 1996. *A Study of Small and Medium Sized Business Financing in New Zealand*. Wellington: Ministry of Commerce.

Baker, G. 2008. Lessons from Yesteryear, *NZ Business: 70th Anniversary Edition* [Online] Available at: http://www.nzbusiness.co.nz/afa.asp?idWebPage=135 79andidAdrenalin_Articles=760andSID=782494321 [accessed: 2 November 2009].

Bertram, G. 2009. The New Zealand Economy 1900–2000, in *The New Oxford History of New Zealand* edited by G. Byrnes. Auckland: Oxford University Press, 537–572.

Birch, D. 1979. *The Job Generation Process, MIT Programme on Neighborhood and Regional Change, 302.* Available at: http://ssrn.com/abstract=1510007 [accessed: 10 April 2010].

Bollard, A. 2005. New Zealand Economic Policy over the Last 20 Years: A Very Personal View, in *The Visible Hand: The Changing Role of the State in New Zealand's Development* edited by A. Ladley et al. Wellington: Institute of Policy Studies, 79–96.

Bollard, A. 1988. *Small Business in New Zealand*. Wellington: Allen & Unwin.

Bollard, A. and Jackson, L.F. 1992. *Economic Stress in the New Zealand Business Sector*. Wellington: New Zealand Institute of Economic Research.

Bolton Report 1971. *Small Firms: Report of the Committee of Inquiry on Small Firms*. London: HMSO.

Campbell, C., Bollard, A. and Savage, J. 1989. *Productivity and Quality in New Zealand Firms: Effects of Deregulation*. Wellington: New Zealand Institute of Economic Research.

Chatterjee, S., Conway, P., Dalziel, P., Eichbaum, C., Harris, P., Philpott, B. and Shaw, R. 1999. *The New Politics: A Third Way for New Zealand*. Palmerston North: Dunmore Press.

Dennis Jr, W. 2005. Research Mimicking Policy: Entrepreneurship/Small Business Policy Research in the U.S., in *Keystones of Entrepreneurial Knowledge*, edited by R. Van der Horst et al. Oxford: Blackwell, 212–230.

Devlin, M. 1984. *The Small Business Sector in New Zealand: An Introductory Perspective, Small Business Research Series Paper No. 1*. Wellington: Development Finance Corporation.

Devlin, M. and Le Heron, R.B. 1977. *Report to the Development Finance Corporation on Dimensions of New Zealand Business*. Palmerston North: Massey University Research Group.

Easton, B. 1997. *In Stormy Seas: The Post-War New Zealand Economy*. Dunedin: University of Otago Press.

Gibb, A. 1999. Creating an entrepreneurial culture in support of SMEs. *Small Enterprise Development: An International Journal*, 10(4), 27–38.

Haines, L. 1991. *Small Business is Big Business: A Review of Trends and Policies*. Wellington: New Zealand Planning Council.

Harper, D. 1994. *Wellsprings of Enterprise: An Analysis of Entrepreneurship and Public Policy in New Zealand*. Wellington: New Zealand Institute for Economic Research.

Harper, D. 1992. *Entrepreneurship in New Zealand: Foundations for a Public Policy Framework*. Wellington: New Zealand Institute for Economic Research.

Jones, R. 1992. *Changes in Business Culture 1960–1990*. Dunedin: University of Otago.

Knuckey, S., Leung-Wai, J. and Meskill, M. 1999. *Gearing Up: A Study of Best Manufacturing Practice*. Wellington: Ministry of Commerce.

Knuckey, S., Johnston, H., Campbell-Hunt, C., Carlaw, K. Corbett, L. and Massey, C. 2002. *Firm Foundations: A Study of Business Practices and Performance in New Zealand*. Wellington: MED.

Le Heron, R.B. 1979. Political practicalities of locating New Zealand's small business agencies. *Growth and Change*, 10(3), 43–51.

Lewis, K. and Massey, C. 2003. Delivering enterprise education in New Zealand. *Education + Training*, 45(4), 197–206.

Massey, C. 2006. Balancing need with potential: A new framework for business development programmes. *Environment and Planning C: Government and Policy*, 24(1), 37–49.

Massey, C. and Ingley, C. 2007. *The New Zealand Policy Environment for the Development of SMEs*. Wellington: New Zealand Centre for SME Research.

Massey, C. and Jurado, T. 2005. The Support Infrastructure for New Zealand Firms, in *Entrepreneurship and Small Business Management in New Zealand*, edited by C. Massey. Auckland: Pearson Education New Zealand, 17–36.

Massey, C., Lewis, K. and Tweed, D. 2003. New Zealand's BIZ training programme: service provider perspectives. *Education + Training*, 45(8/9), 439–448.

Ministry of Research Science and Technology. 2007. *Research and Development R&D Tax Credit*. [Online] Available at: http://www.morst.govt.nz/business/RD-tax-credit/ [accessed: 28 October 2009].

Ministry of Economic Development (MED) 1999. *SMEs in New Zealand: Structure and Dynamics*. Wellington: MED.

Ministry of Economic Development (MED) 2010. *SMEs in New Zealand: Structure and Dynamics*. Wellington: MED.

Ministry of Economic Development (MED) 2008. *Sustainable Business: Eco-Verification Progress Report*. [Online] Available at: http://www.med.govt.nz/upload/59253/777268_1.pdf [accessed: 21 March 2011].

Ministry of Economic Development (MED) 2006. *Expenditure Review of Business Assistance*. [Online] Available at: http://www.med.govt.nz/upload/41646/expenditure-review-report.pdf [accessed: 4 May 2007].

Minniti, M. 2008. The role of government policy on entrepreneurial activity: productive, unproductive, or destructive? *Entrepreneurship Theory and Practice*, 32(5), 779–790.

Morrison, A. 1999. Small business in New Zealand. *Parliamentary Library Background Paper*, 21. Wellington: Parliamentary Library.

NZ Government 1999. *Bright Future: An Overview*. [Online] Available at: http://executive.govt.nz/96-99/brightfuture/overview.htm [accessed: 2 November 2009].

NZ Government 2003. *Whole of Government Small Business Initiatives*. Cabinet Economic Development Committee, EDC 03 262, Wellington: Cabinet Office.

NZ Government 2007. *New Zealand Export Year*. [Online] Available at: www.exportyear.co.nz [accessed: 12 April 2007].

Nyamori, R. and Lawrence, S. 1997. Small business policy in New Zealand. *New Zealand Journal of Business*, 19(1–2), 73–93.

Organisation for Economic Co-operation and Development (OECD) 2000. *The Bologna Charter on SME Policies*. Paris, France: OECD.

Perry, M. 1991. The 1990 small business package: a mirage masquerading as an economic strategy. *New Zealand Geographer*, 47(2), 80–84.

Storey, D. 2005. Entrepreneurship, Small and Medium Sized Enterprises and Public Policy, in *Keystones of Entrepreneurial Knowledge*, edited by R. Van der Horst et al. Oxford: Blackwell, 142–176.

Storey, D. 1994. *Understanding the Small Business Sector*. London: Routledge.

Storey, D. 2008. Entrepreneurship and SME policy. *World Entrepreneurship Forum 2008 Edition*. [Online] Available at: http://www.world-entrepreneurship-forum.com [accessed: 14 October 2010].

Tweed, D. and Cameron, A. 1991. A small business policy for New Zealand. *The Accountant's Journal*, 70 (3), 53–55.

Wigglesworth, R. 2009. *Ten Years of SME Policies in New Zealand: A Retrospective*. Wellington: MED.

Wiltshire F. 1971. *Report of the Committee on Small Business*. Canberra: AGPS.

World Bank Group/International Finance Corporation 2011. *Doing Business 2011 New Zealand: Making a Difference for Entrepreneurs*. [Online] Available at: http://www.doingbusiness.org/~/media/FPDKM/Doing%20Business/Documents/Profiles/Country/DB11/NZL.pdf [accessed: 15 June 2011].

4

Entrepreneurship Policy in Latin America: Trends and Challenges

Hugo D Kantis and Juan S Federico[1]

Chapter Summary

Entrepreneurship policy is booming in Latin America. However, knowledge about this policy development is still limited and is usually based on best practice reports, policy briefs and position papers published by international institutions. As a first step towards filling this gap, this chapter identifies and analyses the characteristics of and main trends in entrepreneurship policy in recent years. It provides a general overview of entrepreneurship policies at the national level, in a sample of nine Latin American countries, and a deeper analysis of the two with most experience in this field, Brazil and Chile.

Overall, the results of this review show that policies in Latin America tend to combine technical assistance provided by business incubators with seed capital provided by governments. National governments usually operate on a 'second floor', outsourcing to a network of specialised institutions the direct assistance to entrepreneurs. Although many steps have been taken, the chapter concludes that to advance further, entrepreneurship policy still requires the implementation of more ambitious initiatives aimed at fostering entrepreneurship education at the different levels, closer integration between entrepreneurship and science and technology policies, reforms to tax and regulatory frameworks, and the development of an adequate supply of entrepreneurial finance.

1   The authors wish to thank Luciano Schwaizer, a specialist at the Multilateral Investment Fund – Brazil, and Adrian Magendzo, Director of Innova Chile (Corfo), for their valuable comments on earlier versions of this chapter. The help of Cecilia Menéndez and Sergio Drucaroff is also greatly appreciated.

Introduction

Many programmes, institutions and policy schemes aimed at supporting entrepreneurs and new ventures have flourished in Latin America over the last decade. However, detailed studies in this field are lacking. Knowledge of this topic is limited and is usually based on best practice reports, policy briefs and position papers published by international institutions (Etchecopar, Angelelli, Galleguillos and Schorr 2006, Kantis 2010, OECD 2010).As a first step towards filling this gap, this chapter identifies and analyses the characteristics of and main trends in entrepreneurship policy in recent years. It provides a general overview of national entrepreneurship policies across nine different Latin American countries, with a detailed focus on Brazil and Chile. It does not focus on policies promoting *subsistence entrepreneurship* (Schoar 2010) that is, micro-enterprises created for subsistence-like motives. Instead, it is mainly concerned with policies for *growth-oriented new ventures* (Kantis, Moori-Koenig and Angelelli 2004).

The chapter is organised as follows: the first section presents some conceptual issues regarding the rationale, purpose and scope of entrepreneurship policies, with special reference to the Latin American context. The second section describes the main characteristics of entrepreneurship policies in the region (such as targets, areas and main instruments) and analyses the most relevant policies in Chile and Brazil. Finally, an analysis of the main trends and future challenges are provided.

Conceptual Issues and the Latin American Context

Before describing the entrepreneurial policy framework in Latin America, some conceptual issues must be considered, such as the rationale of entrepreneurship policy in general. The aim of this section is to establish a basic platform that facilitates understandings of the context for entrepreneurship policies in the region and the particular conditions faced by Latin American countries.

DEFINITION AND SCOPE OF ENTREPRENEURSHIP POLICY

Entrepreneurship policy has evolved significantly during the last decades and constitutes today an important research topic, embracing a number of valuable contributions (see Robson, Wijbenga and Parker 2009). In general, entrepreneurship policy can be defined as

> ... *policy aimed at the pre-start, start-up and early post-start-up phases of the entrepreneurial process, designed and delivered to address the areas of motivation, opportunity and skills, with the primary objective of*

encouraging more people in the population to consider entrepreneurship as an option, move into the nascent stages of taking actions to start a business and proceed into the entry and early stages of the business...

(Stevenson and Lundström 2007: 105).

In addition to other existing typologies (Stevenson and Lundström 2007), entrepreneurship policies can be classified according to their main objectives and time horizons. As such, three different policy groups or types can be identified, as illustrated in Figure 4.1.

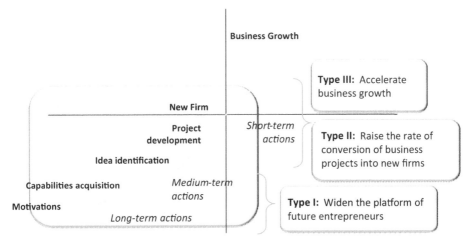

Figure 4.1   The map of entrepreneurship policy
Source: Kantis (2010)

Type I policies seek to *widen the platform of future entrepreneurs*. These policies are focused on those areas that primarily affect the supply side of entrepreneurship in the medium to long term, such as entrepreneurial culture, education and tax reforms. In contrast, Type II policies are aimed at *raising the rate of conversion of business projects into new firms*. By extending Lundström and Stevenson's definition, one can identify a third policy type which seeks to *encourage businesses to achieve a significant growth path* (Type III). Type II and III policies are mainly meant to affect the short to medium term. They often focus on both the provision of 'hard' services, such as those related to finance, and 'soft' assistance, such as training and technical advice (Bridge, O'Neill, and Cromie 1998), and also include networking-related activities among their main instruments. As such, a comprehensive entrepreneurship policy combines short- and long-run actions to generate positive impacts on the entrepreneurial context.

LATIN AMERICA: A SNAPSHOT

Latin America has 580 million inhabitants, or approximately 9 per cent of the world's population. Although there is a remarkable intra-regional diversity, white and indigenous (Native American) people account for the majority of the population, which reflects the importance of European (mainly Spanish) immigration (Lizcano Fernandez 2005). The predominant religion is Christian, notably Roman Catholicism, and the main languages are Spanish and Portuguese.

Latin American legal systems combine features of both US and Western European (mostly Spanish) legal systems. Most countries are organised as republics or federal republics (namely, Brazil and Mexico). According to the Economic Commission for Latin America and the Caribbean (ECLAC), in 2010 Latin America had a gross domestic product (GDP) of nearly US$4 trillion, and a GDP growth rate of 6 per cent, signifying a return to the growth path of the 2003–2008 period. Per capita GDP grew at an average annual rate of 3 per cent reaching 7,000 US$, whilst unemployment fell from 11 per cent to 7 per cent (ECLAC 2010).

World Bank statistics show that between 2005 and 2009 the number of newly registered firms in Latin American countries grew at an annual rate of almost 19 per cent, far above the developed country average of 5 per cent (World Bank 2010a). Similarly, the GEM Report indicates that Latin American countries have the highest Total Early-Stage Entrepreneurship Activity (Kelley, Bosma and Amoros 2010).[2]

However, one of the region's structural features is that necessity entrepreneurs (that is those individuals involved in setting up a new business motivated by negative reasons because they have no other option for work) tend to dominate the landscape (Kelley et al. 2010). There are a number of cultural, social and economic factors that still have a negative influence on the entrepreneurial context compared with other regions (Kantis et al. 2004), as evidenced by the limited numbers of growth-oriented and innovative ventures. In fact, most newly founded businesses are micro-enterprises with low growth expectations, which thus have little impact at the macro-level in terms of innovation, diversification, dynamism and structural change.

Although there is significant heterogeneity among Latin American countries, they share certain features that may justify the establishment of entrepreneurship policies. In general terms, entrepreneurs' social recognition and risk propensity are rather low. Human capital and general educational

---

2   Total Early-Stage Entrepreneurship Activity rate is defined as the percentage of 18–64 population who are either a nascent entrepreneur (people actively involved in setting up a business for more than three months) or owner–manager of a new business with less than 3.5 years (Kelley et al. 2010)

levels are another important constraint on the supply side of entrepreneurship in many countries (UNDP 2010).[3] In addition, Latin American societies tend to be highly fragmented, with the middle classes representing a smaller proportion of the population than in more developed countries (UNDP 2010). As dynamic new ventures tend to be originated in these segments, this is also an inhibiting factor (Kantis et al. 2004). Social fragmentation also negatively affects the existence of network externalities (Audretsch, Grilo and Thurik 2007) and networking process in general, since bridges among different social segments are scarce and trust is limited (Kantis 2010).

Another key argument for policy intervention into new venture creation is the expected contribution by entrepreneurship and new ventures to innovation and job creation (Audretsch et al. 2007, European Commission 2004). These issues are strategic for Latin America since the attitude of business owners and managers towards risk and innovation tend to be rather negative. For instance, research and development investments are lower among firms in Latin America than in more advanced economies (UNESCO 2010). In the same vein, according to the World Economic Forum (WEF 2010), the Latin American business sector is perceived as less sophisticated and innovative than those of Europe and East Asia. As a whole, these features may indicate that Latin American firms are less likely to encourage people to create new (innovative) firms or to promote the emergence of corporate ventures (Kantis and Drucaroff 2009).

In spite of the recent economic growth experienced by most Latin American countries, the labour market still faces structural problems to create jobs in quantity and quality for an increasing population (ILO 2010). In parallel, demand conditions may also be an inhibiting factor, in that they limit the opportunity space for the emergence of innovative and dynamic new ventures. Latin American consumers are perceived to be more price-oriented than quality-oriented compared with those from more developed countries, which may result in lower buyer sophistication (WEF 2010).

The conventional argument about the existence of higher transaction costs for newer and smaller firms (Noteboom 1993) is even stronger in Latin American economies. For instance, despite the efforts being made in some Latin American countries, most are still at the bottom of the *Ease of Doing Business Ranking* (World Bank 2010b). This is related to the existence of higher red-tape burdens for new firms and inefficiencies in factor markets such as labour, information and finance.

Access to financial resources is a particularly significant barrier in most Latin American countries. The venture capital industry in the region is still in its

---

3   According to UNESCO, the tertiary enrolment rate in Latin American countries is half that of more developed countries (UNDP 2010).

very early stages. According to the Latin American Venture Capital Association (LAVCA 2010), the business environment for private equity and venture capital in the region is still underdeveloped.

Finally, institutions currently working for entrepreneurs in the region are relatively weak in both financial and technical terms, and rarely reach the necessary critical mass to face existing challenges. For instance, the number of assisted entrepreneurs and projects is too small to generate a noticeable impact on the general entrepreneurial population (Kantis et al. 2004, Kantis 2010). The quality of the services provided for entrepreneurs and their projects tends to be limited. Moreover, existing institutions in Latin American countries are yet to form an articulated and systemic support network (Kantis 2010).

Overall, these different factors are considered to be sources of systemic failures that affect the number and/or quality of new entrepreneurs and ventures created each year, and thus require public intervention (Verheul, Wennekers, Audretsch and Thurik 2001, Kantis 2010).

Entrepreneurship Policy in Latin America

The previous section provided a conceptual platform and an overview of the entrepreneurial context in Latin America. This section aims to provide a general overview of what is actually being done in the region, based on analyses of about 30 national programmes in nine Latin American countries (Argentina, Brazil, Chile, Colombia, Ecuador, El Salvador, Mexico, Peru and Uruguay). The data was collected principally through interviews with key informants in each country, complemented by information from policy reports and institutional documents. The sample includes the main countries in the region, as well as the most relevant experiences of recent years.

Table 4.1 shows that most programmes aimed at entrepreneurship promotion were implemented in the last five years, one third between 2000 and 2005, and the remaining few in the late 1990s.

The first notable observation is that most of the policies tend to focus on the 'stock' of nascent entrepreneurs and recently created firms (Type II). Policies aimed at generating a long-term flow of entrepreneurs (Type I) are scarce: they are limited to Brazil, Colombia and El Salvador, and to areas such as boosting general motivation to start a business or training courses for would-be entrepreneurs. However, they do not include more ambitious programmes to stimulate entrepreneurship in the long term (such as introducing entrepreneurship programmes at different stages of the educational system or changing the business environment by reforming the tax system, financial

Table 4.1   Main characteristics of entrepreneurship policies in selected Latin American countries

Country	Objective			Target						Main Policy Area					Main role of Government			Year Established		
				Sector			Dynamism													
	Pre-Start Up	Start Up and early development	Growth acceleration	Generic	Innovative	Tech	Generic	Growth-oriented	Institutions	Training	Technical assistance	Networks	Finance	Institutional support	1st floor	2nd floor	Both	Before 2000	Between 2000 and 2005	After 2005
Argentina	0	6	0	2	0	4	2	4	0	1	5	0	3	0	1	4	1	0	2	4
Brazil	1	3	0	1	3	3	2	2	1	1	2	1	4	1	0	4	0	2	0	2
Chile	0	3	0	0	4	0	0	4	3	1	2	1	4	3	1	6	0	0	4	3
Mexico	1	3	1	4	0	1	3	2	0	1	3	0	3	0	0	5	0	0	1	4
Uruguay	0	2	0	0	2	0	0	2	0	0	2	0	2	0	0	2	0	0	0	2
Peru	0	1	0	1	0	0	1	0	0	1	1	0	0	0	0	1	0	0	0	1
Ecuador	0	4	0	0	4	0	0	4	0	1	3	0	1	0	0	4	0	0	0	4
Colombia	1	1	0	1	1	0	1	0	1	1	1	0	1	1	0	2	0	0	2	0
El Salvador	1	1	0	0	1	0	1	0	0	1	1	0	1	0	0	1	0	0	0	1

Note: numbers in cells refer to the quantity of initiatives in each country.

Source: own elaboration based on institutional reports and interviews with key actors.

markets, and/or regulations for entrepreneurs and new firms). Finally, programmes that stimulate the growth of young firms (Type III) are unusual, except in Mexico.

The most typical instruments are seed capital and technical assistance. Policies that include at least some sort of working capital are unusual. The development of business networks for entrepreneurs, on the other hand, is not found as an explicit policy area, but instead depends on the types of support and capabilities available at the institutions delivering technical assistance. The supply of venture capital is one of the least developed policies in the region, although Brazil and Chile are pioneering this field. However, even in these cases, the supply of entrepreneurial finance for young innovative firms is still limited.

A particular type of programme, oriented towards the creation and strengthening of a supportive institutional infrastructure for entrepreneurs, was evident in Chile, Brazil and Colombia, where the government subsidises business incubators. It was noted that the quality of business advisers working with entrepreneurs is crucial to attracting dynamic entrepreneurs, who are not only scarce but also reluctant to request services from institutions whose reputation and sophistication levels do not always suit their needs.

Finally, in most countries the role played by the government is that of a 'second floor' operator. This means that governments concentrate on the design and (in some cases) the evaluation of the programme, whereas direct work with entrepreneurs lies in the hands of a network of specialized decentralised institutions belonging to civil society which constitutes the 'first floor'. These institutions are paid by government, typically on the basis of the number of entrepreneurs they assist.

BRAZIL

Since the late 1970s, Brazil's federal government has been committed to strengthening the development of micro, small-, and medium-sized businesses through the intervention of the Servicio Brasileiro de Apoio as Micro e Pequenas Empresas [Brazilian Support Service for Micro and Small Enterprises] (SEBRAE). This was the context for the launch of the Brasil Empreendedor [Entrepreneurial Brazil] programme in the late 1990s. This programme mainly consists of training and funding for entrepreneurs from all sectors and population segments. But after five years of independent existence, this programme began to lose strategic importance and was eventually absorbed into the broader set of initiatives carried out by SEBRAE.

In parallel, Brazil has implemented a large network of business incubation centres. These centres are supported by different organisations and educational institutions, which are mainly sponsored by the Consejo Nacional de Desenvolvimento Científico e Tecnológico [National Council for Scientific and Technological Development] and SEBRAE.

With regard to financing of new technology-based firms, the most important player in Brazil is the Financiadora de Estudos e Projetos [Funding Unit for Studies and Projects] (FINEP), which reports to the Ministry of Science and Technology. Since the late 1990s, FINEP has taken on a leading role in technological entrepreneurship policies through a series of funds and programmes aimed at stimulating entrepreneurship and innovation. The most noteworthy of these programmes include INOVAR and, more recently, Primeira Empresa Inovadora [First Innovative Enterprise] (PRIME).

The INOVAR programme is an initiative jointly generated by FINEP (2010a) and the Multilateral Investment Fund of the Inter-American Development Bank, which has the objective of creating and strengthening the venture capital industry. To this end, two types of activities have been implemented: first, those aimed at selecting and qualifying entrepreneurial projects (forums); and second, those which select and finance venture capital and private equity funds. In almost ten years, since its creation, INOVAR has organised over 30 forums in which 280 technology companies have participated, 70 of which received investments. Additionally, more than 100 funds have responded to INOVAR's calls, of which 87 are still in the due diligence stage and 18 have been approved. Funds participating in the INOVAR programme represent a total of almost US$3 billion

Although new seed capital funds aimed at financing smaller firms have been launched since 2007, progress in this area is still limited. According to key informants, most investments are concentrated in the growth and consolidation of more mature firms and in private equity in general.This was the context in which FINEP launched the PRIME programme in 2009, which is aimed atsupporting new innovative companies in their early stages (seed capital).

THE PRIME PROGRAMME

The programme's target beneficiaries are companies that are up to two years old, which offer highly innovative products and/or services, and have at least one economically viable product as well as a developed business plan. The programme is carried out through a network of operators, which are basically business incubators. The operational model is largely decentralised, since the government delegates processes (such as the selection and provision of technical support for new companies and the administration of subsidies) to the business incubators. Companies that benefit from the PRIME programme can obtain subsidies of up to

US$70,000 to hire specialist consulting services and human resources for a total period of 12 months. During PRIME's first call, in 2009, 18 operators were selected and 3,154 companies participated, which represented more than 16,000 jobs (FINEP 2010b). The total PRIME programme budget for 2009 was US$138 million. Beneficiary companies that meet their goals in the PRIME programme may apply for another FINEP initiative, the Juro Zero programme, which grants companies access to zero-rate loans to be repaid in up to eight years.

Finally, in 2009, the Ministry of Science and Technology launched the Programa Nacional de Apoio a Incubadoras e Parques Tecnológicos [National Programme for the Support of Incubators and Technological Parks], with the objective of strengthening existing business incubators and technology parks and promoting the creation of new ones.

CHILE

Since the early 2000s, Chile has implemented several public and private initiatives designed to promote new venture creation (Echecopar et al. 2006). The diagnosis at that time was that two major factors were affecting the low entrepreneurial performance of the Chilean economy: the absence of a suitable venture capital industry and the lack of a continuous flow of innovative projects to be invested in. Therefore, a number of measures were adopted to regulate private equity and venture capital funds. The Corporación de Fomento de la Producción [Production Development Corporation] (CORFO) is the main Chilean government agency working in the sphere of innovation and entrepreneurship.

The first initiative began in 1997 and aimed to promote the creation of private venture capital funds with public support from CORFO; the focus was on special loans first and non-reimbursable funds later. However, these funds were not successfully oriented towards the provision of early stage venture capital, and instead concentrated more on private equity and more mature firms.

About five years later, two new initiatives were implemented. In order to increase deal flow, a programme was launched to subsidise the creation and operation of business incubators. From 2003 to 2008, this programme assigned US$11 million to incubators, as a result of which 27 incubators are currently operating (Innova Chile 2010). In parallel, the Seed Capital Programme was designed to support innovative new ventures requiring financial resources at the business concept and commercial and technical validation stages.

THE SEED CAPITAL PROGRAMME

Beneficiary firms must be less than two years old and must be preselected and presented by business incubators, which earn a success fee for each positively evaluated project. The selection is carried out by a committee made up of CORFO and private-sector representatives. Entrepreneurs may be awarded with two non-reimbursable funds: US$20,000 for the first stage and US$80,000 for further development and commercialisation, supplemented by technical assistance provided through business incubators.[1] Up to the end of 2008, 656 projects had been financed under this programme (Innova Chile 2010). The mode of intervention has since been changed: the two phases of the subsidy have been joined, and the total amount awarded has been increased and divided into three different phases, according to the evolution of the project. At the same time, part of the selection process and subsidy administration tasks have been delegated to the incubators, the economic incentives for which were realigned towards results that reflect the performance of incubated companies.

---

1   Beneficiaries are required to contribute 25 per cent of the total project funds.

In 2005, CORFO launched a programme to support the creation and formalisation of angel investor networks. So far, this programme has co-financed the creation of five networks which have provided around US$11 million to new business. In 2009, CORFO created a new initiative to promote the creation of private funds, particularly aimed at co-investing in innovative emerging companies with quasi capital provided by the Government.

In 2010, a new programme aimed at strengthening and invigoratingthe entrepreneurial environment was implemented. This focused mainly on financing institutional strategies that promote the development of entrepreneurial skills and competencies for people in areas including creativity, leadership, business plans, and networking. Finally, a new programme called Start-up Chile was launched in 2010 to entice foreign entrepreneurial teams to locate their businesses in Chile and develop global connections worldwide.

SIMILARITIES AND DIFFERENCES

Some similarities and differences in the development of policy for entrepreneurship policies and initiatives can be observed in the cases of Brazil and Chile. First, financial and technical assistance are the main policy instruments in both cases, and business incubators are the main operational platform. Furthermore, national governments tend to operate at a 'second floor' as it was explained before. Another interesting point in common is the difficulties in developing early stage finance, which arises from a complex set of factors. On the supply side, the need of risk-oriented and skilled investors and fund managers is a key challenge. On the demand side, there is a scarcity of deal flow. After investing large amounts of resources in fostering the creation of private venture capital funds, both countries realised that new initiatives designed to specifically address deficiencies in the provision of seed capital were necessary. Hence, the governments of both Brazil and Chile have implemented specific programmes that supply public subsidies to nascent entrepreneurs, co-investing with different actors in the creation of specific early-stage funds.

However, some contrasts can also be observed. First, the scope of the financial instruments implemented in each country is different. While the Brazilian model simply relies on stimulating the creation of venture funds, Chile also fosters the creation of business angel networks by financing their operational costs. In Brazil, specific efforts aimed at promoting networking among investors and entrepreneurs are concentrated at the organisation of events and forums. Another key difference is the degree of decentralisation in beneficiary selection and subsidy administration. The Brazilian model is more decentralised, although Chile currently seems to be following a similar trend towards decentralisation and flexibility. Chile also stands out for its Government's concern with the behaviour and quality of the services provided by incubators, and is more proactive than Brazil when it comes to implementing incentives aimed at aligning incubators' behaviour with programme expectations.

Entrepreneurship Policy in Latin America: Main Trends and Challenges

The purpose of this chapter has been to present an overview of the main trends in entrepreneurship policy in Latin America, and to identify some lessons and future challenges for the region. One clear common problem is the scarce deal flow of growth-oriented new firms in most countries. This situation constrains the performance and effectiveness of the various institutions supporting entrepreneurs, forcing them to devote significant efforts aimed at identifying and attracting this type of entrepreneurs. One possible lesson from this is that efforts should also be devoted to those initiatives aimed at enlarging the long-term entrepreneurial flow (Type I), not just to those that provide support to the flow of entrepreneurs entering the market (Type II).

The main instruments adopted combine business incubators that provide technical assistance with seed capital provided by governments. However, the development of an adequate supply of financial instruments for entrepreneurs is still pending. Brazil, and to a lesser extent Chile, have already taken steps in this direction, although there is no consolidated intervention model in the region as yet. The development of an adequate supply of private entrepreneurial finance is another challenge, one which requires appropriate financial and human resources, such as risk-oriented and skilled investors and managers. The necessary institutional building process will require a long time horizon. One possible lesson is that governments should play a proactive role in the short-term provision of early-stage finance, while simultaneously fostering a supply of private entrepreneurial finance.

A clear trend concerning the institutional setting of these policies is the outsourcing of services to decentralised institutions. Civil society institutions – universities, business incubators, foundations and chambers of commerce, among others – make up the 'first floor' of such schemes, as they seek and select entrepreneurs and then provide them with direct assistance. Governments, in turn, play a 'second floor' role, which usually includes programme design, final selection of entrepreneurs, funding and follow-up. In this context, the optimal degree of decentralisation is a key issue. Although outsourcing the execution of programmes seems to be a rational strategy in order to gain flexibility and increase proximity to entrepreneurs, some processes remain centralised. As was noted in this paper, in some cases the evaluation and selection of beneficiaries are carried out directly by governments themselves. Even when evaluators from the private sector cooperate with civil servants at this task, it remains troublesome due to the general lack of experience in evaluating innovative and risky projects. One lesson learned from the cases analysed here is that decentralisation itself does not guarantee effectiveness. Rather, effectiveness requires appropriate incentives that influence institutions' behaviour and contribute to an upgrade of their capabilities.

Conclusion

In sum, entrepreneurship has started to occupy a significant space in the policy agenda of many Latin American countries. Over the last ten years, many steps have been taken and a great deal has been learnt. However, a more systemic approach is needed if the development of entrepreneurship policies in the region is to advance further. This will require, in particular, the implementation of more ambitious initiatives aimed at fostering entrepreneurship education at the different levels, closer integration between entrepreneurship and science and technology policies, reforms to tax and regulatory frameworks, and the development of an adequate supply of entrepreneurial finance.

References

Audretsch, D., Grilo, I. and Thurik, R. 2007. *Handbook of Research on Entrepreneurship Policy*. Cheltenham: Edward Elgar Publishing.

Bridge, S., O'Neill, K. and Cromie, S. 1998. *Understanding Enterprise, Entrepreneurship and Small Business*. Basingstoke: Macmillan.

Echecopar, G., Angelelli, P., Galleguillos, G. and Schorr, M. 2006.*Capital semilla para el financiamiento de las nuevas empresas. Avances y lecciones aprendidas en América Latina*. [Seed Capital in Latin America: Advances and lessons learned] Washington, DC: Interamerican Development Bank.

Economic Commission for Latin America and the Caribbean (ECLAC) 2010. *Preliminary Overview of the Economies of Latin America and the Caribbean*. ECLAC: Santiago, Chile.

European Commission 2004.*Benchmarking Enterprise Policy: Results from the 2004 Scoreboard*. Commission Staff Working paper SEC (2004) 1427, Brussels.

Financiadora de Estudos e Projetos (FINEP) 2010a.*INOVA Brazil Internal Report*. [Online] Available at: http://www.finep.gov.br/programas/inovabrasil.asp [accessed: 4 April 2011].

Financiadora de Estudos e Projetos (FINEP)2010b. *PRIME*. Internal Report. [Online] Available at:http://www.portalinovacao.mct.gov.br/pi/prime/ indicadores/ [accessed: 4 April 2011].

Innova Chile 2010.*Datos Emprendimiento Innovador* [Data on Innovative Entrepreneruship] Internal Report, Santiago.

International Labour Office (ILO) 2010. *Labour Overview. Latin America and the Caribbean*.Lima: ILO Regional Office Publications.

Kantis, H. 2010. *Aportes Para el Diseño de Políticas Integrales de Desarrollo Emprendedor en América Latina* [*Insights for the Design of Integrative Entrepreneurship Policies in Latin America*].Washington, DC: Interamerican Development Bank.

Kantis, H. and Drucaroff, S. 2009. *Corporate Entrepreneurship*. Washington DC: Interamerican Development Bank.

Kantis, H., Moori-Koening, V. and Angelelli, P. 2004. *Developing Entrepreneurship. Experience in Latin America and Worldwide*. Washington DC: Interamerican Development Bank.

Kelley, D., Bosma, N. and Amoros, J.E. 2010.*Global Entrepreneurship Monitor – 2010 Executive Report*. [Online] Available at: http://www.gemconsortium.org [accessed: 23 August 2011].

Latin American Venture Capital Association (LAVCA) 2010.*Scorecard: The Private Equity and Venture Capital Environment in Latin America*. [Online] Available at: http://lavca.org/2010/04/21/2010scorecard/ [accessed: 23 August2011].

Lizcano Fernández, F. 2005 Composición étnica de las tres áreas culturales del continente americano al comienzo del siglo XXI [Ethnic composition in the three cultural areas of America at the beginning of the XXI century]. *Convergencia*, 12(38), 185–232.

Noteboom, B. 1993. Firm size effects on transaction costs. *Small Business Economics*, 5(4), 283–295.

Organization for Economic Cooperation and Development (OECD) 2010. *SMEs, Entrepreneurship and Innovation*.OECD Studies on SMEs and Entrepreneurship Series, Paris.

Roberts, E. and Eesley, C. 2009. *Entrepreneurial Impact: The Role of MIT*. Massachusetts: Ewing Marion Kauffman Foundation and MIT Press.

Robson, J., Wijbenga, F. and Parker, S. 2009. Entrepreneurship and policy: challenges and directions for future research. Introduction. *International Small Business Journal Special Issue*, 27(5), 531–535.

Schoar, A. 2010. The divide between subsistence and transformational entrepreneurship. *Innovation Policy and the Economy*, 10(1), 57–81

Stevenson, L. and Lundström, A. 2007. The Fabric of Entrepreneurship Policy in *Handbook of Research on Entrepreneurship Policy*, edited by D. Audretsch et al. Cheltenham: Edward Elgar Publishing.

United Nations Development Program (UNDP) 2010. *Human Development Index Database*. [Online] Available at: http://hdr.undp.org/en/statistics/hdi/ [accessed: 23 August 2011].

United Nations Educational, Scientific and Cultural Organization (UNESCO) 2010.*UNESCO Science Report 2010*. Paris: UNESCO Publishing.

Verheul, I., Wennekers, S., Audretsch, D. and Thurik, R. 2001. An eclectic theory of entrepreneurship: policies, institutions and culture. *Tinbergen Institute Discussion Paper* TI2001-030/3.

World Bank 2010a.*World Bank Group Entrepreneurship Snapshots Entrepreneurship Survey 2010*. [Online] Available at:http://econ.worldbank.org [accessed: 23 August 2011].

World Bank 2010b.*Ease of Dong Business Rankings* 2010. [Online] Available at: http://www.doingbusiness.org/rankings [accessed: 23 August 2011].

World Economic Forum (WEF) 2010. *The Global Competitiveness Report 2010–2011*. Geneva: World Economic Forum.

5

Enterprise Policymaking in the UK: Prescribed Approaches and Day-to-Day Practice

Norin Arshed and Sara Carter

Chapter Summary

Enterprise policy is the main mechanism used by governments to stimulate economic growth, employment and international competitiveness. It is an umbrella term used to describe a plethora of regulatory, fiscal and business support initiatives introduced to support the SME sector. The UK has substantially increased the number of enterprise policy initiatives over the past 30 years, but there are serious concerns about its effectiveness. Critics have suggested that the ineffectiveness of enterprise policy may be attributable to piecemeal policymaking, where a focus on specific initiatives has led over time to a reduction in the overall coherence of enterprise policy. This chapter describes the process of policymaking in the UK, drawing distinctions between the prescribed 'textbook' approach to policymaking and the day-to-day practices of policymakers. While previous studies have explored the public-facing side of policy, its implementation and effectiveness, this chapter focuses on the 'back-office' processes of policy formulation. Four influences (legitimacy, actors, culture and power) evident within the policymaking process may undermine the coherence and consistency of enterprise policy.

Introduction

Just as monetary and fiscal policy were the backbone of creating employment and growth in the post-war economy, so enterprise policy is emerging as the most important policy instrument for a global and knowledge-based economy (Gilbert, Audretsch and McDougall 2004). Enterprise policy includes measures to support individuals moving into business ownership, such as business advice (entrepreneurship policy) as well as measures to improve business performance and growth, such as improving access to growth finance (SME policy) (Audretsch and Beckmann 2007). The overall objective of enterprise policy, regardless of whether it is focused on the individual or the firm, is to increase economic growth, competitiveness, employment and wealth creation. Policy actions across the European Union (EU) include access to finance, maintaining existing jobs and/or integrating unemployed or those at risk into the labour market, facilitating cross-border activities and encouraging tax breaks and financial incentives for purchases of specific sector products (EIM Business and Policy Research 2010).

Within the UK, the context of this chapter, there are growing concerns about both the effectiveness and the cost of enterprise policy. Over the past 30 years, numerous policy instruments have been introduced in the UK with the broad intention of creating an 'entrepreneurial society'. These include the Small Firms Loan Guarantee (SFLG) scheme, which has guaranteed more than 100,000 loans valued at £5 billion since 1981[1] (BERR 2008), and the creation of the Better Regulation Executive (BRE) which led the Government's regulatory reform agenda. More recently, StartUpBritain was launched in 2010 as a major initiative to deliver support and advice to entrepreneurs. Reviewing the previous decade's policy interventions, Huggins and Williams (2009) concluded there had been little improvement in business start-up rates despite the proliferation of policy initiatives. Concerns have also been expressed at the lack of coherence of UK enterprise policy, especially with regard to how specific initiatives fit within the overall policy objectives and the lack of clarity over which objective they are designed to address (Storey 2005). Moreover, a proliferation of initiatives has resulted in an escalation in costs – current estimates suggest that the cost of small business support is in the region of £12 billion[2] (Richard 2007).

Populist concerns about policy effectiveness and cost have been matched by academic criticism which has focused on the visible and tangible elements of enterprise policy, including aims, delivery, evaluation and implementation and delivery mechanisms (Storey 2000, Lenihan, Hart and Roper 2005, Bennett 2008). While previous studies have focused on public-facing aspects of policy, this chapter extends prior research by exploring the 'back-office' process of policy formulation by government ministers and civil servants.

---

1   Equivalent to USD $8 billion/€6 billion.
2   Equivalent to USD $20 billion/€14 billion.

This chapter provides an insight into the reality of formulating enterprise policy in the UK by drawing on original evidence gathered through a three-month period of ethnographic research within a government department. Participant observation allows researchers to uncover, interpret and understand the environment and its hidden rules in which enterprise policy is formulated. Working as a civil servant between October and December 2009 enabled the researcher to become immersed in the policymaking culture and observe the daily working lives and relationships of those involved in enterprise policy. It also actively allowed participation in the formulation of enterprise policy. In practice, the prescribed approaches to policy formulation are rarely followed, and the policy formulation process is unduly influenced by factors that are both less rational and less predictable than previously acknowledged.

The Prescribed Approach to Policymaking in the UK

The UK policymaking process is led by a network of institutions, people and practices gathered at the apex of power around the Prime Minister and the Cabinet, including the most powerful civil servants of Whitehall (the zone of government offices in London), the Cabinet Office and the Prime Minister's Office, known as the core executive. The core executive integrates policy in an otherwise rather fragmented decision-making structure (Dorey 2005). Smith (1999: 5) explains that UK Government departments are headed by ministers who are 'key actors within the institutions of the core executive'. The core executive of Britain is valuable to the policy process because key individuals within the core executive coordinate government activity and provide the resources to implement and deliver public goods.

Best practice in formulating and evaluating UK Government policies is prescribed in the *Green Book* (HM Treasury 2005), which focuses on the flow of the policy process. The ROAMEF Cycle (Rationale, Objectives, Appraisal, Monitoring, Evaluation and Feedback) describes how policy is supposedly formulated and the stages that arise during the process (Figure 5.1). McVittie and Swales (2007) explain that the *Green Book* process starts with a policy action, which must be justified in general terms, usually related to market failure or excessive inequalities (*rationale*) from which more specific *objectives* should then be set. This is followed by an *ex ante* option of *appraisal*. If the policy passes this test, its execution requires *monitoring* and subsequent *ex post evaluation*. An effective evaluation provides *feedback* to policymakers and the opportunity for reflecting on the policy's rationale, thereby starting a further round of policy

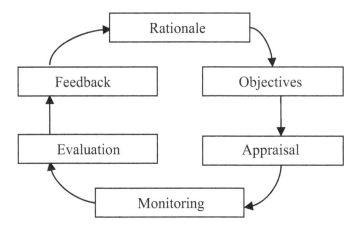

Figure 5.1   ROAMEF cycle
Source: HM Treasury (2005:3)

assessment. This process of continual assessment and feedback is expected to improve policy effectiveness and indicates the key chain of events that lead towards the final decisions and outcomes.

While the ROAMEF process is used extensively within the UK, similar models have been described elsewhere. One of the most common approaches to the study of policymaking derives from the early work of Lasswell (1951), whose original model included seven stages. More recent versions, such as that described by Porter (1995), have reduced the process to fewer steps, as Table 5.1 illustrates. Porter's (1995) model encompasses the key actors involved in the activities and outputs of the policymaking process. This model assumes that policymakers approach the issues rationally, going through each logical stage of the process and carefully considering all relevant information, where there is an emphasis on formal structures in place. If policies fail to achieve the intended outcome, blame is often attributed to political or managerial failure in implementation (Juma and Clark 1995). Critics maintain that policymaking in action is more complicated and less neat than is described in such models, and is actually a continual, iterative process, that is rarely sequentially ordered (Bochel and Duncan 2007).

The Day-to-Day Practices of Policymaking in the UK

The ROAMEF cycle and Porter's policy-in-stages model prescribe desirable approaches to policy formulation, but fail to describe how this process is influenced by other, less predictable forces. The results of participant

Table 5.1   Policy-in-Stages

Stages	Action
1	Identification of policy problems or issues, through demands for action.
2	Agenda-setting or focusing on specific problem or issues.
3	Formulation of policy proposals, their initiation and development, by policy planning organisations, interest groups, and/or the executive or legislative branches of government.
4	Adoption of and rendering legitimating of policies through the political actions of the government, interest groups and political parties.
5	Implementation of policies through bureaucracies, public expenditures and the activities of executive agencies.
6	Evaluation of a policy's implementation and impact.

Source: Adapted from Porter (1995)

observation research within a UK Government department during 2009 revealed four additional influences in the process of formulating enterprise policy: *legitimacy* necessary to establish credibility; the behaviours of individual *actors*; the shared norms and beliefs inherent within the department's *culture*; and the role of political actors with the *power* to overrule civil servants. These influences are discussed below.

LEGITIMACY

It has long been recognised that legitimacy is crucial for the smooth functioning of government (Easton 1965). Legitimacy is defined as a generalised 'perception or assumption that the actions of an entity are desirable, proper, or appropriate within some socially constructed system of norms, values, beliefs, and definitions' (Suchman 1995: 574). In other words, legitimacy is the belief that certain behaviours or practices are common and socially accepted.

In this study, there were three main types of legitimacy that the department fostered: internal legitimacy (predicated on the impartiality of civil servants), external legitimacy (the role of external stakeholders), and media legitimacy (informing the public). Firstly, the impartiality of civil servants remains an important tenet in British governance (Demmke 2005), and strengthens internal legitimacy. Induction into the role of civil servant involved being briefed on the importance of neutrality, regardless of the party in power and its politicians. New recruits entering government are clearly made aware of the importance of impartiality. Secondly, the notion of legitimacy rests on an understanding of the important role played by organisational audiences, external stakeholders and outside referees in influencing the actions of the focal organisations (DiMaggio and Powell 1983). Thus, regional government agencies and delivery partners are involved in creating external legitimacy. Government may be seen to be working alongside these agencies to encourage participation in developing enterprise policy. This was achieved by setting up a number of advisory groups and task forces to advise Government of practical steps to accelerate the start-up and growth rates of certain groups of individuals in the UK and to provide lobbying to raise the profile of the enterprise agenda. By working with these external stakeholders, recognition of the state's legitimacy perceived by external actors enhanced its external legitimacy. Thirdly, the media's broad reach and influence creates a need for media legitimacy. The tone of the media in regard to an organisation has been used as a surrogate measure of an organisation's legitimacy (Bitektine 2011). The department in this study branded itself as an agency that empowers and aids small businesses; however, with budgetary cuts, issues of legitimacy were carefully scrutinised by the media. The new UK coalition Government, which took office in May 2010, announced wide-ranging cuts to the department's budget, to widespread media approval.

Personal legitimacy, such as the charisma of organisational leaders, is also essential. Individuals who are seen to possess personal legitimacy have both linkage legitimacy (links with desirable external social actors) and technical legitimacy (the core technology, quality of services but most importantly the qualifications of the actors) (Bitektine 2011). Reputation and the status of individuals contribute to building pragmatic legitimacy which is an 'instrumental value of the organisation for its stakeholders in terms of how it fulfills their self-interest. Here, legitimacy is assessed in terms of the extent to which the organisation can act to serve the needs and interests of its stakeholders and constituents' (Brinkerhoff 2005: 4). In other words, the reputation and status of individuals, built over the years, becomes interlinked with the legitimacy of an organisation. In contrast, status is awarded on a 'rank-order relationship among people associated with prestige and deference behavior' (Huberman, Loch and Onculer 2004: 104). Status is continuously renegotiated as people assert expertise and claim legitimacy within the organisation's hierarchy. The social identities of influential people in government have an impact both on ordinary citizens and also civil servants. In this study, civil servants openly admitted to being influenced by the charisma and social prestige of certain ministers. Indeed, a minister's status and reputation at times overwhelmed the formulation of coherent enterprise policy. Ideas introduced by a charismatic minister were regarded with greater credibility than was merited simply because of the minister's social prestige.

Furthermore, cognitive legitimacy was widely accepted as it spares the organisation from increased scrutiny and distrust of external social actors, by making the organisation understandable (by denying access to the complex processes) and by providing a perfect example of the outcome (Bitektine 2011). The case study highlights the ROAMEF cycle as the formal procedure undertaken to formulate enterprise policy and from the participant observation this was not the case. Stakeholders were often not involved in process of how the policy was formulated, rather they were excluded and only exposed to the responses to their recommendations.

ACTORS

Institutional actors, sometimes known as institutional entrepreneurs, are those with 'the resources at their disposal to create and empower institutions. Institutional entrepreneurs serve as agents of legitimacy supporting the creation of institutions that they deem to be appropriate and aligned with their interests' (Dacin, Goodstein and Scott 2002: 47). Institutional entrepreneurs have several distinctive attributes. These include identities and roles that allow them to build legitimacy and access resources among diverse stakeholders; the ability to develop lines of argument that appeal to diverse stakeholders; the ability to make connections between existing organisational practices and the new practices; and the capacity to align the new practices with the values of key stakeholders (Maguire, Hardy and Lawrence 2004). Key stakeholders are of great importance to institutional entrepreneurs, as they are seen as individuals who are the providers or holders of legitimacy (Cummings and Doh 2000).

The stakeholder approach for policymaking, planning and management is expected to yield two positive outcomes: realistic, more effective policies and plans and improved implementation. Stakeholders represent interested or affected companies, groups, individuals or systems that the enterprise will impact. Stakeholders should have realistic expectations of their roles and should not be misled in believing that they are involved in a cooperative or consultative process, when in reality, their role may be merely symbolic (Sen 2000). Considerations of stakeholder legitimacy are deemed by nearly all to be important (Freeman 1984), but in the determination of legitimacy, scholars and managers are left largely to their own devices. Annan (cited in Polsby 2001) argues that commissions such as task forces, once enforced, begin to take on a politics of their own and are therefore capable of recommending policies not anticipated or even welcomed by the Government which is free to ignore them. In this study, the two current task forces set up by Government presented their reports and recommendations after three years of consulting and researching. Government then largely ignored the recommendations by aligning non-committal responses to popular attitudes of stakeholders and society to promote the legitimacy of its enterprise agenda.

CULTURE

The role of culture in conditioning organisational activities is a particular concern of new institutionalism within sociology. This perspective views culture and cognition linked as 'internal interpretative processes that are shaped by external cultural frameworks' (Scott 2001: 57). While earlier concepts emphasised shared norms and values, the current emphasis is on shared knowledge and beliefs (Scott 2001). Bawn (1993: 965) argues 'political institutions are explicit products of social choices,' and a culture of job rotation, meetings and a hierarchal structure dominated the government department. Many senior civil servant positions are rotated on a yearly basis. Haldenby, Parsons, Rosen and Truss (2009: 17) call this 'musical chairs with internal positions' and describe the 'central danger of regularly moving individuals between posts (or encouraging them to seek regular moves for themselves)', which it blames for the lack of expertise and institutional memory within the organisation.

The results of this case study suggest that regular job rotation among senior civil servants has consequences for enterprise policy. Certainly, there was little evidence of a deep-seated capacity to build and retain the necessary subject expertise within the department. The lack of subject expertise among senior civil servants also made it difficult for them to rein in the more exuberant demands of government ministers. Government ministers (and taxpayers) often desire grand policies with a wide and immediate social and economic impact to be delivered quickly and effectively; however, hasty implementation often leads to undesirable results. Compliance to ministerial demands and announcements has largely displaced the more mundane but necessary concerns with the fundamentals of improving the quality of business advice and processes. Ministerial demands and announcements led to an abundance of meetings which was common practice within the department. Often meetings had little obvious importance, but were excessively time consuming. The meetings culture can be attributed to the strengthening of internal legitimacy. Civil servants must accept and confirm the work that they do to be credible, reassuring other civil servants of the importance of their work and roles. One of the key themes that arose from the meetings was the importance placed on announcements rather than on the feasibility of the work being undertaken. Allied to the meetings culture was a 'culture of timidity and passivity' in the department, where, to quote an earlier media report, officials had their 'mouths bandaged and their minds switched off' (BBC 2009). The government department studied in this case study had a structured and hierarchical culture – those in senior positions would challenge decisions they thought were not appropriate but junior civil servants were often in fear of making mistakes, saying too much or too little, never questioned senior colleagues nor communicated their own thoughts. In short, there was no desire to challenge existing practices, norms and beliefs.

POWER

Power takes many shapes and forms, with Lukes (1974: 27) offering a wide definition of power: namely, it is a situation where 'A exercises power over B when A affects B in a manner contrary to B's interests.' Although Scott (2001) argues that power certainly matters in supporting legitimacy processes as in other social activities, it is not the absolute arbiter. Nevertheless, power is strongly associated with the legitimacy, actors and culture of the organisation. Social structures are reproduced and continuously modified by the ongoing actions of individual and collective social actors (Giddens 1979). Yet the actions of the most influential and powerful are often those that determine what is socially accepted. For example, Hardy and Philips (1998: 219) argue that 'formal authority, the control of critical resources, and discursive legitimacy' are important sources of power for institutional entrepreneurs. Powerful actors are able to shape the views and needs of other, less powerful actors. In doing so, the nature of the dynamics of power within the organisation leads actors to believe that acting in the interests of more powerful actors is consistent with their own interests.

In this case study, observational evidence from the government department suggests that power is neither balanced nor equal. Powerful actors, such as highly ranked civil servants and Private Secretaries to government ministers who act as ministerial gatekeepers, are regarded as an elite force within the civil service. Private Secretaries yield power that controls areas of the ministerial agenda, and their more junior colleagues perceive the need to build a good working relationship with them in order to access resources and influence agendas. While senior civil servants are popularly viewed as individuals with the ability to control overly enthusiastic politicians and ministers, their lack of subject expertise with regard to enterprise policy rendered them incapable of offering alternatives to the political propensity for high-profile media announcements over prosaic but more effective policy solutions.

Conclusions

Given the heterogeneity of the SME sector, enterprise policy formulation is exceptionally difficult (Dannreuther 2007). Within the UK, a plethora of enterprise-related initiatives have been introduced by successive government ministers. Indeed, enterprise policy formulation has been focused around individual actors who have the authority to ascertain legitimacy, influence the culture of the organisation and have the power to allocate resources in return for announcements. Legitimacy can only be upheld by actors who understand the consequences of their actions and processes. Actors have an interest in specific institutional structures and command resources which can be applied to influence institutionalised rules (Beckert 1999). Power is simultaneously a stabilising force for institutionalisation and a driver of institutional change, just as powerful actors can shape the institutional environment in different directions depending on their particular interests (Pacheco, York, Dean and Sarasvathy 2010). Government can wield public policy, namely the use of tools by policymakers, to influence society in a politically desired manner to stimulate the economy (Henrekson and Stenkula 2010).

In contrast with the prescribed model of policy formulation, the observed process suggests a lack of transparency and the allocation of resources to initiatives with little regard to the overall policy framework.

Figure 5.2 illustrates the actual steps observed within the process of formulating enterprise policy where legitimacy, actors, culture and power played prevalent roles in constructing the process. As a first step, an area of enterprise policy interest is needed to captivate the audience. Once ministers and civil servants have the policy interest, they allocate a team, assign duties, discuss which stakeholders will need to be involved and set deadlines often with 'briefing' meetings providing updates. Data or evidence to substantiate and justify the area of interest is then sought. The team writes a formal report after conducting research followed by a 'clearing' process involving numerous individuals across government who provide comments and feedback. Following this, there is an 'announcement' agenda involving repetitive meetings, brainstorming, gathering stakeholders to gauge their views and ideas and involving as many 'high profile' actors as possible. The main issue in the announcement stage is who will announce and what will be announced either to attract media attention or to appease stakeholders. The announcing facet begins at the briefing stage and follows throughout the procedure, at times overtaking the real matter at hand. The desired policy may then be

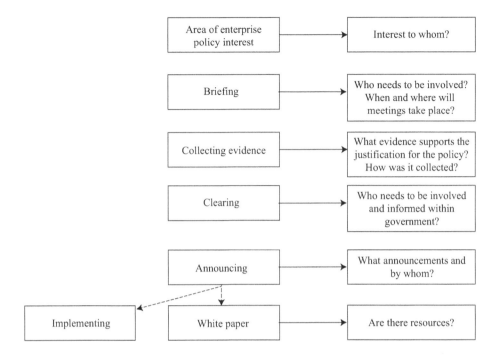

Figure 5.2   Enterprise policy formulation in the UK

implemented either through a White Paper[3] or by allocating resources, setting specific objectives and demanding reviews.

While many critics have focused attention on the ineffectiveness of enterprise policies introduced over the past decades in the UK, this chapter has focused on the relatively unseen 'back-office' function of policy formulation. It is argued that the prescribed process of policy formulation is rarely demonstrated. Instead, policy formulation follows a sequence that starts with ministerial interest, proceeds through a process of briefings and clearing meetings that lead to media announcements, before consideration is given to implementation and resourcing. Focusing attention on the 'back-office' processes and actors formulating policy helps illuminate why so many enterprise policy initiatives have proven to be ineffective. Concentrating attention on the process of formulation, not just evaluation, of enterprise policy will help ensure greater transparency and hence, ultimately improve the effectiveness of enterprise policy.

---

3   A White Paper is a government document put before Parliament. A White Paper allows the Government an opportunity to collect feedback before it formally presents policies as a Bill which, when approved by both Houses of Parliament (Commons and Lords), becomes an Act of Parliament.

References

Audretsch, D.B. and Beckmann, I. A.M. 2007. From Small Business to Entrepreneurship Policy, in *Handbook of Research on Entrepreneurship Policy* edited by D. B. Audretsch et al. Cheltenham: Edward Elgar, 36–53.

Bawn, K. 1993. The logic of institutional preferences: the German electoral law as a social choice outcome. *American Journal of Political Science*, 37(4), 965–989.

BBC 2009. *Civil service 'unfit for purpose'*. Available at: http://news.bbc.co.uk/1/hi/uk_politics/7924008.stm [accessed 12 January 2010].

Department for Business Enterprise and Regulatory Reform (BERR) 2008. *Enterprise: Unlocking the UK's Talent*. Available at: www.hm-treasury.gov.uk/budget/budget_08/documents/bud_bud08_enterprise.cfm. [accessed 18 August 2008].

Beckert, J. 1999. Agency, entrepreneurs, and institutional change. The role of strategic choice and institutionalized practices in organizations. *Organization Studies*, 20(5), 777–799.

Bennett, D. 2008. SME policy support in Britain since the 1990s: what have we learnt? *Environment and Planning C: Government and Policy*, 28,(2) 375–397.

Bitektine, A. 2011. Toward a theory of social judgments of organizations: the case of legitimacy, reputation, and status. *Academy of Management Review*, 36(1), 151–179.

Bochel, H. and Duncan, S. 2007. *Making Policy in Theory and Practice*. Bristol: Policy Press.

Brinkerhoff, D.W. 2005. *Organizational Legitimacy, Capacity, and Capacity Development*: *Proceedings of the 8th Public Management Research Association* (Los Angeles: University of Southern California, School of Policy, Planning, and Development. Los Angeles, California).

Cummings, J.L. and Doh, J.P. 2000. Identifying who matters: mapping key players in multiple environments. *California Management Review*, 42(2), 83–104.

Dacin, T., Goodstein, J. and Scott, W.R. 2002. Institutional theory and institutional change: Introduction to the special research forum. *Academy of Management Journal*, 43(4), 45–57.

Dannreuther, C. 2007. EU SME policy: on the edge of governance. *CESifo Forum*, 8(2), 7–13.

Demmke, C. 2005. *Are Civil Servants Different because They Are Civil Servants?* [Online: European Institute of Public Administration] Available at: http://publications.eipa.eu/en/details/&tid=1417 [accessed 25 April 2009].

DiMaggio, P.J. and Powell, W.W. 1983. The iron cage revisited: institutional isomorphism and collective rationality in organizational fields. *American Sociological Review*, 48(2), 147–160.

Dorey, P. 2005. *Policy Making in Britain*. London: Sage Publications.

Easton, D. 1965. *A Framework for Political Analysis*. Englewood Cliffs, CA: Prentice-Hall.

EIM Business and Policy Research 2010. *European SMEs under Pressure – Annual report on EU small and medium-sized enterprises 2009*; implemented for the European Commission, DG Enterprise and Industry, Brussels 2010 [Online] Available at: http://ec.europa.eu/enterprise/policies/sme/facts-figures-analysis/performance-review/pdf/dgentr_annual_report2010_100511.pdf [accessed 15 August 2009].

Freeman, R.E. 1984. *Strategic Management: A Stakeholder Approach*. Boston, MA: Pitman Publishing.

Giddens, A. 1979. *Central Problems in Social Theory: Action, Structure, and Contradiction in Social Analysis*. Berkeley, CA: University of California Press.

Gilbert, B., Audretsch, D.B. and McDougall, P.P. 2004. The emergence of entrepreneurship policy. *Small Business Economics*, 22(3–4), 313–323.

Haldenby, A., Parsons, L., Rosen, G. and Truss, E. 2009. *Fit for purpose*. [Online: Reform] Available at: http://www.reform.co.uk/Research/Government/GovernmentArticles/tabid/112/smid/378/ArticleID/165/reftab/73/t/Fit%20for%20purpose/Default.aspx [accessed: 27 April 2009].

Hardy, C. and Phillips, N. 1998. Strategies of engagement: Lessons from the critical examination of collaboration and conflict in an interorganizational domain. *Organization Science*, 9(2), 217–230.

Henrekson, M. and Stenkula, M. 2010. Entrepreneurship and Public Policy, in *Handbook of Entrepreneurship Research: An Interdisciplinary Survey and Introduction* (Vol. 5), edited by Z. J. Acs and D. B. Audretsch. New York: Springer, 595–637.

HM Treasury 2005. *The Green Book – Appraisal and Evaluation in Central Government*. Available at: www.hm-treasury.gov.uk/d/green_book_complete.pdf [accessed: 13 April 2009].

Huberman, B.A., Loch, C.H. and Onculer, A. 2004. Status as a valued resource. *Social Psychology Quarterly*, 67(1), 103–115.

Huggins, R. and Williams, N. 2009. Enterprise and public policy: a review of Labour government intervention in the United Kingdom. *Environment and Planning C: Government and Policy*, 27(1), 19–41.

Juma, C. and Clark, N. 1995. Policy research in sub-Saharan Africa: an exploration. *Public Administration and Development*, 15, 121–137.

Lasswell, H. 1951. The Policy Orientation, in *The Policy Sciences*, edited by D. Lerner and H. Lasswell. Stanford, CA: Stanford University Press, 3–15.

Lenihan, H., Hart, M. and Roper, S. 2005. Developing an evaluative framework for industrial policy in Ireland: fulfilling the audit trail or an aid to policy development. *Quarterly Economic Commentary*, Summer 2005, June, 16–85.

Lukes, S. 1974. *Power: A Radical View*. London: Macmillan.

Maguire, S., Hardy, C. and Lawrence, T.B. 2004. Institutional entrepreneurship in emerging fields: HIV/AIDS treatment advocacy in Canada. *Academy of Management Journal*, 47(5), 567–679.

McVittie, E. and Swales, J.K. 2007. The information requirements for an effective regional policy: a critique of the Allsopp Review. *Urban Studies*, 44(3), 425–438.

Pacheco, D.F., York, J.G., Dean, T.J. and Sarasvathy, S.D. 2010. The coevolution of institutional entrepreneurship: a tale of two theories. *Journal of Management*, 36(4), 974–1010.

Polsby, N.W. 2001. Legitimacy in British policy-making: functional alternatives to the civil service. *British Journal of Politics and International Relations*, 3(1), 5–35.

Porter, R.W. 1995. *Knowledge Utilisation and the Process of Policy Formulation: Toward a Framework for Africa*. Washington, DC [Online: SARA] Available at: http://sara.aed.org/publications/cross_cutting/knowledge_utilization/html/utilization.htm#concl [accessed 12 March 2009].

Richard, D. 2007. *Richard Review on Small Business & Government* [Online: The British Library] Available at: http://www.conservatives.com/pdf/document-richardreport-2008.pdf [accessed: 15 August 2008].

Scott, W.R. 2001. *Institutions and Organizations*. Thousand Oaks, CA: Sage Publications.

Sen, S. 2000. *Involving Stakeholders in Aquaculture Policy-making, Planning and Management*. Paper presented at the Technical Proceedings of the Conference on Aquaculture in the Third Millennium, Bangkok, Thailand, 20–25 February 2000.

Smith, M.J. 1999. *The Core Executive in Britain*. Basingstoke: Macmillan.

Storey, D.J. 2000. Six Steps to Heaven: Evaluating the Impact of Public Policies to Support Small Business Developed Economies in *The Blackwell Handbook of Entrepreneurship*, edited by L. Sexton and H. Lundstrom. Oxford: Blackwell Publishers Ltd, 176–194.

Storey, D.J. 2005. *Understanding the Small Business Sector*. London: Thomson Learning.

Suchman, M.C. 1995. Managing legitimacy: strategic and institutional approaches. *Academy of Management Review*, 20(3), 571–610.

6

SME and Entrepreneurship Policies in the Caribbean

Jonathan G Lashley

Chapter Summary

Since the mid-1990s, Caribbean governments have sought to address a number of perceived market failures evident in the support infrastructure for businesses, including access to finance, training and technical assistance. Legislation has also been implemented to specifically address the development of small enterprises and their capacity to generate employment. However, the expected growth in small enterprises has not ensued, despite the existence of numerous incentives, both physical and fiscal.

Two specific constraints have been identified in relation to this lack of policy effectiveness: a lack of proactive behaviour by SMEs, and a public policy framework that embraces entrepreneurship as a panacea for social and economic ills. This chapter argues that this all-encompassing 'vision' for entrepreneurship (which was expected to solve such diverse problems as poverty, gender power imbalances, a lack of national competitiveness and foreign exchange difficulties) led to a diluted policy approach which did not result in any significant SME development in the region. While it is accepted that economic growth, spurred by entrepreneurship, can address many of these socio-economic issues if appropriately designed, it is proposed here that without a clear strategic goal for SME development policy – and one that avoids dilution – none of the desired outcomes will materialise.

Introduction

The Anglophone Caribbean includes the independent countries of The Bahamas, Barbados, Belize, Guyana, Jamaica, Trinidad and Tobago, and the

Organisation of Eastern Caribbean States (OECS)[1] which lie in an archipelago between North and South America. These former British colonies are currently marking approximately 50 years of independence, with Jamaica and Trinidad and Tobago being the first to achieve self-rule in August 1962. Since their independence, Caribbean states have attempted major structural changes to their economies as they sought to move away from a dependence on primary production. Sojourns have been taken through industrialisation by invitation, import substitution, export-orientated industrialisation and, more recently, a push towards developing specific service sectors and the promotion of indigenous enterprise development.[2]

For the most part, industrialisation efforts were historically centred on the attraction of foreign direct investment (FDI) and later a concentration on tourism and the development of offshore financial centres (Moore 2010). The more recent focus on SMEs and entrepreneurship, although viewed politically as a panacea for social ills, has been based on a pragmatic need for employment generation. However, these policies have been implemented in an environment with an entrepreneurial deficit. This deficit is due to antecedent conditions which suppressed individual entrepreneurship and gave primacy to employment, especially in the public sector and the professions (Boxill 2003).

In seeking to examine these issues, the chapter aims to outline the economic situation of the region, especially as it relates to enterprise development, and to provide recommendations for catalysing entrepreneurial development in the Caribbean. Initially, an overview of the economies of the English-speaking Caribbean is presented, followed by a review of the main characteristics of SME development policies initiated by governments across the region in the period 1990 to 2010. An overview of the main issues that constrained the effectiveness of these approaches is accompanied by an analysis of the enterprise creation effects seen in the region. The final section looks at potential avenues for entrepreneurship development policy in the region which have implications for similar small island developing states.

An Overview of the Caribbean Economies

Apart from a common colonial history of plantation slavery and a reliance on the production of primary products for export to the core, the peripheral countries

---

1   Antigua and Barbuda, Dominica, Grenada, St. Kitts and Nevis, St. Lucia, and St. Vincent and the Grenadines.
2   An historical review of Caribbean development policy is provided in Alleyne, Lewis-Bynoe and Archibald (eds.) (2010).

of the Caribbean vary in terms of their size and economic structure. Gross domestic product (GDP) varies substantially across the region from US$21,650 in The Bahamas to US$2,671 in Guyana, while population ranges from 2.7 million in Jamaica to 73,000 in Dominica. Table 6.1 provides an overview of key statistics and, as a comparator, also provides information from some major island–state economies in other parts of the world (namely, Malta and Singapore[3]).

Table 6.1   Economic statistics for the Caribbean and comparators (2009)

Country	GDP per Capita (US$)[1]	Population (millions)[1]	Self-employment (%) (data year)[1]	Average Annual GDP per Capita Growth: 1970 to 2008[2]
Antigua and Barbuda	13,150	0.085	-	3.7
The Bahamas	21,651	0.341	-	-
Barbados	14,105	0.276	15.3 (2008)	1.8
Dominica	4,976	0.073	29.4 (2001)	3.4
Grenada	5,969	0.103	22.9 (1998)	3.8
Guyana	2,671	0.770	-	1.6
Jamaica	4,684	2.699	38.4 (2008)	0.3
St. Kitts and Nevis	10,315	0.054	-	3.7
St. Lucia	5,671	0.172	33.2 (2000)	3.0
St. Vincent and the Grenadines	5,332	0.107	-	3.9
Trinidad and Tobago	15,841	1.339	19.2 (2005)	2.1
Malta	19,238	0.416	13.4 (2008)	4.3
Singapore	36,379	5.009	14.4 (2008)	5.0

[1] *Source:* World Economic Outlook Database, October 2010, International Monetary Fund (http://www.imf.org/external/pubs/ft/weo/2010/02/weodata/index.aspx). Accessed: 26 February 2011.

[2] *Source:* UNDP Human Development Report (2010).

The structure of these economies are also quite varied, ranging from a reliance on the production of primary products such as bauxite/alumina in Jamaica and

---

3   Singapore and Malta are useful comparators for the Caribbean as they are also both small island states and achieved independence from the UK during the same period (1963 for Singapore and 1964 for Malta).

Guyana, and of petroleum in Trinidad and Tobago, to the provision of financial services in Barbados, Antigua and Barbuda and The Bahamas. Tourism is also a key sector for the region due to its tropical location and proximity to major source markets (North America and the UK). Agriculture has also been a mainstay in the region, and preferential trading agreements for bananas and sugar led to overdependence on these sectors for the earning of foreign exchange and the maintenance of livelihoods. However, with the reduction of concessions since the early 1990s, several nations within the region had to restructure their economies away from these sectors, leading to a dislocation of labour. These developments, coupled with the implementation of International Monetary Fund (IMF)-backed structural adjustment programmes[4] (SAPs) in the 1980s and early 1990s, led to high unemployment in many Caribbean nations (see Table 6.2). Although significant decreases in unemployment have been seen since the 1990s, they have remained consistently higher than for the comparator countries of Singapore and Malta.

Table 6.2   **Unemployment rates (%) in the Caribbean and selected comparators**

Country	1991	1995	2000	2007
The Bahamas	12.2	10.8	7.8[1]	7.9
Barbados	17.1	19.7	9.3	7.4[1]
Jamaica	15.7	16.2	15.5	9.4
St. Lucia	na	15.9	16.5	na
Trinidad and Tobago	18.5	17.2	12.1	6.5
Singapore	*1.9*	*2.7*	*6.0*	*4.0*
Malta	*4.4*	*4.9*	*6.8*	*6.4*

Source: World Economic Outlook Database, October 2010, International Monetary Fund (http://www.imf.org/external/pubs/ft/weo/2010/02/weodata/index.aspx). Accessed: 26 March 2011.

[1] Data from Caribbean Centre for Money and Finance (http://ccmfuwi.org/).

Despite the underlying differences between each nation, their approaches to industrialisation have been largely similar. In the immediate post-independence period, governments in the region sought to diversify their economies away

---

4   Structural adjustment in the Caribbean involved domestic market liberalisation, exchange rate correction, tax reforms, labour market reforms and the promotion of trade liberalisation (Melville 2002)

from primary production through the nationalisation of key sectors in tourism, agriculture and finance (Moore 2010). This served to further marginalise indigenous private-sector development in the 1970s. Instead, FDI was sought through fiscal incentives, in addition to the construction of industrial parks and export-processing zones. Countries that did not pursue industrialisation-by-invitation opted instead for import-substitution-industrialisation, with governments utilising tariff barriers to protect domestic manufactures during their early growth (Lashley 2010a, Moore 2010).

Currently, Caribbean industrialisation is mired in the harsh realities of trade liberalisation, catalysed by structural adjustment. However, the enforcement of World Trade Organisation (WTO) commitments from 1995 onwards was somewhat of a watershed for the Caribbean private sector. With the realities of the SAPs, and greater competition occasioned by the implementation of the WTO, governments across the region adopted policies to promote the development of private enterprises to address severe unemployment and contribute to general socio-economic well-being. At the regional level, the Caribbean Community (CARICOM), the region's attempt at an economic/ customs union, ingrained SME development within its 2001 Treaty. Article 53 of the Treaty attempted to provide an overall mission for SME development policy which sought to encourage member states to provide a legal and regulatory environment conducive to enterprise development. In addition to this facilitating environment, the Treaty also sought to encourage capacity development for support agencies; improve access to technical, entrepreneurial and business training; the development of financial institutions to support SMEs through 'innovative instruments'; innovation; and improved access to trade and technology information.[5]

While not ratified until 2001, drafting work on the Treaty was ongoing from 1993. In the intervening period, regional governments implemented a number of programmes to address these regional policy aims. In terms of the legal and regulatory environment, various instruments were implemented to assist in the development and definition of the sector from the late 1990s, as shown in Table 6.3.

This legislative support for SME development in the region was mainly concerned with fiscal incentives in terms of reduced taxes on profits, and exemption from import and stamp duty, although there were variations on this central theme. In addition to reducing the barriers for conducting business, Caribbean governments were also active in the establishment of SME-specific support as it related to the provision of finance, training and technical

---

5   A copy of the Revised Treaty of Chaguaramas is available from: http://www.sice.oas.org/trade/ caricom/caric2a.asp. Accessed: 28 June, 2012

Table 6.3   Caribbean small business legislation and country definitions

Country	Relevant Law	Definition - Employees	Definition - Sales (millions)
Antigua and Barbuda	Small Business Development Act (2007)	<= 25	<=US$0.37
The Bahamas	Guarantee of Loans (Small Business) Act (1998)	<25	<US$1.00
Barbados	Small Business Development Act (1999) (rev. 2006)	<=25	<=US$1.00
Guyana	Small Business Act (2004)	<=25	<=US$0.295
Jamaica[1]	-	<=50	<=US$5.00
St. Vincent and the Grenadines	Small Business Development Act (2007)	<=50	<=US$0.37
St. Lucia	Micro and Small-Scale Enterprise Act (1998)	<=50	<=US$0.37
Trinidad and Tobago[2]	-	<25	<=US$0.78

[1]   Definition from the Jamaica Small Business Association (www.sbaj.org.jm).
[2]   Definition from National Entrepreneurial Development Company (www.nedco. gov.tt).

assistance. This was complemented by financial support for relevant advocacy organisations and non-governmental organisations (NGOs).

SME Development Policy in the Caribbean

Current SME development policy in the Caribbean has its origins in industrial development corporations (IDCs) which governments throughout the region established from the 1960s onwards to catalyse industrial investment. Roles for the IDCs included the management of purpose-built industrial estates and the oversight of fiscal incentives for FDI. Since this early period, IDCs' remits were complemented by other initiatives to support enterprise development with a greater focus on domestic investment. The general approach for SME development in the region included: the original IDCs, whose role was expanded to provide support in relation to business-skills training and technical assistance; debt financing through national development banks or specific financial institutions; and loan guarantees to address the collateral deficit of SMEs seeking loans from commercial sources (Lashley 2010a, Moore 2010).

These financial interventions sought to address perceived market failures in the commercial banking sector which had been characterised as short term and risk-averse (Marshall 2002).

In relation to the revamped IDCs, training schemes provided instruction in accounting/record-keeping, management and stock control, while technical assistance included marketing, product development (marketing and packaging), plant upgrade and international standards certification.

In addition to these generic approaches across the Caribbean, there have also been more innovative, non-traditional, approaches. In terms of financing, The Bahamas, Barbados and St. Lucia provided equity financing options. In addition, the IDC in Barbados offered a Special Technical Assistance Program (STAP) which provided grant funding to exporters and manufacturers to enhance competitiveness. These funds were used to source bespoke technical assistance not internally available to the IDC. Other initiatives included the provision of lease financing by the Business Development Company of Trinidad and Tobago; incubators in Barbados, Jamaica and Trinidad and Tobago; and mentoring in Barbados and Trinidad and Tobago.

While training programmes outside of IDCs were widespread for 'enterprise development', the training provided was mostly in relation to basic business skills. The only countries in the region to break out of this mould were Belize, Grenada and Trinidad and Tobago, where specific entrepreneurship training was undertaken. The National Entrepreneurship Development Company of Trinidad and Tobago is perhaps the best example of this, with modules related to entrepreneurial characteristics, opportunity identification and strategy development. In Barbados there was the Youth Entrepreneurship Scheme which provided basic business skills training to youth, as well as targeting primary and secondary schools. Core elements of this involved soft-skill development, such as building self-confidence, as well as raising awareness of self-employment as a career option. Apart from these more innovative endeavours, there was limited promotion of the core concepts of entrepreneurship, with a preference for training in basic business and management skills.

Effects and Challenges of Policy Approaches

Whilst SME policy appeared uniform across the region, the contribution of self-employment was somewhat varied. In 2009 in Jamaica, self-employment accounted for 38 per cent of total employment, while in 2008 in Barbados this was just 15 per cent. However, despite this variation in levels, the structure of self-employment was similar with the majority of the self-employed being own-account workers[6] rather than employers; 92 per cent and 93 per cent of the self-employed were own-account workers in Jamaica and Barbados respectively. In comparison with extra-regional nations, own-account workers accounted for 64 per cent and 69 per cent of the self-employed in Singapore and Malta respectively. This suggests that self-employment was a more substantial generator of employment in Singapore and Malta than it was in the Caribbean, with own-account workers comprising the majority of the self-employed.

Self-employment as a percentage of total employment in selected countries for selected years is shown in Table 6.4. It appears that despite the implementation of SME development policies by regional governments, the level and structure of self-employment had not changed significantly since the late 1980s, with the exception of Barbados, whose particular case is discussed below.

Table 6.4   Change in self-employment in the Caribbean for selected countries and years

Economy	Own Account: start of period (%)	Own Account: end of period (%)	Employers: start of period (%)	Employers: end of period (%)	Period
Barbados[1]	6	11	3	4	1990–2000
Dominica	26	24	7	5	1991–2001
Grenada	15	17	6	6	1988–1998
Jamaica	35	35	3	3	1997–2008
St. Lucia	24	28	12	5	1994–2000
Trinidad and Tobago	17	15	3	4	1987–2005

Source: World Economic Outlook Database, October 2010, International Monetary Fund (http://www.imf.org/external/pubs/ft/weo/2010/02/weodata/index.aspx). Accessed: 26 February 2011.

[1] Data from 1990 and 2000 Census of Housing and Population (BSS 1994, 2002).

It is clear that there was not a proportional increase in self-employment across the region or a significant change in the structure of self-employment. This is despite the establishment of a more conducive environment for 'doing business'. These results suggest that while there was some employment

---

6   An own-account workers is defined here as a self-employed person that does not employ any other persons on a continuous basis.

generation in these countries, given that unemployment has declined (see Table 6.2), there was limited development of the private sector with own-account workers representing the majority of self-employment.

In contrast to the rest of the region, the data for Barbados shows a different picture. In 1980 and 1990, self-employment was a constant 9 per cent of total employment (BSS 1994, Regional Census Coordinating Committee 1981). Following the implementation of governmental programmes targeted at enterprise development in the mid-1990s, this rose to 13.2 per cent in 2000 (BSS 2002), 14.7 per cent in 2005, and 15.3 per cent in 2008 (Lashley 2010b). However, it appears that the structure of the labour market in Barbados was quite different from the situation in the other countries in the region, as self-employment was growing from a much lower base. This perhaps suggests that the policy approach in Barbados was somewhat conducive given the low levels of self-employment. Policy was able to spur some level of desire to enter self-employment by the marginal entrepreneur. So while there was an effect in Barbados, the other countries in the region, while adopting similar policies, did not see any significant adjustment.

Overall, the effect of government policy in the region for SME development appears to have been limited given the stasis in the level and the structure of self-employment. One of the reasons suggested here for such an occurrence is the lack of concentration on entrepreneurship promotion, and a greater concentration on basic self-employment and the facilitation of business start-ups, regardless of sector. While policies were implemented, there was limited focus in the region on entrepreneurship skills training, the provision of risk-taking capital, innovation/R&D, or assistance with product/market choice for new ventures. In this case, Shane's (2009) proposition that facilitating business start-up attracts the worst entrepreneurs and that they enter the worst sectors, probably holds true: the self-employed were not concerned with growth (they continued to be own-account workers) and entered sectors with the lowest barriers (low value added distributive trades and personal services (ILO 2000)), and hence experienced higher levels of competition. These results suggest that government policies for SME development were not effective in encouraging enterprise growth as there were still a large percentage of one-person operations.

There are perhaps multiple reasons for this lack of effectiveness, with responsibility resting at both the feet of policymakers and enterprise owners. These relate to a level of inertia among enterprise owners and a public policy framework that embraced entrepreneurship as a panacea for social and economic ills. This all-encompassing 'vision' for entrepreneurship led to a diluted policy approach which resulted in a dysfunctional type of entrepreneurship that is characterised by enterprises seeking a 'bigger piece of the pie' rather than attempting to make the pie bigger; a characteristic that Baumol, Litan and Schramm (2007) identify as an anathema to *productive entrepreneurship*. The underlying cause of this dysfunctional type of entrepreneurship is due to a lack of specific market focus for government policy; instead, any business start-up was viewed as beneficial, regardless of sector. With start-ups entering the easiest sectors, they were also entering the most competitive, and hence limited resources (both financial and time-based) were available for undertaking value-added activities or strategic planning (Lashley 2010a); productive entrepreneurship was stifled as enterprises fought amongst themselves to survive.

To further complicate matters, the quality of entrepreneurship in the Caribbean was poor, and hence the 'marginal' entrepreneur was unable to take full advantage of the resources presented through governmental initiatives. Boxill (2003) proposes that one of the main causes of this poor quality of entrepreneurship was a greater concern among the majority of the population for the attainment of status over wealth. Danns and Mentore (1995: 45) support this view, and highlight the education system as a culprit:

> *The region's peoples are job seekers rather than job creators. The brightest and most creative workers seek good jobs and often with the state … It is quite possible that the content of the region's education curricula has induced a trained incapacity in people to adopt values essential to the generation of wealth.*

Griffith (2002), in a similar vein, not only identifies education as a culprit for the lack of an entrepreneurial class, although he also sees it as a solution. Griffith (2002: 102) notes: 'An educational system that does not disdain industrial activity and that encourages risk taking will help to remove the social stigma attached to activities not associated with the professions.' Griffith here points up the main issues that suppressed the development of an entrepreneurial class in the region: an educational system that did not promote industrious activity; and a societal culture that was risk-averse, stigmatised entrepreneurship, and gave primacy to the professions.

Government policy, however, failed to address these educational and cultural issues. Instead, it sought to provide debt financing, technical assistance and business skills training – all activities targeted at promoting business in general, from the micro to the medium, utilising the same instruments, and seeking to achieve multiple goals. This thinly spread policy did not result in any significant increase in the practice of productive entrepreneurship and instead resulted in a labour market structure where the self-employed largely consisted of own-account workers operating in low value added, highly competitive, sectors. The main reason proposed here for this occurrence was the lack of an entrepreneurial class to take full advantage of governmental initiatives.

In effect, there were two main issues that needed to be overcome if the Caribbean is to facilitate a vibrant SME sector: the lack of an entrepreneurial class; and a diluted/unfocused SME policy environment. Although policy was implemented in the Caribbean to promote enterprise development, the lack of an entrepreneurial class was not addressed. The promotion of this entrepreneurial class will need to be one of the main public policy goals in any reorientation of SME policy in the region – assuming, that is, that government intervention is considered necessary for the development of SMEs.

Recent global criticisms of public policy for enterprise development have not so much declared that there is no role for public policy in this area, but rather argued that the form of support provided is misguided (Shane 2009), static and overly complex (O'Neill 2010). In addition, it has been noted that policies that simply encourage business start-up lead to lower quality enterprises (Greene, Mole and Storey 2004). These policy characteristics and effects were also seen throughout the Caribbean.

In his recommendations, Shane (2009) suggests moving away from financial and fiscal incentives that encourage business start-up, and instead focusing on established enterprises and 'picking winners'. However, in the Caribbean, there is a dearth of such established enterprises due to the lack of an entrepreneurial class. O'Neill (2010) follows in this vein of criticism in his questioning of the effectiveness of public policy from a UK perspective, indicating that the 'sameness' of policy and an aversion to revision is a challenge to increasing effectiveness. He suggests that '...problems are often compounded by lack of clarity as to the objectives of any policy' (O'Neill 2010: 7). This was also true of the Caribbean, where clear policy statements were largely absent, and even when present, they were overly complex. The policy statement for SME development in St. Vincent and the Grenadines (Government of St. Vincent and the Grenadines 2010) is perhaps instructive in this regard, where objectives for the provision of support were: employment creation; income generation; rural development; economic competitiveness; greater public-sector responsiveness to the needs of small businesses and the poor; and greater social peace. Such diverse objectives represent what O'Neill (2010) terms a 'scattergun' approach to policy development, and what Klak (1995), in his review of industrial policy in the Caribbean, referred to as 'shatter-shot' approach.

Whilst Shane (2009) and O'Neill (2010) provide recommendations for policy improvement that suggest some form of direct intervention, Bennett

(2008) suggests a more indirect approach for government in addressing market failures. The options proposed include: loan guarantee schemes to commercial banks to address market failures in finance; support for advocacy organisations (trade associations and chambers of commerce) to allow for private sector-led support; and reducing public section inefficiencies that impose barriers to 'doing business'. However, all of these policy actions have been attempted in the Caribbean without the requisite development of the SME sector.

What the above discussion suggests is that public policy in the Caribbean to date has been constrained in promoting enterprise growth due to a lack of focused policy goals and the lack of an entrepreneurial class to take advantage of the resources made available. At the root of this issue are a number of cultural issues related to a preference for the professions and a stigmatisation of self-employment, that are thought to originate from an educational system that emphasises the professional class and does not promote industrious entrepreneurial activity. Overall there was limited productive entrepreneurship in the region, and as noted by Danns and Mentore (1995), the brightest and most creative individuals were job seekers, rather than job creators.

Conclusion

As the case of the Caribbean indicates, policies which seek to promote SME development also perhaps need to be directed at addressing the cultural attitudes of a community (such as a preference for the professions, stigmatisation of self-employment and risk-averseness) that can often restrict entrepreneurship. What has occurred in this region is that governments have implemented production systems for enterprise development without the appropriate human input (entrepreneurs). As a result there has been an underutilised support infrastructure due to a lack of pro-activeness on the part of the self-employed,[7] and a public policy framework where resources have been targeted at achieving a variety of policy goals. This diluted policy approach has led to a lack of development of a truly entrepreneurial class.

While the Caribbean is similar to the developed world with this lack of policy focus, it however lacks a sufficient cadre of productive entrepreneurs and pre-existing enterprises to pursue the sort of focused policies suggested by Shane (2009) and O'Neill (2010), or the indirect approach suggested by Bennett

---

7   Lashley (2010b) in a survey of Barbadian manufacturers shows only 40 per cent of enterprises utilising any form of external support, and 36 per cent being members of the local trade association. In contrast, in the UK, Bennett (2008) showed that 94 per cent of SMEs had utilised external advice services in 2002.

(2008). If public policy is to be reoriented in the Caribbean, and productive entrepreneurship given primacy, then policy should seek to disentangle itself from its diluted approach and address incentives for growth, while seeking to develop the cadre of entrepreneurs that will be required to pursue more enterprise-specific policies in the future. It is clear that supporting entrants into highly competitive, low growth, low value-added sectors will need to be curtailed so that scarce resources can be directed towards the development of productive sectors by way of the promotion of an entrepreneurial class.

Proactive economic stimulation will need to replace the current reactive approach, which supplies support services to the few that demonstrate a desire to grow. Currently, there are limited incentives to grow, although resources are available for the willing few. A shift away from this enterprise-based inertia will only be possible with the development of an entrepreneurial rather than a survivalist culture where the self-employed are competing directly against each other for a larger piece of the pie.

As Caribbean economies seek to move away from a reliance on footloose foreign investment, and competing on low labour costs (which retards development), Griffith (2002: 87) notes that '...if foreign investors must be replaced because they are responsible for underdevelopment, there must be a national manufacturing entrepreneurial class to take their place.' This is an important observation for policymakers in the region and other small developing states; exploitation of indigenous entrepreneurial opportunities requires entrepreneurs. In order to achieve this, there needs to be a move away from the current generic support infrastructure to one that facilitates the development of entrepreneurship as a valid career choice – individually, culturally and regionally. In the Caribbean, such efforts will need to be directed at reorienting an educational system that is considered to be at the root of the poor quality of entrepreneurship seen in the region, and the development of focused enterprise development goals rather than the current diluted approach.

References

Alleyne, F., Lewis-Bynoe, D and Archibald, X. (eds.) 2010. *Growth and Development Strategies in the Caribbean*. Barbados: Caribbean Development Bank.

Barbados Statistical Service (BSS) 1994. *Barbados Housing and Population Census 1990: Volume 1*. Barbados: Barbados Statistical Service.

Barbados Statistical Service (BSS) 2002. *Barbados Census of Housing and Population 2000*. Barbados: Barbados Statistical Service.

Baumol, W., Litan, R. And Schramm, C. 2007. *Good Capitalism, Bad Capitalism and the Economics of Growth and Prosperity*. New Haven, CT: Yale University Press.

Bennett, R. 2008. SME policy support in Britain since the 1990s: what have we learnt? *Environment and Planning C: Government and Policy*, 26(2), 375–397.

Boxill, I. 2003. Unearthing black entrepreneurship in the Caribbean: exploring the culture and MSE sectors. *Equal Opportunities International*, 22(1), 32–45.

Danns, G.K. and Mentore, M.M. 1995. Race and Economic Power in Guyana: A Study of the East Indians, in *Entrepreneurship in the Caribbean: Culture, Structure, Conjecture*, edited by S. Ryan and T. Stewart. Trinidad and Tobago: UWI, ISER, 255–299.

Government of St. Vincent and the Grenadines 2010. *Policy Statement on Small Business Development*. [Online] Available at: http://www.caricomict4d.org/images/stories/docs/svg_small_business1.pdf [accessed: 28 March 2011].

Greene, F.J., Mole, K.F. And Storey, D.J. 2004. Does more mean worse? Three decades of enterprise policy in the Tees Valley. *Urban Studies*, 41(7), 1207–1228.

Griffith, W.H. 2002. A tale of four CARICOM countries. *Journal of Economic Issues*, 36(1), 79–106.

International Labor Organisation (ILO) 2000. *Small Enterprise Development in the Caribbean*. Port-of-Spain, Trinidad and Tobago: ILO.

Klak, T. 1995. A framework for studying Caribbean industrial policy. *Economic Geography*, 71, 297–317.

Lashley, J. 2010a. Productive Sector Development in the Caribbean: Manufacturing and Mining, in *Growth and Development Strategies in the Caribbean*, edited by F. Alleyne, D. Lewis-Bynoe and X. Archibald. Barbados: Caribbean Development Bank, 55–95.

Lashley, J. 2010b. *External Enticements and Internal Inertia: Constraints to Enterprise Growth in Barbadian Manufacturing Enterprises*. Paper presented to the SALISES 11th Annual Conference, Trinidad and Tobago, 24–26 March.

Marshall, D. 2002. At whose service? Caribbean state posture, merchant capital and the export services option. *Third World Quarterly*, 23(4), 725–751.

Melville, J.A. 2002. *The Impact of Structural Adjustment on the Poor*. Paper presented to the Eastern Caribbean Central Bank Seventh Annual Development Conference, St. Kitts and Nevis, 21–22 November.

Moore, W. 2010. Trade and Industrial Policy in the Caribbean, in *Growth and Development Strategies in the Caribbean*, edited by F. Alleyne, D. Lewis-Bynoe and X. Archibald. Barbados: CDB, 125–149.

O'Neill, K. 2010. *Entrepreneurship and SME Policy – No Need to Innovate?* Paper presented to the 36th International Small Business Conference, Taiwan, 2–4 October.

Regional Census Coordinating Committee (RCCC) 1981. *1980–81 Population Census of the Commonwealth Caribbean: Barbados Volume 2.* Barbados: RCCC.

Shane, S. 2009. Why encouraging more people to become entrepreneurs is bad public policy. *Small Business Economics*, 33(2), 141–149.

United Nations Development Program (UNDP) 2010. *Human Development Report 2010.* New York: UNDP.

World Economic Outlook Database October 2010, International Monetary Fund. [Online] Available at: http://www.imf.org/external/pubs/ft/weo/2010/02/weodata/index.aspx [accessed 26 February 2011].

7

Regulatory Reform and the Growth of Private Entrepreneurship in Vietnam

Viet Le and Charles Harvie

Chapter Summary

This chapter discusses the significant growth of private entrepreneurship in Vietnam after the introduction of economic reform in 1986, which triggered the country's transition from a centrally planned to market-oriented economy. In particular, it examines the impact of legislative change on the formal domestic private sector in Vietnam, starting with official recognition of this sector in the early 1990s. Business registrations grew slowly during the 1990s and reached a total of just over 45,000 during the 1992–1999 period. However, business registrations started to grow rapidly after the implementation of the breakthrough *Enterprise Law (EL)* in 2000. Almost 520,000 businesses were registered in the 2000–2010 period, benefiting from the simplified business registration procedures and improved business environment under the new law.

The *EL* recognised the freedom to do business and changed the way in which private enterprises had been governed in Vietnam. It removed administrative and financial requirements which streamlined the business registration process. The time involved in business registration was reduced from 90 days to seven days and the cost reduced by 20 times. The success of this law in Vietnam underscores the importance of regulatory reform for the growth of the domestic private sector, especially in the context of an economy in transition. It demonstrates that developing private entrepreneurship can be done without much direct assistance or subsidies. This chapter also emphasises that adequate mechanisms should be in place to ensure proper implementation of the regulatory reform process, and that continued efforts to improve the business environment are still needed even after the introduction of such major changes.

Introduction

The Vietnamese Government embarked on an economic reform programme known as *Doi Moi* in 1986. This officially heralded the move towards a market-oriented economy from a centrally-planned economy. As a result, Vietnam's economy transformed to become a multi-ownership market economy which includes state, domestic private and foreign-invested sectors. Strong and sustained economic growth characterised economic reform in Vietnam, and annual gross domestic product (GDP) growth averaged 7 per cent during the period 1986–2009 (General Statistics Office of Vietnam 2006, 2009).

With official recognition after *Doi Moi*, the private sector, largely made up of SMEs, experienced considerable growth from the early 1990s. However, the sector faced many legislative and institutional obstacles during the period of the 1990s. As a result, business registrations were modest during 1992–1999. Since 2000, however, SMEs have recorded strong growth after the introduction of the breakthrough EL, which provided simplified registration procedures and created a more enabling business environment. The response to this new law was positive with a rapid increase in business registrations.

This chapter aims to provide an analysis of the growth of domestic private sector enterprises, with a focus on formally registered enterprises in the transition economy of Vietnam. It discusses the growth of the sector in two periods. The first period is the 1990s, after the first set of laws governing the private enterprises sector was introduced. Enterprise registrations were slow during this period due to ongoing regulatory and business environmental barriers. The second period, occurring since the introduction of the EL in 2000, saw a strong increase in business registration. The chapter then discusses the strengths and key features of the *Enterprise Law 2000* and its remarkable contribution to reform of the business environment in Vietnam. The last section of the chapter discusses implications of this landmark regulatory reform in Vietnam, its extension to other ownership categories including the *Unified Enterprise Law* in 2005, and offers lessons for other countries looking to create an enabling business environment.

Growth of the Domestic Non-state Sector in Vietnam after *Doi Moi*

Vietnam is a fast growing economy in Southeast Asia with a large population of over 87 million people in 2009. The country formally started the transformation from a centrally-planned to market-oriented economy from the second half of the 1980s. Together with other significant changes in the economy, formal domestic private enterprises have grown to more than half a million in number by 2010 from being almost non-existent during the period of central planning. The country's government remains controlled by the Communist Party of Vietnam.

Vietnam implemented central planning from the late 1950s in the North after the French defeat and withdrawal in 1954. After the Vietnam War ended in 1975, central planning was expanded to the South. During this central planning period, private sector enterprises were neglected because of the notions that private ownership was a source of personal enrichment and exploitation. Up until the late 1970s, private enterprises in Vietnam were considered by the state to be the 'enemy' of socialism (Dinh 1993).

Although limited forms of private economic enterprise existed during the central planning period, such as sole proprietorship and household enterprises, they were subject to strict regulations and operated in an extremely hostile environment. Small, private sector enterprises received no support from the government, in sharp contrast with state-owned enterprises (SOEs). Nevertheless, a shadow economy existed during this period which helped set the stage for governmental reforms by supporting peasant agriculture, fostering the accumulation and productive investment of local capital, creating urban goods and services, nurturing a spirit of entrepreneurship and proving to the government an alternative path to national development (Freeman 1996).

Reforms after *Doi Moi* led to a significant growth of the private sector outside agriculture. This came as the result of regulations announced in 1988. These were *Decree No. 27* and *Decree No. 28* on ownership and *Resolution No. 16* on renovation and policies towards the non-state sector, which brought the private sector out of the grey zone (Helmlin, Ramamurthy and Ronnås 1998). The new regulations stipulated that the state accepted the positive role and long-term existence of private and individual sectors. At the same time the regulations removed limits to the size of private capital investments and employment of waged labour (Beresford 1993).

Analysts have observed that private sector development has played a crucial role in the reform of the Vietnamese economy (Hakkala and Kokko 2007, Harvie 2004). In particular, a dynamic non-state sector with an emphasis on SMEs in Vietnam was a precondition for attaining the multiple policy objectives of: restructuring and slimming state enterprises; job creation and income growth through expanding non-farm employment and income opportunities; attaining sustainable economic development; improving resource allocation efficiency and productivity growth; expanding exports; attracting foreign invested enterprises; achieving a more equal distribution of income; and assisting in rural and regional development (Harvie 2007).

Private Sector Enterprises in the 1990s

According to Ramamurthy (1998), both pull and push factors were present after *Doi Moi* in the establishment of new enterprises. There were perceived gains because the reforms presumably generated a demand for small-scale units which had greater local reach. The rise in private sector activity was greatest in the services sector, which did well to absorb the gains in purchasing power (Ramamurthy 1998). In addition, there was a pull factor, which was the need for entrepreneurs to create employment for themselves and their family members. This motivation was especially strong in the post-reform period when large amounts of labour were released from state enterprises and soldiers were demobilised (Ramamurthy 1998).

In addition to changes in the macroeconomic environment, there was continual change to the regulatory environment regarding domestic private sector enterprises. Two important laws were passed in 1990 which officially recognised private enterprises: the *Company Law (1990)* and the *Private Enterprise Law (1990)*. The first law governed joint-stock and limited liability companies, while the second governed sole proprietorship companies. In response to the change in legislation, a new formal private sector emerged in the early 1990s. Business registrations gradually increased in the first few years from 1992 to 1994 but began to decline from the mid-1990s. By 1999, total registrations reached just over 45,000 enterprises (see Table 7.1).

It might, therefore, be observed that the development of the private sector in the 1990s was disappointing (Hakkala, Kang and Kokko 2001). Basic business legislation for the private sector was lacking and registration procedures were cumbersome. Before 2000, an estimated 400 various kinds of licences were required to register enterprises in different areas of business. These created a significant administrative burden to businesses, while the discretionary decision-making practices of Vietnamese authorities introduced an element of uncertainty into business planning (Hakkala and Kokko 2007). Public administration was seen to be inefficient with excessive regulation, red tape and corruption (Hakkala et al. 2001). The infrastructure and services to support businesses were also largely lacking (Schaumburg-Müller 2005). Furthermore, private sector growth was stunted by competition from SOEs which benefited from political contacts and privileged access to capital, land and other resources (Hakkala et al. 2001).

Despite a larger number of formally registered enterprises in the private sector, the contribution of this sector to GDP remained fairly constant at around 7.5 per cent until the end of the decade (see Table 7.2). An explanation of this situation is that Vietnam's GDP also expanded substantially during this period. During the 1990s Vietnam was one of the fastest growing economies

Table 7.1   Number of business registration, 1992–1999

	Number	
	Per year	Cumulative
1992	3,985	4,095
1993	7,421	11,516
1994	7,175	18,691
1995	6,158	24,849
1996	5,485	30,334
1997	4,636	34,970
1998	4,252	39,222
1999	5,782	45,004

Source: MPI (2000) as cited in Steer (2001).

Table 7.2   Structure of GDP by ownership (%)

	1992	1995	1996	1997	1998	1999
State	38.1	40.1	40.8	41.4	41.3	40.4
Domestic non-state	61.9	59.9	59.2	58.6	58.7	59.6
Formal private	n/a	7.6	7.7	7.5	7.5	7.5
Household	n/a	35.9	35.0	34.2	33.5	33.1
Collective	n/a	9.7	9.2	8.7	8.5	8.6
Foreign invested	n/a	6.7	7.3	8.2	9.2	10.4

Source: General Statistics Office (GSO) (2001) as used in Steer (2001).

in the world, achieving an annual average GDP growth rate of 7 per cent (Harvie 2001). Thus, it is reasonable to suggest that the formal private sector had expanded not only in terms of number of enterprises but also in terms of economic output. The contribution of formal private enterprises to GDP, however, remained the smallest compared to any other ownership form during the 1990s.

The gradual transformation of the regulatory and legal framework for private enterprises, the fact that SOEs were politically favoured for generating employment, and the weak capacity of private management and capital generation all had their influence on the growth of the private sector in the 1990s (Webster 1999, Webster and Taussig 1999).

Private Sector Enterprises Since 2000

The lack of a dynamic private sector in the 1990s was worrying to many policymakers, as it had become the major source of employment (Hakkala et al. 2001). During the 1990s Vietnamese SOEs reduced their employment while the foreign invested sector contributed very few jobs (Webster 1999). Both of these sectors were primarily capital intensive in nature (Harvie 2007). The need to create employment, the pressures to stop the downturn in exports and foreign direct investment (FDI) capital inflows after the Asian financial crisis, and the need for a level playing field in the domestic business environment, all created an impetus for radical regulatory reform under a new legal framework.

A new *EL* was approved by the National Assembly on 29 May 1999 and became effective from 1 January 2000. This new law combined the *Company Law (1990)* and *Private Enterprise Law (1990)* into one. Thus, the new *EL* provided the legal framework for establishment of all types of formal domestic private enterprises, including sole proprietorship, limited liability and joint-stock companies (JSC). In addition, there were many other important innovations of the *EL* that made it a breakthrough.

The new *EL* was identified as having two major strengths: (i) simplification of bureaucratic procedures involved in enterprise registration, as part of a general shift from the granting of licences to a system of voluntary registration and active regulation; and (ii) clarification of entrepreneurs' basic right to operate in any and all business areas not explicitly forbidden by law (UNDP 2004, Vo and Nguyen 2006). This was the result of a long drafting process, started in August 1996, which required many iterations before final approval by the National Assembly in 1999. The first draft of the *EL* borrowed from Thai and Singaporean Company Law but was not considered suitable for Vietnam. However, after being re-drafted many times following frequent consultations with stakeholders the final draft was quite uniquely Vietnamese (Mallon 2004). Thus, the *EL* is often considered a major symbol of the success of Vietnam's economic and administrative reform processes and is touted as a model for law drafting and enforcement in Vietnam (UNDP 2004).

Since implementation of the *EL* in 2000 the number of new business registrations has increased rapidly (see Table 7.3). Registrations jumped 150 per cent from 5,782 in 1999 to 14,457 in 2000. Business registrations in 2006 alone surpassed the total number of registrations for the entire period 1992–1999. Registrations in 2010 were over 103,000 enterprises, more than double the total registrations in the earlier period. The strong growth trend since 2000 has been maintained throughout the recent global financial crisis (see Figure 7.1).

According to statistics from the National Business Information Centre, over 518,000 enterprises were established from 2000 to 2010 (National

Table 7.3   New registrations 2000–2010

Year	Number	
	Per year	Cumulative from 1999
2000	14,457	59,461
2001	19,800	79,261
2002	21,535	100,796
2003	27,771	128,567
2004	37,230	165,797
2005	39,959	205,756
2006	46,606	252,362
2007	58,196	310,558
2008	65,318	375,876
2009	84,531	460,407
2010(*)	103,170	563,577

(*) Preliminary data.

Source: National Business Information Centre, Agency for SME Development, MPI 2011.

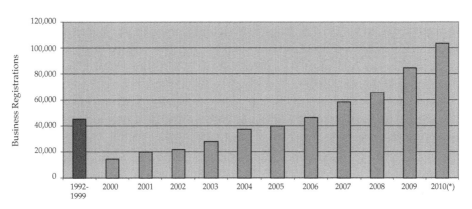

Figure 7.1   Enterprise registration increases sharply from 2000

(*) Preliminary data.

Source: National Business Information Centre, Agency for SME Development, MPI.
(National Business Information Centre of Vietnam 2011)

Business Information Centre of Vietnam 2011). As Table 7.3 indicates, business registrations during the 2000–2010 period increased by more than 11 times the number for the 1992–1999 period. Thus, the accumulated number of business registrations during 1992–2010 reached over 560,000. This is 12.5 per cent more than the target of having 500,000 new business registrations by 2010 as set by the SME Development Plan 2006–2010.

Nevertheless, relying on the number of business registrations as a measure of economic activity should be treated with caution. In the early years after the implementation of the *EL* the increase in registrations was subjected to the question of 'old wine, new bottle'. This refers to the registration of firms that had already existed under other forms, including household enterprises which responded to the changes under the new law and registered as formal businesses. Different surveys revealed that new firms in fact accounted for 55 to 70 per cent of new registrations, depending on locality (World Bank 2005). The registration numbers also did not take into account businesses which would not become operational after registration and businesses that had exited.

Most of the newly registered enterprises were non-state enterprises, accounting for 99.9 per cent of new registrations. New firms in the non-state sector included simple legal forms, such as sole proprietorships and limited liability ventures. Nonetheless, there has been a growing trend towards more complicated forms, such as JSC, among the new registrations. The share of JSCs in new registrations increased from 8 per cent in 2000 to 25 per cent in 2007 (Ministry of Planning and Investment of Vietnam 2008).

It is also noteworthy that most growth has occurred in the urban parts of Vietnam, even though the majority of the population still live in rural and regional areas. A large portion of the newly registered enterprises are based in major cities, with Ho Chi Minh City leading the country in terms of new registrations, followed by Hanoi and Hai Phong. These three cities accounted for almost 55 per cent of total registrations in 2007 (Ministry of Planning and Investment of Vietnam 2008).

The average registered capital per enterprise also increased, from Vietnamese dong (VND) 962 million in 2000 to VND8.14 billion in 2007.[1] This average amount of registered capital gradually approached the limit of VND10 billion according to the SME definition issued in *Decree No. 90* in 2001 (Ministry of Planning and Investment of Vietnam 2008). Newly registered enterprises, however, were small in terms of number of employees. In 2003 the average sole proprietor firm had 15 employees, while the equivalent figures for limited liability companies and JSCs were 38 and 53 respectively (World Bank 2005). These figures were still much lower than the threshold limit of 300 workers for SMEs, according to the 2001 definition.

As discussed above, the share of GDP generated by the formal private sector had been fairly constant during the 1990s. However, unlike the earlier period, its share then increased significantly from 7.3 per cent in 2000 to 11 per cent of

---

1   GBP1=VND34,000; USD1=VND20,000 at the time of writing.

GDP in 2009. Whilst this seems significant, it needs to be looked at in a broader context. Even with the important developments since 2000, the proportion of the formal private sector in GDP remained small relative to other sectors in the economy (see Table 7.4). Its share was just above one-third of the contribution made by household micro-enterprises in 2009. This suggests that there remains huge potential for the dynamic formal private sector to develop further.

Table 7.4   Structure of GDP by ownership (%)

	2000	2001	2002	2003	2004	2005	2006	2007	2008	2009[*]
State	38.5	38.4	38.4	39.1	39.1	38.4	37.3	35.9	35.5	35.1
Domestic non-state	48.2	47.8	47.9	46.5	45.8	45.6	45.7	46.1	46.0	46.6
Formal private	*7.3*	*8.0*	*8.3*	*8.2*	*8.5*	*8.9*	*9.4*	*10.2*	*10.5*	*11.0*
Collective	*8.6*	*8.1*	*8.0*	*7.5*	*7.1*	*6.8*	*6.6*	*6.2*	*5.7*	*5.5*
Household	*32.3*	*31.8*	*31.6*	*30.7*	*30.2*	*29.9*	*29.7*	*29.7*	*29.8*	*30.1*
Foreign invested	13.3	13.8	13.8	14.5	15.1	16.0	17.0	17.7	18.5	18.3

[*] Preliminary.

Source: General Statistics Office (2008, 2009).

Discussion

Implementation of the landmark *EL* facilitated an explosive growth in registrations of formal domestic private sector enterprises and their output after 2000. Several strengths of this innovative law can be highlighted. The first one was a change and simplification of registration procedures. This is the principle often referred to as 'to register first, then to check' by the business community (World Bank 2005). The focus has shifted from the state agency checking that all the requirements are to be in place before a registration could be granted to asking the applicant to take responsibility for the information provided. This represented a fundamental shift in the approach and tools with which the government manages enterprises. Prior to the *EL* it was believed that 'the freedom to do business should only be broadened along with and within the expansion in governance and monitoring capacity of the authorities' (German Technical Cooperation and Central Institute of Economic Management 2006). This view has receded and has been replaced by more innovative thinking under the *EL* (Vo and Nguyen 2006).

As a breakthrough in administrative reforms in Vietnam, the *EL* has three important features. First, simplification of procedures and documentation to register enterprises greatly reduced the time to register a business from 90 days to seven days or less with online registration, and the cost of registration was cut by 20 times from VND10 million to VND500,000. Second, the *EL* has clearly defined the rights of the state, as well as the rights of state officials *vis-à-vis* the rights of the investor and the enterprise, having the effect of gradually reducing the tendency by state bodies to over-administer and create problems for enterprises. Third, 180 licences and permits to do business have been abolished, removing a significant amount of unreasonable administrative barriers on the operations of enterprises that has resulted in a considerably more enabling business environment (UNDP 2004).

The second strength of the *EL* is its recognition of the freedom to do business. According to the law 'citizens are free to do business in all business areas not prohibited by law'. This allows all organisations and individuals (other than those prohibited from conducting business) that have a business initiative or opportunity to establish enterprises appropriate to their circumstances (UNDP 2004). It has helped harness Vietnam's economic potential and removed constraints which hindered innovation and creativity in business. The *EL* has also revitalised entrepreneurship and strengthened the trust of investors and entrepreneurs in the reforms and policies initiated by the Government (Vo and Nguyen 2006). As such, the *EL* is viewed as one of the most fundamental and radical reforms of business law in Vietnam.

In addition, a taskforce was established by the Prime Minister on 29 December 1999, two days before the *EL* was due to come into force, to monitor and supervise the implementation of the *EL*, including the identification of unnecessary business licences. This was the first time a taskforce had been established to oversee the implementation of a law in Vietnam. The taskforce applied a mixture of proactive approaches, combining bottom-up and top-down approaches, inward and outward activities, and administrative and non-administrative measures. Its operations were recognised and backed by the public, the business community and some governmental bodies (German Technical Cooperation and Central Institute of Economic Management 2006).

Perhaps the greatest recognition of the success of the *EL* was that its principles were ultimately also extended to other ownership categories. In 2005 a *Unified Enterprise Law (UEL)* was approved to govern both state and non-state enterprises, including domestic and foreign invested businesses, in an attempt to create a more level playing field across different ownership types (see Figure 7.2). The *UEL* provided a uniform legal framework for all economic actors. It re-affirmed freedom to do business in areas not prohibited by laws with a clearly defined negative list. The *UEL* also demonstrated a continued effort for regulatory and public administrative reform. The impact of the reforms have been recognised and Vietnam was placed among the top 10 most improved economies in terms of ease of doing business, according to the World Bank's *Doing Business 2011* (World Bank 2011). Starting a business in Vietnam has continuously been made easier (see Table 7.5).

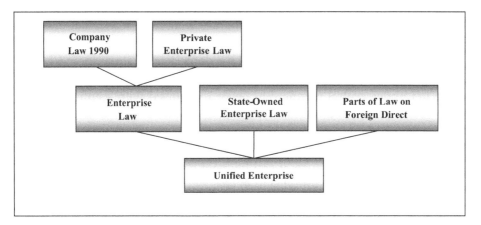

Figure 7.2   Evolution of corporate laws in Vietnam

Source: Adapted from Yu (2008) and Vo and Nguyen (2006)

Table 7.5   Starting a business in Vietnam

Year	Procedures (number)	Time (days)	Cost (% of income per capita)
Doing Business 2004	12	63	31.9
Doing Business 2005	11	56	30.6
Doing Business 2006	11	50	27.6
Doing Business 2007	11	50	24.3
Doing Business 2008	11	50	20.0
Doing Business 2009	11	50	16.8
Doing Business 2010	11	50	13.3
Doing Business 2011	9	44	12.1

Source: World Bank (2011).

Conclusion

This chapter has analysed the growth of formally registered domestic private sector enterprises in the transitional economy of Vietnam. It has emphasised and contrasted the experience of the 1990s with the 2000s. The *EL* of 2000 was found to be a catalyst in terms of its contribution to reform of the business environment, by providing the legislative foundation for the establishment of a modern market driven economy, based upon entrepreneurial endeavour in the private non-state sector. An analysis of its strengths and success suggests that it could offer lessons for other emerging market economies at a similar or earlier stage of development wishing to establish an enabling business environment.

The emergence and development of the domestic private sector in Vietnam after *Doi Moi* is a significant achievement of the economic reforms. From being restricted under central planning to being recognised with scepticism in the early years of *Doi Moi* and actively encouraged since 2000, the domestic non-state sector in Vietnam has grown considerably in the past two decades. The formal sector has experienced a rapid increase in business registrations with an ability to be the major source of employment generation for over one million new entrants to the labour market each year.

Although the growth of the private sector business has been impressive since 2000, the sector remains relatively small in terms of its contribution to GDP in Vietnam. This chapter has demonstrated that it still has considerable further growth potential. To achieve this will require ongoing reform as well as enhancing the private sector's capacity to compete in an increasingly competitive domestic, regional and international market environment. In this context, the acquisition and development of entrepreneurial skills will be critical in facilitating greater involvement in innovative, high value adding, knowledge and skill intensive areas of business activity.

Growth in the number of registered enterprises only reflects a growth in quantity of businesses. The quality aspect of that growth should not be ignored. A recent empirical study about the performance of Vietnamese formal domestic private SMEs found that these enterprises tend to be involved in low skill, low income, and low value-adding activities (Le 2010).

The success of the *Enterprise Law 2000* in Vietnam can offer several lessons for policymakers in other emerging and developing economies. It suggests that regulatory reform can create a significant improvement in the business environment and unleash entrepreneurial potential. By creating a more enabling business environment through simplification of registration procedures and reduction of fees and licensing requirements, it is possible to generate a strong growth of formal enterprises in the private sector. This can be done without much direct subsidies and assistance from the government to the private sector. This chapter has also made clear that it is necessary to ensure that implementation of such reforms is monitored, such as through the establishment of a taskforce. Finally, it is important that continuing efforts are made to keep the momentum for change going, even after major successful regulatory reform is introduced.

References

Beresford, M. 1993. The Political Economy of Dismantling the 'Bureaucratic Centralism and Subsidy System' in Vietnam in *Southeast Asia in the 1990s: Authoritarianism, Democracy and Capitalism*, edited by K. Hewisonet al. Sydney: Allen and Unwin, 213–236.

Company Law 1990. Hanoi: Vietnam National Assembly.

Dinh, X.Q. 1993. Vietnam's policy reforms and its future. *Journal of Contemporary Asia*, 23(4), 532–553.

Enterprise Law 2000. Hanoi: Vietnam National Assembly.

Freeman, D. 1996. *Doi Moi* Policy and the small-enterprise boom in Ho Chi Minh City, Viet Nam. *The Geographical Review*, 86(2), 178–197.

General Statistics Office of Vietnams 2001. *Statistical Yearbook 2000*. Hanoi: General Statistics Office.

General Statistics Office of Vietnam 2006. *Vietnam: 20 Years of Renovation and Development*. Hanoi: Statistical Publishing House.

General Statistics Office of Vietnam 2008. *Statistical Yearbook 2007*. Hanoi: General Statistics Office.

General Statistics Office of Vietnam 2009. *Statistical Yearbook 2008*. Hanoi: General Statistics Office.

German Technical Cooperation and Central Institute of Economic Management 2006. *Six Years of Implementation the Enterprise Law: Issues & Lessons Learnt*. Hanoi: GTZ and CIEM.

Hakkala, K., Kang, O.H.-K. and Kokko, A. 2001. *Step by Step: Economic Reform and Renovation in Vietnam before the 9th Party Congress*, Working Paper No. 114. Stockholm: European Institute of Japanese Studies, Stockholm School of Economics.

Hakkala, K. and Kokko, A. 2007. *The State and the Private Sector in Vietnam*, Working Paper No. 236. Stockholm: Stockholm School of Economics.

Harvie, C. 2001. *Competition Policy and SMEs in Vietnam*, Working Paper 01-10. Wollongong: Department of Economics, University of Wollongong.

Harvie, C. 2004. The contribution of SMEs in the economic transition of Vietnam. *Journal of International Business and Entrepreneurship Development*, 2(2), 1–16.

Harvie, C. 2007. *SME Development Strategy in Vietnam*, 4th SMEs in a Global Economy Conference: Responding to Global Challenges and Opportunities, Shah Alam Selangor, Malaysia, 9–10 July 2007.

Helmlin, M., Ramamurthy, B. and Ronnås, P. 1998. *The Anatomy and Dynamics of Small Scale Private Manufacturing in Vietnam*, Working Paper Series in Economics and Finance No.236. Stockholm: Stockholm School of Economics.

Le, V. 2010. *Technical Efficiency Performance of Vietnamese Manufacturing Small and Medium Enterprises*. Unpublished Doctor of Philosophy thesis, School of Economics, Faculty of Commerce, University of Wollongong, Wollongong.

Mallon, R. 2004. *Managing Investment Climate Reforms: Viet Nam Case Study*. Washington DC: World Bank.

Ministry of Planning and Investment of Vietnam 2008. *Annual Report: Small & Medium Enterprises in Vietnam 2008*. Hanoi: Agency for SME Development, Ministry of Planning and Investment.

National Business Information Centre of Vietnam 2011. *Business Registration from 2000*. Hanoi: Agency for SME Development, Ministry of Planning and Investment.

Private Enterprise Law 1990. Hanoi: Vietnam National Assembly.

Ramamurthy, B. 1998. The Asian Experience II: India and Vietnam, in *Institutional Adjustment for Economic Growth: Small Scale Industries and Economic Transition in Asia and Africa*, edited by P. Ronnås et al. Aldershot: Ashgate, 81–122.

Schaumburg-Müller, H. 2005. Private-sector development in a transition economy: the case of Vietnam. *Development in Practice*, 15(3–4), 349–361.

Steer, L. 2001. *The Private Sector in Vietnam: Facts, Figures, Policy Changes, and a Survey of Research Findings*. Canberra and Sydney: Centre for International Economics.

Unified Enterprise Law 2005. Hanoi: Vietnam National Assembly.

United Nations Development Program (UNDP) 2004. *High Time for Another Breakthrough? Review of the Enterprise Law and Recommendations for Change*. Hanoi: GTZ, CIEM and UNDP.

Vo, T.T. and Nguyen, T.A. 2006. *Institutional Changes for Private Sector Development in Vietnam: Experience and Lessons*, East Asian Bureau of Economic Research Working Paper Series No. 8. Canberra: Australian National University.

Webster, L. 1999. *SMEs in Vietnam: On the Road to Prosperity*. Hanoi: Mekong Project Development Facility.

Webster, L. and Taussig, M. 1999. *Vietnam Undersized Engine: A Survey of 95 Larger Private Manufacturers*. Hanoi: Mekong Project Development Facility.

World Bank 2005. *Vietnam Development Report 2006: Business*. Hanoi: Joint Donor Report to the Vietnam Consultative Group Meeting, December 6–7.

World Bank 2011. *Doing Business 2011: Making a Difference for Entrepreneurs*. Washington DC: The World Bank and the International Finance Corporation.

Yu, S.Q. 2008. Vietnam – Quo Vadis?, *Asia Competitiveness Institute Case Study Series*. Singapore: Lee Kuan Yew School of Public Policy, National University of Singapore.

8

SME Policies and Seasons of Change in the People's Republic of China

Lei Ye, David Tweed and Paul Toulson

Chapter Summary

Over the past 60 years the People's Republic of China (PRC) has shifted its economic structure from a centrally-planned to a socialist-market economy. This change has led to rapid growth in the number of SMEs. According to the latest official statistics, SMEs numbered 42 million by the end of 2009 (Li 2010). However, early conceptions of enterprise, following the 1949 rise of the Chinese Communist Party (CCP) to governance of the nation, branded business as the bane of the people resulting in the total ban of privately held businesses. At the end of this period, new leadership began a series of reforms that have given rise to the 'modern' Chinese economy, by embracing capitalistic ideas within the context of a communist political ideology. The focus of this chapter is on the experience of the SME sector within this political and economic milieu.

Introduction

The purpose of this chapter is to recount the development of SME policies and their impact on the growth of the Chinese SME sector since modern China was founded in 1949. The recent rise of the SME sector in China is impressive. The number of SMEs grew from 2.2 million in 1980 to 42 million by the end of 2009 and now account for 99.8 per cent of the country's enterprises, 60 per cent of exports and 75 per cent of new job opportunities (Li 2010, Wang 2004). Chinese SMEs also exist in various ownership structures, including state-owned enterprises (SOEs), collectively-owned enterprises, joint-stock companies

(JSCs), limited-liability companies, individual proprietorships and family businesses. Today SMEs are a major force in social and economic development; however it was not always this way.

China, the world's fourth largest country by area, has 1.341 billion people and 56 ethnic groups. The country has 34 provincial administrations made up of four municipalities, 23 provinces, five autonomous and two Special Administrative Regions (The Central People's Government of the PRC 2011a, Shan 2011). Although China has become a centre for world manufacturing, agriculture is still its primary economic base. According to statistics provided by the Research Centre of the State Council, 720 million people live in rural areas (Chen 2010).

The last dynastic empire, the Qing, was replaced by the Republic of China in 1912, and was governed by the Nationalist Party (Kuomintang) until 1949. Sun Yat-sen was the first president as China entered political, economic and social turmoil. China was 'bullied' by Western powers in the First World War and later war broke out between China and Japan in 1937 for a period lasting eight years. Civil war between the CCP and Kuomintang then ensued, finally ending with a victory for the CCP in 1949 (Guo 2007). Under Mao Zedong's leadership, the PRC was established in 1949. The new Government focused on building socialism based around public ownership of most assets and organisations in China. After Deng Xiaoping became the Chairman of the Chinese People's Political Consultative Conference in 1978, a wide-ranging series of open door policy and economic reforms were introduced. Since then, the Chinese Government has followed Deng's policies and further reforms have been carried out in subsequent decades.

The fast development of the SME sector has encouraged changing government attitudes towards the private sector. Over the last 60 years government attitudes towards SMEs have been through four stages: vanquished, rediscovery, laissez faire and engine of growth. The CCP's political guidelines have changed from Mao's socialist ideology of public ownership to Deng's socialist system combined with market-based economic ideas. The Chinese economic system has also changed from a centrally-planned to a free-market economy. This chapter examines interactions at the nexus of the political and economic spheres within China and their impact on the growth of SMEs.

Defining SMEs in China

The criteria for defining SMEs in China has been changed many times, making it difficult to compile comparable data for the purpose of identifying trends.

When the PRC was founded, the size of enterprises was determined by value of fixed assets (see Table 8.1). In 1962, the criteria changed to employment size: enterprises that employed more than 3,000 people were considered large enterprises, those that employed 500 or more were considered medium enterprises, and enterprises with fewer than 500 people were considered small enterprises. The criteria were changed to measures of overall production capacity in 1978 (Yao 2005). In 1988, industry-specific criteria were adopted by the Government: enterprises that produced single products were classified by production capacity and enterprises that produced multiple products were categorised based on the value of fixed assets. The criteria were changed yet again in 1999. Sales revenue and total assets became the standard. Enterprises with annual sales revenue of more than 500 million Yuan and total assets of more than 50 million Yuan were categorised as medium enterprises, while those with annual sales revenue and total assets of less than 50 million Yuan were categorised as small enterprises. In 2003, the *Interim Categorising Criteria on Small and Medium-sized Enterprises Regulations* were published. The criteria apply to different industrial sectors, and major elements of consideration include employment size, revenue and enterprise total assets (Yao 2005). In 2011, the new *Criteria on Small and Medium-sized Enterprises* were released by the Chinese State Council. The new criteria include micro-sized businesses and the sectors were expanded to include 16 industries.

Table 8.1   Changing definitions of Chinese SMEs

Year	Criteria
1949	Fixed assets
1962	Employment size
1978	Overall production capacity
1988	Production capacity and fixed assets
1999	Sales revenue and the total assets
2003	Employment size, revenue and total assets

Source: Adapted from Yao 2005: 41.

Yao (2005) notes that size criteria for Chinese SMEs have two features. First, they are subject to ongoing change (five times from 1949 to 2003) and further in 2011. Second, coverage and depth has gradually increased, becoming more industry specific and reflecting Chinese economic development.

In 2011, the *Categorising Criteria on Small and Medium-sized Enterprises (SMEs)* were approved by the Chinese State Council. These criteria were jointly written by the State Development Planning Commission, the State Economic and Trade Commission, National Statistics Bureau and Ministry of Finance. The Government defined 16 industries, each of which has its own size criteria. These criteria are based on sector, headcount and turnover for 13 industries (Table 8.2) and with total assets definitions for the remaining three industries (Table 8.3).

Table 8.2   Industries with employment and annual revenue for SMEs in China

Sector	Employment	Annual revenue (Ten thousand Yuan[1])
Agriculture, forestry, animal husbandry and fisheries	Medium: N/A	500 20,000
	Small: N/A	50–499
	Micro: N/A	< 50
Manufacturing	Medium: 300–1,000	2,00–40,000
	Small: 20–299	300–2,999
	Micro: < 20	< 300
Wholesale	Medium: 20–200	5,000–40,000
	Small: 5–19	1,000–4,999
	Micro: < 5	< 1,000
Retail	Medium: 50–300	500–20,000
	Small: 10–49	100–499
	Micro: < 10	< 499
Transportation	Medium: 300–1,000	3,000–30,000
	Small: 20–299	200–2,999
	Micro: < 20	< 200
Warehousing	Medium: 100–200	1,000–30,000
	Small: 20–99	100–999
	Micro: < 20	< 99
Post	Medium: 300–1,000	1,000–30,000
	Small: 20–299	100–999
	Micro: < 20	< 100
Hotel	Medium: 100–300	2,000–30,000
	Small: 10–99	100–999
	Micro: < 10	< 99

Table 8.2   Industries with employment and annual revenue for SMEs in China *concluded*

Sector	Employment	Annual revenue (Ten thousand Yuan[1])
Food and beverage	Medium: 100–300	2,000–10,000
	Small: 10–99	100–1,999
	Micro: < 10	< 100
Information transmission	Medium: 100–2,000	1,000–100,000
	Small: 10–99	100–999
	Micro: < 10	< 100
The software and IT services	Medium: 100–300	1,000–10,000
	Small: 10–99	50–999
	Micro: < 10	< 50
Property management	Medium: 300–1,000	1,000–5,000
	Small: 100–299	500–999
	Micro: < 100	< 500
Other non-specified industries	Medium: 100–300	N/A
	Small: 10–99	N/A
	Micro: < 10	N/A

Source: Chi, Chen, Xie and Ye, 2011: 63

SME Policies in China

The development of SMEs in China is closely connected with the degree of recognition accorded to the non-state sector by the Government, as non-state enterprises are mainly SMEs. Urio (2010) suggests that the state plays a very important role in deciding and orienting the development of countries in transition. This is especially true for a one-party country like China, as all initiatives for politics, economy and culture are planned and monitored by the CCP. The rapid growth of SMEs in both number and economic significance since Deng's reforms in 1978 provides strong evidence on the downstream impact of government policies.

During the first period of government post the revolution (1949 to 1977) all enterprises in the private sector were converted into state ownership. During this period, the Chinese development model was built on Marxist philosophy

Table 8.3   **Industries with employment, annual revenue, and total assets for SMEs in China**

Sector	Employment	Annual revenue (Ten thousand Yuan[1])	Total assets (Ten thousand Yuan[2])
Construction	Medium: N/A	6,000–80,000	5,000–80,000
	Small: N/A	300–5,999	300–4,999
	Micro: N/A	< 300	< 300
Real estate development and management	Medium: N/A	1,000–200,000	5,000–10,000
	Small: N/A	100–999	2,000–4,999
	Micro: N/A	< 100	< 2,000
Leasing and business services	Medium: 100–300	N/A	8,000–120,000
	Small: 10–99	N/A	100–7,999
	Micro: < 10	N/A	< 100

[1] One US dollar equals approximately 6.5 Yuan

[2] One US dollar equals approximately 6.5 Yuan

Source: Chi, Chen, Xie and Ye, 2011: 63

and political economy, which required a centrally planned economic system and socialist public ownership. The results of this process were that non-agricultural industries in cities were aggregated into single enterprises and people living in urban areas became employees of the Government (Wu 2005). The private sector gradually disappeared as the state ownership system became dominant during this period. At the same time, agrarian reforms were also carried out. All rural households and farmers were organised into people's communes, which were large publicly-owned organisations (Dreyer 2007, Wu 2005). Unfortunately, this process resulted in overstaffed Chinese organisations and under-motivated people. To make matters worse, the Cultural Revolution, a ten-year hiatus, was launched by Mao in 1966. Factories came to a standstill, students dropped out of the school, and public institutions were in total disarray. The Chinese political and economic order was largely destroyed by the Cultural Revolution.

The year 1978 has become pivotal in modern Chinese history, as it marks the point when Deng Xiaoping became the leader of CCP. China initiated a series of reforms intended to reverse the decline of the preceding era and usher in a new age of economic liberalisation. The destruction of the Cultural Revolution left two important issues for Deng: how to improve the living standard of the Chinese people and how to restore governmental legitimacy to the CCP (Urio 2010). The private sector, which had been treated as a vestigial remnant of capitalism, was then marked for a revival. One major motivator was a tsunami of internal migration. A large number of educated urban youth returned to cities, as they had been unable to find employment when forced to work in rural areas during the Cultural Revolution. In response, in 1980 the CCP issued a circular which stated that the urban individual business sector should be encouraged and fostered. Even so, recruiting employees was strictly forbidden and was considered exploitation at that time (Wu 2005), and an individual business owner could only have a maximum five employees.

Rural areas experienced the rapid development of family farms which was accompanied by the growth of Township and Village Enterprises (TVEs). In 1980, the Government established a general quota system moderated by local conditions (Wu 2005). The TVE contracting system aimed to stimulate output by instituting a quota. Output that exceeded the quota could be retained by the family. The predecessors of TVEs were commune enterprises (Chen 1993), which in many localities had set up enterprises to produce simple agricultural machines or provide repair services. The introduction of the contracting system released surplus labour from the rural sector and the commune system, and provided the labour force for TVEs. Furthermore, the increasing living standard of farmers and demand for exchange of goods between rural and urban areas provided markets for the development of TVEs. In China, the vast majority of TVEs were located in coastal regions, such as the Pearl River Delta, Yangtze River Delta, central Zhejiang and the Jiaodong Peninsula. To some extent TVEs can be seen as the pioneers of the development of SMEs, and those regions have now become the richest regions in China (Wu 2005). TVEs and individual businesses played an increasingly important role in the economy, which in turn encouraged the state to change its guiding principles.

Major reform of SOEs began in the 1990s after Jiang Zemin ascended to power. SOEs had been criticised for their sluggish rates of development, low economic efficiency and budget problems (Cao 2007), so the Government decided to privatise small and medium-sized SOEs. In 1993, the CCP Party Committee promulgated the *Decision on Issues Regarding the Establishment of a Socialist Market Economic System*, which allowed inefficient small SOEs either to be sold to individuals, or transformed into limited-liability and JSCs. Privatisation of SOEs resulted in the loss of 53 million jobs through lay-offs and early retirements. As a result, the proportion of state ownership dropped dramatically from 90 per cent in 1978 to 60 per cent in 1994. Bolotinsky and Jiang (2008) argue that the encouragement of SME growth by Government was the most effective way to absorb former SOE workers while at the same time improving economic development.

Since 2000, the SME sector in China entered into a new and dramatic development phase. In 2001, there were 29.3 million SMEs employing 174 million people. At that time the SME sector contributed 50.5 per cent of China's gross domestic product (GDP) (Ai and Zhu 2002). As noted earlier, in 2009 SMEs numbers reached 42 million and provided 75 per cent of job opportunities as well as 60 per cent of GDP. Hence, Chinese SMEs have become a major force in social and economic development. The ongoing development of SMEs has now become an important factor supporting the rapid growth of the national economy, promoting social stability and providing people's livelihood. In the third development stage, the political status of SMEs and their owners was officially recognised by the Government. President Jiang announced in 2001 that private businessmen and entrepreneurs were now welcome to join the Communist Party. This meant the Government affirmed the political status of SME owners since, in China, only 'advanced elements' of the masses could become Party members. Secondly, the SME Promotion Law, promulgated in 2003, clarified the legal status of SMEs and also identified the legal responsibilities of the Government with respect to the development of SMEs. Furthermore, in 2007, the Government stressed a change of economic development model from relying solely on manufacturing industry to relying on the coordinated development of the primary, manufacturing and tertiary industries. At the same time, the Government recognised private entrepreneurs and small business owners as a new social stratum (Pan 2007).

Chinese SME Policies over Time

Government policy has a strong influence on the nature of economic development in China. Similarly, SME policies in China have been strongly influenced by the political ideology of the state and reflect social and economic changes in modern Chinese history. Policy for SMEs can be usefully grouped into four periods based on the modern historical development of China and summarised as follows.

PERIOD 1 – VANQUISHED (1949–1977)

Government policies towards private enterprises changed from using and supporting to denying and banning. In 1953 legislation was passed which called for the elimination of capitalist industry and commerce. The underlying assumption was that socialist ownership was the only legitimate economic base for China.

PERIOD 2 – REDISCOVERY (1978–1983)

China entered a period of reform. One of the areas of change was in ownership structure. Legislation between 1981 and 1982 encouraged the development of urban business, allowed individual business owners to hire a small number of employees, freed up employment in the collective and individual business sectors, and began to recognise individual businesses as a supplement to the socialist public sector.

PERIOD 3 – LAISSEZ FAIRE (1984–1999)

In the early part of this period, Government policies affirmed the importance of large business and ignored small enterprises. SOE reform became the priority of economic reforms. Policy developments included moving economic reform from rural to urban areas, emphasising the importance of scientific and technological advances, and the affirmation of the private sector as an important component in the modern socialist economy.

PERIOD 4 – ENGINE OF GROWTH (2000 ONWARDS)

This stage marks the expansion of earlier ideas, the formal recognition of SMEs, the formation of SME policy and the establishment of SME support systems. The *SME Promotion Law* (2003) laid the groundwork for Government support for SMEs and ensured the legal rights of SMEs were protected. Subsequently high taxes and sourcing capital have become major impediments to the further development of SMEs. Therefore, Government has focused on policy announcements in these two areas over the last few years in order to stimulate the ongoing development of SMEs.

Government policy initiatives establishing a more favourable environment for SME owner/operators began in 2000 as local government bodies were tasked to support SMEs through structural adjustments and technological innovation. A credit guarantee scheme was mooted, along with expanded financing channels and the establishment of more social services for SMEs.

In 2002 a framework designed to support the development of SMEs was established by the Government, while in 2003 the importance of non-public sector economic activity was made explicit. Individual and private enterprise economic activity was recognised as important to ongoing social development and economic productivity and was no longer the pariah of the communist state. In 2004, this view was further emphasised by a decree that the state would now protect the lawful rights and interests of the private economy.

In 2005 the Government sought to establish an environment even more conducive to the development of the private sector. In this regard the state cast itself in the role of ensuring that all private sector institutions operated according to the law. The state also communicated its expectation that enterprises behave in a trustworthy manner and improve their management systems. In addition the state took on a greater role in providing improved services to the private sector.

A new five-year plan, promulgated in 2006, contained specific proposals for the promotion and implementation of SME support projects at all levels of government and sought to improve the competitiveness of SMEs in all markets. More recently the state has called for open, fair and competitive markets within China that will assist SMEs in achieving improved and sustainable growth with its helpful side benefit of increased employment (Li 2009b).

SME Administration and State Services

To understand how SME policy is developed and delivered, it is also necessary to understand the structures of government within the PRC. Major national institutions in China are the National People's Congress, the Chairman and Vice Chairman of China, the State Military Commission, the Supreme People's Court, the Supreme People's Procuratorate and the State Council, the local people's congresses and the local people's governments at various levels, and autonomous local self-government authorities (The Central People's Government of the PRC 2011b).

The State Council, or the Central People's Government, is the highest administrative organ of the country and the executive organ of state power. It has 27 Ministries and Commissions, one special organisation, 15 other organisations, four administrative offices, 14 institutions, and 16 State Administrations and Bureaus under Ministries and Commissions (The Central People's Government of the PRC 2011c).

As SMEs have become the major players in China's economic growth, the Government has set up five central state organisations to administer and promote the development of SMEs. Figure 8.1 shows governmental agencies that have an interest in SMEs.

DEPARTMENT OF SMEs IN THE NATIONAL DEVELOPMENT AND REFORM COMMISSION: (NDRC)

The NDRC is responsible for overall planning and policy coordination for SMEs and the non-SOE sector. The main functions of the NDRC include formulating and implementing strategies for SMEs; setting up and improving the entrepreneurial environment for SMEs; directing SMEs' reforms and improving their management and productivity. It also has responsibility for developing policies to help SMEs solve financial problems (NDRC 2011).

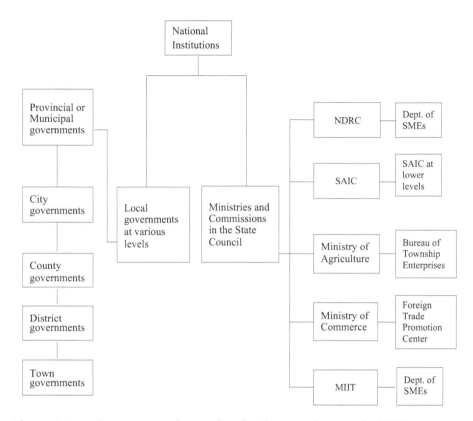

Figure 8.1   Governmental agencies that have an interest in SMEs

ADMINISTRATIVE AUTHORITIES FOR INDUSTRY AND COMMERCE AT DIFFERENT LEVELS (SAIC)

The State Administration for Industry and Commerce investigates and studies the developmental and managerial issues of self-employed people and private businesses, and develops policies and laws to supervise and administrate these types of businesses. administrative authorities for industry and commerce at the provincial, district and county levels are responsible for monitoring and providing guidance for the self-employed and private businesses within their respective jurisdictions (SAIC 2011).

THE BUREAU OF TOWNSHIP ENTERPRISES

The main functions of the Bureau are to draft laws and regulations for rural and township enterprises and organise their implementation; guide the administration of these enterprises and related foreign trade; guide the reform of rural and township enterprises; and monitor and analyse their economic operations (Ministry of Agriculture 2011).

FOREIGN TRADE PROMOTION CENTER FOR SMEs

This agency is under the jurisdiction of the Trade Development Bureau of the Ministry of Commerce, and assists SMEs active in importing or exporting. The SME foreign trade advice centre, set up in 2004, provides information, business training and international communication opportunities to SMEs in order to improve their competitiveness in the international market (Foreign Trade Promotion Center 2011).

THE DEPARTMENT OF SMES IN THE MINISTRY OF INDUSTRY AND INFORMATION TECHNOLOGY (MIIT)

The main target group of this department is scientific and technologically-based SMEs. Its core function is to provide funds for technology innovation to technology-based SMEs (MIIT 2011).

Government Services

In recognising the crucial role that SMEs play in national economic growth, the Chinese Government is pursuing a range of measures, from supporting international cooperation and adopting more favourable SME policies to strengthening SME development. Exhibitions and projects supported by the Government reduce the process costs for SMEs seeking business opportunities and provide a mechanism for SME owners/managers to learn about management skills and technology innovation.

The China Association of SMEs, launched in 2006, is under the charge of the state-owned Assets Supervision and Administration Commission. The major functions of this association are to facilitate collaboration and cooperation between SMEs, set up a bridge between SMEs and government organisations, and also to arrange international cooperation and communication for SMEs (CASME 2011).

The China International Cooperation Association of SMEs is also directed by the Assets Supervision and Administration Commission. The aim of the association is to organise and promote cooperation and trading opportunities between Chinese SMEs and small firms in the rest of the world. It has hosted numerous international economic and trade events in China and other countries since it was founded in 1990, such as the China International SME Fair in Suzhou (CISMEF 2009).

The All China Federation of Industry and Commerce (ACFIC) is the largest business association in China, as its organisational network covers all government agencies above the county level. The ACFIC at all levels serves as a bridge between government and the private sector. It informs the private sector of government laws and regulations, and informs the government of private sector views and suggestions (ACFIC 2011). There are also some industry-specific associations in China. These associations are formed either at the local or national levels, such as the Wenzhou Garment Chamber of Commerce or the China National Association of Automation. They provide information and interactions to their members (Garnaut, Song, Yao and Wang 2001).

Table 8.4 shows some of the changes in government attitudes towards SMEs and the key institutions in each policy phase.

Table 8.4   Government policy for SMEs

	Government Attitudes Towards SMEs	The Role of SMEs	Key Institutions
Stage 1 (1949–1977)	Vanquished	None envisaged	Central government
Stage 2 (1978–1983)	Rediscovery	A supplement to the socialist public sector	Government at all levels
Stage 3 (1984–1999)	Laissez faire	Part of the national economy	Local government; Department of SMEs under the State Economic and Trade Commission
Stage 4 (2000 onwards)	Engine of growth	An important and growing sector of the economy with special requirements	Local government; Department of SMEs in the National Development and Reform Commission; Bureau of Township Enterprises; Department of SMEs under the Ministry of Commerce; The administrative authorities for Industry and Commerce at various levels; Department of SMEs in the Ministry of Industry and Information Technology

As the above discussion indicates, there are a number of central-level organisations involved in SME administration. This fragmented system can result in problems due to overlapping functions, duplicated laws and regulations, and conflicting authority interests, which can cause confusion for SMEs. Since 2010, the central Government has required all industries and the many different governmental organisations working in this field to coordinate their services and provide an integrated platform. The goal is that SMEs might be able to more effectively access institutional support, information and services (Tan, Yang and Veliyath 2009).

Conclusion

This chapter has sought to examine the development of Chinese SME policies over the last 60 years. An examination of China's relationship to the SME sector highlights a number of important issues. The first is that the SME sector has been strongly influenced by the ideology of the state apparatus, as in other countries. When considering China's post-revolution experience it becomes clear that the disastrous interventions of the 1950s impacted severely on small business, because of the state's intention to eliminate private sector activity in favour of collective organisations. The remainder of the twentieth century and first decade of the twenty-first century has seen a reversal of that philosophy. The consequential impacts on small business have been enormous and form a useful case study for other developing economies in transition.

The second point policymakers can take from the Chinese experience is that SMEs have a very important role to play in an economy, irrespective of political ideology. Massive gains in economic development in China have been possible because of the rise of private enterprise and small businesses in particular. The Chinese experience highlights the SME sector's potential to provide employment, providing new job opportunities even as privatisation of SOEs in the 1990s lead to major job losses. The encouragement of the growth of the SME sector by Government has helped to absorb the excess workforce while ensuring social stability (Bolotinsky and Jiang 2008).

Third, the rapid rise of the modern economy in China has been accompanied by numerous attempts to assist SMEs. The Chinese experience highlights the difficulty of offering a seamless service to SMEs when a plethora of agencies become involved. Recent thinking in China has recognised the need for an integrated service that reduces overlap and improves the environment for SME development (MIIT 2010).

A fourth issue revolves around the kinds of policies that provide enabling conditions for SME success. Early interventionist policies in China have given way to the realisation that the role of the state is to provide enabling conditions. For Chinese SMEs these include access to capital, avoiding excessive taxation, providing a level playing field for SMEs versus large enterprises, providing legal certainty and protection, and demonstrating a commitment to longer term economic policy.

Overall, the Chinese experience has shown that SMEs can be a major force to improve economic conditions in a developing country. However, two important conditions are needed. The first is government recognition of the importance of SMEs in achieving economic and social objectives. Secondly, governments need to implement economic policies that improve the business and market environment of SMEs.

References

Ai, F. and Zhu, X.P. 2002. *Zhongxiao Qiye: Rongzi Jiujing Nanzaina*(SMEs: Is It Hard to Get Loans.). Beijing: Jingji Ribao.

All-China Federation of Industry and Commerce (ACFIC) 2011. *About ACFIC*. [Online] Available at: http://www.acfic.org.cn/publicfiles/business/htmlfiles/qggsl/gsljj/index.html [accessed: 25 May 2011].

Bolotinsky, M. and Jiang, H.D. 2008. *SMEs in Russian and China: A Comparison*. [Online] Available at: http://www.acg.ru/english/news2.phtml?m=2866 [accessed: 13 March 2010].

Cao, S.Y. 2007. The homogenization and decline of China's state-owned economy. *Chinese Law and Government*. 40(6), 22–30.

Central People's Government of the PRC 2011a. *About China*. [Online] Available at: http://www.gov.cn/test/2005-08/11/content_27116.htm [accessed: 19 May 2011].

Central People's Government of the PRC 2011b. *System of National Institutions of the PRC*. [Online] Available at: http://www.gov.cn/gjjg/2005-08/28/content_27083.htm [accessed: 19 May 2011].

Central People's Government of the PRC 2011c. *The State Council of the PRC*. [Online] Available at: http://www.gov.cn/gjjg/2005-08/01/content_18608.htm [accessed: 19 May 2011].

Chen X.W. 1993. *Zhongguo Nongcun Gaige: Huigu yu Zhanwang*. (China's Rural reforms: Review and Prospect). Tianjin: Tianjin Renmin Chubanshe.

Chen, Y. 2010. *Expert of the State Council Says Chinese Rural Population Will Reduce to 400 Billion in 30 Years*. [Online] Available at: http://news.xinhuanet.com/politics/2010-02/24/content_13035879.htm [accessed: 20 May 2011].

Chi, R.Y., Chen, C., Xie, H.M. and Ye. C.L. 2011. *Zhongguo Zhongxiao qiye jingqi zhishu yanjiu baogao*. (Climate Index Report of Chinese SMEs). Beijing: Jingji Kexue Chubanshe.

China Association of SMEs (CASME) 2011. *Brief Introduction*. [Online] Available at: http://www.acfic.org.cn/publicfiles/business/htmlfiles/qggsl/gsljj/index.html [accessed: 15 January 2011].

China International SME Fair (CISMEF) 2009. *About CISMEF*. [Online] Available at: www.smefair.org.cn/en/html/CISMEF/AboutCISMEF/index.html [accessed: 17 November 2009].

Dreyer, J.T. 2007. *China's Political System: Modernization and Tradition*, 6th edition. New York: Pearson Longman.

Foreign Trade Promotion Center 2011. *About Us*. [Online] Available at: http://www.smetrade.org.cn [accessed: 25 May 2011].

Garnaut, R., Song, L.G., Yao, Y. and Wang, X.L. 2001. *Private Enterprise in China*. Sydney: Asia Pacific Press.

Guo, R.X. 2007. *How the Chinese Economy Works*. 2nd edition. New York: Palgrave Macmillan.

Li, Z.B. 2009a. *The Blue Book of SMEs in China: The Current Situation and Policies*. Beijing: Zhongguo Fazhan Chubanshe.

Li, Z.B. 2009b. *Zhongguo Zhongxiaoqiye Fazhan Baogao*. (Report on the development of SMEs in China). Beijing: Zhongguo Jingji Chubanshe.

Li, Z.B. 2010. *The Blue Book of SMEs in China: Development, Financing, Service and Policies*. Beijing: Zhongguo Fazhan Chubanshe.

Ministry of Agriculture 2011. *Main Functions*. [Online] Available at: http://english.agri.gov.cn/ga/amoa/organs/200906/t20090625_1169.htm [accessed: 13 January 2011].

Ministry of Industry and Information Technology (MIIT) 2010. *Guiding Opinions on Promoting SME Public Service Platform*. [Online] Available at: http://www.gov.cn/zwgk/2010-04/21/content_1588478.htm [accessed: 8 August 2011].

Ministry of Industry and Information Technology (MIIT) 2011. *The Department of SMEs*. Available at: http://www.miit.gov.cn/n11293472/n11293832/n11294147/index.html [accessed: 13 January 2011].

National Development and Reform Commission (NDRC) 2011. *Organisation Structure*. [Online] Available at: http://zxqys.ndrc.gov.cn/jgsz/default.html [accessed: 13 January 2011].

Pan, L.T. 2007. *Senior Official: New Social Stratum Important for Development*. [Online] Available at: http://english.gov.cn/2007-02/14/content_527590.htm [accessed: 5 January 2011].

Shan, J. 2011. *By the End of 2010, Chinese Population Grew to 1.341 billion*. [Online] Available at: http://www.chinadaily.com.cn/china/2011-03/01/content_12091922.htm [accessed: 25 May 2011].

SME Promotion Law 2003. Standing Committee of the National People's Congress (ed.) *69*. Beijing.

State Administration for Industry and Commerce of the PRC (SAIC) 2011. *Main Functions*. [Online] Available at: http://www.saic.gov.cn/zzjg/zyzz/ [accessed: 13 January 2011].

Tan, J., Yang, J. and Veliyath, R. (2009). Particularistic and system trust among small and medium enterprises: a comparative study in China's transition economy. *Journal of Business Venturing*, 26(4), 544–557.

Urio, P. 2010. *Reconciling State, Market and Society in China: The Long March toward Prosperity*. Oxford: Routledge.

Wang, Y.Z. 2004. Financing difficulties and structural characteristics of SMEs in China. *China & World Economy*, 12(2), 34–49.

Wu, J.L. 2005. *Understanding and Interpreting Chinese Economic Reform*. Mason: Texere.

Yao, S.X. 2005. *Zhongri Zhongxiao Qiye Bijiao* (Comparison Between Chinese and Japanese SMEs). Chengdu: Sichuan Renmin Chubanshe.

9

Small Business Support and Enterprise Promotion: The Case of France

Rita Klapper, Mahamadou Biga-Diambeidou and Arto Henrikki Lahti

Chapter Summary

The purpose of this chapter is to provide an analysis of how the French Government deals with entrepreneurial activity, in terms of new venture creation and small business development. Contrasting institutional and cultural dimensions, which are two sources of authority that influence the process of economic change over time, this chapter discusses how France, which is generally perceived as hostile to entrepreneurship and enterprise creation, is now accepted as one of the three leading European countries in terms of its support for entrepreneurship and small business development. However, there still remains a level of cultural resistance which limits the institutional will to make France an entrepreneurial society.

Introduction

While entrepreneurship is viewed as an essential ingredient of wealth creation and social justice (Van Praag and Versloot 2007), a major paradox of the literature on entrepreneurship is that the process of opportunity recognition and exploitation (Kraus and Kauranen 2009) has been analysed separately from market structures.

Entrepreneurship is understood differently by different scholars. For some researchers (Gartner 1988: 11) entrepreneurship is about 'the creation of organizations, the process by which new organizations come into existence'. This contrasts with Davidsson, Delmar and Wiklund (2006), who view entrepreneurship as venture development. Arguably, such differences have been detrimental to the understanding of the specificities of entrepreneurship and have affected the development of framework conditions for both entrepreneurship and for small business development in different contexts.

Research at a country level (see for instance Audretsch, Grillo and Thurik 2007, Storey 2003) suggests that policymakers are faced with a number of choices that may influence entrepreneurial processes. In general, empirical evidence shows that 'macro' policies are seen as more effective than 'micro' policies in promoting entrepreneurship (Ahmad and Hoffman 2007). In addition, there is a great variation in policy effectiveness between countries and according to economic circumstances (Storey 2008). This suggests that the ability of policymakers to design effective policies that favour the sustainability of entrepreneurship and small business development is a key element in economic and social decision-making processes. Despite the importance of policy effectiveness for stimulating entrepreneurship, to date little research has focused on the framework conditions for entrepreneurship and small business development (Dennis 2011) and even less is known about the French context (Klapper 2008).

The purpose of this chapter is to provide an analysis of how French Government has dealt with entrepreneurial activity, in terms of new venture creation and small business development. Contrasting institutional and cultural dimensions, which are two sources of authority that influence the process of economic change over time (Dennis 2011), the chapter discusses how France, which has been generally perceived as hostile to entrepreneurship and enterprise creation, is now accepted as one of the three leading European countries in terms of its support for entrepreneurship and small business development (Eurostat 2008). The chapter also examines how particular cultural framework conditions have the potential to limit, or influence negatively, the will to change to an entrepreneurial society and to hinder the creation of dynamic and favourable institutional structures. Finally it is suggested that the heterogeneity of entrepreneurship definitions, or conceptualisations, may affect or constrain the vision of policymakers.

The remainder of the chapter is structured as follows. A short review of entrepreneurship literature is presented, with a particular focus on French contributors, followed by a discussion of France-specific developments since the end of the Second World War period, up to the present situation. Some statistical information is provided about the importance of the SME sector and enterprise creation, as well as some critical analysis of existing policy tools. The final section concludes by underlining the importance of tensions that impact on the creation of an entrepreneurial culture in France.

Definitional Heterogeneity

One of the key problems in entrepreneurship research relates to the lack of consensus regarding a definition, or conceptualisation, of entrepreneurship. In fact, many authors such as Davidsson, Delmar and Wiklund (2006), Fayolle (2005), Verstraete (2003), Shane and Venkataraman (2000), Bygrave and Hofer (1991), Cunningham and Lischeron (1991), and Gartner (1990) have emphasised the lack of an agreed definition of entrepreneurship and what entrepreneurship constitutes as a field of research. Gartner (1988) undertook an analysis of a range of normative and empirical definitions of entrepreneurship, which ranged from economics (Schumpeter 1934) and psychology (McClelland 1961) to examples of empirically-derived definitions such as that of Brockhaus (1980). Gartner concluded by advocating two different approaches to defining entrepreneurship: the behavioural approach and the traditional trait approach.

In the French context, different types of definitions have been used for different purposes. INSEE, Institut National de Statistique et des Etudes Economiques (National Institute for Statistics and Economic Studies) has developed an official definition used for statistical purposes, that is, for data gathering and data analysis. This definition suggests that enterprise creation can be understood: (i) as new ways of producing; (ii) as the entrepreneur restarting an activity after more than one year of interruption; (iii) as the entrepreneur restarting an activity after an interruption of at least a year, but with change in activity; or (iv) as the takeover of the activities of an existing enterprise by a newly created business (INSEE 2010a). This definition contains both Gartner's understanding of the term enterprise creation (see i), but also the notion that entrepreneurship is of a developmental nature, with the possibility of starting, stopping and re-launching at different stages in time (see ii,iii and iv).

In comparison, within the French academic community, seminal authors such as Fayolle (2005) and Bruyat (2001, 1993) have created their own definitions appropriate to the diverse research contexts that they have investigated. Fayolle (2005: 40), for example, emphasised the importance of entrepreneurship as a developmental process and developed the following definition: 'Entrepreneurship concerns essentially the emergence and transformation of human organisations. It is not just about the reasons of this emergence, rejoining economists, sociologists, political scientists but is also interested in the way we can conceive and construct new activities or new organisations.' Unlike Fayolle, for Bruyat (2001, 1993) entrepreneurship is about the relationship between the individual and the value creation aspect of entrepreneurship. He suggested the following: 'The scientific object studied in the field of entrepreneurship is the dialogue between the individual and the creation of value' (Bruyat 1993: 57). Bruyat's conceptualisation is interesting as it suggests that new value is created in terms of more, or less, intense change in the environment directly connected with the entrepreneurial process (Verstraete and Fayolle 2005). Bruyat's theoretical developments are based on Gartner (1985) who viewed entrepreneurship as a system involving four key ingredients: the individual, the enterprise, the process and the environment.

In summary, this short review of relevant literature underlines that it is important to understand entrepreneurship both as an act of the creation of a business, but also as a growth orientation, implying a developmental process.

The Development of French Institutions Over Time

This section gives a short overview of the history of the support for entrepreneurship and small business, starting with the Trentes Glorieuses after the Second World War through to the 1980s.

LES TRENTES GLORIEUSES: THE '30 GLORIOUS YEARS' AFTER THE SECOND WORLD WAR

There has been a long tradition of French state involvement in the economy which goes back to Jean-Baptiste Colbert (1619–1683). Colbert's intellectual legacy has been associated with a long-standing tradition of state intervention through discriminatory fiscal and public procurement policies, intended to develop and nurture public and private national champions as well as nascent industries (Gordon 1993, Cohen 1992). As MacLean (2002) suggested, at the heart of French business culture is the concordat between the state and business, which '…is held together by the shared ideology of a relatively homogeneous national elite' (p. 21). Gordon (1993) critically pointed out that French market forces have never been allowed to function freely due to a long tradition of interventionist policies affecting all aspects of economic and industrial activities. As a result, in the post-Second World War period the state acted both as 'director, catalyst, initiator and regulator' of growth (MacLean 2002).

Bruyat (1993) pointed out that during the 'trente glorieuses' – the glorious 30 years after the Second World War – numerous economic and social indicators suggested that the entrepreneur and the small enterprise, and in consequence enterprise creation, were just a remainder from the past and that only large enterprises could supply the needed employment and economic wealth in an economic context dominated by international competition. In fact, in the postwar period France's ruling elite was concerned with growth, with national economic strength and with the extension of the national business system.

As Goyer (2001) states, there were two alternatives open to policymakers: the creation of large firms through mergers, or the emergence of SMEs through internal growth. The French state opted for the first option, with the support of a generalist education provided by the French Grandes Ecoles system, which provided the strategic vision and organisational capabilities for running conglomerate firms (Fridenson 1997). Special policy measures were developed to support industrial concentration, convert inefficient industries and develop those of the future. This resulted in mergers and acquisitions as an integral part of de Gaullist industrial policy. This policy of national champions was supported by tax incentives, mid to long-term credits and direct government intervention (Boltho 1996). As a result, by the beginning of the Giscard era (1974–1981), France had the highest rate of corporate mergers in Western Europe whilst the number of firms with ten or fewer employees had dropped by 20 per cent (Hall 1986). A similar trend could also be observed in the UK, with the Industrial Reorganisation Corporation in the 1960s, which promoted structural change to improve the efficiency and profitability of British industry (HC Deb 1968).

BUSINESS SUPPORT IN THE 1970S AND 1980S: EARLY BUSINESS SUPPORT MEASURES

Most of the French initiatives in favour of enterprise creation and SMEs originated in the 1970s. Similar to the Bolton report in the UK in 1971 and the Wiltshire report in Australia (Landström 2005), it was the Miliaret report in 1973 that triggered interest in small business and enterprise creation, pointing out the inadequate level of renewal of the economic and industrial fabric of the country (APCE 2002). As Léger-Jarniou (2005) highlighted, this was the first time that the concept of firm creation received attention in the French economy, arguably inspired by foreign examples, in particular American. Indeed, it took six years to establish the first government institution dedicated to venture creation: *Agence Nationale de Création d'Entreprise* (ANCE, the National Agency for Venture Creation) in 1979 which later in 1996 became the *Agence Pour la Création d'Entreprise* (APCE) (APCE 2002).

As Boutillier and Uzunidis (1995) emphasise, in the period from 1976–1980 the French state started to discover the importance of SMEs in terms of employment generation and export potential. Several types of business support aiming to promote enterprise creation were created during the period from 1977–1987 (Léger-Jarniou 2005). First, purely financial support targeted specific groups such as the unemployed (Abdesselam, Bonnet and Le Papen 2004) and specific sectors of the economy such as food processing (APCE 2002). Second, counselling and training networks offered personalised training and counselling programmes, aiming to encourage business start-ups. Centres for Company Formalities (CFE, the Centre de Formalités des Entreprises) were set up to facilitate the administrative burden associated with the start-up process (APCE 2002). Finally, support activities were developed within the framework of an emerging incubator system, with the first incubator opening at the beginning of the 1980s (APCE 2002, Léger-Jarniou 2005).

In addition, from the early 1980s onwards, French public-sector policies gave preferential support to the development of innovative companies in high-technology sectors such as biotechnology. As Boutillier and Uzinidis (2000) commented, collaboration between research institutions and industry was actively encouraged (APCE 2002). Later at the end of the 1980s, support was extended to all types of businesses. As Boutillier and Uzinidis (2000) explained, this period saw a multiplication of social laws in favour of non-profit organisations, as the French state perceived the need for a social objective to support enterprise creation (APCE 2002).

SUPPORT FROM THE 1990S ONWARDS

From the mid 1990s, support for entrepreneurship and enterprise creation was increasingly recognised as vital for French post-industrial society due to the contribution of both to economic regeneration, regional economic development and employment generation (APCE 2002, Fayolle 1999). As a result many different programmes and initiatives were developed and in 1995 the ANCE identified 30 types of assistance for enterprise creation at both national and local level. Such assistance was available in the shape of subsidies, social charges and tax exemptions, enterprise finance and general business support (APCE 2002). The following sections point out the different legal support structures created by the French Government to encourage enterprise creation and small business development.

LOI DE L'INNOVATION OR LAW OF INNOVATION

At the end of the 1990s the *Law on Innovation* was passed to further promote entrepreneurship and enterprise creation. This law authorised: (i) researchers to set up their own business; (ii) helped create public incubators (innovation centres) for hosting these new firms; (iii) launched a national competition for the creation of high-tech firms; and (iv) defined measures to simplify the creation and operation of new firms. In 1999 at national and regional level, funding for enterprise and enterprise creation amounted to 2.6bn Francs in 1999, compared to 2.1bn in 1998 (in 2010 terms these values would correspond to approximately USD $464m and USD $349m respectively).

LOI DU DUTREIL OR LAW OF ECONOMIC INITIATIVE

In 2003, building upon the recent interest in entrepreneurship, the French Government under President Jacques Chirac announced its ambitious objective to create one million new enterprises over a five-year period. To achieve this goal the French National Assembly passed the *Loi du Dutreil* or *Law of Economic Initiative* in August 2003. The law consisted of five different elements intended to facilitate enterprise creation, one of which was company creation via the Internet for the price of just one euro. In addition, the law was intended to facilitate a change from employee to entrepreneur status, finance economic initiatives, facilitate entrepreneurial projects and enable the take-over of existing companies. As Fayolle and Sénicourt (2005) critically commented, it would, however, be naïve to believe that a business could be created with one euro, as 210 euros are needed to register a firm as SARL (societé à responsabilité limitée – limited liability corporation).

LOI DE LA MODERNISATION DE L'ECONOMIE OR LAW OF THE MODERNISATION OF THE ECONOMY

In Spring 2008 President Nicolas Sarkozy's Government introduced the *Loi de La Modernisation de l'Economie (Law of the 'Modernisation of the Economy)*, which contained a number of initiatives to encourage enterprise creation. The underlying motivation was to create a Small Business Act 'à la française', that is, a legal support framework inspired by the American Small Business Act, implemented and adjusted to the French context. One of the important measures was the creation of a simplified status for the individual entrepreneur (the so-called 'auto-entrepreneur') who could create their own enterprise and earn an annual turnover up to 80,000 or 32,100 euros respectively, depending on whether the activity was of a commercial or service/liberal nature (INSEE 2010a, Radu and Redien-Collot 2008). A further major change was that the entrepreneur was no longer expected to make social security contributions prior to making any sales. The new law offered better protection of the property of the entrepreneur in case of failure, and reduced the need to register with different government authorities, thus lowering the overall administrative burden (INSEE 2010a).

REDEFINITION OF THE TERM 'ENTERPRISE'

Up to 2008 the term enterprise was defined from a legal point of view. Decree no.2008-1354 changed this situation, by outlining four economic categories: micro-enterprises, SMEs, enterprises of intermediary size (ETI) and large enterprises. These categories were based on the number of employees, turnover and balance sheet total (INSEE 2010b) (see Table 9.1).

Table 9.1   Four new categories of enterprise

	Microenterprises	Small and Medium-Sized Enterprises (SMEs)	Enterprise of Intermediary Size (ETI)	Large Enterprise
No of employees	< 10 people	<250 people	< 5,000 people	>5,000 people
Turnover (annually)	Either <2m euros annually	<50m euros annually	<1,500 million euros	>1,500 million euros
Balance sheet total (annually)	Or <2m euros annually	<43m euros annually	<2,000 million euros	>2,000 million euros

Source: INSEE (2010a).

At the end of 2010 INSEE (2010b) published the latest statistics of enterprises in France, applying the above criteria. In total there were 2.9 million enterprises in 2007, of which 2.7 million or 96 per cent were microenterprises. These companies employed 3.2 million employees, representing 21 per cent of the French working population. There were 164,000 SMEs, (that is, excluding microenterprises), which employed 29 per cent of the workforce, and 4,600 companies of intermediary size that employed another 20 per cent. In comparison, some 240 large companies employed 4.4 million people (29 per cent of the French working population).

In 2009 the number of business start-ups in France reached a record high of 580,200, which represented an approximately 75 per cent increase in comparison with 331,400 in 2008. Much of this increase can be attributed to the 320,000 auto-entrepreneur (one person) start-ups. These companies were primarily created in the services sector, two-thirds of which were of an auto-entrepreneur type (INSEE 2010a). Following the publication of the *Loi du Dutreil*, the number of creations slowly increased from 2003 onwards, peaking in 2009.

Obstacles to New Venture Creation and Small Business Development

As the above discussion indicates, recent French Government initiatives have focused on the facilitation of enterprise creation through the removal of administrative barriers. Significantly less attention has been devoted to the promotion of small business development. The following section discusses some of the obstacles to enterprise creation and small business development, with particular reference to specific cultural and educational features of French society.

THE FRENCH EDUCATION SYSTEM

In France the higher education system has a key role to play in the promotion of small business and entrepreneurship. Higher education operates in a tripartite structure consisting of universities, Grandes Ecoles, and other Higher and Further Education institutes. Some of the oldest Grandes Ecoles, such as the Polytechnic and ENS, were established during the French revolution (Maclean, Harvey and Press 2006). These Grandes Ecoles are very prestigious establishments, represent avenues to the highest social positions and have been carriers of national and regional policy initiatives. The recent government focus on entrepreneurship has given the Grandes Ecoles a new role in promoting entrepreneurship in management and engineering schools (Klapper 2008, European Commission 2003). This has resulted in the creation and expansion of entrepreneurship teaching, whether through dedicated centres, as add-ons in other departments or courses, or as profile and awareness raising exercises (Fayolle 1999). The question is, however, whether the Grandes Ecoles are up to this challenge (see Klapper 2004).

ENTREPRENEURIAL VALUES

In French society, nascent entrepreneurs are confronted with a lack of acceptance of entrepreneurship and entrepreneurial values (Fayolle and Sénicourt 2005). In particular, the close relationship between business and government which has been promoted by '…the main actors being cast in the same mould of the Grandes Ecoles and preserving a lasting web of interlocking formal and informal relationships' (Gordon 1993: 129). This has, as Maclean et al. (2006) argue, fostered a common worldview or '*pensée unique*' on the part of the state elite. Arguably, this worldview has been particularly influenced by the Grande Ecoles' mission to educate and train managers for the French state or French multinationals, yet not to start their own business and become entrepreneurs (Klapper 2010a, 2010b, 2008). As Klapper (2010a, 2010b, 2008) shows, this has clearly worked to the disadvantage of enterprise creation and small business development.

WAGE VERSUS ENTREPRENEURIAL CULTURE

Several commentators have noted that French society is characterised by a wage culture, where salaried workers have greater historical advantages in terms of social security and relative job stability (Abdesselam et al. 2004, Frugier and Verzat 2005). This is in stark contrast to the UK, where private entrepreneurial initiative is socially valued. Hence, staying an employee is a rather attractive option, while becoming an entrepreneur may involve high opportunity costs. In fact, as Béranger, Chabral and Dambrine (1998) has suggested, young French people think that it is the Government's and the overall system's responsibility to provide job security and work. As a result, enterprise promotion becomes a difficult task.

ESTABLISHED/TRADITIONAL COGNITIVE STRUCTURES

Carayannis, Evans and Hanson (2003) argue that traditional French society wants its children to enter 'noble' professions, instead of seeking self-employment. In other words, it is acceptable to become a doctor or lawyer, but most parents would strenuously try to dissuade their children from being an entrepreneur. The authors also argue that French culture seems to equate creating an activity with the destruction of the normal pattern of wealth distribution in a collectivist society. The idea that an individual and not the nation as a whole would benefit from this creation seems to be the norm. Arguably some of this thinking may be rooted in Jean-Jacques Rousseau's *Social Contract* (1762). Rousseau was interested in how individual citizens with their individual needs could live together in harmony within a community and within society. He argued that individuals should neglect their natural, possibly harmful inclinations (*le moi humain*) and instead support the 'general will' (*la volonté générale*) of the community (*le moi commun*), which would not allow for different points of view (Klapper 2008, MacLean 2002). In short, arguably French society has, to some extent, counter-entrepreneurial cognitive structures with deep historical roots.

RISK AVERSENESS OF FRENCH CULTURE

As MacLean (2002) and Gordon (1997) have underlined, French business culture is characterised by a search for organisational security which is linked to a deep-rooted need to avoid uncertainty and remove ambiguity. Referring to Hofstede's work (1983) on cultural values, Fayolle and Sénicourt (2005) and MacLean (2002) have emphasised the risk-averseness of French business culture. For example, in Hofstede's study, France scored particularly high on this aspect, compared with the UK. As Fayolle and Sénicourt (2005) emphasised, the French cultural context promotes risk awareness and a fear of failure, which does not encourage the individual to take personal risks, such as those needed for setting up a business. MacLean et al. (2006) argued that for the past few decades France has preferred to prioritise employment security to risk-taking. The fear of failure seems to dominate and paralyses many entrepreneurial initiatives, which may be rooted in an education system that does not teach individuals how to manage failure (Masclot 2003). An unsuccessful French entrepreneur would not only lose material possessions, but also self-esteem, professional opportunities and possibly his/her well-established place in French society (Carayannis et al. 2003).

Conclusion

This chapter has provided an overview of French entrepreneurial literature, outlined some of the recent trends in French small business development, and examined some of the social features that arguably work in favour of – and against – the development of an entrepreneurial society in France. These features are identified as an education system that aims to produce senior managers required for large state-run conglomerates; a wage-oriented rather than entrepreneurial culture, possibly underpinned by a long historical tradition of collectivism; and risk-aversion in business thinking. There are no easy solutions to these issues. Whilst some measures, such as entrepreneurship education, may help address the matter, French society is unlikely to change in the short term.

References

Abdessalam, R., Bonnet, J. and Le Papen, N. 2004. An explanation of the life span of French firms. *Small Business Economics*, 23 (3), 237–254.

Agence pour la Création d'Enterprise (APCE) 2002. *Politique Locales de Soutien à la Création d'Entreprise*: *Attendus et Résultas* (Local policies to support business creation: expected results). Paris: APCE.

Ahmad, N. and Hoffman, A. 2007. *A Framework for Addressing and Measuring Entrepreneurship*. Paris, OECD Entrepreneurship Indicators Steering Group.

Audretsch, D.B., Grillo I. and Thurik R.A. 2007. Explaining Entrepreneurship and the Role of Policy: A Framework, in *Handbook of Research on Entrepreneurship Policy*, edited by D.B. Audretsch and R.A. Thurik. Cheltenham: Edward Elgar Publishing, 1–17.

Béranger, J., Chabral, R. and Dambrine, F. 1998. *Rapport sur la Formation Entrepreneuriale des Ingénieurs (Report on the Entrepreneurial Training of Engineers)*. Paris : Ministère de l'Economie, des Finances et de l'Industrie.

Boltho, A. 1996. Has France Converged on Germany? in *National Diversity and Global Capitalism* edited by S. Berger and R. Dore, New York: Cornell University Press, 89–104.

Bolton, J.E. 1971. *Small Firms: Report of the Committee of Inquiry on Small Firms*, Cmnd 4811. London: HMSO.

Boutillier, S. and Uzinidis, D. 1995. *L'Entrepreneur Une Analyse Socio-économique (The Entrepreneur A Socio-Economic Analysis)*. Paris: Economica.

Boutillier, S. and Uzinidis, D. 2000. Les Dimensions socio-économique et politique de l'entrepreneur (The Socio-economic and political dimensions of the entrepreneur) in *Histoire d'Entreprendre* edited by T. Verstraete, Caen: EMS, 21–33.

Brockhaus, R.H. 1980. Risk taking propensity of entrepreneurs. *Academy of Management Journal*. 23(3), 509–520.

Bruyat, C. 1993. *Création d'Entreprise: Contributions Épistémologiques et Modélisation (Creating Company: Epistemological Contributions and Modeling)* Thèse pour le Doctorat de Sciences de Gestion, ESA, Grenoble: Université Grenoble II.

Bruyat, C. 2001. Creer ou ne pas creer? Une modelisation du processus d'engagement dans un projet de creation d'entreprise (Creating or not creating? Modeling the process of engagement in a project to create business). *Revue de l'Entrepreneuriat*, 1(1), 25–37.

Bygrave, W.D. and Hofer, C.W. 1991. Theorising about entrepreneurship. *Entrepreneurship, Theory and Practice*, 16(2), 13–22.

Carayannis, E.G., Evans, D. and Hanson, M. 2003. A cross-cultural learning strategy for entrepreneurship education: outline of key concepts and lessons learned from a comparative study of entrepreneurship students in France and the US. *Technovation*, 23, 757–777.

Cohen, E. 1992. *Le Colbertisme High tech: Economie des Telécom et du Grand Projet (The Colbertism High tech: Economy of Telecom and Grand Project)*. Paris: Hachette Pluriel.

Cunningham, J.B. and Lischeron, J. 1991. Defining entrepreneurship. *Journal of Small Business Management*, 29 (1), 45–61.

Davidsson, P., Delmar, F. and Wiklund, J. 2006. *Entrepreneurship and the Growth of Firms*. Cheltenham: Edward Elgar Publishing

Dennis, W. 2011. Entrepreneurship, small business and public policy levers. *Journal of Small Business Management*, 49(1), 92–106.

European Commission 2003. *European Commission (2003) SME Package: Thinking Small in an Enlarging Europe*, Enterprise Europe, April–June, No. 11/2003, Luxembourg: Office des Publications Officielles des Communautés Européennes.

Eurostat 2008 *L'Europe en Chiffres (Europe in figures)*, Luxembourg: Office des Publications Officielles des Communautés Européennes.

Fayolle, A. 1999. *L'enseignement de l'entrepreneuriat dans les Universités Françaises: Analyse de l'existant et Propositions pour en Faciliter le Développement (The teaching of entrepreneurship in French Universities: Analysis of existing and Proposals to Facilitate Development)*. Lyon: EM.

Fayolle, A. 2005. *Introduction à l'Entrepreneuriat (Introduction to Entrepreneurship)*. Paris: Dunod.

Fayolle, A. and Sénicourt, P. 2005. Peut-on former des entrepreneurs? (Can we train entrepreneurs?) *Expansion Management Review*, March, 34–48.

Fridenson, P. 1997. Who is Responsible for the French Economic Miracle (1945–1960)? In *Revolution, Society and the Politics of Memory*, edited by M. Adcock, E. Chester and J. Whiteman. Melbourne, University of Melbourne Press, 309–313.

Frugier, D. and Verzat, C. 2005. Un defi pour les institutions educatives (A Challenge for educational institutions). *l'Expansion Management Review*, March, 42–48.

Gartner, W.B. 1985. A framework for describing the phenomenon of new venture creation. *Academy of Management Review*, 10, 696–706.

Gartner, W.B. 1988. "Who is an entrepreneur?" Is the wrong question. *American Journal of Small Business*, 12(4), Spring, 11–31.

Gartner, W.B. 1990. What are we talking about when we talk about entrepreneurship. *Journal of Business Venturing*, 5(1), 5–28.

Gordon, C. 1993. Business Culture in France in *Business Culture in Europe*, edited by W.C. Brierley et al. Oxford: Butterworth-Heinemann, 86–137.

Gordon, C. 1997. The Business Culture in France in *Business Cultures in Europe*, edited by C. Randlesome et al. 2nd edition. Oxford, Butterworth Heinemann, 86–133.

Goyer, M. 2001. Corporate governance and the innovation system in France, 1985–2000. *Industry and Innovation*, 8(2), 135–158.

Hall, P.A. 1986. *Governing the Economy: The Politics of State Intervention in Britain and France*. Cambridge, Polity Press.

HC Deb 30 January 1968. *Industrial Reorganisation Corporation*, House of Commons Debates, 757, cc278_9W.

Hofstede, G. 1983. National Cultures in Four Dimensions. *International Studies of Management and Organization* 13(1), 46–74.

Institut National de Statistique et des Etudes Economiques (INSEE) 2010a. *La création d'entreprise en 2009 dopée par les auto-entrepreneurs (Business creation in 2009 boosted by auto-entrepreneurs)*, No. 1277, January. Paris: INSEE.

Institut National de Statistique et des Etudes Economiques (INSEE) 2010b. *Quatre nouvelles catégories d'entreprise (Four new categories of business)*, INSEE, 1321, November, Paris: INSEE.

Klapper, R. 2004. Government goals and entrepreneurship education – an investigation at a Grande Ecole in France. *Education and Training*, 46(3), 127–137.

Klapper, R. 2008. *The Role of Social Capital in French Entrepreneurial Networks at the Pre-organisation Stage*, PhD dissertation. Leeds: Leeds University Business School, UK. [Online]. Available at: http://etheses.whiterose.ac.uk/1259/

Klapper, R. 2010a. Innovations in entrepreneurship teaching: the use of repertory grids within the French Grande Ecole context. *International Journal of Euro-Mediterranean Studies*, 3(1), 113–133.

Klapper, R. 2010b. Innovating entrepreneurial pedagogy – examples from France and Germany. *Journal of Small Business and Enterprise Development*, 17(4), 552–568.

Kraus, S. and Kauranen, I. 2009. Strategic management and entrepreneurship: friends or foes? *International Journal of Business Science and Applied Management*, 4(1), 37–50.

Landström, H. 2005. *Pioneers in Entrepreneurship and Small Business Research*, International Studies in Entrepreneurship. Boston: Springer Science and Business Media Inc.

Léger-Jarniou, C. 2005. Learning in French Higher Education in *The Dynamics of Learning Entrepreneurship in a Cross-cultural University Context*, edited by P. Kyrö and C. Carrier. Tampere: University of Tampere, 322-354.

MacLean, M. 2002. *Economic Management and French Business From de Gaulle to Chirac*. Basingstoke: Macmillan.

MacLean, M., Harvey, C. and Press, J. 2006. *Business Elites and Corporate Governance in France and the UK*. Basingstoke: Macmillan.

Masclot, T. 2003. La crainte d'entreprendre, une exception culturelle Française (Fear to undertake, a French cultural exception). *Le Nouvel Economiste*, 17(2), 18.

McClelland, D.C. 1961. *The Achieving Society*. Princeton, NJ: van Nostrand.

Radu, M. and Redien-Collot, R. 2008. The social representation of entrepreneurs in the French press. *International Small Business Journal*, 26(3), 259–298.

Rousseau, J.J. 1762. *The Social Contract*. London: J. M. Dent and Sons Ltd.

Schumpeter, J.A. 1934. The theory of economic development, an inquiry into profits, capital, credit, interest and the business cycle. *Harvard Economic Studies*, XL VI, Harvard.

Cambridge, MA (first edition in German in1909).

Shane, S. and Venkataraman, S. 2000. The promise of entrepreneurship as field of research. *Academy of Management Review*, 25(1), 217–226.

Storey, D.J. 2003. Entrepreneurship, Small and Medium Sized Enterprises and Public Policies in *The Handbook of Entrepreneurship*, edited by D. Audretsch and Z. Acs, London: Kluwer, 473–511.

Storey D.J. 2008. *Entrepreneurship and SME Policy*, World Entrepreneurship Forum. [Online] Available at: http://www.world-entrepreneurship-forum.com. [accessed July 2011].

van Praag, C.M. and Versloot, P.H. 2007. *What Is the Value of Entrepreneurship? A Review of Recent Research*. Discussion Paper Series, Forschungsinstitut zur Zukunft der Arbeit (Institute for the Study of Labor), Bonn.

Verstraete, T. 2003. *Proposition d'un cadre théorique pour la recherche en Entrepreneuriat (Proposed a theoretical framework for research in Entrepreneurship)*. Editions de l'ADREG, Dec. [Online]. Available at: www.editions-adreg.net. [accessed July 2011].

Verstraete, T. and Fayolle, A. 2005. Paradigmes et entrepreneuriat (Paradigms and Entrepreneurship). *Revue de l'Entrepreneuriat*, 4(1), 33–552.

PART TWO

Practical Tools To Foster Small Firm Development

10

Business Incubators: Their Genesis, Forms, Intent and Impact

Phillip Kemp and Paull Weber

Chapter Summary

This chapter explains the rationale behind business incubators, describes their forms, and examines them in multiple countries and contexts. An incubator is an organisation that supports the development of new businesses, helping them to survive and grow during the start-up phase, then ejecting them after a period of time. Ancillary (but important) outcomes of business incubation include job creation, the fostering of growth and diversity in local industry and strengthened local economies. Incubators typically provide incubatees with support such as subsidised accommodation; access to capital; business advice; personal mentoring; networking opportunities; and secretarial and office services. If market acceptance is any indication, incubators are a policy success story. They can be a relatively cost-effective method of creating employment and stimulating a diversity of new economic activity. However, it remains a vexed question as to whether incubators 'add value' to their host economies and communities or only to the incubator and incubates.

Introduction

This chapter explains the rationale of the business incubator, identifies their forms and provides examples of the outcomes and modes of delivery in multiple countries and contexts. The purpose of this approach is to highlight their convergent and divergent forms globally. According to the National Business Incubator Association (NBIA 2009), the term 'business incubator' probably originated in the US in the late 1950s when the Mancuso family in New York purchased a former Massey-Ferguson factory, with the intention of leasing it out as a manufacturing space. The property was divided into ten rentable spaces, thus reducing the capital required to refit each section. The family helped founding tenants to raise capital, formulate strategy and facilitate growth within their business networks. Within five years, the incubator had reached capacity and was eventually responsible for the creation of thousands of new jobs. Included in the initial list of tenants was a chicken hatchery, and over time the connection to incubation became ingrained (NBIA 2009).

Business incubators of various forms have proliferated globally since that time, as public and private stakeholders have sought to innovate and create entrepreneurial ventures. The various forms of supported business environments now go by many different names: business incubators; business accelerators; technology parks; start-up incubators; enterprise centres; shared workshops; technology incubators; community incubators; small business incubators; bio-incubators; kitchen incubators and virtual incubators.

There is convincing evidence in the US that incubators are highly effective and relatively low-cost job creation vehicles (Monkman 2010). In the European Union (EU), it was estimated that in 2002 over 900 business incubators made a significant contribution to job and wealth creation, being directly responsible for some 40,000 new (net) jobs per annum (Centre for Strategy and Evaluation Services 2002). There is also evidence in both the US and the UK that technology business incubation programmes such as Boston's Route 128 and Cambridge's Silicon Fen result in strong regional growth (Mian 2011). That is not to say that all incubation is effective. For example, 80 per cent of university-founded incubators in Canada are not expected to return a profit to their sponsoring university (Maxwell and Levesque 2011).

Ateljevic and Dawson (2010) identify five areas where incubators can create value: encouraging regional economic diversity; increasing entrepreneurial activity; aiding new firm formation; attracting capital from investors; and providing direct employment opportunities within the incubator. However, there is mixed evidence on whether these impacts are achieved. For example, in the literature reviewed by Hackett and Dilts (2004), the finding related to community impact was that incubators were not good job creators, even though they were more cost-effective than other government initiatives to attract firms to a region. When specifically examining the impact of science parks (as one form of incubator), there is evidence that many parks funded substantively from the public purse are not particularly effective at either employment creation or the commercialisation of university-created intellectual property (IP) (Massey, Quintas and Wield 1992).

What is Business Incubation?

Schaper, Volery, Weber and Lewis (2011) explain that an incubator typically has management experienced in working with new growing ventures offering low (subsidised) rent that includes start-up support. They identify three broad types of incubator: embedded incubators which are co-located with some other complimentary business support facility; independent incubators that serve no other purpose than to create new firms; and specific purpose incubators, supporting a particular industry.

Some definitions of incubation simply describe the actual premises (Fry, as cited in Hackett and Dilts 2004), whereas more recent descriptions incorporate community and economic benefits, such as jobs created and local economic development (AusIndustry 2003, NBIA 2010). The NBIA (2009) highlights three consistent success-related features of business incubation – the *age of the business*, the *delivery of assistance* and the *goal of graduation*. According to the NBIA, the incubation programme must have a mission to provide business assistance to early-stage companies. It must also have staff that provides business assistance to clients and is designed to lead companies to self-sufficiency.

If there is such a thing as a 'typical' incubator it would embody these three principles of dealing with new firms, by providing start-up assistance for a limited time span (two to three years) to businesses that are expected to eventually graduate and leave the facility.

The Rationale of Business Incubation

It is a central assumption wherever incubators are encouraged that that they will improve small business start-up volume and quality. Policymakers often regard new business start-ups as a way to increase the level of innovation, by commercialising new ideas, technology and science (Hannon 2005). The nature of start-ups is such that most are small businesses. This creates challenges, as small businesses can be fragile in the early years. New small firms may have limited access to financial resources; rely on fewer customers for the majority of their income; operate in a single market; only offer one or two products; and display an over-reliance on personal relationships (Storey 1996). This fragility, combined with the overall impact of small business on the economy, has meant that business incubators can play an important role in economic development programmes (Campbell and Allen 1987). This is based on the finding that incubators can help reduce the failure of start-up small businesses, create jobs and build wealth within an economy (Hackett and Dilts 2004).

Business incubators are primarily designed to assist start-up firms that are small in terms of employment, capital and turnover. Together, however, their numbers mean they have a major effect upon the economy. Numerically, small businesses represent a significant proportion of the economy in most Organisation for Economic Co-operation and Development (OECD) countries. To illustrate this, research by the Kauffman Foundation shows nearly all net job creation in the US has occurred in firms of less than five years old (Stangler and Litan 2009). A further, two-thirds of all new jobs added to the US economy in 2007 were created by businesses started that year, of which 85 per cent could be defined as small business. Bayhan (2006: 8) also concludes that incubators are a useful policy tool '…in more successful economies, as one of the important instruments to develop effective employment and sustainable new start-ups to support knowledge-based enterprise development'.

Types of Business Incubators

There are numerous types of incubators that vary at the margins in their form, primarily as a consequence of the industry they support. Examples include biotechnology incubators, fashion incubators, agricultural incubators, food business incubators and manufacturing incubators (Monkman 2010). Incubators can also vary based on the incubator's primary financial sponsorship (is it a for-profit or non-profit venture?); whether tenants are spin-offs or start-ups; the business focus of the tenants; and the business focus of the incubator (Hackett and Dilts 2004).

The OECD (1999) suggests that there are fundamentally three types of business incubators, based upon the role they play in the economy, namely: mixed, economic and technology incubators. General or mixed-use incubators have a main imperative to promote continuous regional industrial and economic growth through general business development. Support is focused on access to local or regional sources of technical, managerial, marketing and financial assistance. A second group, 'economic development' incubators, have a main aim of stimulating specific economic objectives such as job creation, whilst the third group – 'technology' incubators – are primarily designed to promote the development of technology-based firms.

Barrow (2001) suggests five types of incubators defined by the motives and goals of constituent stakeholders. These are summarised in Table 10:1.

Table 10.1   The varying goals of differing types of incubators

Goals \ Type	For-profit Property Focused	Non-profit Arm of State Development Corporations	University Spin-offs	For-profit Investment	Corporate Ventures
Main Goals	Rental investment maximising returns Add services for a fee	Job creation Encourage entrepreneurship Diversify economic base	University/ industry collaboration Commercialise university research	Make substantial capital gain	Get into related markets quickly and inexpensively A window into related technologies
Sub-Goals	More property investment opportunities Expand and/ or open new incubators	Generate sustainable income, break-even Use vacant community premises for social good	Exploit investment opportunities Create goodwill in community	Identify profitable synergies in the investment portfolio	Entrepreneurial opportunities for staff Make money

Incubation around the Globe

In Australia, business incubators are predominantly self-funded organisations, relying on their own resources for survival once established (Schaper and Lewer 2009). Government has invested some funds in bricks and mortar to establish facilities but largely expects these to generate enough revenue to be self-sufficient. State governments began this seed funding of incubator sites in the middle to late 1980s. The federal government became involved in 1991 with the creation of a funding scheme to create community based, not-for-profit business incubators. The Business Incubator Scheme originated in the Department of Employment, with its main focus being to assist in the creation of jobs. Over 15 years, some A$50 million was invested in the creation of business incubators to establish incubators in both inner city areas and small communities in regional Australia (ANZABI 2004). Currently, a network of approximately 60 business incubators receives some federal funding but supplements this with other business advisory contracts to ensure financial survival.

Israel is a different example of a recent and successful strategy in this field. Beginning its business incubator programme in the 1990s, as a response to a large influx of technically skilled migrants from the former Soviet Union, incubation was used as an economic development tool designed to help transform these migrants into entrepreneurs (Dutta, Lopez-Claros and Mia 2006, Nordfors and

Shalit n.d). The services provided included determining the potential market for the technology; assisting the business to form a management team; general business advisory services; mentoring of the entrepreneur; and legal advice, especially regarding IP (Dutta et al. 2006). Israel has subsequently been dubbed the 'start-up nation', producing the highest number of technology based start-ups per capita in the world (Senor and Singer 2009). More Israeli companies are listed on the NASDAQ exchange than all other mainland European firms combined (Senor and Singer 2009).

In mainland Europe, interest in incubation has waxed and waned. One country that does have a significant and somewhat stable incubation heritage is Sweden. An overview of incubation activity is provided by their member association Swedish Incubators and Science Parks (SiSP 2010). In 2010, this organisation claimed its network of technology business incubators represented 3,320 companies employing over 64,000 people. Nearly three-quarters of all incubators were privately funded and of the 1,700 ideas investigated by the association members in 2009, fewer than 100 were accepted. Just over half of ideas came from university research programmes. The strong growth of incubators in Sweden can in part be traced to the Swedish Governments' support of innovation through Vinnova, the government agency responsible for innovation systems since 2003. The programme was based upon the same strategy and process as the Israeli model (Petersen and Schmerber 2008).

Chinese business incubators are quite large by global standards, and perhaps best thought of as a cross between technology incubators and technology parks, often occupying large spaces in good quality, high-rise buildings. An example of this is the Shanghai International Business Incubator. This incubator network (which consists of six incubators) was formed in the late 1990s and uses the model of 'one incubator, many bases'. This network plays a significant role in promoting and coordinating domestic and overseas SME hi-tech start-ups (Shanghai Technology Innovation Center 2005).

In the USA, there have been funding programmes from both federal and state governments over the past 50 years, leading to a vibrant incubator sector (Chandra and Fealey 2009, Hansen, Chesbrough, Nohira and Sull 2000). There have also been many private and corporate philanthropic initiatives supporting incubation, including the creation of incubators by venture capital funds and internally-funded corporate research incubators. The diversity of business incubators located within the US has meant that incubation has been used for many different goals: to assist in the creation of jobs; to support urban renewal; to commercialise research and IP; to drive local economic development and industry adjustment; to assist minority groups and ethnic entrepreneurship initiatives; and to develop specific industries such as defence, aerospace and bioscience.

Business incubation began in the UK in the late 1980s, mostly as a part of economic development and urban renewal strategies. There has also been involvement from universities and science parks in business incubation, research institutes and private sector companies. As at the beginning of 2011 there were approximately 300 business incubators operating in the UK, providing services to sectors including ICT, science, technology, creative industries, social enterprises and all manner of entrepreneurs (UK Trade and Investment 2011). Funding has come from the national government, regional agencies, local communities, universities and research institutes (UK Business Incubation n.d.).

It seems that the business incubation community is quite international in terms of adopting best practice. New Zealand's incubation model appears to have been influenced by the Israeli incubator system, and also guided by best practice from the US, UK and Australia. These incubators vary in terms of their ownership structure, the pre- and post-incubation programmes they run, relationships with stakeholders, tenants, and financial model. Incubators in New Zealand all have pre-incubation processes and a structured incubation programme for occupants. The incubator takes an equity stake in the tenant firm, and managers work with the owner of the firm, developing the business and matching angel investors to the venture.

South Korea's first incubators started in 1993 as science park incubators with a regional development imperative. These facilities have been referred to as technoparks and have strong government support. Whilst the technoparks were shown to be quite successful at an individual level, there has been some evidence of rent seeking and waste as tenants shift from one incubator to another around the country in search of various financial incentives on offer (Kim and Jung 2010).

A range of business incubator associations and other economic development agencies that have a focus on business incubation are listed in Table 10.2.

Effectiveness and Impact of Business Incubation

What separates incubator success from failure? Researchers have described incubators as a 'black box', in the sense that often the internal workings are somewhat of a mystery (Hackett and Dilts 2008). One of the reasons for the limited examination of incubators is that incubation is both place and a process (Voisey, Gornall, Jones and Thomas 2006). These two ideas are often mixed and confused in the literature, with a focus on incubator place (and type) frequently occurring at the expense of effort in understanding the process and effects of

Table 10.2   A selection of incubator organisations

Geographic Scope	Organisation	Website
Asia Pacific	Asian Association of Business Incubation	www.aabi.info
Australia	Business Innovation and Incubation Australia	www.businessincubation.com.au
Canada	Canadian Association of Business Incubation	www.cabi.ca
China	Chinese Business Incubator Association	
Europe	European Business and Innovation Centre Network	www.ebn.be
Global (developing economies)	World Bank	www.idisc.net
Global (technology parks)	Science Park and Innovation Center Association Science Park and Innovation Center experts	www.spica-directory.net www.spicegroup.de
India	Indian Business Incubators	www.isba.in
Israel	Israeli Technology Business Incubators	www.incubators.org.il
Japan	Japanese Association of New Business Incubation Organisations	www.janbo.gr.jp
New Zealand	Incubators New Zealand	www.incubators.org.nz
Sweden	Swedish Incubators and Science Parks	www.sisp.se
UK	United Kingdom Business Incubation	www.ukbi.co.uk
USA	National Business Incubation Association	www.NBIA.org

incubation. Outcomes are rarely explored, as the value or effect of business incubators is believed to be difficult to measure (Erlewine 2007, Voisey et al. 2006, National Agency for Enterprise and Construction 2004, Bearse, 1998). However, there have been some attempts to analyse their effects.

The US National Business Incubator Association has identified two principles that characterise effective business incubation: externally, by having a positive impact on economic health by maximising the success of emerging companies and internally, by being a dynamic model of a sustainable, efficient business operation (Erlewine 2007). Understanding these principles requires an examination of the external impact of an incubator. For example, Monkman (2010) explains that incubators create new jobs for a low subsidy cost, estimated to be in the order of US$1,100 per job. Incubation programmes also contribute to their client companies' success and expand community entrepreneurial resources, as well as improving local community image (Monkman 2010).

The Economic Development Administration (EDA) of the United States Department of Commerce estimates that for every US$10,000 in EDA funds invested in business incubation programs, 47 to 69 local jobs are generated. The EDA also estimates that incubators provide up to 20 times more jobs than community infrastructure projects at a cost per job of between US$126 and US$144, compared with between US$744 and US$6,972 for other infrastructure projects (Arena, Adams, Noyes, Rhody and Noonan 2008).

New Zealand is one nation that has developed an evaluation methodology for their incubators. In 2008, after spending approximately NZ$5 million on supporting their business incubators, a Government evaluation found over NZ$500 million in economic impact to the New Zealand economy with over 1,000 people employed nationwide (Ministry of Economic Development 2008).

Sweden is another country that evaluates its national technology business incubator programme in a systematic way. Over 100 businesses graduate from their incubator system every year, with some SEK$500 million of capital investment generated within those firms (SiSP 2010).

A challenge exists in using traditional financial performance metrics, given that the majority of business incubators are not-for-profit entities (Hackett and Dilts 2004). Sipos and Szabo (2006) propose eight measures of business incubator success that can be applied to not-for-profit incubators. They are:

1. the survival of the business incubator;
2. political and regional effects;
3. finance and sustainability of the incubator;
4. characteristics of the management team;
5. range of services offered;
6. infrastructure and sources of funding for the incubator;
7. research potential and networks; and
8. business success of tenants.

This list mostly defines the incubator's success by internal organisational outcomes, with only one measure of incubatee performance, albeit a core measure. The NBIA also has a set of benchmarks, designed to improve incubator performance more broadly (Bearse 1998). It recommends members measure ten basic metrics to determine success (Erlewine 2007). These measures are:

1. number of clients in the incubator;
2. total number of graduates since the beginning of the incubator;

3.   number of graduate firms still in business (or have been merged or acquired);

4.   number of people currently employed full time by current clients and graduate firms;

5.   number of people currently employed part time by current clients and graduate firms;

6.   current monthly salaries and wages paid by client and graduate firms;

7.   gross revenues for the most recent full year for client and graduate firms;

8.   dollar amount of debt capital raised in the most recent full year for client and graduate firms;

9.   dollar amount of equity capital raised in the most recent full year for client and graduate firms; and

10.   dollar amount of government grant funds raised in the most recent full year for client and graduate firms.

While useful as internal benchmarks, these measurements are difficult to compare across different industries. Those searching for a more rigorous methodology for assessing the effectiveness of incubator policy are encouraged to read Kim and Jung (2010). They employ a combination of qualitative and quantitative measures to assess the influence of incubators in South Korea on a regional economy.

Implementing an Incubator Programme: Issues for Policymakers

While incubators are often recognised as a success story in economic development terms, they are not a cure-all for employment and innovation policy challenges. In fact, it can be argued that in some situations the support framework of business incubation encourages a weak business environment that is dependent upon artificial support, such as cheap rentals and poor quality standardised or inappropriate 'advice' from resident incubator managers (Lalkaka 2001). There are potential problems when any non market-driven methods are used to select 'winners' after applicants go through an application process to receive subsidised support. The policy of many incubators to evict their tenants after a pre-determined period of time is recognition that some high-performing firms could have their long-term competitive capabilities weakened by dependency upon the sheltered incubator environment. Indeed, some research on business incubators has shown that erstwhile successful facilities have fallen for this trap, by not allowing the fledgling to leave the nest

(Kim and Jung 2010). Location certainly appears an important success factor: for example, in the 1980s and 1990s, private sector investment in the UK was somewhat limited to highly defined territories (mostly in the south east), with other incubator regions described as '...at best risky and at worst unprofitable' (Massey et al. 1992: 215).

After considering the potential pitfalls, policymakers who are intent upon implementing an incubation programme should consider carefully the type of incubator that is appropriate for their intended outcomes. This choice will drive the extent, cost and type of support offered. For example, will there be a need to provide capital for bricks and mortar premises, ongoing operational funding or legislative assistance (such as export or research and development tax concessions)?

Successful incubators will have demonstrable linkages to a sound knowledge-base via technology clusters, universities or other professional networks. Lalkaka (2001) suggests that incubator physical spaces should be designed to stimulate creativity and interaction whilst allowing a positive rental income cashflow, possibly through securing a few anchor tenants who provide support services to incubatees. They will house a careful mix of entrepreneurs and management who are growth focused and market oriented. The services delivered will add value to the incubatee and should include a plan to facilitate access to market-based capital. Furthermore, the organisation will need to benchmark and measure performance of self and clients, and keep a close eye on future trends (Lalkaka 2001). There is also evidence to suggest that the tacit knowledge possessed by the actors within incubator networks can take several years and even multiple career positions within the network of the incubator to have a definitive impact upon an individual innovator or entrepreneur (Cooper and Park 2008). Thus, it is important to have a career progression plan and retention strategy for incubator managers.

Conclusion

This chapter has sought to provide an overview of various business incubation forms, intents and impact, highlighting the successes as well as exposing some of the problems that have been encountered. Incubators are a popular means of small business start-up promotion and job creation, but are not without their pitfalls. The successful implementation of an incubator strategy allows for local economic conditions to be taken into consideration, along with the political and social context in which incubation will occur. Business incubation has grown quickly over the past two decades in most developed and some developing economies. This has resulted in a diversity of incubation models as commercial operators, community stakeholders and policymakers have reacted to different opportunities and pressures. However, there is now a certain level of best practice emerging in the maturing global network of incubator organisations.

As discussed, there are a range of measures that can be used to quantify an incubator's economic impact, such as employment numbers in graduating firms, capital raised or annual revenue. Determining the exact impact that an incubator intervention has had on these measures remains difficult. In many cases, the ability for an incubator to leverage networks, university expertise and other small businesses in a cluster also exceed that of less intense economic development interventions. By acting as a focal point for expert advice, support and ongoing business assistance, incubators can and do act as an effective launch pad for businesses with employment and growth potential.

References

Arena, P., Adams, J.A., Noyes, K., Rhody, S. and Noonan, M. 2008. *Construction Grants Program Impact Assessment Report 2008*, US Department of Commerce, Economic Development Administration. [Online] Available at: http://www.eda.gov/PDF/EDAConsImpactStudyVolume1FINAL.pdf [accessed: 4 May 2011].

Ateljevic, J. and Dawson, A. 2010. Business incubators: new mechanisms for economic/enterprise development or passing fad? Exploring complex relationship of the growing phenomenon in the context of Scotland. *International Journal of Entrepreneurship and Innovation Management*. 12(2), 217–240.

AusIndustry 2003. *Fact sheet: Small Business Incubator Program*. Canberra: AusIndustry.

Australian and New Zealand Association of Business Incubators (ANZABI) 2004. *Incubation Works: Case Studies of Australian Small Business Incubators and Their Impacts*. Fremantle: Australian and New Zealand Association of Business Incubators.

Barrow, C. 2001. *Incubators: A Realist's Guide to the World's Business Accelerators*. Chichester: Wiley.

Bayhan, A. 2006. *Business Incubator Process: A Policy Tool for Entrepreneurship and Enterprise Development in a Knowledge-based Economy*. [Online] Available at: http://competitiveness.org.pk/downloads/BusinessIncubatorConceptPaper_Modified_23Nov06.pdf [accessed: 5 May 2011].

Bearse, P. 1998. A question of evaluation: NBIA's impact assessment of business incubators. *Economic Development Quarterly*, 12(4), 322–333.

Campbell, C. and Allen, D.N. 1987. The small business incubator industry: micro-level economic development. *Economic Development Quarterly*, 1(2), 178–191.

Centre for Strategy and Evaluation Services (CSES) 2002. *Benchmarking of Business Incubators*. European Commission Enterprise Directorate General, Brussels. [Online] Available at: http://webcache.googleusercontent.com/ search?q=cache:http://www.bii.ge/eng/studies_%26_Papers/%5B1%5D. benchmarking_bi_part_one_2002.pdf [accessed: 16 March 2011].

Chandra, A. and Fealey, T. 2009. Business incubation in the United States, China and Brazil: a comparison of role of government, incubator funding and financial services. *International Journal of Entrepreneurship*, 13(special issue), 67–86.

Cooper, S.Y. and Park, J.S. 2008. The impact of incubator organizations on opportunity recognition and technology innovation in new entrepreneurial high-technology ventures. *International Small Business Journal*, 26(1), 27–56.

Dutta, S. Lopez-Claros A. and Mia, I. 2006. *Israel: Factors in the Emergence of an ICT Powerhouse*. World Economic Forum, Geneva Switzerland. [Online] Available at: http://www.investinisrael.gov.il/NR/rdonlyres/61BD95A0- 898B-4F48-A795-5886B1C4F08C/0/israelcompleteweb.pdf [accessed: 7 May 2011].

Erlewine, M. 2007. *Measuring Your Business Incubator's Economic Impact: A Toolkit*. Athens, Ohio: National Business Incubator Association.

Hackett, S.M. and Dilts, D.M. 2004. A systematic review of business incubation research. *Journal of Technology Transfer*, 29(1), 55–82.

Hackett, S.M. and Dilts, D.M. 2008. Inside the black box of business incubation: Study B – scale assessment, model refinement and incubation outcomes. *Journal of Technology Transfer*, 33(5), 439–471.

Hannon, P. 2005. Incubation policy and practice: building practitioner and professional capability. *Journal of Small Business and Enterprise Development*, 12(1), 57–75.

Hansen, M.T., Chesbrough, H.W., Nohira, N. and Sull, D.N. 2000. Networked incubators: hothouses of the new economy. *Harvard Business Review*, September–October, 74–84.

Kim, H.Y. and Jung, C.M. 2010. Does a technology incubator work in the regional economy? Evidence from South Korea. *Journal of Urban Planning and Development*, 136(1), 273–284.

Lalkaka, R. 2001. *Best Practices in Business Incubation: Lessons (Yet to be) Learned*. European Union – Belgian Presidency International Conference on Business Centers: actors for economic & social development, Brussels, 14– 15 November 2001. [Online] Available at: http://zunia.org/uploads/media/ knowledge/EU_belgium_conf_041101.pdf [accessed: 6 May 2011].

Massey, D., Quintas, P. and Wield, D. 1992. *High Tech Fantasies*. London: Routledge.

Maxwell, A. and Levesque, M. 2011. Technology incubators: facilitating technology transfer or creating regional wealth? *International Journal of Entrepreneurship and Innovation Management*, 13(2), 122–142.

Mian, S.A. 2011. University's involvement in technology business incubation: what theory and practice tell us? *International Journal of Entrepreneurship and Innovation Management*, 13(2), 113–121.

Ministry of Economic Development 2008. *Incubator Support Program Evaluation Report*. Wellington, New Zealand: Ministry of Economic Development.

Monkman, D. 2010. Full committee hearing on business incubators and their role in job creation: hearing before the committee on small business, United States House of Representatives, one hundred eleventh congress, second session, hearing held March 17, 2010. Washington: U.S. G.P.O.

National Agency for Enterprise and Construction 2004. *Benchmarking Incubators: Background Report for the Entrepreneurship Index, 2004*. Copenhagen, Denmark: National Agency for Enterprise and Construction.

National Business Incubator Association (NBIA) 2009. *Founder Award Honors Joseph Mancuso*. [Online] Available at: www.nbia.org/about_nbia/founders_awards/mancuso.php [accessed: 21 November 2010].

Nordfors, D. and Shalit, O. n.d. *Technology Incubators in Israel – Immigrants Start up Hi-tech Companies*. [Online] Available at: http://www.nordfors.com/incubators/statteng.htm [accessed: 9 March 2011].

Organisation for Economic Co-operation and Development (OECD) 1999. *Business Incubation: International Case Studies*. Paris: OECD.

Petersen, K. and Schmerber, L. 2008. *Mid-term Evaluation of the Swedish National Incubator Programme*. [Online] Available at: http://www.vinnova.se/upload/EPiStorePDF/Midterm%20Evaluation%20NIP.pdf [accessed: 15 March 2011].

Schaper, M.T. and Lewer, J. 2009. Business incubation in Australia: policies, practices and outcomes. *Asia-Pacific Journal of Innovation & Entrepreneurship* 3(3), 37–46.

Schaper, M., Volery, T., Weber, P.C. and Lewis K. 2011. *Entrepreneurship and Small Business*, 3rd Asia-Pacific edition. Milton, Queensland: John Wiley and Sons.

Senor, D. and Singer, S. 2009. *Start-up Nation: The Story of Israel's Economic Miracle*. New York: Twelve Publishing.

Shanghai Technology Innovation Center 2005. *About STIC*. [Online] Available at: www.incubator.sh.cn/en/about.asp [accessed: 16 March 2011].

Sipos, Z. and Szabo, A. 2006. *Benchmarking of Business Incubators in CEE and CIS Transition Economies*. Budapest, Hungary: The Foundation for Scientific and Industrial Research.

Stangler, D. and Litan, R.E. 2009. *Where Will the Jobs Come From?*, Ewing Marion Kauffman foundation research series, firm formation and economic growth, paper No.1. [Online] Available at: www.energizingentrepreneurs.org/site/images/research/erpr/policy/policy4.pdf [accessed: 14 March 2011].

Storey, D.J. 1996. *Understanding the Small Business Sector*. London: Routledge.

Swedish Incubators and Science Parks (SiSP) 2010. *SiSP: Swedish Incubators and Science Parks*. [Online] Available at: http://np.netpublicator.com/?id=n88592986 [accessed: 16 March 2011].

UK Business Incubation n.d. *Who We Are*. [Online] Available at: http://www.ukbi.co.uk/about-ukbi/who-we-are.aspx [accessed: 7 May 2011].

UK Trade and Investment 2011. *Science Parks and Business Incubators in the UK*. [Online] Available at: www.ukti.gov.uk/investintheuk/whytheuk/localisation/107013.html [accessed 17 August 2011].

Voisey, P., Gornall, L., Jones, P. and Thomas, B. 2006. The measurement of success in a business incubation project. *Journal of Small Business and Enterprise Development*, 13(3), 454–468.

11

Understanding Self-Employment: The Opportunities and the Challenges for Good Policy

Ken Phillips and Tui McKeown

Chapter Summary

This chapter examines SMEs from the unit of analysis of the self-employed individual. Specifically narrowing the view of SMEs to this perspective reveals the challenge to policymakers who are used to operating an environment oriented towards businesses as entities that are run, controlled and managed by employees. Traditionally, business development is an environment where policymakers play an important role in intervening to isolate or protect the personal lives of individual employees from the risk associated with doing business. However, the notion of business as being bigger than any individual and the desire or even the need for intervention and protection may be in stark contrast to the realities faced by the individual in self-employment.

This chapter will address two of the fundamental policy challenges presented by the self-employed. The first is the problem of defining clearly and accurately, what self-employment actually is and is not. The second is how to implement an appropriate regulatory framework for the self-employed which maximises rather than constrains their skills, creativity and innovation. The chapter concludes with a review of several practical responses in Australia specifically designed to enable self-employment and its associated positive benefits. These may provide a useful guide for future initiatives.

Introduction

Whilst it is commonly assumed that small business operates within an environment where businesses are regarded as formal entities with a distinct legal structure, operated by managers and employees, policymakers need to be aware that a business can be just one individual. Further, collapsing SMEs into a homogeneous category is often not helpful. Terms such as freelancer, micro-business, contractor, sub-contractor, independent contractor, small business, SME, home-based business, free agent and consultant, are often applied interchangeably in public policy discourse, yet they often have quite discrete boundaries and definitions (Leighton and Wynn 2011). This has resulted in confusion and has made understanding the sector difficult. The focus of this chapter is on the individual self-employed person – those who work for themselves – as it is this simplest view which provides the clearest contextualisation about both the challenges and the opportunities the self-employed provide. Understanding these people as 'businesses of one' brings greater clarity to SME policy.

Over the last 30 years, views on self-employment have changed and it is now recognised as a major part of the dynamic and changing world of work within developed economies (ILO 2011, OECD 2010a, Haunschild 2003). For instance, although there are significant variations, overall about 15 per cent of the European Union's (EU's) labour market is self-employed. The percentages for the US, Australia, China and several emerging economies are far higher and growing (ILO 2011, OECD 2010b, ABS 2008). While often heralded as an indicator of economic vitality and creativity, the reality is that the self-employed represent a challenge to prevailing orthodoxies, because they fall through regulatory and conceptual gaps created by systems based on the notion of traditional employment. The self-employed are individuals who bridge the divide between employee and employer, and consumer and businesses, in a way that both of these dichotomies find hard to comprehend. As a consequence, the self-employed provide a challenge to the traditional regulatory and administrative processes covering areas such as taxation, work safety and labour laws and even, according to some, to the social order (Aldrich 2006).

The key to understanding self-employed people is that the business is an individual, that is, the individual is the business. As simple as it is, this is the critical conceptual point to be grasped. However, until now, the reality has been that such a seemingly simple task has proven both legally and behaviourally complex and is well illustrated by the issue of definition (Benz and Frey 2008, Parker 2004).

Defining Self-employment

The extant literature on self-employment generally falls into one of two groupings. First, there are legal definitions. These are important because they are known to determine the scope of the legislative and regulatory design under which the self-employed can operate (for example, Stanworth and Purdy 2008). The second are the behavioural identifiers, which are important because they enable an appreciation of the different perspectives self-employed people can have to work and to understand how and why they do things (Scase 2003a).

Courts around the world have struggled to find coherent and compelling tests to differentiate the employee from the self-employed and this situation is compounded by the increasing complexity and diversity within employment relationships themselves (Leighton and Wynn 2011). The legal debate revolves around identifying the difference between who and what an employee is when compared with who and what a self-employed person is. The most authoritative global identifier comes from the International Labour Organisation (ILO) which, in June 2003, passed a resolution separating the three concepts of employee, worker and self-employment:

> *The term employee is a legal term which refers to a person who is a party to a certain kind of legal relationship which is normally called an employment relationship. The term worker is a broader term that can be applied to any worker, regardless of whether or not she or he is an employee. Self-employment and independent work based on commercial and civil contractual arrangements are by definition beyond the scope of the employment relationship.*

> *(ILO 2003: 52).*

The discourse surrounding self-employment has been dominated by the issue of defining self-employment and a pre-occupation with perceived problems. This includes weeding out 'sham', 'pseudo', or 'disguised' employment, leading – it is argued – to vulnerability and denial of access to employment and other protective rights for many (Casale 2011, Blanpain and Nakakubo 2010, Sutherland and Riley 2010, Wynn and Leighton 2009).

Further work by the ILO (2006) has provided evidence of the commonality in legal processes and definitions used to determine employment and self-employment across the globe. As a result, Phillips (2008) suggests that a self-employed person is someone who earns their income through the commercial or civil contract and not the employment contract. This is where the reality of the disparate terms covered under the umbrella 'self-employed' coalesce in the commercial contract. It does not mean that debates over definition have ceased, but only that the arguments are now more clearly focused. Concerns remain about 'the opportunity for 'disguising' the dependent (employment) work-relationships as self employment to avoid the regulatory, social and fiscal costs associated with subordinate work relationships' (Countouris in Casale 2011: 35). The main point is that the need for greater clarity in legal definitions cannot be understated because statutes directly create the design and reach of the regulatory oversight of self-employed people. Further, the regulations covering self-employed also affect their ability to be entrepreneurial, their preparedness to take risks and their potential for employing other people (Bridges 2010). Governments need to be alert and responsive to this point.

Although legal definitions provide a fundamental basis around which regulation is created, the literature on self-employment clearly identifies that an understanding of the behaviour, motivations and desires of self-employed people is also needed (Bridges 2010, Blackburn and Kovalainen 2009, Carsrud and Brännback 2009). The most commonly identified single motivation is a desire to have control of their own work and their career (see, for example, McKeown, Bryant and Cochrane 2011, Hessels, van Gelderen andThurik 2008, Lammiman and Syrett 2004).Interestingly, there is another way to view this motivation. As Shane (2008: 7) states, 'the most common reason why people start businesses is to avoid working for others'. Thus, they seek to be their own boss, working in and subject to their defined marketplace of consumers and clients (Stanworth and Purdy 2008, Scase 2003b, Goffee and Scase 1995). There are also other common themes, such as the perceived value of the autonomous nature of their work and the sense of freedom – even if it is an illusion, that comes from being able to adapt their work to their lifestyle and vice versa (Garrett and Henley 2009, Benz and Frey 2008,Felfe, Schmook, Schyns and Six 2008). Many self-employed people actively choose and may even take great risks to be self-employed (EC 2010a, McMullen, Bagby and Palich 2008, Shane 2008). Put these things together and it is no wonder that self-employed people consistently report being happier in both work and life than employees (Eurofound 2010). Overall, the consensus seems that if you feel you have higher levels of control over your work, you are happier (Andersson 2008, Benz and Frey 2008).

Self-employed individuals also display high levels of pride and confidence in their own abilities and the services they can supply; they are also optimistic about the future (McKeown et al. 2011, Burke 2010, Eurofound 2010, Rousseau and Schalk 2000). They are heavy networkers and active information-gathers who see a strong need to be multi-taskers and holistic in their approach to work. They are likely to believe it important to think outside the square and to be ready to 're-invent' themselves to adapt to changing market requirements (Shane 2008, Lammiman and Syrett 2004).

When the legal and behavioural identifiers are combined and contextualised with the basic demographic elements which emerge as universals it becomes possible to understand self-employed people with greater clarity. This includes the tendency to be home-based, to be male, married and older, and to cover a heterogeneous group 'embracing high level professionals through to low-skilled manual workers'(EC 2010a, OECD 2010a, Stanworth and Purdy 2008: 5). This ability makes it easier first, to implement appropriate regulatory frameworks for the self-employed, and second, to ensure the maximisation of their skills, creativity and innovation. The role of behavioural identifiers is especially important here.It provides a focus on 'people management' and strategies for managing self-employment which, necessarily, have to be different from those for managing employees. The focal point is on the self-employed as individuals who earn their income via a commercial contract, who *are* the business and whose personal and business lives are intimately intertwined. They strive to create for themselves, an environment that enables them to flourish.

Self-employed people may benefit from their actions and decisions but they also suffer some negative consequences. This is work at its most individual and basic level.

The Contribution of the Self-employed Sector

There is increasing recognition and appreciation of the value the self-employed bring to the workplace (Bridges 2010, EC 2010a, 2010b, OECD 2010a, Scase 2003b). The perspective of the individual provides a window into understanding that the primary tasks for governments in enabling self-employment are twofold. These are the need to:

- accommodate self-employed people within regulatory design, rather than discriminate against them through regulation; and to
- facilitate the effective creation and enforcement of commercial contracts under which self-employed people conduct their business.

A key feature of the important link between self-employment and a dynamic economy is emerging in recent research. For instance, research from the EU (Eurofound 2010), found increases in self-employment, is predominantly in high-skilled occupations. For example there has been a dramatic increase of over 20 per cent in skilled self-employment in the Nordic states. Even countries such as Germany and France that have a strong tradition of well-rewarded and protected employment have also seen similar major changes (Eurofound 2010). Alongside the increase in skilled self-employment is a general rise in one-person enterprises throughout the EU (Casale 2011, ILO 2011, ONS 2011).

These results encapsulate the policy challenge, as they are indicative of a worldwide and significant growth in skilled self-employment, balanced by a decline in less-skilled occupations. This growth in skilled self-employment has occurred in many countries even where some regions experienced marginal declines in overall self-employment. It appears, this trend is not correlated with geography, industrial relations traditions or economic policies. The results also support the contention of writers like Shane (2008) and Sarasvathy and Venkataraman (2011) that the dynamic capabilities, entrepreneurship and creativity that self-employment can produce should be recognised as something common, not a rarity. Understanding how to foster and stimulate the positives of self-employment is often linked to the regulatory environment individuals operate in and whether this environment stifles or enables such activity.

Government, Regulations and Self-Employed People

Despite the proliferation of government policies and programmes to regulate self-employment, many analysts agree that the approaches have not contributed to the ability to be self-employed (Sarasvathy and Venkataraman 2011, Bridges 2010). Ideologically, it can be argued that there is an institutional, even cultural, bias that presumes that employment is moral and that self-employment is somehow inferior, even immoral (see, for example, Casale 2011, where terms such as 'subordinate work' and 'economically dependent work' are key themes). A major problem is that regulation and policies are based around the view that a 'good job' is fulltime and permanent. Such views mean that self-employment is an inconvenient nuisance to legal, fiscal and societal systems ostensibly established to be fair and just to all. This quite often results in regulations preventing or even outlawing self-employment. In spite of this self-employment has continued to rise.

Backing for this view is found in a recent survey covering 36 countries, including EU, the European Free Trade Association (EFTA), US, Japan and China, which found that a wide gap between those who would prefer to be self-employed and those who considered it 'feasible' (EC 2010a). The reasons given for its not being 'feasible' are instructive. Unsurprisingly, lack of finance featured strongly, as did a lack of information and perceived lack of skills. However, some two-thirds reported they were deterred by 'complex administration', including fiscal matters, and a wide range of regulatory issues. Overall, people were clear about the opportunities as well as the risks. Of graver concern was the universal finding that many believe there are increasing formal deterrents created by regulations. This result is perplexing given the general political and policy rhetoric identifying self-employment as a key aspect of revival (see for example ILO 2011, EC 2010a, 2010b, OECD 2010a, 2010b).

Examples Where Regulation Does Work

While many examples exist where regulation has hampered and even killed off entrepreneurship (see Bridges 2010 for an excellent summary), this chapter focuses on what has worked and why. The five examples provided are Australian but this is not the result of a parochial bias of the authors. It is reflective of the fact that, since the passing of specific federal independent contractor legislation very much aligned with the ILO (2006) recommendations, Australia appears to be at the forefront of developing institutional understandings of self-employed people and how to work with them, even if it is a work in progress.

The first example is the *Independent Contractors Act (2006)*. This makes it clear that the definition of an independent contractor is that applying under common law. Its primary intent is to ensure that independent contractors are subject to commercial law and not industrial relations law. It overrides state and federal laws that try to treat independent contractors as employees for industrial relations purposes. It also created measures for protecting independent contractors from unfair contracts. Finally, parallel legislation made illegal the practice of sham contracting – that is, treating employees as if they were independent contractors. To our knowledge, each of these measures are world firsts and have not yet been replicated elsewhere.

The second example comes from the Australian Taxation Office (ATO). As background, the 19 per cent of the Australian workforce who are self-employed pay some 25 per cent of Australia's federal goods and services tax (GST) and constitute some 60 per cent of the ATO's bad and doubtful debt (ATO 2008a). This type of tax debt scenario is common throughout developed economies and provides some backing for taxing authorities' tendency to view self-employed people as a problem for the integrity of their taxing systems. The problem is that it is more difficult administratively to collect tax from millions of self-employed people than it is to collect tax from relatively much smaller numbers of large employers. Until about a decade ago, the ATO took a highly aggressive stance towards self-employed people in their collection processes. The income tax collection laws were revised around 2000–2001 with changes designed to embrace rather than exclude the self-employed (ATO 2009). The ATO concurrently began a relationship change programme in realisation that the self-employed were simply too large to 'beat' and that it was better to work with them.

Aligned with this, the ATO has undertaken considerable research into how self-employed people see them and how they should relate to and with them (ATO 2009, 2008a, 2008b). Key initiatives which have resulted include free accounting support services for start-up businesses, a reconfigured language of its published information, replacing 'tax talk' with plain English and an extensive micro-business consultative programme focused on understanding the basic, practical problems of the self-employed. This latter programme has even connected with an Australian government anti-depression help service (Beyond Blue). The ATO recognises that a business problem or a family problem and/or mental illness of a self-employed person can affect the (tax) relationship that person has with the ATO. This new approach to self-employed people is based on the ATO seeing itself in partnership with self-employed people rather than being 'at war' with them. This example shows how the design and administration of regulations can either destroy, or work with and assist, small business entrepreneurs.

The third example has to do with reforms of Australian Occupational Health and Safety (OHS) laws. OHS laws have held that employers have a responsibility to keep employees safe at work. But self-employed people are by definition both employer and employee all in one. Consequently they 'fell through' a legislative crack in OHS legislation. Legislation failed to accommodate workplace realities and was mostly ignored as an inconvenient 'truth' too hard to handle. But as the realisation sank in that the self-employed had come to constitute one in five workers in the workplace it could not be ignored if safety was to be improved. Legislative changes now are progressing through the seven different jurisdictions in Australia needed to progress the reform. Changes are designed to ensure that self-employed people are accommodated within OHS laws. Specifically the laws are moving away from being structured around the employer–employee relationship to a structure focused on those who undertake business activity. This embraces self-employed people, who are, as discussed above, engaged in business and is reflective of the fact that 'business' within this OHS framework is broad and includes government activity.

However, government can also have a positive impact on enabling self-employed entrepreneurship through ensuring the effective rule of commercial law. This notion provides the fourth example and introduces the concept of contract integrity. As already noted, self-employed people exist because of the commercial contract. It is the vehicle by which they run their business but, perversely, because of their size, they also suffer from a practical disadvantage. If they are in dispute over a contract, the legal costs associated with enforcing the contract and/or resolving the dispute frequently exceed the value of the contract (Garrett 2008, French 2007). This means that self-employed people are easy prey for fraud and intimidation. This is not government's fault but it is something government could resolve by providing cheap, quick, dispute-resolution processes for contract disputes.

One way to overcome the problem of dispute resolution is to create statutorily independent mediation and dispute resolution services for SMEs and the self-employed. This is the final example. The Victorian Small Business Commissioner (SBC) is an independent authority charged with looking after the interests of small business people. One of the most important functions of the Commissioner is contract dispute-resolution.

A small business in dispute with a large business (say, is owed money) can go to the SBC. A nominal dispute lodgement fee is required. The SBC will look at the dispute and try to resolve it informally with a phone call, correspondence and discussions with both parties. If no resolution is achieved, the SBC organises a mediation hearing. It cannot enforce decisions but has a powerful influence. The SBC issues a yearly report to the Victorian Parliament and does 'name and shame' organisations that have treated small business people unfairly (SBC 2010a).

Small business owners who are owed money usually have to resort to litigation but the cost of litigation in Australia is such that it is probably not worth suing if the debt is under $10,000. The SBC has a success rate in excess of 70 per cent of cases brought to it (SBC 2010b: 21). The Small Business Commissioner demonstrates how government can play an important institutional role in encouraging entrepreneurship. This is an encouraging environment within which SME/self-employed entrepreneurship is able to grow. Instructively, Small Business Commissioners are being established in three other jurisdictions in Australia replicating the Victorian model.

Conclusion

This chapter has sought to expand the idea of 'business' – something that is normally considered to be systems of collectives involving managers and employees. Yet this traditional understanding does not fit the reality of the bulk of small businesses which are in fact self-employed people – 'businesses of one.' When this is grasped public policy can gain a deeper understanding of business and create approaches that more effectively accommodate and even assist small business people to contribute to economic development.

Given this framework, self-employment must be contextualised within both legal definitions and behavioural characteristics. This combined perspective provides some insight into explaining why self-employment is growing as a global phenomenon, particularly within the high-skilled occupations. The legal and behavioural perspectives also provide insight into both the advantages and disadvantages of being self-employed and why the traditional rules governments implement to regulate employment emerge as strong negatives. Examples and suggestions provided highlight ways in which policymakers and governments can help support and encourage the self-employed. This can occur though both the provision of practical services as well as more inclusive accommodation in key areas of policy recognising that the self-employed person is a 'business of one'.

This concept disrupts standard approaches to the regulation of economies including expectations of employment being bounded by organisational systems. Some may ask, can an individual be a business? It's a conceptual challenge! The research presented supports the concept and reveals the high levels of motivation and innovative behaviour demonstrated by self-employed people. But more research is needed to create a fuller profile of the heterogeneous nature of the self-employed workforce if regulatory and managerial approaches are to keep pace.

The challenge is one of opportunity or opportunity lost. If entrepreneurship and its resultant innovative potential is a common rather than a rare human trait, then societies and economies have much to gain by understanding and accommodating the individual as an entrepreneur. The challenge sits most heavily, but not exclusively, on government, to review and adjust administrative and regulatory systems to ensure that self-employed people are accommodated and not stifled. If responded to, the potential offered through self-employed people may be enhanced.

References

Aldrich, H. 2006. Trends and Directions in Entrepreneurship Research in *Entrepreneurship Research: Foundations and Trends in Entrepreneurship*, 2(1), 49–62.

Andersson, P. 2008. Happiness and health: well-being among the self-employed. *Journal of Socio-Economics*, 37(1), 213–236.

Australian Bureau of Statistics 2008. *Australian Social Trends*, (Cat. No. 4102.0). Canberra: ABS.

Australian Taxation Office (ATO) 2008a. *Understanding the Characteristics of Micro Business Tax Debtors by IPSOS Eureka*.[Online] Available at: http://www.ato.gov.au/content/downloads/cor00161745debtrprt.pdf [accessed 7 May 2009].

Australian Taxation Office (ATO) 2008b.*Profiling the Micro Business Segment Communication and Information Needs November 2008* by GfKbluemoon. [Online] Available at: http://www.ato.gov.au/content/downloads/cor 00182325.pdf [accessed 7 May 2009].

Australian Taxation Office (ATO) 2009.*Understanding Preventative, Facilitative and Punitive Payment Measures for Micro Businesses* by GfKbluemoon. [Online] Available at: http://www.ato.gov.au/content/downloads/cor00227004.pdf [accessed 7 May 2009].

Benz, M. and Frey, B. 2008. Being independent is a great thing: subjective evaluations of self-employment and hierarchy. *Economica*, 75(298), 362–383.

Blackburn, R. and Kovalainen, A. 2009. Researching small firms and entrepreneurship: past, present and future. *International Journal of Management Reviews*, 11(2), 127–148.

Blanpain, R. and Nakakubo, H. 2010. *Regulation of Fixed-Term Employment Contracts*. The Netherlands: Kluwer Law International.

Bridges, S. 2010. *Re-thinking Enterprise Policy: Can Failure Trigger New Understandings*. London: Palgrave Macmillan.

Burke, A. 2010. *The Economic Role of Freelance Workers in the Construction Industry*. Cranfield: Hudson.

Carsrud, A. and Brännback, A. (eds) 2009. *Understanding the Entrepreneurial Mind: Opening the Black Box*. New York: Springer.

Casale, G. (ed) 2011. *The Employment Relationship: A Comparative Overview.* Geneva: ILO/Hart Publishing.

Eurofound 2010. *2010 Survey of Working Conditions in the EU*, European Foundation for the Improvement in Living and Working Conditions.

European Commission (EU) 2010a. *Entrepreneurship in the EU and Beyond*, Flash Barometer 2010 No 283, European Commission DG Enterprise/Gallup.

European Commission (EU) 2010b. *Employment in Europe*, European Commission, DG Employment.

Felfe, J., Schmook, R., Schyns, B. and Six, B. 2008. Does the form of employment make a difference? *Journal of Vocational Behavior*, 72(1), 81–94.

French, B. 2007. *Australian Charter of Employment Rights The Australian Institute of Employment Rights*. Melbourne: Hardie Grant Books.

Garrettt, G. 2008. *Cost Estimating and Contract Pricing: Tools Techniques and Best Practices*. Chicago, IL: CCH-Wolters Kluwer, Law & Business.

Garrett, G. and Henley, A. 2009.*Switching Costs and Occupational Transition into Self-Employment*, Bonn: Institute for the Study of Labor Discussion Paper No. 3969.

Goffee, R. and Scase, R. 1995. *Corporate Realities: The Dynamics of Large and Small Organisations*. London: International Thomson Business Press.

Haunschild, A. 2003. Managing employment relationships in flexible labour markets: the case of German repertory theatres. *Human Relations*, 56(8), 899–929.

Hessels, J., van Gelderen, M. and Thurik, R. 2008. Drivers of entrepreneurial aspirations at the country level. *International Entrepreneurship and Management Journal*, 4(4), 323–339.

ICA Act 2006. *Independent Contractors Act 2006* (Commonwealth) No 162 of 2006. [Online] Available at: http://www.comlaw.gov.au/Search/Independent%20 Contractors%20Act [accessed 26 June 2006].

International Labour Organization (ILO) 2003. *International Labour Conference. Provisional Record. 91st Session*, Geneva.

International Labour Organization (ILO) 2006. *International Labour Conference, 95th Session, Report V(1) The employment relationship*, Geneva.

International Labour Organization (ILO) 2011. *Employment Trends 2010*, International Labour Office.

Lammiman, J. and Syrett, M. 2004. *CoolSearch: Keeping Your Organisation in Touch and on the Edge*. Chichester: Capstone Wiley.

Leighton, P. and Wynn, M. 2011. Classifying employment relationships: more sliding doors or a better regulatory framework? *Industrial Law Journal*, 40(1), 5–44.

McKeown, T., Bryant, M. and Cochrane, R. 2011. The Role of Emotions in Supporting Independent Professionals in Härtel, C., Ashkanasy, N. & Zerbe, W. (ed.) *What Have We Learned? Ten Years On (Research on Emotion in Organizations, Volume 7)*, Emerald Group Publishing Limited, pp. 133-147.

McMullen J.S., Bagby, D.R. and Palich, L.E. 2008. Economic freedom and the motivation to engage in entrepreneurial action. *Entrepreneurship Theory and Practice*, 32(5), 875–895.

Office for National Statistics United Kingdom (ONS) 2011. *Labour Market Statistics April 2011*. [Online] Available at: http://www.statistics.gov.uk/ pdfdir/lmsuk0411.pdf [accessed 1 May 2011].

Organisation for Economic Co-operation and Development (OECD) 2010a. *SMEs, Entrepreneurship and Innovation*, OECD.

Organisation for Economic Co-operation and Development (OECD) 2010b. *Employment Outlook 2010*, OECD.

Parker, S. 2004. *The Economics of Self-employment and Entrepreneurship*. Cambridge: Cambridge University Press.

Phillips, K. 2008. *Independence and the Death of Employment*.Melbourne: Connorcourt Publishing.

Rousseau, D. and Schalk, R. (eds) 2000. *Psychological Contracts in Employment: Cross National Perspectives*. Newbury Park: Sage Publications.

Sarasvathy, S. and Venkataraman, S. 2011. Entrepreneurship as method: open questions for an entrepreneurial future. *Entrepreneurship Theory and Practice*, 35(1), 113–135.

Scase, R. 2003a. Entrepreneurship and Proprietorship in Transition: Policy Implications for the SME sector in *Small and Medium Enterprises in Transitional Economies*, edited by R. McIntyre and R. Dallago. London: Palgrave Macmillan, 64–77.

Scase, R. 2003b. Employment Relations in Small Firms in *Industrial Relations Theory and Practice*, edited by P Edward. Oxford: Blackwell, 470–488.

Shane, S. 2008. *The Illusions of Entrepreneurship*. Yale: New Haven.

Small Business Commissioner of Victoria (SBC) 2010a. *Small Business Commissioner Annual Report 2009*. [Online] Available at: http://www.sbc.vic.gov.au/latest/annual-report-2009-10-tabled-in-parliament [accessed 2 May 2009].

Small Business Commissioner of Victoria (SBC) 2010b. *Small Business Commissioner Annual Report 2010*. [Online] Available at: http://www.sbc.vic.gov.au/images/stories/vsbc_AnnualReport_2009_10.pdf [accessed 2 May 2010].

Stanworth, J. and Purdy, D. 2008. *SME Facts & Issues: A Compilation of Current Data & Issues on U.K. Small and Medium-sized Firms*. [Online] Available at: http://www.scribd.com/doc/45733619/SERTeam-Stanworth-and-Purdy-Oct-2008-SME-Facts-and-Issues [accessed 23 April 2010].

Sutherland, C. and Riley, J. 2010. Industrial legislation in 2009. *Journal of Industrial Relations*, 52(3), 275–287.

Wynn, M. and Leighton, P. 2009. Agency workers, employment rights and the ebb and flow of freedom of contract. *The Modern Law Review*, 72(1), 91–102.

12

Promoting Environmentally Sustainable Enterprises: Some Policy Options

Richard Blundel, Adrian Monaghan and Christine Thomas

Chapter Summary

Governments around the world are taking an increasing interest in promoting environmentally-sustainable economic activity. They have developed a variety of policy approaches in an effort to address environmental issues that range from localised pollution incidents to global climate change. This chapter examines the kinds of intervention tools that are being used to improve the environmental performance of SMEs, and to guide entrepreneurial energies towards more environmentally benign goals. The chapter aims to: outline the main options available to policymakers; compare specific intervention tools, noting their strengths and limitations; and discuss the case for adopting more holistic approaches to address the pervasive, complex and often deeply-rooted challenges of sustainable development. Key lessons are that policymakers need to select appropriate combinations of tools based on careful reviews of the evidence, and that well-integrated, context-sensitive policies are likely to prove the most effective.

Introduction

Until recently, sustainable development initiatives tended to focus on the environmental performance of large public and private sector organisations, with smaller firms attracting less attention (Schaper 2002). However, over the last two decades there has been increasing interest in the role played by SMEs (Calogirou, Sørensen, Bjørn Larsen, Alexopoulou 2010, Parker, Redmond and Simpson 2009).

Many different policy tools have been introduced in an attempt to control against environmentally damaging economic activities and to encourage them to adopt more environmentally benign practices. It is a vast policy arena, which extends from relatively modest local conservation projects to ambitious 'green new deals' that span national and regional economies. This chapter provides an analysis of the main types of policy developed in the last 20 years to influence the environmental performance of SMEs and to promote more sustainable forms of entrepreneurial activity. To understand the context in which sustainability policies are framed, it begins by reviewing arguments used in support of intervention.

The Case for Intervention

The main argument for intervention in relation to becoming environmentally sustainable is that SMEs have a substantial environmental impact. The nature and scale of this impact can be illustrated by the findings of a recent study conducted by European researchers (Calogirou et al. 2010) who calculate that SMEs are responsible for 64 per cent of the overall environmental impact in Europe, including greenhouse gas emissions (Figure 12.1). Though some impacts, such as energy use, are roughly related to their share of the economy, smaller firms have a disproportionate impact in some sectors (Revell and Blackburn 2007). Small firms have generally been slower to adopt environmental improvements compared to their larger counterparts, with research evidence suggesting that this is due to a combination of internal and external barriers (Parker et al. 2009, Vickers, Vaze, Corr, Kasparova and Lyon 2009, Environment Agency 2003). One reason is that they are often more difficult to regulate than larger organisations. In addition, they may lack the necessary awareness, motivation, capabilities, financial resources, or capacity to innovate (Daddi, Testa and Iraldo 2010, Schaper 2002, Tilley 1999).[1]

Sources include Eurostat's Structural Business Statistics (SBS) database and DTI's (Danish Technology Institute) own estimations for the EU27. Aggregated at level 3 data (equals the average share of employees in the SME size companies per country).

It follows that governments require radical changes in the performance and impact of SMEs if they are to meet their own environmental targets. For example, the European Union (EU) has formally committed to reduce greenhouse gas emissions by 80–95 per cent by 2050 compared to 1990. This requires intermediate

---

1   For example, in the UK, almost a third of SME expenditure on energy is wasted through inefficient practices (Vickers et al. 2009: 15). SMEs also cause about 43 per cent of serious industrial pollution incidents and generate 60 per cent of commercial waste in England and Wales (Environment Agency 2006: 11).

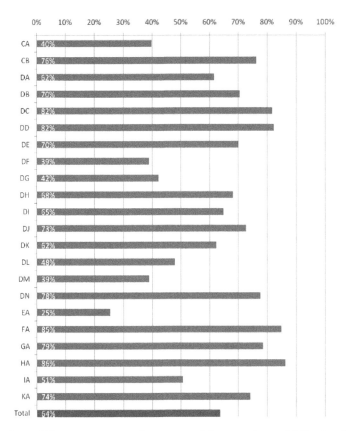

Figure 12.1   The average environmental impact from SMEs in the EU27 per sector

Source: Calogirou et al. 2010: 60 (Table 31)

cuts in emissions of 25 per cent by 2020, 40 per cent by 2030 and 60 per cent by 2040. The EU recognises that SMEs are integral to its transformation into a competitive low-carbon economy (European Commission 2011, Calogirou et al. 2010). The preceding arguments are often reinforced with reference to the 'business case' for sustainability. Support for eco-efficiency is seen as a 'win–win' because by generating firm-level cost savings, it can make SMEs more competitive, though the evidence remains mixed (Revell and Blackburn 2007, Cambridge Econometrics 2003). Investing in technological innovation and new entrepreneurial activity can offer other rewards, particularly in emerging 'eco-industry' sectors[2] such as waste management, soil remediation, environmental

2   Eco-industries have been formally defined as 'activities which produce goods and services to measure, prevent, limit, minimise or correct environmental damage to water, air and soil, as well as problems related to waste, noise and eco- systems' (Organisation for Economic Cooperation and Development/Eurostat 1999: 9).

monitoring, renewable energy generation and eco-construction. For example, by supporting clean technology start-ups, a regional government can both modernise its industrial base and enhance its international competitiveness (United Nations Environment Programme 2009).

The Main Policy Options

Policy options are usually categorised in terms of broad types of measure (for example, regulation), and more specific instruments or intervention tools, such as the introduction of an emissions standard. The range of options can be illustrated by considering a single environmental policy arena, energy efficiency (see Table 12.1).[3] In practice, there is some variation in terminology and overlaps between categories. For example, while product labels are generally associated with particular standards (that is, regulation), they are also market-based instruments, designed to influence consumer demand.

There are a number of factors to consider when selecting between different options. Firstly, what environmental issues are being prioritised? The focus may be on particular arenas, such as climate change mitigation, climate change adaptation, biodiversity, water, air and waste, or on sectors with particular

Table 12.1   Policy measures and intervention tools – some examples

Type of Measure	Intervention Tools Applicable to SMEs and Entrepreneurship
Regulation	**China**: new national building standards require 50% reduction in energy use compared to the 1980s, with sanctions including fines on non-compliant construction firms. **Australia**: construction firms affected by revised building codes to meet carbon reduction targets and new Nationwide House Energy Rating Scheme (NatHERS).
Economic and market-based	**France**: energy management fund (FOGIME) guarantees loans to SMEs for energy efficiency and renewable energy investments. **Japan**: an Emission Credit Scheme whereby reductions achieved by small and medium-sized companies with financial, technical or other assistance from large companies helps the latter to meet their emissions targets.
Capacity building	**United States**: Small Business Innovation Research (SBIR) and Small Technology Transfer (STTR) programmes, which fund competitions for small firms. **Norway**: the Norwegian Energy Efficiency Network (IEEN) encourages cooperation and networking of SMEs, demonstration programmes and assistance with environmental management systems.

Sources: International Energy Agency 2011, Vickers et al. 2009

---

3   For more examples of measures currently in operation, see the online databases of the European Environment Agency and International Energy Agency (European Environmental Agency 2011, International Energy Agency 2011).

environmental impacts, including transport, energy, agriculture, fisheries (European Environmental Agency 2010). Secondly, how do these issues relate to other policy goals? For example, the EU's 'Europe 2020' combines economic and environmental aims in pursuit of 'sustainable growth'; these include: 'building a competitive low-carbon economy that makes efficient, sustainable use of resources'; 'protecting the environment and preventing biodiversity loss'; and 'capitalising on Europe's leadership in developing new green technologies and production methods' (European Commission 2011). Thirdly, what obstacles are likely to stand in the way of achieving sustainable growth? These are likely to differ depending on the social and economic conditions in the countries concerned. Table 12.2 illustrates one way in which these considerations might translate into policy options (Organisation for Economic Cooperation and Development 2011a).

The following are some of the tools that are most commonly applied to SMEs and entrepreneurship, highlighting particular strengths and limitations.

Environmental regulations and standards are widely used for high energy-using products, such as vehicles and heating systems, and for waste management, particularly in more hazardous forms, including clinical and radioactive waste. SMEs operating in such areas can be 'pushed' into compliance through minimum standards, which may be combined with certification or labelling schemes. Regulations and standards are often seen as essential to drive behaviour change. They can be particularly effective when combined with fiscal and informational intervention. However, effective enforcement is also necessary in order to gain

Table 12.2   Possible policies to address green growth constraints

Green Growth Constraints	Policy Options
Inadequate infrastructure	Taxes, tariffs, transfers, public–private partnerships
Low human and social capital and poor institutional quality	Taxes, subsidy reform/removal
Incomplete property rights, subsidies	Review and reform or remove
Regulatory uncertainty	Set targets, create independent governance systems
Information externalities and split incentives	Labelling, voluntary approaches, subsidies, technology and performance standards
Environmental externalities	Taxes, tradable permits, subsidies
Low returns on R&D	R&D subsidies and tax incentives, focus on general-purpose technologies
Network effects	Strengthen competition in network industries, subsidies or loan guarantees for new network projects
Barriers to competition	Reform regulation, reduce government monopoly

Source: Organisation for Economic Cooperation and Development 2011b: 9 (Table 2)

legitimacy and to ensure that compliant firms are not adversely affected by the activities of 'rogue' traders (Thomas, Lane, Oreszczyn, Schiller and Yoxon 2009). Research evidence suggests that regulators should adopt a variety of tools, ensuring that they are sector-specific and well integrated with other enterprise policies (Hansen, Søndergård and Meredith 2002). There is also evidence that formal Environmental Management Systems (EMS) and eco-labelling can assist SMEs to achieve legal compliance by making them more aware of their environmental impacts (Centre for Research on Energy and Environmental Economics and Policy 2006). Only a small minority of SMEs have adopted EMS, but their use can be promoted with the help of other intervention tools. For example, inter-organisational EMS programmes are now being promoted through sector-based networks or 'clusters' involving local government agencies, firms and non-governmental organizations (NGOs) (Daddi et al. 2010).

Online information and support services have created new possibilities for engaging directly with SMEs, which can complement and extend more traditional face-to-face and paper-based approaches. For example, the German national waste prevention plan seeks to support and encourage pro-environmental actions through an online database, which facilitates coordination and networking. Users can consult the database to see what measures are being used to support SMEs in areas such as eco-design (Environmental Technologies Action Plan 2011). UK environmental agencies operate a similar online tool, *NetRegs*, which provides clear and concise information on legal compliance and environmental good practice with the aim of reducing the amount of environmental harm caused by SMEs. Networking between different actors, such as SME manufacturers and their suppliers, is recognised as a key requirement for learning. This can now be delivered more widely through online tools; networks can be built around institutions, such as the Swedish Waste Council, enabling participants to exchange experiences (Environmental Technologies Action Plan 2011).

Though such tools can be effective, penetration of information-based support services has often been limited. Many small firms are still failing to recognise the environmental impact of their activities (for example, Environment Agency 2009, 2003) and converting pro-environmental attitudes into operational changes has been identified as a further obstacle (Revell and Blackburn 2007, Schaper 2002, Tilley 1999). In addition, evaluating the impact of such interventions remains difficult. For example, to measure the success of a waste prevention initiative, it is necessary to make assumptions about the so-called 'counterfactual', or level of waste that would have been generated in its absence (Dehoust, Küppers, Bringezu and Wilts 2011).

Taxation, tax credits and funding packages can be used to influence SMEs. They can be levied directly on the firm through landfill or carbon taxes, or indirectly by targeting particular product categories, such as applying differential taxes based on CO_2 emissions. Financial incentives can be also used to promote sustainable entrepreneurial activities, such as 'retrofitting' of existing buildings by SMEs to reduce energy demand (for example, Burch, Shaw, Zerriffi and Meyer 2011, Natural Resources Canada 2011). However, careful design and implementation is crucial to avoid distortion and disruption of markets. For example, while public subsidies in Denmark encouraged nascent wind turbine manufacturers to develop, the introduction of tax breaks in the United States led to a speculative 'wind rush' of large-scale construction projects, most of which collapsed following fiscal changes in the mid-1980s (Garud and Karnøe 2003, Asmus 2001). Successful interventions often make use of multiple tools. For example, Danish Government support for wind energy combined subsidies with regulation and research, underpinned by a strong political coalition in favour of this technology. In the UK, the rapid expansion of SMEs operating anaerobic digestion (AD) plants for organic wastes was supported by two fiscal tools: a funding package to support new composting and AD facilities and two Renewable Obligation Certificates (ROCs), funded by energy suppliers, to promote the dissemination of AD technologies (Department for Environment, Food and Rural Affairs 2009a). The policy was reinforced by pressures on local authorities to reduce the amount of biodegradable waste sent to landfill and a national drive to become less reliant on energy from fossil fuels (Department for the Environment, Food and Rural Affairs 2009b).

Research services and research funding can be provided as a way of promoting eco-innovation and the growth of more sustainable enterprises. In making these investments, governments may decide to favour larger or smaller-scale enterprises. For example, in the case of wind energy, the Danish approach (that is, founding a small wind turbine testing station at Roskilde and working closely with small manufacturers and community-based networks), contrasts with that of the United States, where the aerospace industry was identified as the best source of expertise on turbine design (Department of Environment 2011, Garud and Karnøe 2003). Research funding can be effective where innovation is blocked by specific knowledge gaps. For example, the UK New Technologies Development Programme provided financial assistance to new waste treatment demonstration projects. The programme was intended to overcome the real and perceived risks of introducing alternative technologies by generating accurate and impartial technical, environmental and economic information for key decision makers (Department for the Environment, Food and Rural Affairs 2011). Governments can also support knowledge creation and innovation by facilitating inter-organisational interaction via sector-based networks and geographic clusters (Daddi et al. 2010); such activities are increasingly coupled with web-based information and support services (see above).

Selecting Appropriate Tools

Policymakers need to consider a number of factors when selecting specific intervention tools. As with broad policy options, these choices are likely to be influenced by current political priorities. For example, a decision to pursue energy efficiency through regulation may be driven by the need to achieve national carbon reduction targets. Tools also need to be matched to the characteristics and requirements of the firms, sectors and markets that are being addressed. Hence, information, research services or educational support may be appropriate where SMEs are seen as lacking essential knowledge or capabilities. It is also important to take into account potential inter-actions with other policies and tools (for example, firm-level subsidies may undermine competition policy goals). Lastly, there are many contextual factors to consider, including political institutions, economic conditions, physical infrastructures and educational levels (Daddi et al. 2010, Hansen et al. 2002, Revell 2003, Spence, Jeurissen and Rutherfoord 2000). While some tools may be shared across national and regional borders, such as pan-European emissions regulations and carbon trading schemes, there are also significant variations in the policy landscape, both between different geographic locations and over time. These differences can be illustrated with a brief overview of recent developments in waste management. Earlier policies tended to be based around public health issues, but the emphasis has since shifted towards a broader concern with environmental protection. In the past, regulatory tools such as pollution controls and local planning rules were the most widely-used. However, by the 1990s there was an increasing interest in achieving waste prevention and increasing recycling rates (Wilson 2007). This led to the adoption of new tools, including fiscal measures, target-setting for local authorities, communications campaigns, and programmes to stimulate growth in recovered materials markets. The exact form and combination of tools varies by country. As a case in point, in Switzerland high disposal charges are complemented by provision of free recycling facilities, while in Hong Kong similar tools are combined with public education initiatives, financial support for the recycling industry and a labelling scheme for local businesses (Federal Office for the Environment 2011, Government of Hong Kong 2011). In some cases, the proliferation of tools has resulted in SMEs being confronted by a complex and often confusing array of regulations and fiscal incentives (Netregs 2011). However, it has also created opportunities for policy diffusion and convergence as governments share their experiences and learn from the more successful policy innovations of environmental 'pioneer countries' (Jänicke 2005).

Towards a More Integrated Approach?

It is clear that, while some policies and intervention tools may prove more effective than others, there are no 'magic bullets'. Given the scale, complexity and pervasiveness of today's environmental problems, the central challenge is to identify the best *combination* of tools and to implement it in a context-sensitive way (Organisation for Economic Cooperation and Development 2011b, Calogirou et al. 2010). Governments around the world are being encouraged to develop more coherent, better-integrated enterprise policies (Audretsch and Beckman 2007) and environmental policies (Hansen et al. 2002, Nilsson and Persson 2003). Similar calls have been heard from environmental campaigners, industry bodies and entrepreneurs, particularly in relation to global issues such as climate change. For example, leading Australian firms in the built and natural environment sectors have expressed concern that 'fragmented' public policies on climate change are compromising the country's economic and environmental prospects (Consult Australia 2011). There are indications that greater integration of environmental, innovation and enterprise policies is becoming a reality. Several countries, including Austria, Belgium and Finland, are adopting more holistic, systems-based approaches to achieve sustainable production and consumption goals (Geels, Monaghan, Eames and Steward 2008).[4]

The application of systems thinking is most fully developed in the Netherlands, where the 'transitions management' (TM) approach has been formally adopted (Loorbach and Rotmans 2010, Elzen, Geels and Green 2004). TM widens the scope and ambition of innovation policy beyond traditional 'end-of-pipe' solutions, process efficiency measures and product life cycle evaluations. It aims to introduce more radically eco-efficient ways of meeting society's needs (such as energy, food and transport). TM policies typically combine two dimensions: i) increasing pressure on particular industrial sectors through mechanisms such as financial and regulatory measures and; ii) stimulating and supporting the emergence and development of new 'niches' (that is, protected environments where entrepreneurs can develop new concepts and radical innovations). Success in the first dimension should create windows of opportunity for diffusion and mainstreaming of niche innovations. TM policies recognise the need for a variety of actors, including entrepreneurs, SMEs, larger firms, community organisations and government agencies. To achieve breakthrough, niche innovations require critical mass.

---

4   Other examples include the German national waste prevention programme, which creates, 'a strategic reference framework', to coordinate actions at federal, state and municipal level (Dehoust et al. 2011: 18) and the proposal for a Commission for a Sustainable Australia to drive, 'innovation and new technology pathways for a sustainable future' (Consult Australia 2011: 9).

Their technical, practical, economic and political feasibility can be supported by intervention tools designed to promote learning (for example, subsidies for pilot projects); the formation of networks (for example, using participatory methods with stakeholders who have positive or negative vested interests in an innovation); the development of long-term visions; and their translation into short-term actions (Geels et al. 2008, Kemp, Schot and Hoogma 1998). The move towards more integrated policies is still in its early stages. Many issues remain open to debate, including the ways that transitions are governed, how they can be adapted to fit different contexts, and the role that entrepreneurs of various kinds might play in facilitating or resisting change (Blundel and Monaghan 2011, Grin, Rotmans and Schot 2010, Smith, Stirling and Berkhout 2005). The unfolding of sustainability transitions is typically measured over several decades, making it difficult to evaluate their strengths and limitations, based on current evidence. However, TM's holistic approach provides a useful starting point for policy reviews that take SMEs and entrepreneurship into account, and which promote more coherent portfolios of intervention tools.

Conclusion

This chapter has examined environmental policies related to SMEs and entrepreneurship. It reviewed a range of intervention tools and discussed how they might be selected and combined to address specific impacts. It has also considered the main lessons and implications for practice.

Having established the importance of SMEs and entrepreneurship in relation to current environmental concerns, a strong case for public policy intervention was outlined, based on a number of factors. Addressing SME environmental impact will be necessary in order to achieve current and future sustainability targets. It may also generate new opportunities to reduce costs, improve other performance measures and promote innovative entrepreneurial activities in emerging 'green' industries. When framing policy, it is important to clarify the environmental goals to be pursued and their relationship to other goals, such as supporting smaller businesses or enhancing competitive advantage. In some cases, the economic, social and environmental arguments may coincide, but in others there may be unavoidable trade-offs. The chapter has provided several examples of the kinds of research evidence that are available to inform these policy debates.

Turning to the main policy options, three broad types of environment-related policy measure were identified (that is, regulation, economic and market-based, capacity building), along with an extensive range of more specific intervention tools. Where policymakers have discretion in selecting tools, it is important to consider their respective strengths and limitations. In practice, the quality of evaluation data remains variable and it is not always possible to assume that tools will transfer readily from one context to another. However, policy choices can be better informed by drawing on the best available research evidence and being ready to select – and if necessary adapt – tools to address particular regional or sectoral requirements. The final section indicated that attempts to identify the 'best' intervention tool are being replaced by a new focus on how different tools can be combined most effectively. The challenge for policymakers is to develop more holistic and joined-up approaches that match the scale, complexity and pervasiveness of today's environmental challenges. The Dutch TM perspective exemplifies these developments, requiring policymakers to consider the needs of SMEs and entrepreneurship alongside those of other actors, including public-sector bodies, larger businesses and community groups. Intervention may be necessary to coordinate and drive sustainability transitions, but there is also considerable scope for governments to engage SMEs and entrepreneurial actors of various kinds in shaping new visions of a more sustainable future.

References

Asmus, P. 2001. *Reaping the Wind: How Mechanical Wizards, Visionaries, and Profiteers Helped Shape Our Energy Future*. Washington DC: Island Press.

Audretsch, D.B., and Beckmann, I.A.M. 2007. From Small Business to Entrepreneurship Policy, in *Handbook of Research in Entrepreneurship Policy*, edited by D.B. Audretsch et al. Cheltenham: Edward Elgar, 36–53.

Blundel, R.K. and Monaghan, A. 2011. *Teaching Tigers to Dance?: Evaluating the Role of Enterprise Policies in Purposive Sustainability Transitions*, 2nd European Conference on Sustainability Transitions. Lund, 13–15 June 2011.

Burch, C., Shaw, A., Zerriffi, H. and Meyer, R. 2011. *Harnessing the Entrepreneurial Power of Small Business: New Strategies for Reducing Greenhouse Gas Emissions* (Briefing Note 2011-28). University of Victoria: Pacific Institute for Climate Solutions.

Calogirou C., Sørensen, S.Y., Bjørn Larsen, P. and Alexopoulou, S. 2010. *SMEs and the environment in the European Union. PLANET SA and Danish Technological Institute for European Commission*, DG Enterprise and Industry. [Online] Available at: http://ec.europa.eu/enterprise/policies/sme/business-environment/ [accessed: 9 March 2011].

Cambridge Econometrics 2003. *The Benefits of Greener Business*. Cambridge Econometrics and AEA Technology. [Online] Available at: www.environment-agency.gov.uk/business [accessed: 19 March 2011].

Centre for Research on Energy and Environmental Economics and Policy 2006. *EVER: Evaluation of Eco-Label and EMAS for their Revision*. European Commission. [Online] Available at: http://ec.europa.eu/environment/emas/pdf/eversummary.pdf [accessed: 25 May 2011].

Consult Australia 2011. *Seizing the Sustainability Advantage*. Consult Australia. [Online] Available at: http://www.consultaustralia.com.au [accessed: 19 March 2011].

Daddi, T., Testa, F. and Iraldo, F. 2010. A cluster-based approach as an effective way to implement the Environmental Compliance Assistance Programme: evidence from some good practices. *Local Environment*, 15(1), 73–82.

Dehoust, G., Küppers, P., Bringezu, S. and Wilts, H. 2011. *Development of Scientific and Technical Foundations for a National Waste Prevention Programme* (Summary). (UBA-FB) 0014427/E. Öko-Institut e.V., Darmstadt. [Online] Available at: http://www.uba.de/uba-info-medien-e/4044.html [accessed: 19 March 2011].

Department for Environment, Food and Rural Affairs, United Kingdom 2009a. *Waste Strategy: Annual Progress Report 2008/09*. London: Department for the Environment, Food and Rural Affairs.

Department for Environment, Food and Rural Affairs, United Kingdom 2009b. *Anaerobic Digestion – Shared Goals*. London: Department for the Environment, Food and Rural Affairs.

Department for Environment, Food and Rural Affairs, United Kingdom 2011. *New Technologies Demonstrator Programme* (NTDP) Department for Food and Rural Affairs. [Online] Available at: http://archive.defra.gov.uk/environment/waste/residual/newtech/index.htm [accessed: 21 May 2011].

Department of Environment, 2011. *A National Offshore Wind Strategy: Creating an Offshore Wind Energy Industry in the United States*. Washington DC, US: Department of Energy.

Elzen, B., Geels, F.W. and Green, K. 2004. *System Innovation and the Transition to Sustainability*. Cheltenham: Edward Elgar.

Environment Agency, United Kingdom 2003. *SME-nvironment 2003: A Survey to Assess Environmental Behaviours among Smaller UK Businesses*. Environment Agency, NIEA and SEPA. [Online] Available at: www.netregs.gov.uk [accessed: 9 March 2011].

Environment Agency, United Kingdom (2006) *Spotlight on Business: Environmental Performance in 2006*. [Online] Available at: http://publications. environment-agency.gov.uk/pdf/GEHO0707BMMX-e-e.pdf [accessed: 7 November 2011].

Environment Agency, United Kingdom 2009. *SME-nvironment 2009: UK Summary*. Environment Agency, NIEA and SEPA. [Online] Available at: www.netregs.gov.uk [accessed: 9 March 2011].

Environmental Technologies Action Plan 2011. *Germany: Laying the Foundations for a German National Waste Prevention Plan. Environmental Technologies Action Plan*. [Online] Available at: http://ec.europa.eu/environment/etap/inaction/showcases/germany/642_en.html [accessed: 9 March 2011].

European Commission 2011. *A Resource-Efficient Europe – Flagship Initiative Under the Europe 2020 Strategy*. COM(2011) 21. European Commission.

[Online] Available at: http://ec.europa.eu/resource-efficient-europe/pdf/
resource-efficient_europe_en.pdf [accessed: 9 March 2011].

European Environmental Agency 2010. *The European Environment – State
and Outlook 2010: SOER 2010 in a Policy Context.* European Environmental
Agency. [Online] Available at: www.eea.europa.eu/soer/policy-makers
[accessed: 9 March 2011].

European Environmental Agency 2011. *Climate Policies and Measures in Europe.*
European Environmental Agency. [Online] Available at: www.eea.europa.
eu/themes/climate/pam/ [accessed: 9 March 2011].

Federal Office for the Environment 2011. *Waste Treatment Processes: Recycling
Federal Office for the Environment.* [Online] Available at: http://www.bafu.
admin.ch/abfall/01495/01498/index.html?lang=en [accessed 28 March 2011].

Garud, R. and Karnøe, P. 2003. Bricolage versus breakthrough: distributed and
embedded agency in technology entrepreneurship. *Research Policy*, 32(2), 277–300.

Geels, F.W., Monaghan, A., Eames, M. and Steward, F. 2008. *The Feasibility of
Systems Thinking in Sustainable Consumption and Production Policy.* [Online:
Department for Environment, Food and Rural Affairs] Available at: http://
randd.defra.gov.uk/Document.aspx?Document=EV02030_7726_FRP.pdf
[accessed: 28 March 2011].

Government of Hong Kong 2011. *Waste Reduction and Recycling.* [Online:
Government of Hong Kong] Available at: http://www.gov.hk/en/residents/
environment/waste/wasteredrecyc.htm [accessed: 29 March 2011].

Grin, J., Rotmans, R. and Schot, J. 2010. *Transitions to Sustainable Development: New
Directions in the Study of Long Term Transformative Change.* London: Routledge.

Hansen, O.E., Søndergård, B. and Meredith, S. 2002. Environmental innovations
in small and medium sized enterprises. *Technology Analysis and Strategic
Management*, 14(1), 37–56.

International Energy Agency 2011. *Energy Efficiency Policies and Measures*
[Online: International Energy Agency] Available at: http://www.iea.org/
textbase/pm/default.aspx?mode=pm [accessed: 25 May 2011].

Jänicke, M. 2005. Trend setters in environmental policy: the character and role
of pioneer countries. *European Environment*, 15(2), 129–142.

Kemp, R., Schot, J. and Hoogma, R. 1998. Regime shifts to sustainability through
processes of niche formation: the approach of strategic niche management.
Technology Analysis and Strategic Management, 10(2), 175–198.

Loorbach, D. and Rotmans, J. 2010. The practice of transition management:
examples and lessons from four distinct cases. *Futures*, 42(3), 237–246.

Natural Resources Canada 2011. *EcoENERGY Retrofit Grants and Incentives.*
Natural Resources Canada. [Online] Available at: http://oee.nrcan.gc.ca/
corporate/retrofit-summary.cfm?attr=0 [accessed: 19 March 2011].

Netregs 2011. *Current Environmental Legislation: Free Environmental Guidance for
SMEs.* Environment Agency/Scottish Environment Protection Agency/Northern

Ireland Environment Agency. [Online] Available at: http://www.netregs.gov. uk/netregs/legislation/current/default.aspx [accessed: 19 May 2011].

Nilsson M. and Persson, S.A. 2003. Framework for analysing environmental policy integration. *Journal of Environmental Policy and Planning*, 5(4), 333–359.

Organisation for Economic Cooperation and Development (OECD) 2011a. *Tools for Delivering on Green Growth* [Online: Organisation for Economic Cooperation and Development]. Available at: http://www.oecd.org/ dataoecd/32/48/48012326.pdf [accessed: 25 May 2011].

Organisation for Economic Cooperation and Development (OECD) 2011b. *Towards Green Growth*. Paris: Organisation for Economic Cooperation and Development.

Organisation for Economic Cooperation and Development/Eurostat (1999) *The Environmental Goods and Services Industry – Manual for Data Collection and Analysis*. Paris: Organisation for Economic Cooperation and Development/Eurostat.

Parker, C.M., Redmond, J. and Simpson, M. 2009. A review of interventions to encourage SMEs to make environmental improvements. *Environment and Planning C: Government and Policy*, 27(2), 279–301.

Revell, A. 2003. Environmental policy and the small firm in Japan: comparisons with the Netherlands. *Journal of Environmental Policy and Planning*, 5(4), 397–413.

Revell, A. and Blackburn, R. 2007. The business case for sustainability?: An examination of small firms in the UK's construction and restaurant sectors. *Business Strategy and the Environment*, 16(6), 404–420.

Schaper, M. 2002. Small firms and environmental management. *International Small Business Journal*, 20(3), 235–251.

Smith, A., Stirling, A. and Berkhout, F. 2005. The governance of sustainable socio-technical transitions. *Research Policy*, 34(10), 1491–1510.

Spence, L.J., Jeurissen, R. and Rutherfoord. 2000. Small business and the environment in the UK and the Netherlands: towards stakeholder engagement. *Business Ethics Quarterly*, 10(4), 945–965.

Thomas, C., Lane, A., Oreszczyn, S., Schiller, F. and Yoxon, M. 2009. *Attitudes to the Use of Organic Waste Resources on Land* [Online: Department for Environment, Food and Rural Affairs]: Available at: http://randd.defra.gov.uk/Document. aspx?Document=WR0510_8620_FRP.pdf [accessed: 31 May 2011].

Tilley, F. 1999. The gap between the environmental attitudes and the environmental behaviour of small firms. *Business Strategy and the Environment*, 8(4), 238–248.

United Nations Environment Programme 2009. *An Introduction to the Green Economy Report*. Geneva: United Nations Environment Programme/Green Economy Initiative.

Vickers, I., Vaze, P., Corr, L., Kasparova, E. and Lyon, F. 2009. *SMEs in a Low Carbon Economy* (URN 09/574). [Online: CEEDR, Middlesex University] Available at: www.berr.gov.uk/files/file49761.doc [accessed: 9 March 2011].

Wilson, D.C. 2007. Development drivers for waste management. *Waste Management Research*, 25(3), 198–207.

13

Government Advice Services for SMEs: Some Lessons from British Experience

Robert J Bennett

Chapter Summary

This chapter assesses the form of market gap for external advice, focusing on how SMEs select advisors, what they expect and how outcomes are evaluated. Using Britain as an example, the chapter reviews the history of policy to provide advisory support to SMEs. It looks at the expectations that small business have for government-based services, the outcomes achieved, and issues of design, management, branding, marketing and use of fees. The chapter seeks to offer a guide to practitioners about where the boundaries lie between government services and market suppliers of advice. Key conclusions are that simple and uniform structures for government provision offer superior management of expectations, quality control and much lower costs. A strong differentiation between intensive and non-intensive services helps clients to route enquiries and manage their expectations, especially for intensive government advice which often carries significant deadweight and raises expectations that cannot be met. Government self-provision should be avoided due to high unit costs and often low satisfaction levels compared with market and not-for-profit suppliers.

Introduction

Government advice schemes for SMEs have become one of the most widely used means by which to encourage small firm development across most western economies. This is because a lack of information and technical know-how has been identified as one of the main areas where gaps in market provision may exist that governments can fill. In particular, it has been frequently claimed that government advisory services may be able to offer a strategic vision that individual SMEs and independent consultants cannot themselves provide, and hence fill a market gap in the provision of information. It has also been argued that most private consultants and advisors are themselves small businesses that may lack a wider vision and expertise, and so there is scope for a government role drawing consultants into a wider network of support and knowledge.

These features were fundamental to the case made in Britain by the Bolton Report (1971) that SMEs were disadvantaged compared to larger firms and hence some intervention from government was justified. This, in turn, led to the evolution of government-sponsored advisory services, which are the subject of this chapter. At the level of the European Union (EU), the European Commission (2003, 2008) *Green Paper on Entrepreneurism* and subsequent *Small Business Act* have advocated an expansion of advice across all EU countries, and also suggested that their range of objectives be widened (so as, for example, to help reduce entry barriers to starting a business, help reduce risk and increase reward levels, and foster small firm capacity and skills). Similar policies have been suggested more widely across OECD and other countries (OECD 1995, Bannock 2005).

Selecting and Assessing Advisors

The most frequently used methods by which small businesses select advisors are 'previous use' and 'recommendation' from personal contacts; these usually account for over 70 per cent of choices in most surveys (for example, Davies, Dowling and Patterson 1992, Bennett and Smith 2004). This derives from the high information asymmetry inherent in using advisors: they are offering a largely intangible service in an unregulated market with difficulties of evaluating quality, both *ex ante* and *ex post*. Hence trusted routes limit asymmetries, because clients know what to expect. Other routes to overcome information asymmetry may include the brand identification of advisors (for example, by professional institutes and business associations) and referral from established advisors that a firm is already using (such as banks and lawyers). Government advisory centres may play a role in this referral process by offering an independent perspective on this market. A well-marketed government initiative may also gain brand identity as a nationwide service with advantages of costs underwritten by the state.

Once received, advice is usually evaluated for most market-based advice services by assessing whether it satisfies customer expectations. This mode of assessment is central because of the information 'soft' nature of most advice, which involves learning and experiential development. 'Hard' outcomes are certainly the underlying purpose: to expand markets and increase turnover, enhance asset values or increase profitability. But advice most commonly offers an intermediate support. It applies external expertise to the solution of a problem or enhancement of a business practice, which then subsequently delivers the desired 'hard' outcomes. Hence, when seeking to assess outcomes of government-based advice, it is crucial to understand the processes and intensity of service delivery. Much of the debate about government advice services to SMEs has centred on the intensity of service that is needed or wanted. Government advice services are often criticised either for providing what politicians think SMEs need, rather than what SMEs expect, or for meeting political rather than business objectives (Bennett 2012).

The Evolution of Government Advice Services in Britain

The way in which governmental advice systems have been implemented varies considerably between countries, and in most cases have changed substantially over time. Britain provides an important example with international interest because it has experimented with a range of different policies. The developments fall into five distinct periods where different models of provision have been attempted, as summarised in Table 13.1, based on more detailed discussions in Bennett (2008, 2012), Bennett and Robson (2004), and a recent policy overview by Richard (2008) that has underpinned reforms since 2010.

Over 1973–1988 the main Government-supported information and advice service directly followed the recommendations of the Bolton Report (1971), called the Small Firms Service (SFS). This provided a two-level service, consisting of:

- An *extensive* telephone-based help-line staffed by civil servants in regional offices. This attracted high volumes of enquiries, with callers referred on to specialist suppliers mainly in the private sector.
- An *intensive* Business Development Service offering specialist counselling to SMEs. The aim was to follow up basic information requests with designated ('accredited') counsellors. It thus sought to aid selection of advisors through quality controls.

This approach was expanded over 1988–93 by the Government's Enterprise Initiative. This retained the SFS help-line, but replaced the Business Development Service with an expanded intensive service that provided higher levels of Government grant support to use external consultancy. Market-based

Table 13.1   Advice and consultancy schemes in Britain, 1973–2011

Main Schemes	Period	Point of Management	Administration	Delivery	Client Fees	Intensity of Advice
Small Firms Service (SFS) and Business Development Service	1973–1988	Central and government regional offices	Civil servants	Referral and market consultants	Free advice, subsidised consultants	Mainly low, a few high
SFS and Enterprise Initiative	1988–1993	Central and government regional offices	Civil servants	Referral and market consultants	Free advice, subsidised consultants	Mainly low, more high
Business Link	1993–2005	Local: county and districts level	Contracts to government agencies, partner bodies	Internal, PBAs, and some referral	Complex mix of with fee targets	Targeting high, also low
RDAs and Business Link	2005–2010	Regional and county level	RDAs, partner bodies, and specialist contractors	Internal, PBAs, and some referral	Complex mix of with some fee targets	Targeting high, also low, varied
Local Enterprise Partnerships in England	2010–	Local: city-region and county	Local strategy boards	Partners and private sector	Existing supplier fees, with some subsidies	Mainly low, a few high, very varied

Note: SFS: Small Firms Service; PBA: personal business advisor; RDA: Regional Development Agency

consultants replaced counsellors (who were largely voluntary secondees). There was a particularly strong focus on consultancy for SME internal staff development, managerial learning, and support for design and technological innovation. A key feature of the Enterprise Initiative was nationwide marketing and high-profile brand development.

The system was restructured from 1993 to become Business Link. This had three fundamental differences from the Bolton design. First, rather than having centralised management, it was decentralised to local partner bodies; second, the emphasis on intensity was reversed – high-intensity services were prioritised over basic information and referral; and thirdly, rather than responding to client demand raised by high-profile marketing, there were targets set to offer SMEs intensive support and 'sell' government advice services. The local delivery points were composed (in England) of 85 'hub' offices with over 200 'satellites' offices that sought to integrate a wide range of central government small business advice and other support services. Two SME groups were targeted: (i) 10–200 employee firms 'with growth potential', where intensive consultancy services were offered through a new group of employees called 'personal business advisors' (PBAs); and (ii) all other SMEs were offered a general support system for basic information through referrals and low-intensity services. There was no major effort at national marketing or brand development.

During 1999–2001 the Business Link system was restructured. This reduced the number of local delivery points to 45, giving a little more attention to general support services and referrals over internal PBAs, whilst the Scottish and Welsh devolved governments adopted a different mix of services after 2001. Over 2005–2007 management of Business Link was again changed, with policy management passed to English Regional Development Agencies (RDAs). This led to a variety of systems and intensities of services between regions. With the abolition of RDAs in England (which occurred over 2011–2012) the responsibility for local support to SMEs was passed to Local Enterprise Partnerships (LEPs) (HM Government 2010). LEPs are bottom-up partnerships formed between business leaders (usually including chambers of commerce) and public partners; they have the purpose of bidding for public funds and developing a strategy for their areas. Significantly this change has removed almost all funding from local SME supports and centralised it into a single web-based toolkit.

Expectations

The experience of the varied British Government advice schemes offers an opportunity to assess different approaches. The starting point of this discussion is expectations. Ideal and normative performance, which define what performance should be, were used as the main targets for Business Link development (DTI 1996, 2003), as they fitted readily into the Government's general approach to centralised targets. Early targets included volume (of market penetration), responsiveness, accuracy, appropriateness, professionalism, repeat business and impact, but also incentivised PBAs to raise fees from clients (DTI 1996: 52). Later targets were narrowed by DTI (2003) to measure the contribution of advice to improving productivity and competitiveness, and increasing employment, with some fee incentives retained, as well as a wide range of policy targets to increase workforce skills, contribute to social inclusion and other political objectives.

There was never any development by Business Link of methods to assess client expectations based on derived experience. This is the normal means by which SMEs themselves make judgements about services: based on costs, endorsements, recommendations and prior experiences with similar or related suppliers (Bateson and Wirtz 1991, Priest 1998). Two large-scale evaluations were made of business expectations about Business Link: one by Priest (1998, 1999) and the other by Bennett (2007). Expectations-based approaches were recommended by Ci Research (2002), but were never been taken up by Government. A central conclusion of these evaluations for early stages of Business Link was that actual performance was the main means used by SMEs to assess whether expectations were met, reflecting a lack of prior knowledge and expectation about government services, with 'only limited evidence of the relevance of some of the DTI client-focused quality dimensions of promoting the "brand". Customers do not have a strong perception of using the ... services ... as a quality assured service' (Priest 1998: 442). Nor was 'the core feature of PBAs providing the effective link to a range of services' (Priest 1998: 97).

For the later period, when Business Link was more fully developed, Bennett (2007: Tables 1–4) confirmed these findings. Most SMEs had multiple expectations (about 60 per cent of cases), with a wide and somewhat conflicting range: from technically specific, such as wanting a particular service or response to a particular query, through to general advice and very broad-ranging business information needs. However, the main expectations were to receive a detached view and technical input, with the government advisor sought as a sounding board rather than offering final service delivery. In addition, there was an important secondary expectation by nearly one-fifth of users that Business Link would provide or broker grants or other financial assistance. Overall about 75 per cent of services fully or partially met expectations, but the mean for *fully* meeting expectations was only 40 per cent. Performance was best for narrow and focused services where quality was properly assured, but wider offers frequently disappointed, especially *internal* referral to PBAs and other advisors.

One crucial finding was that only 3 per cent of Business Link users had any expectation of being referred to other sources of advice. Business Link was marketed as a hub from which other providers could be accessed, but in practice it primarily sought to retain clients (Bennett 2007, see also Tann and Laforet 1998, Mole, Hart, Roper and Saal 2008, Bennett and Robson 2004). This undermined its quality, since some services were provided with little expertise. Much of the difficulty focused on the role of the PBAs, who acted as the gatekeepers of the system as well as the actual advisors. Several studies of PBAs questioned their quality, and found that most were targeting clients to meet government objectives (including fee levels that had to be achieved) rather than actual needs: only 22 per cent of PBAs selected clients on the basis of need (amongst multiple criteria: Sear and Agar 1996). This was also found in government surveys, such as those by MORI, and resulted in a parliamentary committee recommending a complete redefinition of the role of PBAs, reducing bureaucracy and improving referrals to partners (House of Commons 1996). Underlying these difficulties was mis-selling: 'raising expectations about the availability of grants and start-up finance, for which small businesses often found themselves ineligible' (Thomas, Rajkumar and Chadwick 2004: 15). Moreover, the targets set by Government for evaluation did not reflect SME client views. The main Treasury targets of increasing employment, profits, turnover and productivity, did not match SME expectations which mainly sought intermediate objectives (such as improving management knowledge and skills) (Bennett 2007).

As a result of these failures, there were various attempts to re-focus Business Link to better manage expectations and improve its brokerage. The brokerage model has a number of potential advantages for SME support services (Mole 2002: Chapter 5). Brokers act to facilitate markets by using know-how to signpost contacts, build relationships and help to manage expectations, which encouraged greater clarity of what is on offer and monitoring that it is delivered effectively. However, by the time Business Link was re-launched in this way many opportunities had already been lost. Mole (2002: 43) identified a number of dilemmas: first, there remained confusion and scepticism about impartiality when it offered its own services as well as signposting the services of others; and second, brokerage was not a simple add-on: 'it offers a way to work with the market for business support and keeps Business Links from mushrooming … (but) it does require difficult issues of market and knowledge managing to be solved' (Mole 2002: 44). Hence, Business Link was difficult to improve unless the advisor structure itself was radically reformed.

Use, Satisfaction, Impact and Cost-effectiveness

Taking an overview of British developments, shown in Table 13.2, the early period of SME schemes had limited ambitions and achieved a relatively low level of market penetration; about 8 per cent of SMEs used the SFS. However, the more ambitious centralised scheme of the Enterprise Initiative, and the subsequent development of decentralised schemes focused on Business Link and regional bodies, lifted the market penetration to 38–49 per cent of SMEs (and this against a background of a steadily rising number of SMEs in the economy as a whole). However, the satisfaction levels achieved from the decentralised form of the service generally fell. The overall satisfaction levels achieved over 1973–1993 were almost comparable to market-based services. However, decentralisation over 1993–2007 led to falls in satisfaction. The satisfaction levels were remarkably consistent through each phase of Business

Table 13.2   Market penetration and satisfaction from different advice and consultancy schemes in Britain, 1973–2010

Main Schemes	Period	Use (% of SME population)	Satisfaction (%)
Small Firms Service (SFS) and Business Development Service	1973–1988	8	95
SFS and Enterprise Initiative*	1988–1993	38	95
Business Link hubs and satellites*	1993–2001	49	79
Business Link partnerships*	2001–2005	44	79
RDAs and Business Link*	2005–2010	45	79

Source: quoted in Bennett, 2007, 2008.

* Includes Business Link and all other government schemes.

Link re-design, although this disguises fluctuations. But most importantly, satisfaction never reached that achieved under the centralised service of the SFS or Enterprise Initiative. For most commentators, including government ministers, the primary drawback of the decentralised system after 1993 was the considerable *variability* of the system. This has generally been attributed to the different quality of the local outlets, but was chiefly due to the very wide range of quality among individual advisors. Client evaluations ranged from eulogies from highly satisfied customers, to highly dissatisfied experiences that focused on 'waste of company time' and 'lost us business' to 'low expectations – they have grants they want to push regardless of results', and 'no relevant knowledge' or 'self-serving extortionists' (quoted in Ramsden and Bennett 2005, Bennett, 2007). Other concerns about the decentralised system were, first, the greatly increased costs, and second, the effects of using different management models.

The estimated costs of the decentralised schemes after 1993 were about 10–12 times higher than the centralised ones before 1993. The total expenditure was estimated at £12bn across Britain in 2006 (Richard 2008), with about 34 per cent of this funding spent on administration within the complex set of agencies involved. Inefficiencies also arose from fragmentation into about 3,000 different programmes (DTI 2007, Richard 2008), each with its own funding 'silo' and targets. Decentralisation was also enormously complex, with different business support strategies operated in each English region, Scotland, Wales and Northern Ireland. Various assessments in England referred to a 'patchwork quilt', 'chaos', 'labyrinth of initiatives' or 'muddle' (Audit Commission 1999, Treasury 2002, DTI, 2007).

Four different management models were used for Business Link schemes in different local areas:

- through independent operators dedicated to the Government's objectives as their only line of business;
- through pre-existing enterprise agencies, local government and related partner bodies;
- through chambers of commerce; and
- through a private company.

The desired model for Government policy was the use of independent operators, where it was thought that a lack of conflicts of interest would lead to superior performance. However, several evaluations found independent operators to be the least effective means of delivery, largely because they had no other expertise or synergies of advice services to draw on, they needed to hold on to clients to survive, and hence were reluctant to make referrals. The most effective local outlets (in terms of use, impact and satisfaction) were operated by local chambers of commerce and the private company (A4E) involved. This was because both offered synergies with their existing services. In the case of chambers this was with their exports and other advice services, general information bureaus and networking; in the case of A4E there were synergies with their training business. Services linked to enterprise agencies and other partners were intermediate in effectiveness, but highly variable in quality (Bennett and Robson 2004).

Chambers of commerce and similar market providers were effective because they offered economies of scale and scope (Bratton, Bennett and Robson 2003: Figures 1 and 2). Chambers of commerce in Britain are voluntary, private law bodies (in contrast to much of Europe), that only exist because of business member demands. Where such bodies have other market-based business services there are synergies and advantages of 'bundling'. This results in reduced transaction costs, and is reflected in *lower costs per unit* as scale of use increases. For government-based advice services the more bureaucratic regimes of delivery and limited business synergies usually result in higher unit costs. Mixed models for Business Link provision, using both independent and market-based suppliers, was thus bound to lead to variable quality, brand identity and sustainability. Use of entirely market-based suppliers would have resulted in significant increases in quality overall and reduced variability.

The Bratton et al. study (2003) also confirmed the expectation, going back to the Bolton Report, that there is only a limited market gap for intensive government-backed advice. If a service is attempted at a level of intensity beyond that level, then the effectiveness declines. Hence, it appears that Business Link was a service that was expanded beyond its scale of usefulness for many clients, which meant that even for partner bodies such as chambers there were diminishing returns to scale in terms of impact achieved, and for the whole system there were massive inefficiencies and lack of value for money. Similarly, Mole et al. (2008) found that the intensive brokerage model ('pipeline forcing') used by Business Link, whilst capable of achieving high impacts, was only successful when focused on a very narrow category of SMEs (chiefly high-growth SMEs). Hence, high overall costs were usually wasted in much deadweight and searching for the 'right' clients – although, for the right firms, the benefits could be considerable.

Fees for Government Advice

The use of fees for receiving advice from government schemes was a specific target for British schemes after the 1993 decentralisation. Over the preceding period a distinction was drawn between free information and advice at low intensity (as well as using referral), and the marketing of consultants from the general market of suppliers for which subsidies were offered. This latter approach has tended to return since 2010, but with variation between areas depending upon the level of other government supports available (through regeneration initiatives, EU structural and social funds, and other sources). However, between 1993 and 2010 the core objective of the system was a fee-based and intensive government advice service chiefly delivered through PBAs.

The motives behind using fees were partly to help finance the system; but there was also a belief that clients would perceive better value for what they paid for (DTI 1997). The chair of the group overseeing Business Links stated that: 'Charging is about credibility, demonstrating value and setting the right culture … small companies value much more those services for which they are paying' (Grayson 1996: 133). DTI (1999: 20) stated that 'Charging for value-added service remains an important principle … [with contractors] expected to have an effective charging policy … including the current broad assumption of 25 per cent of income from customers.' However, a significant body of criticism suggested that fees can distort SME behaviour, acknowledged by SBS (2001: 14) noting that 'charging … has been a contentious issue, as it can distort priorities'.

The only detailed evaluation of the impact on clients from 'fee regimes', by Robson and Bennett (2010), indicates the strengths and pitfalls of the policy. The most critical finding was that there was no significant relationship of the use of fees with either impact or satisfaction, once service type was controlled for (because service type is interrelated with service intensity, and hence the scope to charge a fee). Hence, there were no grounds for arguing that clients more strongly valued Business Link services that were charged for. Rather, Business Link often achieved most where it offered least: providing information with minimal or no fees (Robson and Bennett 2010: Tables 3 and 4).

Conclusion

This chapter has sought to assess how government advice services to small firms are best organised and delivered. The different experiments with modes of delivery in Britain suggest that the SFS model (to provide large-scale non-intensive information, advice and referral) was highly successful. When combined with a large-scale offer of subsidised consultancy through the Enterprise Initiative, and widespread marketing, brand development and accreditation of market-based consultants, this approach offered the best outcome achieved for SME advice in Britain. There was a high level of market penetration and levels of satisfaction approaching market suppliers. However, when the model was decentralised, quality levels became highly variable and satisfaction levels plummeted. Even after considerable improvements, small firm satisfaction never matched the earlier SFS and Enterprise Initiative models. On the positive side, market penetration was increased by decentralisation, from about 38 per cent to 45–49 per cent; that is, by an increment of between one-fifth and one-quarter. But this occurred at costs levels that were about ten times greater.

The lessons offered by the British experience, for those seeking to develop SME advisory services, are sixfold. First, centralised structures for government provision, covering a whole country, with simple and single branding, offer superior management of expectations, simpler means of quality control and much lower costs of provision. Second, a strong differentiation between intensive and non-intensive services is beneficial (as occurred between the SFS and Enterprise Initiative). Clients can clearly see different routes to satisfy their specific needs, develop appropriate expectations, and the management and monitoring of each type of service can be appropriately tailored. Third, efforts to target intensive advice through tailored PBAs or 'pipeline forcing', as well as inevitably having high costs, are bound to carry significant deadweight and raise expectations that cannot be met in many cases. Fourth, in-house provision of intensive government support is bound to produce a higher cost per unit outcome, and have more highly varied outcomes, than use of market suppliers, resulting in average satisfaction levels that are low. Fifth, lower costs and higher satisfaction levels are achieved by utilising the synergies from 'bundling' of service provision with market suppliers and not-for-profits such as chambers of commerce. Sixth, whilst fee income offers some scope to mitigate government costs, fee targets distort the behaviour of both manager and advisor, and limits effectiveness.

References

Audit Commission 1999. *A Life's Work: Local Authorities, Economic Development and Economic Regeneration*. London: Audit Commission.

Bannock, G. 2005. *The Economics and Management of Small Business: An International Perspective*. London: Routledge.

Bateson, J.E.G. and Wirtz, J. 1991. *Modelling Consumer Satisfaction: A Review*, Working Paper 99. London: London Business School.

Bennett, R.J. 2007. Expectations-based evaluation of SME advice and consultancy: an example of Business Link services. *Journal of Small Business and Enterprise Development*, 14, 435–457.

Bennett, R.J. 2008. Government SME policy since the 1990s: what have we learnt? *Environment and Planning C: Government and Policy*, 26(3), 375–397.

Bennett, R.J. 2012. Government and Small Businesses in *Enterprise and Small Business*, edited by S. Carter and D. Jones-Evans, 3rd edition. London: FT Pitman, Chapter 5.

Bennett, R.J. and Robson, P.J.A. 2004. Support services to SMEs: does the 'franchisee' make a difference to the Business Link Offer? *Environment and Planning C: Government & Policy*, 22(6), 859–880.

Bennett, R.J. and Smith, C. 2004. The selection and control of management consultants by small business clients. *International Small Business Journal*, 22(5), 435–462.

Bolton, J.E. 1971. *Small Firms: Report of the Committee of Inquiry on Small Firms*, Cmnd 4811. London: HMSO.

Bratton, W.J., Bennett, R.J. and Robson, P.J.A. 2003. Critical mass and economies of scale in the supply of services by business support organisations. *Journal of Services Industry Management*, 17(3), 730–752.

Ci Research 2002. *Development of a Model for Measuring the SBS Client Experience: Final Report*. London: Ci Research Market Intelligence, for Small Business Service.

Davies, P.A., Dowling, G.R. and Patterson, P.G. 1992. Criteria used to select management consultants. *Industrial Marketing Management*, 21(1), 187–193.

Department of Trade and Industry 1996. *Business Link Accreditation Booklet*. London: Department of Trade and Industry.

Department of Trade and Industry 1997. *Business Link Service Guide*. London: Department of Trade and Industry.

Department of Trade and Industry 1999. *Guidance for Proposals to Deliver Local Services*. London: Department of Trade and Industry.

Department of Trade and Industry 2003. *DTI: The Strategy*. London: Department of Trade and Industry.

Department of Trade and Industry 2007. *Simplifying Business Support: A Consultation*. London: Department of Trade and Industry.

European Commission 2003. *Green Paper: Entrepreneurship in Europe*. Brussels: European Commission, COM (2003) 27.

European Commission 2008. Small Business Act. Brussels: European Commission. [Online] Available at: www.europa.eu/legislation.

Grayson, D. 1996. Building a network for business co-operation. *Financial Times*, 9 December. Reprinted in Mastering Enterprise, edited by S. Birley and D. F. Muzylea. London: F.T. Pitman, 131–135.

House of Commons, United Kingdom 1996. *Trade and Industry Committee 5th Report*, Business Links. 3 Vols, HC302. London: HMSO.

HM Government 2010. *Local Growth: Realising Every Place's Potential*, Cm 7961. London: The Stationery Office.

HM Treasury 2002. *Cross Cutting Review of Services to Small Businesses*. London: HM Treasury.

Mole, K. 2002. *International Review of Business Support and Brokerage: A Report for the Small Business Service*. [Online] Available at: www.sbs.gov.uk.

Mole, K., Hart, M., Roper, S. and Saal, D. 2008. Differential gains from Business Link support and advice: a treatment effect approach. *Environment and Planning C: Government and Policy*, 26(3), 315–334.

Organisation for Economic Co-operation and Development (OECD) 1995. *Best Practice Policies from Small and Medium Sized Enterprises*. Paris: Organisation for Economic Co-operation and Development.

Priest, S.J. 1998. *Stimulating the Performance of SMEs through Business Link: An Assessment of Customer Satisfaction and Dissatisfaction and Policy Implication*. Unpublished PhD. Cambridge: University of Cambridge.

Priest, S.J. 1999. Business Link services to small and medium-sized enterprises: targeting, innovation and charging. *Environment and Planning C: Government and Policy*, 17(2), 177–194.

Ramsden, M. and Bennett, R.J. 2005. The benefit of external supports to SMEs: 'hard' versus 'soft' outcomes and satisfaction levels. *Journal of Small Business and Enterprise Development*, 12(2), 227–243.

Richard, D. 2008. *Small Business and Government*. The Richard report: Submission to shadow cabinet. London: Conservative Central Office.

Robson, P.J.A. and Bennett, R.J. 2010. Paying fees for government business advice: an assessment of Business Link experience. *Applied Economics*, 42(1), 37–48.

Small Business Service (SBS) 2001. *SBS Strategy 2001/04: Making the UK the Best Place in the World to Start and Grow a Business, Small Business Service*. London: Department of Trade and Industry.

Sear, L. and Agar, J. 1996. *A Survey of Business Link and Personal Advisers: Are They Meeting Expectations?* Durham: Durham University, Small Business Centre.

Tann, J. and Laforet, S. 1998. Assessing consultant quality for SMEs – the role of Business Links. *Journal of Small Business and Enterprise Development*, 5(1), 7–18.

Thomas, A., Rajkumar, R., and Chadwick, M. 2004. *Small Business Experience of Using Government Services: Case Study Results*. Proceedings of ISBA Conference (Newcastle Gatehead).

14

Enterprise Agencies: An English Model of Small Business Advice and Support

Andrew Maville

Chapter Summary

The Local Enterprise Agency (LEA) model of business support has operated in England for over 30 years. In that time, it has offered solutions to policy problems posed in widely differing economic and political climates. This chapter explores the longevity of the model and draws out transferable lessons from the experience. At the core of the model's ethos is the intention to positively affect local economies by working with individuals, offering them a flexible, responsive service based around face-to-face business advice from experienced advisers. Clients of an LEA are enabled to explore the possibilities of self-employment and obtain information, advice and guidance, often together with access to finance and premises, to help them move towards starting a business. Crucially, it is also seen as a positive outcome if the client decides that starting a business is not appropriate for them at that time.

As the chapter reviews how small business support has been implemented in government policy over time, the effect on LEAs is considered. The changing political and economic environment within which LEAs operate takes in the range from self-employment as a route out of unemployment, through to the concept of the enterprise journey, and back again. The external stresses placed on LEAs have stimulated flexible responses, not least in the way that surviving LEAs have found income to enable them to maintain their services. Parallel examples of enterprise support agencies in Australia and Uganda are outlined for comparison.

Introduction

This chapter aims to explore the development and delivery of the LEA model of business support, setting it within the context of a changing economic and political environment over a 30-year period. The intention is to provide the reader with insight into what LEAs do, how external factors affect them and how they handle change. As the development of local enterprise support has followed alternate paths in different parts of the UK, this chapter focuses on the picture in England.

Local Enterprise Agencies

At its simplest, an LEA is an organisation delivering free information, advice and guidance to pre-start and start-up small business clients. The UK definition for an 'approved' LEA, evaluated and recognised as fulfilling that role, is: an organisation recognised by the Government for having as a primary objective 'the promotion or encouragement of industrial and commercial activity or enterprise in a particular area in the United Kingdom with particular reference to encouraging the formation and development of small businesses' (Finance Act 1982: s48).

LEAs are not just providers of pre-start business advice, although that is an important part of their work. Grayson and Irwin (2001), significant players in forming and developing the LEA movement, describe a process of enthusing and educating people to think about enterprise; to understand that they need to learn; and to learn how to learn. LEAs have helped pilot many of the main types of training intervention aimed at businesses in their various stages of development (for example, Johnstone, Hayton, Macfarlane and Moore 1988, Maville, Nelson and Atterton 1993), with some, like The Tyneside Economic Development Company Ltd (TEDCO), going beyond the core provision of information, advice and guidance to deliver targeted services around ideas, motivation, knowledge gaps, personal barriers, coaching, mentoring and advice.

A 'typical' Enterprise Agency is a not-for-profit company limited by guarantee; it has a management team who report to a board of directors. This legal form suits their nature and purpose, enabling the management to retain profits within the organisation and to attract finance, sponsorship and involvement in governance from a broad range of private and public-sector bodies. It is not unusual to see management boards that include voluntary members from local government, big businesses, small businesses, the clergy, academics, lawyers and accountants. In return, the LEA will provide a range of services geared towards promoting self-employment and the formation of new businesses, taking local needs and circumstances into account. The staff of an LEA can be employees; secondees from banks, big businesses or government departments; self-employed sub-contractors; volunteers; or any mixture of these.

Importantly, LEAs are flexible in being able to tailor support to circumstances. Looking at national policy, Derbyshire (2009) noted that business support programmes designed in boom times are not always appropriate in a recession, when there is a rise in 'necessity' entrepreneurs whose needs are different. With experience of developing and running support programmes in the recession of the 1980s as well as during the following two decades, LEAs have amassed a cumulative wealth of knowledge of what works. Concerns have been raised that government policy can easily disperse such accumulated professional expertise (Cobweb Information Ltd 2010). The distinction needs to be understood, at policy level, between business support for established businesses and the practical support required by people starting new businesses. Whilst LEAs have been involved in both areas, pre-start and early stage support are their natural field of expertise; Bennett (1995) noted that in the 1980s around 80 per cent of the firms LEAs worked with were pre-start and start-up ventures, and over 50 per cent of LEA clients were previously unemployed.

History

Probably the first organisations in England to appear as business support agencies in this mould were in 1976 in Bridgewater, Somerset and St Helen's, Merseyside. They were a local response to the closure of major employers. In St Helen's' case, the local Trust was established by Pilkington, a firm that was closing its plant (National Federation of Enterprise Agencies 2006: 22–29). Responding to inner-city issues, London Enterprise Agency was established in 1978 as an independent project by the London Chamber of Commerce, supported by a consortium of major businesses and banks (Hansard 1981). The government of the day recognised these early LEAs' contributions towards tackling a range of social and economic problems, largely brought about by increasing unemployment but differing in nature because of varied regional and local circumstances. To encourage the creation of more private sector-led LEAs across the country, tax breaks were introduced by legislation (Finance Act 1982: s48), alongside a process for gaining government approval. By November 1982 there were 83 approved LEAs and by December 1985, 308 approved LEAs had been established (Hansard 1982, 1985).

The organisation Business in the Community (BiTC), which was founded in 1982 and now specialises in promoting corporate social responsibility, played a significant part in brokering sponsorship arrangements for many of the new LEAs and used its network of high-level contacts, including the Prince of Wales, to encourage their board members, staff and sponsors. BiTC also looked for ways to promote the spread of best practice and the setting of professional standards for business advisers. By 1993, BiTC had other priorities and handed over its role in promoting the interests of LEAs and their clients to the newly formed National Federation of Enterprise Agencies (NFEA) (rebranded in 2011 as the National Enterprise Network), which also managed the LEA approval process on behalf of government. In the same year, Business Link came into being in England as part of a government push to offer consistent, one-stop access to small business support across the country. The intention was for Business Links to be partnerships of LEAs, Chambers of Commerce (which have voluntary membership in the UK), Local Authority Economic Development Units (there was then a statutory requirement for all Local Authorities to have an EDU) and the Training and Enterprise Councils (TECs). TECs were local bodies established to oversee delivery of publicly funded training schemes and enterprise support programmes.

The introduction of TECs and then Business Links reflected a change in Government approach, moving from centralised to decentralised control of business support policy implementation (Bennett and Robson 2001). Prior to this, Government had catered for business support through the Small Firms Information Service (from 1971), which then changed in 1977 to the Small Firms Counselling Service in recognition that information without advice was insufficient. By 1979, the service was being referred to as the Small Firms Service; it was part of the Government's Department of Trade and Industry, reflecting the focus on supporting existing businesses and increasing belief in the importance of SMEs to the national economy. This differentiated it from the employment generating pre-start programmes supported by the Employment Department.

The relationship between LEAs and Business Links was complicated by the fact that LEAs were obvious candidates to provide contracted services to Business Links for the delivery of enterprise support, but Business Links also had a remit to earn income from some of their services. On top of this, Business Links were accountable for their use of public funds and came under pressure to be seen to put their contracts out to open tender. Nevertheless, many LEAs were assessed as best value contractors to deliver pre-start and start-up services for Business Links, even though in some areas LEAs were obliged to form consortia to tender, adding a management layer to the costs.

The original Business Link arrangement was sub-regional, but after 2005, the Business Link network was managed by the Regional Development

Agencies and reorganised into larger organisations with regional remits. As significant numbers of LEA business advisers were employed specifically to deliver Business Link contracts with responsibilities the new Business Links were taking on themselves, many LEA staff transferred to Business Link jobs under protection of employment legislation. Subsequently, a 'brokerage model' was adopted whereby Business Link staff would act as brokers, pointing clients to specialist service providers whose services would be wholly or partly funded from available grants. This worked well for existing businesses and was effective for pre-start businesses with complex needs (for example, technology research spin-outs) but the brokerage of general pre-start support had flaws. The approach made an assumption that LEAs had an independent income stream that would keep them trading and enable them to take clients as and when they were referred. In reality, however, pre-start clients were sometimes assisted in-house by Business Link advisers and they could also be referred to any private-sector provider on the Business Link register who had indicated their ability to produce business plans for clients. Most surviving LEAs had alternative income streams – some for their core pre-start activity, but others had diversified, often using fee-earned income to cover losses on business support services.

As Business Links took over provision for existing businesses and they or other agencies received funding to support start-ups with higher growth potential, LEA activity was reduced and overheads (especially administration and audit) became proportionally higher. With pre-start service funding open to private-sector competition, LEAs were forced to compete for a share of an ever smaller pot of business support funding. To survive, LEAs had to take a commercial stance and look further afield for fee-earning income. The strain was greater because most LEAs were operating frugally, playing on goodwill and social conscience to make things happen, yet were rightly having to demonstrate ever higher standards of service, which added to overhead costs.

From a free-market perspective it appeared that LEAs were no longer needed because private-sector firms were taking up the challenge. This view proved illusory when grant funding criteria tightened as the value-for-money of pre-start brokered support was evaluated. Many private firms no longer found the revised revenue stream attractive.

Following mergers, closures and changes of role, by March 2011 there were 77 approved LEAs remaining in England (National Federation of Enterprise Agencies 2011). These survivors face major uncertainties from a combination of local and national government spending cuts together with the effects of restructuring. Regional Business Link services and the RDAs that control them cease operation in 2011/12. It appears that current government policy favours a return to centralised, remotely accessed information provision from the public sector, combined with voluntary mentoring by the private sector. Interestingly, Mark Prisk, the Government Minister for Business and Enterprise has said, '...Enterprise Agencies have a vital role. That's why I don't believe that government running competing Business Links helps good private and third sector providers' (The Guardian 2011). Along with LEAs, other ideas being proposed as good for the economy in February 2011, like improving small firms' access to public-sector tendering opportunities or making sure that enterprise development activity is responsive to local situations, were also being similarly discussed in Parliament in the early 1980s (Hansard 1981, 1982). Institutional memory is not a Government strong point; the average tenure of Ministers for small business is around 18 months, making advocacy about the role of LEAs an important consideration. However, central funding for LEAs is unlikely to return and local government funds may be called upon. It is proposed that local government will be allowed to retain local business rate revenue, instead of remitting it to central government, and that each local authority will have the option to use these funds to support businesses in their area or to cover other priorities (Department for Communities and Local Government 2011).

Funding

Many LEAs were created by like-minded individuals who came together through their mutual interests in tackling severe economic deprivation and helping others to achieve their own potential through self-employment (Grayson and Irwin 2001). They typically started on minimal budgets, seeking initial funding through corporate donations and in-kind sponsorships such as providing premises or seconding personnel; indeed, most of the staff in early LEAs were secondees from industry, often part of an outplacement programme being run by a restructuring employer (National Federation of Enterprise Agencies 2006: 22–29).

The model of funding based on private-sector sponsorship was effective where large corporations could be persuaded to be involved and the Government tried to encourage this with the 1982 tax changes. At the same time, the restructuring and de-nationalising of the coal and steel industries provided funding to offset the economic impact in their core areas. Some modest 'pump-priming' funding was made available by Government to help establish 78 LEAs (Hansard 1986); however, some agencies struggled to obtain all the funding they needed. In 1986 the Government introduced the Local Enterprise Agencies Grant Scheme (LEAGS) to offer grant assistance towards core costs for smaller LEAs, decreasing over five years, on the condition that private-sector funds could be found by each agency to match the value of the grant they received (Hansard 1988).

Further funding became available in 1988 with the Local Enterprise Agencies Project Scheme (LEAPS) providing matched funds for special projects targeting inner-city regeneration. The availability of additional funding encouraged LEAs to take on more work in line with Government policy on employment and economic development, but the effect noted by Bennett and McCoshan (1993) was that by 1988 LEAs were obtaining the bulk of their funding from public-sector sources (18 per cent from local government and 45 per cent from central government). Bennett (1995) went on to point out that these public funds were leveraging in significant value from the private sector, consisting of not just money, but also the in-kind support of free services and provision of secondees.

In 1988, LEAs were called upon to bring their expertise in supporting new businesses to the delivery of the Enterprise Allowance scheme that was introduced by the Government to encourage jobless people into self-employment. The approach was considered effective and by 1990 over 540,000 people had started businesses under the scheme, at an average net cost to the Government of £1,900 per person (Hansard 1990a, 1990b). However, from 1991, subsequent contracts to supply self-employment services for the unemployed (such as the Business Start-up Scheme) were awarded to single organisations for large geographical areas. The effect of this was to attract funding away from the established local delivery provided by LEAs, impairing their financial sustainability. This coincided with reduced availability of secondees. Whilst some LEAs took on paid directors and looked for alternative income streams, others closed (National Federation of Enterprise Agencies 2006: 22–29).

By 1992, LEAGS and LEAPS funding had ceased. A radical shake up of employment and enterprise programme delivery in the late 1980s had produced new public-sector bodies with sub-regional remits; these were called Training and Enterprise Councils (TECs) in England and Wales. The nature of the funding relationship had changed; grants and project funding from government departments was replaced by contracts with TECs for the delivery of their programmes. In fairness, some LEAs had already been delivering Enterprise Allowance and other schemes on a contractual basis since 1988. Bennett (1995) noted that this change reflected the successful promotion by BiTC of LEAs as the ideal solution to TECs' need for suppliers of enterprise services.

Since then, many LEAs have looked to diversify their coverage and revenue generating activities to survive and thrive. The list of such activities has included consultancy (in many forms), business workspace portfolios, fund management, publishing, supporting third sector organisations and business incubation.

National and regional policymakers talk about responding to local need and simplifying business support. These are not mutually exclusive, despite many demonstrations to the contrary, but funding regimes imposed from above usually promote fragmentation as key projects are designed to meet funders' criteria and organisations design separate projects to fill gaps in provision. Repeated personnel changes and discontinuity in commissioning have left the role and expertise of LEAs poorly understood and solutions reinvented. For example, as approved delivery agencies, LEAs obtained a block exemption from *de minimis* restrictions on the amount of European Union (EU) state aid an organisation could receive; this was crucial in sustaining intervention levels, but no longer applies systematically.

Examples in England

To demonstrate the flexibility of the LEA model, it is useful to look at some examples that are currently operating.

Business Insight is based around Birmingham's business library service. It was founded in 1919 as the Birmingham Commercial, Technical and Patent Library, a business support service helping people build up the post-First World War economy by providing free business information services. It merged with Birmingham Central Library in 1973 whilst remaining part of the national network of business reference libraries. The rebranded Business Insight, established as a not-for-profit, Community Interest Company, gained Enterprise Agency status in 2006 and provides a range of information, advice and guidance services around enterprise, creativity and innovation, and learning (Laird 2009).

Project North East (PNE) was launched in Newcastle upon Tyne in 1980 at a time of rising unemployment as traditional industries declined. Its two individual founders, David Irwin and David Grayson, wanted to encourage people to consider working for themselves by giving them access to the information, advice and finance they needed. Starting with a board chaired by an industrial chaplain, Canon Peter Dodd, PNE was heavily involved in piloting self-employment initiatives, including early examples of specialist centres for information technology and youth enterprise, and operating its own start-up loan fund (Project North East 2011). Promoting good practice for advisers, PNE produced training videos and written materials for use by other agencies. Its specialist information arm, publishing materials for small businesses and their advisers, became a new business, Cobweb Information Ltd, in 1997 and is now independent. As well as advising pre-start clients, running several incubator/workspace units and managing the Shell Livewire youth enterprise programme, PNE has positioned itself as an innovator in supporting third-sector organisations.

TEDCO was established in South Tyneside in 1984 by private-sector business Reyrolle in close cooperation with the local council; its constitution originally required a Council member to chair the board. TEDCO operates pre-start advisory services and has developed award-winning business incubators and workspaces in South Tyneside and Northumberland. In North Tyneside, it currently (August 2011) delivers a full programme of enterprise promotion, ideas generation, enterprise coaching, workshops on business topics and one-to-one start-up advice under contract to the local council, as well as delivering pre-start workshops on behalf of Business Link. TEDCO also provides pre-start advice for students under contract to a local university.

Overseas Parallels

Variations on the LEA model can be found around the world. Two examples reflecting adaptation to markedly different economic and geographical conditions come from Australia, which exemplifies joined-up policy, and Uganda, which demonstrates independent intervention from outside the state.

The Australian version of an LEA is the Business Enterprise Centre (BEC). The local BECs resemble LEAs, and BEC Australia carries out a similar networking and promotional role to that of NFEA. In many respects, the BEC network in Australia is like a mixture of the UK Government's Business Link, the NFEA and LEAs, but whereas Business Links were imposed upon and became both customers and competitors to the existing network of LEAs, Australia's Government has sought to work with the BEC network in a more cohesive, lighter touch approach, centralising nationally applicable information resources and contributing only some of the funding needed to keep the BECs going. Funding comes from a range of sources: delivering business services under contract to national, state and local government; in-kind support from local government; and private-sector sponsorship. BEC income streams include training programmes, events and fee-based activities, and, in some cases, membership fees. Although BEC Australia resembles the UK's NFEA, BEC Australia is used as a national brand for local business support and clients are signposted to the BECs for support by government (business.gov.au 2011). This joined-up relationship favours the ongoing existence of the BECs. An example BEC is Hunter Business Centre (HBC) in Newcastle, New South Wales. It is a not-for-profit organisation, owned and supported by the local community and funded by the state and Commonwealth governments (Hunter Business Centre

2011). Its governance is through a board of directors. HBC has been running for over 20 years, operating incubator office space and providing training, information and advice to its clients.

Uganda Gatsby Trust (UGT) also operates like an enterprise agency (Irwin 2011, Uganda Gatsby Trust 2009). Founded in 1994 with initial funding from the UK-based Gatsby Charitable Foundation, UGT tailors its activities to suit its economic environment. UGT focuses on supporting small-scale manufacturing businesses whose activities add value, as opposed to trading businesses. Support measures range from training and counselling, through making workspace or simple production facilities available, to providing businesses with access to university services for developing new products and new ways of working. Access to support is facilitated by a number of Business Clubs spread across Uganda, enabling members to receive business development support and apply for micro-loan funding. Irwin's evaluation suggests that UGT's activities have generated tangible economic benefits.

The Enterprise Agency Ethos

Over 40 years ago, the Bolton Report on the role of small firms in the economy set the tone for policy interventions aimed at encouraging small businesses. Bolton (1971: 83–85) suggested that the few justifications for supporting business activity included establishing a way for 'new entrepreneurial talent' to enter business and providing a 'seedbed' for future large firms. Ever since, UK enterprise activity has had an eye on counting outputs in the form of business starts, particularly where high growth is anticipated. However, the LEA perspective is that outcomes can be more important than outputs. Positive outcomes, for clients and the economy, can include someone not starting; it is not unusual for an LEA client to say, 'Four years ago your support helped me realise I wasn't ready to run a business; I'm ready now.' Bennett and Robson (1999) have pointed out that start-up businesses generate a special demand for advice services. Derbyshire (2009) notes how the 'necessity' entrepreneurs of a recession need a different style of service – personal, local, face-to-face and empathetic, which can be at odds with an output focus.

Although UK enterprise policy may deprecate 'lifestyle businesses', many LEA advisers see them as a valid form of economic activity that should be encouraged as people's positive attempts to make the most of their own potential. To that end, business plans are not treated as a product or output, but are part of the learning process a client goes through. Cobweb Information Ltd (2010) noted that the would-be business owners with the most to gain from a support programme tend to be those least capable of finding and acting upon it independently. Some prospective business owners prefer to seek out support or advice rather than be told that they need it. LEAs understand that homogenous categories of small business owner are hard to define and harder still to target because of their very individual and often localised needs.

Potential Pitfalls

The LEA model is not without problems. They can be established cheaply, but increased sophistication and accountability raises their running costs. Their funding streams are vulnerable to external influences. There are often mismatches between funders' targets or policies and the nature and needs of individual clients. Localised geographical coverage leads to gaps in service. Clients can question the quality and value to themselves of a free service.

There are other possible pitfalls too. Commenting on the LEA role in increasing the private sector's involvement in economic development, Smallbone (1991) considered their links with local authorities and raised concern over the apparent lack of local democratic accountability. Conversely, Bateman (2000), evaluating the impact of business support centre networks on economic development in Central and Eastern Europe, lamented the disappointing results compared to previous local state initiatives. Bateman suggested that private-sector leadership and the push to be financially self-sustaining had emphasised short-term imperatives over longer-term strategies.

Conclusion

This chapter has shown that LEAs represent an adaptable and cost-effective model of business support, but one which is vulnerable to the consequences of changes in public policy and the economic shifts affecting corporate social investment.

The history of LEAs demonstrates that they can work as a useful policy intervention under certain conditions. These are: a joined-up approach across national government to provide coherent policies that encourage self-employment and new business formation; the existence of strong drivers or champions operating at both national and local level to promote LEA establishment and activities; the LEAs' management teams operating in a flexible and innovative way to ascertain clients' needs before developing services; a conducive policy environment that encourages private-sector sponsors to be actively involved in, but not wholly responsible for, service delivery; the opportunity to develop diverse income streams; and a supply of good quality advisers who understand pre-start businesses.

References

Bateman, M. 2000. Neo-liberalism, SME development and the role of business support centres in the transition economies of central and Eastern Europe. *Small Business Economics*, 14(4), 275–298.

Bennett, R.J. 1995. The re-focusing of small business services in enterprise agencies: the influence of TECs and LECs. *International Small Business Journal*, 13(4), 35–55.

Bennett, R.J. and McCoshan, A. 1993. *Enterprise and Human Resource Development: Local Capacity Building*. London: Paul Chapman.

Bennett, R.J. and Robson, P.J.A. 1999. The use of external business advice by SMEs in Britain. *Entrepreneurship & Regional Development*, 11(2), 155–180.

Bennett, R.J. and Robson, P.J.A. 2001. *Changing Use of External Business Advice and Government Supports by SMEs in the 1990s*. Working Paper No. 210, ESRC Centre for Business Research, University of Cambridge.

Bolton, J.E. 1971. *Report of the Committee of Inquiry on Small Firms*. Cmnd 4811, London: HMSO

Business.gov.au 2011. *How can I get advice & support?* [Online] Available at: http://www.business.gov.au/Howtoguides/Thinkingofstartingabusiness/Pages/HowcanIgetadviceandsupport.aspx [accessed: 24 March 2011].

Cobweb Information Ltd 2010. *What UK Small Businesses Don't Need in 2011*. [Online 23 December 2010] Available at: http://www.cobwebinfo.com/site/article_detail/item14430/?link_466=14430 [accessed: 14 March 2011].

Department for Communities and Local Government 2011. *Councils to Lead Local Path to Growth Boosting Jobs and Firms*. [Online 19 August 2011] Available at: http://www.communities.gov.uk/news/localgovernment/1969220 [accessed: 23 August 2011].

Derbyshire, G. 2009. *Business Support in a Recession*. [Online 6 March 2009] Available at: http://www.nfea.com/blog/business-support-in-a-recession.html [accessed: 11 February 2011] NFEA.

Finance Act 1982. (Section 48). [Online] Available at: http://legislation.data.gov.uk/ukpga/1982/39/enacted/data.htm [accessed: 27 February 2011]. London: HMSO.

Grayson, D. and Irwin, D. 2001. *Educating Entrepreneurs*. Lecture given to the RSA, London, 21 November 2001.

The Guardian 2011. *Live Q&A: Small Business Minister Mark Prisk Takes Your Questions*. [Online 16 February 2011] Available at: http://www.guardian.

co.uk/money/blog/2011/feb/12/small-business-minister-mark-prisk [accessed: 25 February 2011].

Hansard 1981. House of Lords Debate 06 May 1981 (vol 420 cc136-86): *New and Smaller Businesses*. [Online] Available at: http://hansard.millbanksystems.com/lords/1981/may/06/new-and-smaller-businesses#S5LV0420P0_19810506_HOL_104 [accessed: 28 February 2011].

Hansard 1982. House of Commons Debate 26 Nov 1982 (vol 32 cc1111-75): *Small Businesses*. [Online] Available at: http://hansard.millbanksystems.com/commons/1982/nov/26/small-businesses#S6CV0032P0_19821126_HOC_65 [accessed: 03 March 2011].

Hansard 1985. House of Commons Debate 03 Dec 1985 (vol 88 cc143-5): *Local Enterprise Agencies*. [Online] Available at: http://hansard.millbanksystems.com/commons/1985/dec/03/local-enterprise-agencies-1#S6CV0088P0_19851203_HOC_54 [accessed: 03 March 2011].

Hansard 1986. House of Commons Debate 18 Feb 1986 (vol 92 c145W): *Local Enterprise Agencies*. [Online] Available at: http://hansard.millbanksystems.com/written_answers/1986/feb/18/local-enterprise-agencies#S6CV0092P0_19860218_CWA_381 [accessed: 15 March 2011].

Hansard 1988. House of Commons Written Answers for 08 Mar 1988 (vol 129 c117w 117w): *Local Enterprise Agency Grant Scheme*. [Online] Available at: http://hansard.millbanksystems.com/written_answers/1988/mar/08/local-enterprise-agency-grant-scheme [accessed: 27 February 2011].

Hansard 1990a. House of Commons Debate 20 November 1990 vol 181 c110W: *Enterprise Allowance Scheme*. [Online] Available at: http://hansard.millbanksystems.com/written_answers/1990/nov/20/enterprise-allowance-scheme#S6CV0181P0_19901120_CWA_297 [accessed: 22 March 2011].

Hansard 1990b. House of Commons Debate 19 February 1990 vol 167 c498W: *Enterprise Allowance Scheme*. [Online] Available at: http://hansard.millbanksystems.com/written_answers/1990/feb/19/enterprise-allowance-scheme#S6CV0167P0_19900219_CWA_143 [accessed: 22 March 2011].

Hunter Business Centre 2011. *Hunter Business Centre: About Us*. [Online] Available at: http://www.businesscentre.com.au/site/index.cfm?display=158223 [accessed: 27 March 2011].

Irwin, D. 2011. Learning from business support in Africa. *Management Research Review*, 34(2), 207–220.

Johnstone, D., Hayton, K., Macfarlane, R. and Moore, C. 1988. *Developing Businesses: Case Studies of Good Practice in Urban Regeneration*. London: Department of the Environment/HMSO.

Laird, D. 2009. *Business Insight: BestForBusiness*. [Online 22 May 2009] Available at: http://web.fumsi.com/go/au/3934 [accessed: 25 February 2011] FUMSI.

Maville, A., Nelson, E. and Atterton, T. 1993. *A Directory of Small Business Management Training Experience in the UK 1970–1990*. London: Department of Trade and Industry.

National Federation of Enterprise Agencies 2006. *The Effective Board*. Bedford: NFEA.

National Federation of Enterprise Agencies 2011. *BIS Approval*. [Online] Available at: http://www.nfea.com/membership/bis-approval.html [accessed: 22 March 2011].

Project North East 2011. *PNE Timeline*. [Online] Available at: http://www.pne.org/about/pne-timeline [accessed: 22 February 2011].

Smallbone, D. 1991. Partnership in economic development: the case of UK local enterprise agencies. *Review of Policy Research*, 10(2-3), 87–98.

Uganda Gatsby Trust 2009. *Who We Are*. [Online] Available at: http://gatsbyuganda.com/index.php?prgm=who-we-are [accessed: 03 February 2011].

15

Social Enterprise Support Policies: Distinctions and Challenges

Fergus Lyon and Leandro Sepulveda[1]

Chapter Summary

This chapter examines the support infrastructure for a specific segment of the SME market, namely social enterprises. The first section briefly examines the different definitions of social enterprise found in different countries. There is a spectrum of types of organisations ranging from commercial enterprises with social objectives, to voluntary or community sector organisations that have an element of trading activity. The second section discusses the rationales for public-sector interest in support, examining how this differs between countries and over time. Particular attention is given to the emergence of social enterprise policies in the UK. The third section examines the different types of support that are commonly provided. This includes: encouraging social entrepreneurship and attitudes to starting a social enterprise; training and advisory services for start-ups and for those wanting to grow or survive; social investment and finance; social enterprises and public-sector procurement; and the transfer of public assets to social enterprise organisations. The final section examines the challenges of evaluating the effectiveness of these policies. Since social enterprises provide a combination of social, environmental and financial objectives, evaluation measures have to address both economic benefits and broader social value.

1   The support of the UK's Economic and Social Research Council (ESRC), the Office of the Civil Society (OCS) and the Barrow Cadbury UK Trust is gratefully acknowledged. The work was part of the programme of the Third Sector Research Centre but all views are those of the authors.

Introduction

Social enterprises are often presented as alternative approaches to delivering benefits to communities, linking both the themes of enterprise and social inclusion (Peattie and Morley 2008, Borzaga and Defourny 2001).This interest has resulted in a wide range of policy measures across the globe aimed at helping those setting up and running social enterprises. This chapter introduces the concept of social enterprise and discusses how the term is evolving in different contexts. It also examines the support policies that have been developed in different countries.

There are a variety of types of organisations that have been brought under the umbrella term 'social enterprise' in order to form a coalition of similar organisations influencing policy agendas. A common definition used is that developed by UK's Department for Trade and Industry in 2002: 'A social enterprise is a business with primarily social objectives, whose surpluses are principally reinvested for that purpose in the business or in the community, rather than being driven by the need to maximise profits for shareholders' (DTI 2002: 7).They are differentiated from the conventional private sector by having social and environmental aims as a core mission. Social enterprises can originate from a variety of sources. Some may be new start-ups trading as enterprises from the beginning (such as a community nursery or café), while others, who start as voluntary-sector organisations or charities with income from grants or donations, may develop trading enterprises. Thirdly, there are a small number of cases where social enterprises have come about through transfers from public sector. Examples of this are found in the UK and include housing associations, leisure services or the recent trend of encouraging people in the health services to 'spin out'. Finally, social enterprises can evolve from conventional private-sector for-profit organisations that shift their objectives to take on primarily social aims.

Social enterprises, it is argued, have the potential to transform communities and find solutions where others cannot (DTI 2002, HM Treasury 1999). Successful case studies have been shown to have a range of possible benefits, including: providing quality and accessible services; finding ways to deliver where the state or market cannot; understanding the needs of the community; mobilising community members; providing community support through volunteers; building 'social capital' in a community; creating local employment and training; and retaining wealth within a community (Lyon 2009).

Social enterprise has become a truly global phenomenon in recent years. Over the last 15 years, it has moved from its past modest position on the fringes of social and economic development policy to occupy an increasingly important position within wider debates on social and economic development and state reform. This trend can be observed in the northern and southern hemispheres and from East to West (Defourny and Nyssens 2010, Kerlin 2009, AISMER 2007).

For example, the European Commission has created the European Council of Associations of General Interest which has been developed to integrate and support social enterprises and the social economy more generally. Social enterprise policy documents have also emerged from multilateral organisations including the Organisation for Economic Co-operation and Development (OECD) (Mendell and Nogales 2009). The regional banks of the World Bank Group operating in less-developed countries (such as the African Development Bank, the Asian Development Bank and the Inter-American Development Bank) have all established social entrepreneurship-related programmes for economic and social development activities. The Inter-American Development Bank, for instance, claims that it has supported projects that fall under the rubric of 'social enterprise' since the Small Project Fund was created in 1978 to support income generating nonprofits and cooperatives (IDB 2010).

Types of Social Enterprise

The definition of social enterprise is strongly debated, and in many countries it has been kept 'loose' and open intentionally to allow a range of organisations to be included within a widening social enterprise movement umbrella. However, many organisations may claim to be social enterprises when they are predominantly motivated by profit for owners (for example within the private/ commercial sector) and many organisations that meet the definition (typically within the voluntary and third sectors) may not like the language of enterprise and therefore reject the label (Lyon and Sepulveda 2009). The range of types of social enterprise can be seen as a continuum from the more profit oriented to the more socially oriented, with organisations demonstrating hybrid natures drawing on both the voluntary/community sector and business models. There is agreement among scholars that the element that defines the quintessence of social enterprise is its social values and mission (Peattie and Morley 2008, Nicholls and Cho 2006, Nyssens 2006, Pearce 2003). However, what is or can be considered 'social' and what is not is a matter of hot debates and a very politically sensitive issue as well (Dart, Clow and Armstrong 2010, Arthur, Keenoy and Scott Cato 2006).

There are also discernable differences both within and between countries regarding the definition. In particular there are differences with regard to the importance of democratic governance and profit distribution. In the US, there has been a focus on the entrepreneur with moves to encourage social entrepreneurship rather than a social enterprise form (Defourny and Nyssens 2010:39).

The social enterprise tradition in continental Europe has evolved out of the cooperative movement and so there is a greater emphasis on democracy in the organisation's governance (Defourny and Nyssens 2010:43). The Work Integration Social Enterprises (WISEs) are at the core of recent developments within continental Europe and comprise cooperatives, mutuals and associations. The aim of policy initiatives within this tradition is to tackle chronic problems of unemployment and worklessness through either the integration of low-qualified unemployed in a productive activity or their access to opportunities for training and work experience (Defourny and Nyssens 2010). The UK draws on the traditions of both continental Europe and the US, as the social enterprise movement originally developed out of the cooperative movement. However, the democratic criterion has eventually faded away to embrace a range of organisations that might have a greater role for the social entrepreneur, and to include charitable organisations that are also trading enterprises (Teasdale 2012).

In less-developed countries, the term social enterprise is used much less frequently. Non-governmental organisations (NGOs) in Latin America, Africa and Asia often operate on business lines, using income from trading and contracts to deliver public services (Werker and Ahmed 2008, Etchart, Davis and O'Dea 2005). In India, NGO social enterprises which raise funds through some commercial activity to support their social mission can be registered as a society under the *Indian Societies Registration Act* or as a trust registered under several *Trust Acts* (Edward and Hulme 1996). Similarly, a large proportion of African NGOs use business models to support their activities and mission and can therefore be seen as social enterprises, although the term itself is not widely used. Apart from the work developed by NGOs, it is also necessary to highlight the role in social enterprise development played by the small business sector (Etchart et al. 2005), worker coops (Amin 2010) and fair trade organisations (Murray and Raynolds 2007) in the southern hemisphere.

Rationales for Public Policy

Social enterprise has emerged as an innovative institutional response to perceived market and government failure, addressing the needs of the most socio-economic vulnerable and disadvantaged individuals and communities (Amin, Cameron and Hudson 2002, Borzaga and Defourny 2001, Spear 2001). This has been used to justify a range of policy initiatives aimed at scaling up and increasing the capacity of social enterprises.

While much is written on the activities of social enterprises, critical voices question claims made about their potential to fulfil their social or environmental mission (Dart 2004, Foster and Bradach 2005). Others query the financial sustainability of this business model (Hunter 2009) and its innovative capacity to design and deliver public services (Westall 2007).

In the US tradition, social enterprise development is largely related to the long-standing market-based business activities developed by non profits (notably, foundations). These were initially conducted in order to support the organisations' social mission but then expanded to goods and services not directly related to their mission–mainly to fill the gap left by substantial cutbacks in federal funding from the late 1970s onwards (Kerlin 2006, Salamon 1997). In the UK, social enterprise development has been most actively pursued in relation to the development of alternative forms of public service delivery (Cabinet Office 2010, DTI 2002, HM Treasury 1999). This process has been characterised as the 'social enterprisation' of former public services (Sepulveda 2009) with a growing reliance on (quasi) market principles of competition, tendering, commissioning and subcontracting (Carmel and Harlock 2008).

Types of Support Policies

In those countries with social enterprise-specific policies, a range of different approaches have been set up to support the sector. In some countries, there are specific units with the central government to coordinate and lobby other parts of the public sector. The Office for Civil Society (formerly the Office of the Third Sector) covering England and the US Office of Social Innovation and Civic Participation have been examples of this form of institutional development.

BUILDING SOCIAL ENTREPRENEURSHIP CULTURES AND HELPING START-UPS

Behind all the successful cases can be found entrepreneurs or entrepreneurial teams willing to take risks, think laterally, challenge the status quo and do things differently. Policies to encourage social entrepreneurship aim to raise awareness of opportunities, with programmes aimed at both children (notably within the education system) and adults (publicising the potential of social enterprise).

While awareness raising can encourage people to think about social enterprises, other forms of public policy intervention include advisory services for those starting up organisations and attempts to reduce the barriers of those starting up. There is also an argument for having support to put people off starting an enterprise. A good adviser will spend much time encouraging those thinking of starting an enterprise to think through issues so they are not putting themselves and others at risk. Performance measures for support providers, such as the number of social enterprises started, result in people being pushed into being 'reluctant entrepreneurs' who are less likely to be successful (Lyon and Ramsden 2006).

Other support from policymakers has come from changes to legislative frameworks making it easier to start-up. New laws and regulation have been recently introduced in several countries to legally recognise social enterprises and differentiate them as a new subject of public policy. Examples include the law on *Social Purpose Business* in Belgium (2005), the *Community Interest Company* legislation in the UK (2005), the *Law on Social Enterprise* in Italy (2005), the *Social Enterprise Promotion Act* in South Korea (2006), and the *Finnish Act on Social Enterprise* (2003).

TRAINING AND ADVISORY SERVICES

Those wanting to set up or grow an enterprise may lack knowledge or experience and can benefit from advisory support and training. Like business support, research has shown that those receiving social enterprise support prefer a more personalised approach of one-to-one advice, or mentoring rather than training. However, this has considerable cost implications (Lyon and Ramsden 2006). There are innovative ways of reducing the cost through using groups and online methods but the personal relationship is usually preferred. In the UK, a range of social enterprise support providers have evolved, as well as private-sector support providers and programmes as part of the Business Link services for SMEs (Hines 2006). In other countries, such as South Korea, there are policies to support social enterprise through subsidised consultancy (Kim 2009). Social enterprises can use mainstream SME support but research in the UK (Lyon and Ramsden 2006) and Canada (ENP 2011) has found that such programmes are not tailored to social enterprise and social entrepreneurs may perceive them to lack empathy and knowledge of their approach.

Where resources are scarce, a key challenge for providers is to target their resources on those they feel are most likely to succeed. How success is defined may vary but can include financial sustainability as well as maximising social and environmental outcomes. However, the process of targeting presents challenges in terms of 'picking winners,' just as it does in mainstream SME policy development (Freel 1998).

INNOVATION EXCHANGE

An example of a UK-based advisory service is Innovation Exchange that aims to support innovative social enterprises to grow and access public-sector contracts. The pilot programme which ran between 2007 and 2010 provided expert advisors who helped social enterprises to develop their programmes and brokered the organisation's access to key commissioners and politicians. One award-winning social enterprise that was supporting children to tackle online cyber-bullying was then able to rapidly engage approximately 200,000 new users and reduce bullying in participating schools by 37 per cent. This resulted in a strategic partnership with Google and several UK government departments (CEEDR 2010).

SOCIAL INVESTMENT AND FINANCE

Access to finance can be a major constraint, especially for those enterprises that are growing or which intend to grow (SEC 2010, Hynes 2009). Some may be looking for grant finance while others may be interested in loans. As with many smaller enterprises, social enterprises often do not have sufficient assets which can be used as collateral, and mainstream banks may be unwilling to lend. Specific funds lending to social enterprises has been termed 'social investment'. This can be based on what is termed 'patient capital' with less onerous conditions and a combination of loans and grant finance. While these interventions can tackle the supply of finance, there is often resistance from risk-*averse* trustees or board members to taking out loans for enterprises.

In many countries there are grant programmes to encourage innovation and service delivery. For example, the 'Chinese Development Marketplace' initiative, in a partnership with the World Bank, provided US$ 1.2 million in grants to 50 innovative development projects by non-profits working on issues of poverty alleviation and the environment, and so supporting innovative business-like solutions to address social problems (Yu 2011). Different degrees of state involvement and provision of financial support to social enterprise development are observed in the European Union (EU) ranging from north European experiences (including France and Germany), where the state has been more instrumental and supportive to it, to south European experiences (such as Italy and Portugal) where the provision of public services financed by the state is underdeveloped and civil society organisations have instead played more instrumental roles in social enterprise development.

In order to meet the gap in access to loan finance, there are a number of social investment banks (such as Triodos or Charity Bank in the UK) that have developed products for social enterprises. There are also public-sector-supported funds, such as the Social Enterprise Development and Investment Fund in Australia or the Social Enterprise Investment Fund in the UK. These products range from grant-like funds to more commercially-focused forms of loans and/or equity finance. There are also innovative approaches to accessing capital through community shares and bonds, raising money from local people who may also be users of any services (Brown 2008). In all of these approaches there is a combination of social and financial returns, with innovative accounting systems developed to measure these social and economic impacts.

SOCIAL ENTERPRISES AND DELIVERY OF PUBLIC SERVICES

The public sector can play a key role in sustaining social enterprise by purchasing their goods and services. Similarly, international donors can purchase services of indigenous social enterprises and NGOs. The interest in social enterprises from policymakers is due to their perceived innovative approaches and value for money, thereby giving benefits to the public sector and service users alike. In South Korea, service delivery opportunities have come from the *National Basic Livelihood System Act* in 2000 – a form of active labour market policy to support work integration of the unemployed and disadvantaged (including the elderly and disabled), and the 2003 social work programme which placed greater emphasis on the role of civil society organisations as service providers (Kim 2009). In the UK there has been a rapid growth in outsourcing to social enterprises from the public sector, as well as a policy of transferring assets such as leisure centres from public to social enterprise ownership (Hunter 2009).

Social enterprises offer a wide range of social benefits (economic, social and environmental) and make contributions to a range of public-sector goals. However there are particular challenges in changing attitudes of the civil servant officers responsible for commissioning or buying of public services, as they may prioritise short-term financial value rather than longer-term social impacts when making decisions over who should deliver a service. There are a range of programmes working with public servants to build their understanding of social enterprises (Hunter 2009). Whilst a useful development, there are also dangers for social enterprises from such close relationships with the state. Many organisations are highly dependent on contracts from government and there are risks of changing government priorities or cut backs. Furthermore, the commissioning process (the buying of public services from outside of the public sector) can restrict the very innovation it seeks to support as bidders have to meet the expectations of the commissioners in order to win the contract. Finally, the advocacy role of organisations can be muted as those receiving contracts may be unwilling to 'bite the hand that feeds'.

Evaluating Social Enterprise Support

Assessment of social enterprises is an important issue for government agencies and policymakers. Evaluations need to consider the multiple objectives of social enterprise policy which may combine social, environmental as well as economic objectives. This emphasis on measuring the social and environmental impacts presents specific challenges to evaluations of social enterprise policies. There is a lack of rigorous evaluation of impact of different policies, despite the scale of the support provided to social enterprises. Evaluations of policies in the UK (such as the Phoenix Fund or Capacity Builders) have been carried out soon after programmes have finished. However, there has been limited research on the impact of these policies on the beneficiaries of the social enterprises themselves (Rocket Science 2011, DFES 2005, Ramsden 2005). The lack of clear definition of what is a social enterprise and the lack of clear objectives of policies has also affected the quality of evaluations of support. Furthermore, in many countries, such as the UK, social enterprise policy has also been closely linked to wider public-sector reform agendas, particularly those related to opening up public service provision to a range of providers and competitive markets. Again, evaluations may not have explicitly considered the impact (both positive and negative) of such changes to public service delivery and the extent to which social enterprise policy has played a role.

In addition to challenges of defining what is to be evaluated, there are future challenges in measuring the social and economic impacts of social enterprises and the policies supporting them. The instruments and methodologies commonly used to measure social outcomes, such as social accounting and social return on investment (SROI), are currently under intense scrutiny, owing to problems with data gathering and subjectivity bias observed in the evaluation process (Arvidson, Lyon, McKay and Moro 2010, Leighton and Wood 2010). Furthermore, evaluations of support need to measure both the impact of the support on the social enterprises themselves and also assess the impact of the social enterprises on the actual intended beneficiaries. For example, evaluations of programmes to provide loan finance to social enterprises need to assess their impact on the growth of organisations receiving support, as well as the impact on those using the social enterprise's services. There are further complications when attempting to put a monetary value on less tangible social impacts such as creating social capital and raising confidence or well-being. There is a risk that evaluations will only focus on what is measurable and quantifiable.

Conclusion

This chapter has set out to examine the support policies for social enterprises. In order to understand this, it is first necessary to understand what is meant by social enterprise, and the multiple rationales for support. The discourse around social enterprise is shown to be varied, with a lack of clarity over definitions in different countries resulting in a lack of clear objectives of policies and policies being interpreted in different ways. While many social enterprises themselves have little interest in debates over definitions, these issues are likely to become more of a concern where policies give social enterprises specific advantages in terms of contracts, taxation or access to finance. There is therefore a need for a degree of clarity in the development of support policies for social enterprises. The following recommendations can be drawn to inform future policy development.

Firstly, there is a need to distinguish between different types of social enterprises and to segment support accordingly. Some welcome the use of business models and the language of enterprise, while others find the labels of enterprise, business and entrepreneurship alien. Further distinctions can be made between those with democratic governance systems as found in the cooperative sector, and those with a more traditional hierarchical system. Support needs to be sensitive to this and provide help in the form that is acceptable.

Secondly, there is a risk of taking the idea of 'best practice' to extremes and looking for a 'one size fits all approach'. Local success is more likely to occur through adaptation with good practice lessons coming from understanding what is needed and developing suitable ways of meeting the need for that locality, while minimising confusion from a proliferation of approaches.

Thirdly, the public sector has considerable influence on social enterprise through its procurement policies or purchasing of public services. The roles of procurement officers or commissioners are central in encouraging social enterprises to deliver services and being invited to bid for contracts.

Finally, there is a lack of clear evidence concerning the impact of social enterprise support on beneficiaries, communities and the environment. The challenges go beyond those found in measuring the impact of SME support, with additional difficulties arising from the lack of a clear definition of social enterprise and complications in measuring social and environmental value. As it stands, current support for social enterprise can often be seen as policy based on an act of faith or expectation, rather than being based on solid evidence.

References

Amin, A. (ed) 2010. *The Social Economy: International Perspectives on Economic Solidarity*. London: Zed Books.

Amin, A. Cameron, A. and Hudson, R. 2002. *Placing the Social Economy*. Oxford: Routledge.

Arthur, L., Keenoy, T. and Scott Cato, M. 2006. *Where is the 'Social' in Social Enterprise?* Paper presented at the 3rd Annual Social Enterprise Research Conference, South Bank University: London.

Arvidson, M., Lyon, F., McKay, S. and Moro, D. 2010.*TheAmbitions and Challenges of SROI*, Third Sector Research Centre, Working Paper 49, Birmingham.

Austrian Institute for SME Research (AISMER) 2007. *Study on Practices and Policies in the Social Enterprise Sector in Europe*, Final Report, on behalf of the EU/DG Enterprise and Industry, Vienna, June 2007.

Borzaga, C. and Defourny, J. (eds) 2001. *The Emergence of Social Enterprise*. London: Routledge.

Brown, J. 2008.*Community Investment–Using Industrial & Provident Society Legislation*. Manchester: Cooperatives UK

Cabinet Office 2010. *Modern Commissioning: Increasing the Role of Charities, Social Enterprises, Mutuals and Co-operatives in Public Service Delivery*. London: Cabinet Office.

Carmel, E. And Harlock, J. 2008. Instituting the 'third sector' as a governable terrain: partnership, procurement and performance in the UK. *Policy & Politics*, 36(2), 155–171.

Centre for Enterprise and Economic Development Research (CEEDR) 2010. *External Evaluation of Innovation Exchange Brokerage Model*, funded by OTS–Cabinet Office. [Online] Available at: http://eprints.mdx.ac.uk/7102/1/ie_evaluation_report[1].pdf. [accessed: 17 October 2011].

Dart, R. 2004. The legitimacy of social enterprise. *Nonprofit Management and Leadership*, 14(4), 411–424.

Dart, R., Clow, E. and Armstrong, A. 2010.Meaningful difficulties in the mapping of social enterprises. *Social Enterprise Journal*, 6(3), 186–193.

Defourny, J. and Nyssens, M. 2010. Conceptions of social enterprise and social entrepreneurs in Europe and the United States; convergences and divergences. *Journal of Social Entrepreneurship*, 1(1), 32–53.

Department for Education and Skills (DFES), United Kingdom, 2005. *Evaluation of the Support for Enterprising Communities Pilot Project*, DFES Research Report RR653. [Online] Available at: https://www.education.gov.uk/publications/eOrderingDownload/RR653.pdf [accessed: 26 June 2012].

Department of Trade and Industry (DTI), United Kingdom, 2002. *Social Enterprise: A Strategy for Success*. London: Social Enterprise Unit, DTI.

Edward, M. And Hulme, D. (eds) 1996. *Beyond the Magic Bullet: NGO Performance and Accountability in the Post-Cold War World*. Hartford, CT: Kumarian.

Enterprising Non-Profits (ENP) 2011. *Social Enterprise Access to Government SME Services: Challenges and Opportunities*. [Online] Available at: http://www. enterprisingnonprofits.ca/resources/social-enterprise-access-government-sme-services-challenges-and-opportunities-2011 [accessed: 05 September 2011].

Etchart, N., Davis, L. and O'Dea, C. 2005. *Social Enterprise in Latin America*. Santiago: Nonprofit Enterprise and Self-sustainability Team (NESsT).

Foster, W. and Bradach, J. 2005. Should nonprofits seek profits? *Harvard Business Review*, 92–100.

Freel, M.S. 1998. Policy, prediction and growth: picking start-up winners? *Journal of Small Business and Enterprise Development*, 5(1), 19–32.

Hines, F. 2006. Viable social enterprise: an evaluation of business support to social enterprise. *Social Enterprise Journal*, 1(1), 13–28.

HM Treasury 1999. *Enterprise and Social Exclusion*, London: HM Treasury National Strategy for Neighbourhood Renewal Policy Action Team 3.

Hunter, P. (ed.) 2009. *Social Enterprise for Public Service: How Does the Third Sector Deliver?* London: The Smith Institute.

Hynes, B 2009. Growing the social enterprise–issues and challenges. *Social Enterprise Journal*, 5(2), 114–125.

Inter-American Development Bank (IDB) 2010. *The Four Lenses Strategic Framework: Towards an Integrated Social Enterprise Methodology*. Washington, DC: IDB.

Kerlin, J. 2006. Social enterprise in the United States and Europe: understanding and learning from the differences. *Voluntas: International Journal of Voluntary and Nonprofit Organizations*, 17(3), 246–262.

Kerlin, J. (ed) 2009. *Social Enterprise: A Global Comparison–Civil Society: Historical and Contemporary Perspectives*. New England, CT: University Press of New England.

Kim, H.W. 2009. Formation of Social Enterprise Policy and Prospects for Social Enterprises in Korea, in *Labor Issues in Korea 2009*, edited by M-S Jun. Seoul: Korean Labor Institute, 162–195.

Leighton, D. and Wood, C. 2010. *Measuring Social Value: The Gap between Policy and Practice*. London: Demos.

Lyon, F. 2009. Measuring the Value of Social and Community Impact, in *Social Enterprise for Public Service: How Does the Third Sector Deliver?*, edited by P. Hunter. London: The Smith Institute, 30–38.

Lyon, F. and Ramsden, M. 2006. Developing fledgling social enterprises? A study of the support required and the means of delivering it. *Social Enterprise Journal*, 2(1), 27–41.

Lyon, F. and Sepulveda, L. 2009. Mapping social enterprises: past approaches, challenges and future directions. *Social Enterprise Journal*, 5(1), 83–94.

Mendell M. and Nogales, R. 2009. Social Enterprises in OECD Member Countries: What Are the Financial Streams?, in *The Changing Boundaries of Social Enterprises* edited by N. Antonella. Paris: Local Economic and Employment Development (LEED), OECD, 89–138.

Murray, D.L. and Raynolds, L.T. 2007. Globalization and its Antinomies: Negotiating a Fair Trade Movement, in *Fair Trade. The Challenges of Transforming Globalization*, edited by L.T. Raynolds and D.L. Murray. London: Routledge.

Nicholls, A. and Cho, A. 2006. Social Entrepreneurship: The Structuration of a Field, in *Social Entrepreneurship: New Models of Sustainable Social Change* edited by A. Nicholls. Oxford: Oxford University Press, 99–118.

Nyssens, M (ed.) 2006. *Social Enterprise: At the Crossroads of Market, Public Policies and Civil Society*. London: Routledge.

Pearce, J. 2003. *Social Enterprise in Any Town*. London: Calouste Gulkenkian Foundation.

Peattie, K. and Morley, A. 2008.*Social Enterprises: Diversity and Dynamics, Contexts and Contributions*, ESRC Centre for Business Relationships, Accountability, Sustainability and Society (BRASS), Cardiff University, and Social Enterprise Coalition.

Ramsden, P. 2005. *Evaluation of The Phoenix Development Fund*, Freiss for Department of Work and Pensions, July 2005.

Rocket Science 2011. *Capacity builders Social Enterprise Programme Evaluation. Evaluation National Report*. [Online] Available at: http://www. rocketsciencelab.co.uk/pdfs/SEP_national_report.pdf [accessed: 10 June 2011].

Salamon, L.M. 1997. *Holding the Center: America's Nonprofit Sector at a Crossroads*. New York: Nathan Cummings Foundation. [Online] Available at: http://www.ncf.org [accessed: 12 October 2009].

Social Enterprise Coalition (SEC) 2010. *State of Social Enterprise Survey 2009*. London: SEC.

Sepulveda, L. 2009. *Outsider, Missing Link or Panacea? Some Reflections about the Place of Social Enterprise (With)in and in Relation to the Third Sector*. Third Sector Research Centre (TSRC), Working Paper 15, Birmingham.

Spear, R. 2001. A Wide Range of Social Enterprises, in *The Emergence of Social Enterprise* edited by C. Borzaga and J. Defourny. London: Routledge, 252–269.

Teasdale, S. 2012. What's in a Name? Making Sense of Social Enterprise. *Discourses Public Policy and Administration*, 27(2), 99–119.

Werker, E. And Ahmed, F. 2008. What do non governmental organizations do? *Journal of Economic Perspectives*, 22(2), 73–92.

Westall, A. 2007. *How Can Innovation in Social Enterprise be Understood, Encouraged and Enabled? A Social Enterprise Think Piece for the Office of the Third Sector.* London: Cabinet Office, OTS. [Online] Available at; http://www.eura.org/pdf/westall_news.pdf [accessed: 10 October 2008].

Yu, X. 2011. Social enterprise in China: driving forces, development patterns and legal framework. *Social Enterprise Journal*, 7(1), 9–32.

16

Government Policy to Support Franchisees

Jenny Buchan

Chapter Summary

Franchising is a form of organisational structure that enables a business to grow by licensing other parties (franchisees) to operate a version of the original business. Whilst there are different types of franchising models, this chapter focuses on business format franchising. Key aspects are discussed, as are the challenges it poses for franchisees and governments. This chapter starts with an outline of franchising, examines the rationale for government intervention to support franchisees, and then briefly discusses the tools currently used to support the franchise sector. It concludes by recommending policymakers focus on five areas: making data accessible, improving liaison across regulatory silos and across jurisdictions, involving all stakeholders in policy, empowering franchisees as a distinct group, and providing accessible and affordable dispute resolution.

Introduction

At its most simple, franchising is a business expansion model where a business operator, the franchisor, licenses franchisees to clone a facet of its business. Three commonly recognised types of franchised business exist. *Product* franchising entails a distributor acting as an outlet for a manufacturer's or supplier's products within a specific market. Petroleum retailing is an example. In *processing or manufacturing* franchising, the franchisor provides an essential ingredient or know-how. The franchisee contracts with the franchisor to meet agreed criteria, but otherwise runs its business as it chooses. Examples of this type are found in the soft-drink industry. *Business format* franchising is the third, and entails a franchisor granting a license to franchisees to create and run entire turn-key businesses. A typical example of this approach is often found in the fast-food sector.

Franchising enables entrepreneurs to penetrate markets quickly at low personal risk, by quarantining valuable assets such as trademarks and then achieving economies of scale through investment by franchisees. Franchisors can expand their branded businesses rapidly and uniformly by creating a distribution channel that harnesses the energy, local knowledge, equity and access to debt of individual franchisee owner–operators. Business format franchising in particular has become a significant part of the SME landscape in both developed and developing economies, and is the type of franchising that most poses new challenges for policymakers and regulators. This chapter thus focuses on business format franchising.

The first challenge for governments seeking to understand franchising is to understand the key elements of the franchise model. Curran and Stanworth (1983) have identified these as: an organisation (franchisor) with a market-tested (branded) business package, which is centred on a product or service and continuing contractual relationships with its franchisees. Franchisee businesses are independently owner-managed small firms operating under the franchisor's brand to produce and/or market goods or services according to the format specified by the franchisor. Each franchisor has one to thousands of franchisees ultimately contractually bound to it. Typically, the franchisor controls the franchise's strategy and its look and feel, sources suppliers and sets standards, in exchange for franchisees making payments, signing contracts and creating and operating their franchises.

However, any definition of franchising is imperfect. Every element may be adapted to suit each franchisor, resulting in a relationship that is slightly different for franchisees of each brand. For instance, whilst all franchisors require franchisees to sign non-negotiable franchise agreements, these vary in terms of what is included and what is left out. Some contracts are 'harder' and some 'softer' than others (Felstead 1993). What needs to be borne in mind, regardless of the wording of the contract, is that it locates ownership and risk with the franchisee and control in the franchisor (Hadfield 1990). Risk that would be borne by an employer in a traditionally modelled business is outsourced to franchisees in the franchise model.

Franchising is replete with loose terminology and different legal interpretations. Franchisors often portray their relationship with franchisees as a 'partnership', although the franchisor/franchisee relationship is not a partnership recognised by the law. Franchising comprises elements of several other legal relationships: agency, joint venture, investment, employment and supplier/consumer. A franchisee's relationship status on Facebook would most accurately not be 'single' or 'in a relationship' but 'it's complicated'. In law, franchisees are variously identified as consumers (South Africa), business consumers (Australia), a business entity (Japan), employees (some US court cases), or parties to contracts that are assets or liabilities (of an insolvent franchisor, in most jurisdictions).

At a national level, franchising benefits the economy through providing employment, easy entry into business for a wide range of people, and export opportunities. In Britain in 2009, for example, it was estimated that there were some 840 franchise systems worth approximately £11.8 billion, and employing 465,000 people (NatWest 2010). In South Africa, Woker (2005) has noted the value of franchising for its role in creating jobs, alleviating poverty and creating black empowerment. These qualities stem from its capacity to address many of the problems which make it difficult for a stand-alone new business to get started.

Franchising offers growth opportunities for many entrepreneurially-minded small business operators. It enables franchisors to compete with big business, by licensing out their model and achieving significant size. There are no particular barriers to entry for franchisors: any small business operator with a big vision can become a franchisor.

For franchisees the principal barriers to entry may be accessing funding, and meeting franchisors' criteria. For them, franchising is an alternative to independent business ownership and employment. The model provides a path to self-employment (Felstead 1993, Frazer, Weaven and Wright 2008), and has been especially popular amongst retiring armed forces personnel, immigrants unable to find work using their original skills or qualifications, risk-averse individuals seeking to 'buy themselves a job', and others. Many are attracted by a ready-made business idea, a tried and tested format, and access to the help and support of the franchisor (Felstead 1993). This support can include comprehensive start-up assistance, initial site selection, fit-out and staff hiring guidelines drawing on what has worked for previous franchisees in the network. Through franchising, franchisees can gain access to premium retail locations and favourable supplier terms. Ideally, franchisors also supply ongoing product/service development, assistance with management and operational issues, and marketing (Gardini 1994).

On the other hand, franchising has a number of potential drawbacks for the franchisee. These include lack of independence, the need to make a significant investment before having had the opportunity to fully understand the business, the need to follow the franchisor's instructions (even if flawed), and the difficulty of selling a franchised business (compared to the ease of quitting a job) if the franchisee wishes to exit.

The Rationale for Government Intervention

Franchising challenges policymakers in the fields of consumer protection, small business, competition and corporate affairs. The challenges arise out of its relative newness as a business form, the absence of legally meaningful checks and balances on franchisors, the consequences of franchise system failure, unchecked risk-shifting to franchisees, asymmetry of information, differences in power and access to courts, difficulty in accessing the perspectives of stakeholders other than franchisors, and the inability of franchisees to protect themselves from a franchisor's exploitative conduct.

In terms of positioning franchising within the law, the business format franchise model evolved only after laws regulating other types of business relationships (such as partnerships, company structures, joint ventures, contracts, creditors and debtors, and employers and employees) were settled. Consequently, there are multiple disconnects for franchisees within existing legal frameworks. For example, whereas business failure law recognises employees and creditors, it has not adapted to accommodate the franchisees' stake in a failed franchisor. Franchise agreements become assets or liabilities and the franchisees become parties to contracts without rights that mirror their role or their vulnerability.

Traditional business forms have checks and balances through clear levels of authority, and a management structure (Lessing 2009) underpinned by corporate governance principles and legislation overseen by regulators. These are absent in the franchise context in most jurisdictions. For example, some decisions taken by a board of a company have to be explained to shareholders and voted on. In contrast, most franchisors do not have to secure their franchisees' consent or sign-off to any of their decisions, even though they have a significant effect on the franchisees and their success. A franchisor's strategy may damage the system and the franchisees. For example, a franchisor may finance experimentation through franchise fees generated by selling more franchises, unchecked by the need to prove to a financier that it can fund extra debt. Franchisees have limited options in the face of any detrimental decision by their franchisor (Croonen and Brand 2010). In some respects, a franchisor is like a monopolist, unburdened by the laws that typically regulate anti-competitive conduct. In a franchise network the franchisor creates a tightly controlled but lightly regulated monopoly, where the franchisee-consumers are contract bound to deal with the monopolist, the franchisor supplier; there is often no external regulator to moderate their behaviour.

It is also worth noting that the ownership of franchise systems has changed in many cases to reflect current investment practices. Traditionally franchisors were proprietary companies, trusts or even partnerships or sole traders. A recent trend has been for some existing franchisors to be bought by public companies or venture capitalists. Whilst new owners provide an exit strategy for founder–franchisors, these latter stakeholders purchase a franchise system as an investment that must generate a competitive return, or be wound up, which means that franchisees are often needed simply as commodities, not participants in a joint business activity.

Not all franchisors succeed. For example, of 952 French franchisors operating over the period 1992–2002, only 42 per cent survived (Perrigot and Cliquet 2004). Despite franchisor lobby group rhetoric that would suggest otherwise, not all franchisees can continue trading if the franchisor fails or exits. The franchisees may not be able to secure ongoing rights to use the brand. An Australian study showed that the trademarks licensed to franchisees are owned by franchisors in only 26 per cent of networks (Buchan 2009). Liquidators cannot force brand owners, landlords or other third-party suppliers to deal with former franchisees.

Franchisee vulnerability also arises because the franchisor controls the legal and financial structure of its network. Franchise opportunities are sold on a 'take it or leave it' basis. This may include requiring franchisees to provide personal guarantees for head leases held by franchisors, despite franchisees having no control over how their franchisor meets its obligations under that head lease (Buchan and Butcher 2009). Franchisors may require franchisees to be commission agents where a franchisee's customers make payment directly to the franchisor that then pays a commission to its franchisees. However, franchise agreements rarely incentivise franchisors to pay commissions promptly to their franchisees.

Asymmetry in all dimensions works against franchisees. Franchisors control the availability of information about themselves and their networks, engage specialist 'big end of town' advisers, transfer risk, protect personal assets and draft franchisor-biased contracts. Even legislation designed to protect franchisees can deliver superior rights to franchisors (Buchan 2010). Franchisors choose which aspects of the network are owned by the franchisor entity and which are corralled in other entities that have no direct contractual relationship with franchisees. Where pre-contract disclosure is made, it often centres on 'the franchisor', and provides little or no information about related entities the franchisee may have to contract with. The information that is supplied may be impossible for franchisees to verify objectively because of a dearth of information in the public arena. Aspiring franchisees are required to 'tell all', but cannot find out much about what they are buying beyond what franchisors disclose. Although franchisees have little power to achieve amendments to franchise contracts, they are cast as the authors of their own misfortune for failing to conduct adequate pre-purchase due diligence.

Despite the clear disadvantages that beset franchisees, it is often hard for governments to locate and engage with them as a group. Franchisors, on the other hand, are strongly represented by well-resourced industry associations. These are effective lobby groups that claim to also represent franchisees interests, although in reality this is only the case when there is no conflict between the interests of franchisors and franchisees. Franchisee class-actions are rare, even though systemic issues within a network would lend themselves well to such group actions.

The erroneous view that franchise agreements are 'negotiated' is a strong deterrent to regulatory, and judicial, intervention. In reality, as explained above, the agreement is a standard form, relational contract providing much discretion to a franchisor in the performance of the contract. It exposes franchisees to significant uncertainty and risk, but grants them few absolute rights (Felstead 1993). As Hoy (2008: 152) observes, '[t]here is little doubt as to who the senior party is in the contractual agreement'. Franchisees are seldom able to protect themselves by negotiating better contracts.

Hence, effective franchising policy requires both an understanding of the risks and roles franchisees assume, and an acceptance of their inability to measure, or mitigate these risks. How, then, have policymakers responded to date?

Government Assistance for Franchisees

Many countries have developed specific franchising policies and regulatory responses, and some 30 countries (Spencer 2010: 215) now have either formal voluntary measures or legislation to assist franchisees. These follow a number of common themes which are discussed below. The nations that have franchise specific legislation include Australia, Canada, Italy, the USA, Ukraine and Vietnam.

Some regulators provide free information on websites and at franchise shows. For example the US Federal Trade Commission, and the Australian Competition and Consumer Commission, publish guidance material for franchisees as part of its education mandate under the *Competition and Consumer Act 2010* (Cth). Advice and assistance to franchisees is also available through the various small business advisory networks provided by government, such as Business Enterprise Centres (2011) in Australia, and Business Link (2011) in Britain. Generic information is useful, but is no substitute for tailored advice about specific franchise systems.

Tailored education can help people understand franchising. Hoy, Gough, Orlando and Morgan (2006: 2) however, caution against 'commonly available [franchise information/education] 'seminars' by vendors and suppliers ...

[as they] are ... primarily intended to solicit clients, [and contain] minimal educational content'. Governments can have strong input into education programmes that they fund, thus ensuring the content is even-handed. For instance, in Australia government-funded pre-entry franchise education (http://www.franchise.edu.au/pre-entry-franchise-education.html) is delivered online by Griffith University under contract to the national franchising regulator. The programme is 'in line with research which suggests improved pre-entry education can ... create a sector where people enter franchising with more realistic expectations' (Frazer, Weaven and Bodey 2010: 2). Similarly, Malaysia tasked its Ministry of Domestic Trade, Co-operatives and Consumerism with formulating directions and policies for the development of the franchise sector, including sponsoring education programmes (iFranchise Malaysia 2011). Likewise, some American face-to-face programmes aim to provide 'a thorough, balanced review of the fundamentals of franchising' (Hoy et al. 2006: 1), and there is a high level of demand from students, existing business owners, managers and self-employed people. Hoy also noted that many seeking education about franchising in America are Hispanic (Hoy et al. 2006). Where prospective franchisees are migrants who are not fluent in a country's official language(s), both information and education would be of greater benefit in their language.

Warnings and advice provided by government through information, education and even through statutorily mandated wording on disclosure documents may help address any lack of awareness, but will only be effective if advisers understand how to 'read between the lines' of the franchise agreement. Warnings cannot stop exploitation of franchisees by franchisors complying with the letter of the franchise agreement, but not the spirit of the relationship. Nor does awareness translate into an ability to negotiate changes to the proposed agreement.

Voluntary codes of conduct are another approach. These are non-binding rules which industry players agree to abide by. Their strengths are that they can be modified quickly and can avoid an overly general 'one size fits all' legislated solution. However, opportunities for opting-out and for special interests to control the process sometimes mean that such voluntary measures are insufficient (Spencer 2010). Furthermore, where numerous players exist, achieving widespread 'buy-in' to voluntary codes is difficult. For example, in 1993 Australia introduced a voluntary code requiring disclosure of prescribed information by franchisors. A manager was funded to secure widespread compliance. Voluntary compliance proved unsatisfactory because both ethical and rogue franchisors refused to participate, claiming they were exempt or attributing their refusal to lawyers' advice. Some franchisors advertised themselves as being 'code compliant', but were not. Some used the required disclosure document as a marketing tool, withholding key information and instead filling the document with marketing hype. On being targeted for a compliance audit, some franchisors threatened to sue the government-appointed directors of the code governing body for defamation. Without government indemnity from prosecution, the role of 'watchdog' became untenable (Gardini 1994). Governments choosing voluntary codes could thus boost compliance by indemnifying the managers of the process against prosecution.

Mandatory measures have since replaced earlier voluntary measures in some jurisdictions. Today, formal franchising legislation exists in a wide variety of countries, including those in Table 16.1.

Table 16.1   Selected examples of national franchise laws, with regulators

Country	Law	Regulator
Australia	Franchising Code of Conduct 1998	Australian Competition and Consumer Commission
Italy	Law on Commercial Affiliation (Franchising) 2004 Regulation Setting Up Rules On Franchise 2004	Ministry for Production Activities
South Korea	Act on Fairness in Franchise Transactions, 2002	Ministry of Industry and Trade
Malaysia	Franchise Act 1998	Ministry of Domestic Trade, Consumerism and Co-operatives

One mandatory requirement is pre-sales disclosure: that is, providing prospective franchisees with a standardised snapshot of the current and past status of the franchisor, details of its existing franchisees, and the financial and legal fitness of the franchisor. As of 2010, 19 countries required mandatory disclosure, while a further nine imposed a more generalised requirement on franchisors to provide 'information necessary for a franchisee to exercise its exclusive rights under the agreement' (Spencer 2010: 227).

Disclosure is not perfect. It is expensive for the franchisor to keep up to date. If information turns out to be misleading, franchisors may be sued. Franchisees faced with reading long documents sometimes find the amount of information indigestible, and in practice a high proportion of franchisees will admit that they did not read the disclosure documents. It is also difficult for a franchisee to test the accuracy of information disclosed. Existing franchisees, theoretically a source of information, may be silenced by confidentiality agreements, or may be intimidated or unwilling to be honest about an investment they themselves misjudged. Problems within the franchise network may be hidden in other companies related to the franchisor that are not required to make disclosure.

Whilst effective disclosure ideally balances the positions of contracting parties during the formation of the contract, it can never redress the imbalance of power in performance. Moreover, disclosure cannot demonstrate what the network will look like in the future.

Another government response is to require formal registration of the franchise system, franchise consultants or brokers, and/or of the offering prospectus. Approximately ten countries (including Malaysia, Mexico and Russia) currently require registration of the franchise agreement, whilst registration of disclosure documents has been adopted in three countries and about 14 American states (Spencer 2010: 249). Franchisors sometimes argue that confidentiality of commercially sensitive material will be compromised by registration, but such claims need to be balanced against the potential benefits of greater transparency and the fact that, in practice, most franchise agreements contain significantly similar clauses. In America, websites such as www. freefranchsiedocs.com host searchable catalogues of disclosure documents and franchise agreements, as do American state government websites. Their existence proves that accessibility does not doom a franchise.

Cooling-off periods (that is, short time periods in which a prospective franchisee can opt out of a franchise agreement they have just signed on to) are relatively low-intervention and inexpensive, can mitigate irrational consumer behaviour, and may cure market failures in situational monopolies (Spencer 2010). Cooling-off periods are mandated in several jurisdictions, including Australia and China. A brief cooling-off opportunity, however, may provide a false sense of security for franchisees still experiencing the afterglow of the end of a long search for 'the one', while a long cooling-off period may be unworkable for franchisors.

Legislation may provide franchisees with the right to sue a franchisor that makes misleading representations, or behaves unconscionably, or it may entrench rights that franchisors have otherwise tended to remove via contract. Accordingly, legislation can alter the parties' rights to freedom of contract by making rules about aspects of their relationship such as dispute resolution, discrimination, changes in management, encroachment, termination, non-renewal and the franchisees' rights to form associations (Barkoff and Selden 2008).

Dispute resolution provisions are uncommon in franchise legislation, despite the fact that many franchisees complain to government about so-called 'unfair' behaviour by the franchisors. Resolving such business relationship issues in court is often inappropriate, as litigation is slow and expensive, and seldom provides a good foundation for repairing a damaged long-term relationship. As a result, alternate dispute resolution mechanisms are now mandated in some national regimes, such as the Australian Franchising Code of Conduct.

Interestingly, in most countries both legislated and contractual termination provisions exacerbate asymmetry by allowing the franchisor to terminate the franchise agreement following breach by a franchisee, but not permitting the franchisees to terminate for a breach by their franchisor. Vietnamese legislation (*Decree No 35/2006/ND-CP* 2006) is an exception that provides termination rights to franchisees.

Future Policy Initiatives

It has been recognised that '[a]n effective regulation-making and administrative system for franchising should mediate the impact of … demands that arise from an increasingly risk averse society' (Banks 2006: 12). This is necessary because, in general, franchisors will try to pass as much risk as possible to franchisees. Policymakers and regulators could implement five strategies to reduce the risks of franchising for franchisees.

First, there is a need for more comprehensive data on franchising systems. This can facilitate a better understanding of the sector, helps inform prospective franchisees and their advisers, and leads to better informed policy responses. In the absence of public databases of franchisors and franchisees, research to inform policy can never be optimal. As already noted, access to objective data assists due diligence. More effective disclosure would start with a requirement that franchisors supply an organisational chart of its network naming and identifying both the roles of each entity the franchisee will depend on and the flow of money between franchisee and the network players. This would enable franchisees to verify from the public record and to purchase credit ratings for the network players rather than depending on franchisors as sole sources of information.

Second, seamless policy solutions will only be achieved if consumer protection, small business, corporations and taxation regulators at all levels of government within a country and across jurisdictions work together to identify gaps in knowledge, policy and regulation and address them. Seamless policy would help franchisees to conduct effective due diligence, to be protected from risks they cannot manage alone, and possibly to survive a franchisor's early exit.

The third area for improvement is stakeholder participation. In many countries, franchisees, professional advisers and other parties with an interest in the sector (such as mediators and accountants) are under-represented in franchise policy discussion (Buchan and Harris 2010). Mediators can provide insights into underlying causes of disputes which never become public because mediation is seen as a confidential process. The role of accountants is significant as they advise potential franchisees about the financial viability of a proposed business. Once a client becomes a franchisee, the accountant is the advisor who is consulted first and frequently as the business develops. The 'hot tub' method, a facilitated private conference where '[e]xperts are brought together to endure rigorous questioning [from policymakers] and debate' from the other experts (Victorian Bushfires Royal Commission 2009: 20) can assist policymakers fill gaps in their understanding.

Fourth, governments need to improve access to the collective voice and views of franchisees. Franchise representative organisations exist in about 45 countries (Spencer 2010); they give priority in their lobbying efforts to franchisor concerns. This is despite the fact that the number of franchisees is significantly greater than the number of franchisors. Few working in government have personal experience of franchising; few understand the full extent or the causes of the franchisee's vulnerability. Franchisees tend to have limited input into policy or advocacy, because they have little discretionary free time to devote to lobbying activities, even though their interests are distinct from franchisors. Organising a collective voice for franchisees is not easy. The franchisor is often the only one aware of which outlets are franchisee-operated and which are franchisor-operated. Even where franchisees are meant to register their business name, many do not. As a group, franchisees are indistinguishable from any other business from the public record, except in those countries that require formal registration of franchisees. If required to register on a government database they would be identifiable. Alternatively, although the idea ignites dissent from franchisor-focused groups, governments could support franchisee union membership as a policy initiative to enable the franchisees' voice to be accessed. For example, Japan permitted individual owners of franchised convenience stores to become members of an existing union (Anderson, Mori and Tomotsune, 2009). If franchisees are consumers, the European Union's (EU) recognition of the difficulties of finding time and money for consumers to self-represent effectively is instructive and has led it to 'subsidise consumer group representation' (European Union 2007). Governments could subsidise the establishment of similar representation channels for franchisees whose most persistent outlets currently in Australia and the US are blogs and the high-profile strategies of lobbying politicians and the media.

Finally, recognising the burdens litigation place on franchisors and franchisees, governments can assist by supporting low-cost, low-intervention dispute resolution procedures such as the Australian Government-funded Office of the Franchise Mediation Adviser, and Small Business Commissioners. Both franchisors and franchisees benefit from having an alternative to litigation. The financial and emotional cost and time commitment is lower than required for a court case, the dispute can be resolved at a time and place convenient to both parties, and the mediator will be a person who understands franchising. Governments benefit from being involved as they can require the dispute manager to file reports identifying problems in the sector. This helps governments assess whether their level of intervention is appropriate.

Conclusion

Franchising is a powerful and effective business model, but it is not perfect. Government involvement is necessary because of the absence of meaningful checks and balances on franchisors, the consumer-type transaction that the purchase and conduct of a franchise business mirrors, the asymmetry of information that exists between parties, the difficulty in accessing the perspectives of stakeholders other than franchisors, and the cost of access to courts.

Any attempt to regulate contractual relationships presents risks for a government. If the market is left to its own devices, freedom of contract remains intact, no costly processes of regulatory intervention and review are required, and there is no public criticism of the intervention.

Effective franchising policy depends on governments understanding the numerous risks and roles franchisees assume, and accepting franchisees' and their advisers' inability to accurately measure or mitigate these risks. So long as policymakers address franchising as a simple, contract-based, commercial relationship government responses will miss the mark. Franchisors will continue to act in their own interests, relatively unchecked. Policymakers instead need to develop a more sophisticated understanding of the nuances of twenty-first century business format franchising.

Determining the correct mix of checks and balances which permit the franchise model to thrive, whilst protecting franchisees, is the central challenge for policymakers. It is one which governments will continue to grapple with for some time to come.

References

Anderson Mori and Tomotsune. 2009. *Formation of Labour Union by Convenience Store Franchisees*. [Online] Available at: http://www.amt-law.com/en/ [accessed: 5 January 2011].

Banks, G. 2006. *Reducing the Regulatory Burden: The Way Forward*. Paper to the Monash Centre for Regulatory Studies: Melbourne, 17 May 2006.

Barkoff, R.M. and Selden, A.C. 2008. *Fundamentals of Franchising*, 3rd edition. Chicago: American Bar Association.

Buchan, J. 2009. Franchisors' registered trade marks – empirical surprises. *Australian Intellectual Property Law Bulletin*, 21(7), 154–157.

Buchan, J.M. 2010. *Franchisor Failure: An Assessment of the Adequacy of Regulatory Response*. PhD Thesis, Queensland University of Technology.

Buchan, J. and Butcher, B. 2009. Premises occupancy models for franchised retail businesses in Australia: factors for consideration. *Australian Property Law Journal*, 17(2), 143–177.

Buchan, J. and Harris, J. 2010. *Stakeholder Input into Franchise Inquiries: an Australian Exploratory Study*. Paper to the 24th Annual International Society of Franchising Conference: Sydney, 8–9 June 2010.

Business Enterprise Centres Australia 2011. *Franchising*. [Online] Available at: http://www.becnt.com.au/SyndicationPHP/BECAustralia/HTML/3460.htm [accessed 16 August 2011].

Business Link UK 2011. *Buy a Franchise*. [Online] Available at: http://www.businesslink.gov.uk/bdotg/action/layer?topicId=1073947364 [accessed 16 August, 2011].

Competition and Consumer Act 2010. (Commonwealth) Australia. Act No. 51 of 1974 as amended.

Croonen, E.P.M. and Brand, M.J. 2010. Dutch druggists in distress: franchisees facing the complex decision of how to react to their franchisor's strategic plans. *Entrepreneurship Theory and Practice*, 34(5), 1021–1038.

Curran J. and Stanworth, J. 1983. Franchising in the modern economy – towards a theoretical understanding. *International Small Business Journal*, 2(1), 8–26.

European Franchise Federation 2008 *National Regulation by Country*. [Online] Available at: http://www.eff-franchise.com/spip.php?rubrique21 [accessed 19 August 2011].

European Union 2007. *European Union Consumer Policy Strategy 2007–2013, Empowering Consumers, Enhancing Their Welfare, Effectively Protecting Them*. [Online] Available at: http://ec.europa.eu/consumers/overview/cons_policy/doc/EN_99.pdf [accessed 11 June 2011].

Felstead, A. 1993. *The Corporate Paradox: Power and Control in the Business Franchise*. London and New York: Routledge.

Frazer, L., Weaven, S. and Bodey, K. 2010. *Franchising Australia 2010*. Brisbane: Griffith University.

Frazer, L., Weaven, S. and Wright, O. 2008. *Franchising Australia 2008*. Brisbane: Griffith University.

Gardini, R. 1994. *Review of the Franchising Code of Practice. Report to Senator Schacht, Minister for Small Business, Customs and Construction*. Canberra: Australian Government.

Hadfield, G.K. 1990. Problematic relations: franchising and the law of incomplete contracts. *Stanford Law Review*, 42(4), 927–992.

Hoy, F. 2008. Organizational learning at the marketing/entrepreneurship interface. *Journal of Small Business Management*, 46(1), 152–158.

Hoy, F., Gough, C., Orlando, T. and Morgan, K.B. 2006. *Recognizing Opportunities in Franchising*. Paper to the 51st International Council of Small Business World Conference: Melbourne, 18–21 June 2006.

iFranchise Malaysia 2011. *Government to the Fore*. [Online] Available at http://www.ifranchisemalaysia.com/government-to-the-fore.html [accessed 16 August 2011].

Lessing, J. 2009. The Checks and Balances of Good Corporate Governance. *Corporate Governance ejournal*. [Online] Available at: http://works.bepress.com/john_lessing [accessed 10 June 2011].

NatWest/BFA Survey. 2010 *Highlights from the 2010 NatWest/BFA Franchise Survey*. [Online] Available at http://www.natwest.com/business/services/market-expertise/franchising/natwest-bfa-survey.ashx [accessed 16 August 2011].

Perrigot, R. and Cliquet, G. 2004. *Survival of Franchising Networks in France from 1992 to 2002*. Paper to the 18th Annual International Society of Franchising Conference. Las Vegas, 6–7 March 2004.

Spencer, E.C. 2010. *The Regulation of Franchising in the New Global Economy*. Cheltenham: Edward Elgar.

Victorian Bush Fires Royal Commission Practice Note 5 Letters Patent 2009. Melbourne, Government of Victoria, Australia. [Online] Available at: http://www.royalcommission.vic.gov.au/Prac-Notes [accessed 13 March 2011].

Vietnam 2006. *Decree No 35/2006/ND-CP detailing the Provisions of the Commercial Law on Franchising 2006*.

Woker, T. 2005. Franchising – the need for legislation. *South African Mercantile Law Journal*, 17(1), 49–55.

PART THREE

Evaluating and Assessing Policies and Programmes

17

SME Policy Evaluation: Current Issues and Future Challenges

Paul Cowie

Chapter Summary

This chapter aims to explain what SME policy evaluation is, its purpose and who is responsible for such assessments. It then explores the challenges and current issues facing those involved in the evaluation of SME policy. Drawing on current research and evaluation models from both developed and developing economies, this chapter then examines the future issues and challenges for evaluation practice and policy development, highlighting potential areas for future research both by academics and practitioners either developing policy or conducting its evaluation.

It is acknowledged that evaluation of SME policy is no easy task. Using the logic model to illustrate the evaluation process, the various issues currently facing evaluators are discussed. These include the problem of measuring the additional benefits any policy programme delivers; difficulties understanding the complex causal links between a programme's inputs and its likely overall impact; issues relating to the timing of evaluations; and how to ensure impartiality when, as is ordinarily the case, the budget holder or the body responsible for policy implementation is the body responsible for evaluation.

Finally, the chapter also seeks to highlight two possible challenges facing evaluators of SME policy in the future. The first is that caused by an increased need to evaluate the more subjective aims and outcomes of SME policy (for example, how policy stimulates more innovation or an entrepreneurial business environment). The problem for assessors evaluating these programmes is finding suitable metrics to demonstrate success or failure. The second challenge for evaluators is in developing real-time evaluation models. In an increasingly fluid and complex economic situation, there is a need by policy developers and politicians to continuously monitor progress of a programme against its intended outcomes and adapt policy if those outcomes are likely to be missed.

Introduction

The development of policy evaluation is inextricably linked to recent developments in the rationale underpinning policy development. Specifically, two key shifts in SME policy can be seen to have influenced the development of evaluation theory and practice. The first of these reflects the move away from the interventionist industrial policy, often sectoral in nature, in the UK (Blackburn and Smallbone 2008), the USA (Ketels 2007) and in Europe (Aiginger 2007) to more holistic policies which concentrate on the general business environment. An example of this is the trend to create policies designed to stimulate 'enterprise' or 'innovation' (SBS undated). Whilst most policy is developed using a rationale, the underlying basis for that logic is not always clear. Gibb (2000) contends a number of the rhetorical arguments put forward to justify these policy rationales are based on mythical concepts.

Secondly, policy development has moved into a new era of managerial-style politics (Molas-Gallart and Davies 2006). Policy makers now see it as their role to correct market failures and information asymmetries and therefore ensure free market conditions (Bennett 2008). The development of policy programmes to counteract such flaws needs to be backed up by evidence, both to support the rationale and to demonstrate that policies have achieved desired effects.

Yet it is no easy task to undertake effective evaluation. This chapter aims to explain what SME policy evaluation is, its purpose and who is responsible for such activity. It then explores the challenges and current issues facing those involved in the evaluation of SME policy. Drawing on current research and models from both developed and developing economies, the chapter also examines the possible future issues for evaluation practice and policy development, highlighting potential areas for future research both by academics and practitioners either developing policy or conducting its evaluation.

Current Evaluation Practice

Evaluation is the measurement of the performance of a particular policy programme. It aims to link the programme actions with overall impacts. An evaluation often takes place in the initial stages of a policy programme. It will then tend to focus on the delivery of the programme and satisfaction levels of participants: an *ex ante* or process evaluation. The policy programme can also be evaluated once it has been completed. Evaluation then assesses whether the policy programme has delivered its intended outputs or aims, its impact on the wider economy, and its value for money: an *ex post* or impact evaluation.

Evaluation should and indeed often does form an integral part of many countries' policy development life cycles. For example in the UK, evaluation forms part of the Treasury's ROAMEF (Rationale, Objectives, Appraisal, Monitoring, Evaluation and Feedback) policy cycle (HM Treasury 2003: 3). This is a continuous process with each previous iteration informing the next. The Organisation for Economic Co-operation and Development's (OECD) (2008) guidance on evaluation also stresses that 'evaluation is not a "once-off" activity, undertaken once a particular programme has been completed. It is an integral element of a *process* of improved policy or service delivery' (OECD 2008: 16).

The question of who is responsible for the evaluation of SME policy is a key one. Around the world different agencies and actors are driving the need for better evaluation of policy. In the context of SME policy evaluation there tend to be two main actors: the body that holds the purse strings, and the body responsible for the policy itself. For example, in India the evaluation of SME policy is undertaken by the government department developing the policy, the Ministry of Micro, Small and Medium Enterprises (NIMSME 2008). In the UK, however, the evaluation process is overseen by the Treasury, although the actual evaluation is carried out by the department responsible for the policy. The Treasury details the evaluation framework it expects all departments to adhere to in the 'Green Book' (HM Treasury 2003). In the case of European Union (EU) policy programmes, the requirement to carry out an evaluation is often written into EU regulations themselves (Gore and Wells 2009). In developing countries, policy programmes are often funded through external aid and the evaluation of those programmes is driven by institutions such as the World Bank (Leeuw and Vaessen 2009).

This proximity between the body responsible for developing, implementing and evaluating policy has led some to question the impartiality of the evaluation process (Smith and Spenlehauer 1994). Whilst evaluation is often presented as being a neutral or managerial process, this may not always be the case. Smith and Spenlehauer (1994) argue evaluation can be manipulated to serve the purpose of the controlling government department. This may even be the case when a third-party consultancy is commissioned to carry out the evaluation. A close working relationship between the government department and the consultancy may mitigate against the consultancy painting a realistically harsh picture of the outcomes of a particular policy programme.

The Evaluation Process

One useful tool for developing evaluation frameworks is the logic model. Although various forms of the logic model have been developed over time, the most often used is the methodology developed by the W.K. Kellogg Foundation (2004). The logic model consists of a framework which shows each stage of a policy programme and the expected results. An example is shown in Figure 17.1.

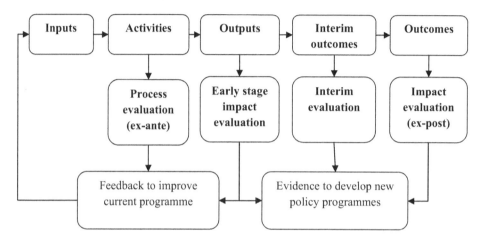

Figure 17.1   Typical logic model with corresponding evaluation stages

A distinction needs making between a *process* evaluation (sometimes known as *ex ante*) and an *impact* evaluation (sometimes known as *ex post*). A process evaluation seeks to understand how the policy was implemented. It investigates the selection criteria for participants, the speed at which the policy was implemented and satisfaction with the programme for those taking part. A process evaluation by its nature takes place at an early stage of the programme, often before there are any concrete outputs from the intervention. In contrast, an impact evaluation takes place on the partial or complete completion of the programme and seeks to investigate the wider economic benefits of a programme and whether the intended outcomes have been achieved.

However, as already noted above, evaluation should not be a one-off activity. It must be a continuous process, undertaken throughout the delivery of any policy programme. Figure 17.1 illustrates how an evaluation cycle can be integrated into the logic model and demonstrates where each evaluation type sits within that model.

The type of evaluation method used will influence the data collection methods used. A quantitative methodology has the benefit of being able to capture large amounts of information and is suitable for detailed statistical analysis and econometric modelling to identify trends and relationships. On the other hand, qualitative methods yield a richer and more detailed understanding of the processes involved in the programme. Qualitative methods are often used in the early stages of a policy programme, with quantitative methods subsequently used to assess impact. There is an increasing trend amongst commentators to suggest that a mixed methods approach (one which uses both qualitative and quantitative methods) at all stages as this can give a more balanced and detailed understanding of the programme's impacts (Leeuw and Vaessen 2009, OECD 2008).

Practical Issues in Evaluation Practice

When evaluators investigate a particular policy programme they frequently seek answers to questions, including:

- Would the businesses have achieved the desired outputs even if the programme had not taken place?
- How can we show the policy programme caused the observed outcomes and impacts?
- Is the evidence provided by the evaluation cost effective?
- Has the evaluation captured all the activity taking place?

The way in which evaluation can be used to answer these questions is outlined below.

MEASURING ADDITIONALITY

In answering the first question, evaluators are seeking to measure the additional benefits brought by the programme over and above those which would have happened anyway. This is known as additionality. In a scientific experiment additionality is known as the treatment effect. In other words, what difference has a particular treatment made to the participant? This is measured by having a treatment group and a control group. Both groups are treated identically save for the element being tested. The experiment is run on a 'double blind' basis; neither the participant nor the researcher knows which group a particular participant has been assigned to. In relation to SME policy this scientific approach is not practical and indeed is often not politically acceptable, although there has been recent call for this approach in the implementation of public policy generally (Haynes et al. 2012). Therefore a number of ways of evaluating additionality in terms of policy programmes have been developed. The OECD (2008), in their 'six steps to heaven' assessment of evaluation quality, detail six elements which need to be included if an evaluation is to provide robust evidence of a programme's impact:

- Step 1. Take up of schemes.
- Step 2. Recipients' opinions.
- Step 3. Recipients' views of the difference made by the assistance.
- Step 4. Comparison of the performance of the assisted with typical firms.
- Step 5. Comparison with match firms.
- Step 6. Taking account of selection bias.

The closer the evaluation is to reaching step 6, the better the measurement of additionality is. This improvement in the quality of the evaluation was tested in a research paper by Greene (2009). Greene used the UK business support programme run by the Prince's Trust for the period 1993–2003 and the various evaluations of those programmes to investigate the influence of evaluation methodology on evaluation results. Greene also used the OECD 'six steps' measure to rate the quality of the evaluations considered. The conclusions of the paper were that different evaluation methods will give differing conclusions and that the higher an evaluation is made up the six steps ladder, the clearer the results were.

A further example of an evaluation using econometric methods to establish additionality is the Inter-American Bank's evaluation of SME policy in Argentina (Castillo, Maffiolo, Monsalvo, Rojo and Stucchi 2010). Here the evaluators used propensity score matching and 'difference in differences' econometric models to establish a control group of SMEs to match against the performance of the treatment group. This allowed them to evaluate the impact of a programme to provide professional business support to SMEs.

By contrast, however, the UK Trade and Investment Department (UKTI) uses telephone surveys of programme participants to estimate additionality through their Performance Impact and Monitoring Surveys (UKTI 2010). Participants are asked to confirm whether they would have behaved as they did without the support of UKTI. This is then backed up by *ex post* evaluations which seek to utilise more rigorous evaluation methods to independently assess additionality (OMB Research, 2010). This approach of an initial self-reporting of additionality, followed up with a more detailed *ex post* evaluation, arguably suggests that the OECD's six steps may be too simplistic. An alternative approach might be to use the different steps at different points within the life cycle of the policy programme.

CAUSALITY

Causality is the link between the input and the output and outcome. When dealing with policy programmes which offer support and assistance to SMEs, there will inevitably be a large number of sometimes minor interventions to evaluate. This makes it difficult to isolate the effect of an intervention on the individual firm and problematic to trace the combined effects at a regional or national scale. The key difficulty is in showing the casual link between the policy programme and the observed outcomes and outputs.

Toulemonde (1995) highlights the complexity inherent in evaluation of any economic system. For Toulemonde there are four typologies of causality: linear; circular; reflexive; and irreversible. The simplest, linear causality, where the input directly influences the output, is arguably the form most often used in current policy evaluations. Circular causality simply means the outputs become inputs. Circular causality can have a multiplier effect, with small initial changes resulting in large unpredictable impacts. Reflexive causality incorporates a self-organising element. Reflexive causality may be seen where a programme results in a greater skill base or better network connections, which then enable businesses to develop without further intervention. Reflexive and circular causality have an element of feedback in them and can therefore pose problems relating cause to effect. Circular and reflexive causality are arguably most relevant to the current policy practice where policy makers are seeking to influence wider economic structures. Irreversible causality occurs when a policy programme causes changes of such significance that the situation is completed changed, for example, when the policy results in closure of a business fundamental to an area's economy.

White (2010) argues that understanding the causal chain is vital. Although White's guidance is aimed at social development programme evaluations, his suggestion that early process evaluations should include measures to assess the causal link between inputs and outcomes is equally relevant to economic policy programmes. This again reinforces the need for a life cycle approach to evaluation, with each of the evaluation stages feeding into the next as well as giving meaningful results in their own right.

However, mapping the causal links and hence the impacts of a policy is not always easy in practice. An evaluation of an Indian enterprise programme for SMEs, the Entrepreneurship Development Institution Scheme (EDIS) (NIMSME 2008), measured direct outputs of these Entrepreneurship Development Institutions; the number of people trained; and the number who went on to find work or start a business. It did little to measure what impact these people had on the national or even regional economy. One of the reasons for this, as outlined in the EDIS Evaluation Report (NIMSME 2008), was a lack of data available from the participants. Issues around data and data collection will be discussed in more detail below.

OPENING THE BLACK BOX OF POLICY PROGRAMMES

Greene and Storey (2007) highlight the lack of a coherent understanding of the way in which SME policy leads to the intended impacts. They argue most policy evaluations treat the process by which the inputs lead to the outputs and impacts as a 'black box' not to be opened. This means the mechanism by which the input results in the output is not understood or revealed through evaluation (Astbury and Leeuw 2010). This is illustrated in relation to innovation policy by Molas-Gallart and Davies (2006). They argue developments in the broad policy assumptions made about the linkages between inputs and outcomes in relation to innovation policy, the policy theory, have not been matched by developments in evaluation practice to enable evaluators to capture and measure those linkages, the programme theory (Molas-Gallart and Davies 2006: 65). Molas-Gallart and Davies also argue this lack of an understanding of the processes involved is exacerbated by conflict between the twin goals of evaluation. Evaluation is needed to both provide the clear quantitative outputs politicians need to defend policy decisions, as well as qualitative data which can be used to inform future policy development. This lack of a concern for the processes taking place between the provision of support and the observed outcomes may be a reflection of the dominance of Gibb's (2000) 'Mythical Concepts' which underpin policy makers' assumptions. For example policy makers take it as a given that more entrepreneurship education in schools leads to a more entrepreneurial society without any thought as to how this may come about.

PARSIMONY

Data collection is a key issue for any evaluation body. This is because there often needs to be a trade off between the costs of carrying out the evaluation and the relevance or usability of the information it provides. The information provided by the evaluation should add sufficient value to the policy intervention to warrant the cost of the evaluation. A thorough evaluation is research intensive. This can therefore be costly both for the government carrying out the evaluation and for the firm whose time is spent in the process of collating the required information.

As noted above, in *ex ante* evaluations the data collected is relatively straightforward: it relates to the speed at which the policy is being delivered and the satisfaction rates of those taking part in the policy programme. The focus is on the process of delivering the policy rather than the outcome of the policy.

It usually takes the form of a questionnaire or telephone survey. The data can then be analysed using simple quantitative methods. *Ex post* evaluations are, however, carried out following completion of the programme to establish the impact and therefore significantly more data is required particularly to address the question of additionality.

What is missing from these evaluations is an ability to track progress of a policy programme during its delivery. This form of continuous evaluation has been developed by humanitarian relief agencies and is known as Real-time Evaluation (Herson and Mitchell 2005). It offers the opportunity to estimate changes to the overall outcome resulting from alterations in the delivery of the policy programme. One way in which this could be done is through data matching. This is using data collected by a government during the normal course of its activities (such as via tax or employment records) and matching that data to the firms participating in the particular policy programme. This is particularly useful for SMEs, given the relatively high burden of collecting detailed financial data on a small number of staff. The main reason that this has not happened is the quality of the data held, privacy issues, and political competition between the departments holding the data and those wishing to access the data.

TIMING OF EVALUATION

The timing of the evaluation is important. Each policy programme will have an impact at a different rate. Some policy programmes are able to get up and running quickly. They soon start to deliver outputs and outcomes that can be measured. Others have a longer gestation period. There may be complex institutional arrangements to initiate or the inputs are such that the impacts take longer to manifest themselves. As part of the evaluation process it is therefore important to understand the timescales involved and how quickly the inputs will lead to observable outputs and impacts (King and Behrman 2009). A false impression of the policy's impact may be created if an evaluation is initiated too soon or too late.

An example of a programme which took longer to become established would be the Indian EDIS (NIMSME 2008). The process of establishing the physical institutions and then recruiting participants to the programme meant the programme took time to establish itself. The inputs in relation to this programme were the educational courses provided to the budding entrepreneurs. To establish the institute and develop the courses took some time, as did attracting people to participate in the courses. The outcomes for the programme were the number of new businesses started by those budding entrepreneurs. This also had the potential to delay any observed outcomes. Moreover, just having the entrepreneurial knowledge to start a business was only part of the equation. An entrepreneur will also need access to capital, for example. These intervening elements may slow the cumulative impact of the policy programme.

An example of a programme establishing itself quickly would be the Manufacturing Advisory Service (MAS) run by the Department for Business, Innovation and Skills in the UK. Support programmes such as this are able to make an impact shortly after their start, if the advisors are quickly in place and can start connecting with firms and providing support. In the case of the MAS programme there was a short chain of events to be completed before impacts were seen. The MAS Programme therefore contrasts with a programme such as EDIS, where there is a longer chain of events before the impacts of the intervention are felt.

Future Issues and Challenges for Evaluation

To date most evaluations of policy have focused on objective measures of impact: gross value added, productivity and employment. However, there is a growing awareness that this does not necessarily give the whole picture. This was highlighted by the British Prime Minister (Cameron 2010) in a recent speech announcing the need to measure GWB (general well-being) as well as gross domestic product (GDP). Evaluation may therefore be called upon to start quantifying the impact of policy programmes using subjective measures in addition to the traditional objective measures.

Linked to the need for more subjective measures of impact is a move to more holistic policy aims. Simple single sector policy programmes have given way in many agencies to complex policy initiatives often concentrating on subjective outcomes such as a more enterprising economy or greater innovation (Luengas and Ruprah 2009). At the present time evaluations of these types of policy programmes use proxy measures for the intended policy aim. For example, new VAT registrations in the United Kingdom are taken as a proxy for a more entrepreneurial society; likewise, research and development spending is taken as a proxy for innovation (Bakhshi, Edwards, Roper, Scully and Shaw 2011). At best, though, these proxy indicators can only offer a partial picture of the impact of a policy programme. They also fail to offer an understanding of the process by which the input leads to the observed outcome and impact.

THE NEED FOR A REAL-TIME EVALUATION METHODOLOGY

At the moment all evaluations only give a snapshot of the situation at the time of the evaluation. In an increasingly complex and fluid economic environment this can mean evaluations become rapidly out of date and irrelevant. Increasingly policy makers require real-time evidence of the impact a programme is having and an ability to gauge the likely overall impact the policy will have in future. As mentioned above, this concept of real-time evaluation was originally developed in relation to humanitarian relief programmes, where up-to-the-minute information on a programme's impact and it anticipated outcomes is vital (Herson and Mitchell 2005). A key challenge for evaluators will be to introduce a similar methodology to the evaluation of SME policy, which could then allow policy makers to fine tune policy programmes as they are implemented. This would need to be more than just a series of *post hoc* evaluations. Real-time evaluation would ideally be a continuous process of collecting and analysing data to give a picture of the current outcomes and the progression towards delivering the overall intended impact.

Conclusion

This chapter has attempted to provide an overview of current evaluation practice, and to highlight the challenges facing evaluators operating in an economic environment which is changing with ever greater speed and intensity. Evaluation is seen as an integral part of the policy development cycle. However, there is a risk that if evaluations are carried out by the same government department that developed the policy, they may be perceived as having been manipulated to provide an overly favourable picture of the impact of the policy.

This is not, however, the only challenge for evaluators. Current evaluation frameworks need to be developed to better deal with issues such as additionality and the timing of evaluations. A better understanding of the processes which link the inputs, outputs and outcomes of a particular policy initiative are also required. Opening this black box will give policy makers greater opportunities to develop future policy in a more targeted way. In light of the shift in focus of policy, away from single sector and simple policy programmes to policy programmes which are more holistic in nature and which exhibit greater complexity in relation to their causal links, evaluation frameworks need rethinking. This creates a substantial challenge: how can we establish suitable proxy measures for what are often subjective outcomes in a policy programme?

Finally, there is a growing need to undertake real-time evaluations. The ability for policy makers to continuously track progress of a programme as it is implemented and gauge its ability to deliver the intended impact would be a significant step forward in evaluation practice. This will allow policy makers to fine tune policy programmes, or even cancel them at an early stage, if they are failing to deliver the intended outcomes.

References

Aiginger, K. 2007. Industrial policy: a dying breed or a re-emerging phoenix? *Journal of Industry, Competition & Trade*, 7(3-4) 297–323.

Astbury, B. and Leeuw, F. 2010. Unpacking black boxes: mechanisms and theory building in evaluation. *American Journal of Evaluation*, 31(3) 363–381.

Bakhshi, H., Edwards, J., Roper, S., Scully, J. and Shaw, D. 2011. *Creating Innovation in Small and Medium-sized Enterprise: Evaluating the short term effects of the Creative Credits Pilot*. London: NESTA. [Online] Available at: http://www.nesta.org.uk/library/documents/Creating_Innovation_in_SMEs_v13.pdf [accessed: 16 August 2011].

Bennett, R. 2008. SME policy support in Britain since the 1990s: what have we learnt? *Environment and Planning C: Government and Policy*, 26(2) 375–397.

Blackburn, R. and Smallbone, D. 2008. Researching small firms and entrepreneurship in the UK: development and distinctiveness. *Entrepreneurship Theory and Practice*, 32(2), 267–288.

Cameron, D. 2010. *PM Speech on Wellbeing*. [Online] Available at: http://www.number10.gov.uk/news/speeches-and-transcripts/2010/11/pm-speech-on-well-being-57569 [accessed: 20 June 2011].

Castillo, V., Maffiolo, A., Monsalvo, A., Rojo, S. and Stucchi, R. 2010. *Can SME Policies Improve Firm Performance? Evidence from an Impact Evaluation in Argentina*, Washington: Inter-American Development Bank. [Online] Available at: http://idbdocs.iadb.org/wsdocs/getdocument.aspx?docnum=35545433 [accessed 20 June 2011].

Gibb, A. 2000. SME policy, academic research and the growth of ignorance, mythical concepts, myths, assumptions, rituals and confusions. *International Small Business Journal*, 18(3), 13–35.

Gore, T. and Wells, P. 2009. Governance and evaluation: the case of EU regional policy horizontal priorities. *Evaluation and Program Planning*, 32(2), 158–167.

Greene, F. 2009 Assessing the impact of policy interventions: the influence of evaluation methodology. *Environment and Planning C: Government and Policy*, 27(2), 216–229.

Greene, F. and Storey, D. 2007. Issues in Evaluation: The Case of Shell Livewire in *Handbook or Research on Entrepreneurship Policy*, edited by D. Audretsch et al. Cheltenham: Edward Elgar, 213–233.

Haynes, L, Service, O., Goldacre, B. & Torgerson, D. 2012 *Test, Learn, Adapt: Developing Public Policy with Randomised Controlled Trials*. London: Cabinet Office Behavioural Insights Team

Herson, M. and Mitchell, J. 2005. Real-time evaluation: Where does its value lie? *Humanitarian Exchange Magazine*, 32. [Online] Available at: http://www.odihpn.org/report.asp?id=2772 [accessed: 20 June 2011].

HM Treasury, United Kingdom 2003. *The Green Book: Appraisal and Evaluation in Central Government*. London: TSO.

Ketels, C. 2007. Industrial policy in the United States. *Journal of Industry, Competition and Trade*, 7(3-4), 147–127.

King, E. and Behrman, J. 2009. Timing and duration of exposure in evaluation of social programs. *The World Bank Research Observer*, 24(1), 55–82.

Leeuw, F. and Vaessen, J. 2009 *NONIE: Impact Evaluation Guidance*. [Online] Available at: http://www.worldbank.org/ieg/nonie/guidance.html [accessed 20 March 2011].

Luengas, P. and Ruprah, I. 2009. *Should Central Banks Target Happiness? Evidence from Latin America*. Working paper: OVE/WP-02/09. Washington: Inter-American Development Bank.

Molas-Gallart, J. and Davies, A. 2006. Toward theory-led evaluation: the experience of European science, technology, and innovation policies. *American Journal of Evaluation*, 27(1), 64–82.

National Institute for Micro, Small and Medium Enterprises, Government of India (NIMSME) (2008) *Report on the Evaluation of Entrepreneurship Development Institution Scheme*. MMSME, Hyderabad

Organisation for Economic Co-operation and Development (OECD) 2008. *OECD Framework for the Evaluation of SME and Entrepreneurship Policies and Programmes*. Paris: OECD

OMB Research 2010. *PIMS 12-14 Follow-up Report. UKTI, London*. [Online] Available at: http://www.ukti.gov.uk/uktihome/aboutukti/ourperformance/ performanceimpactandmonitoringsurvey/followupsurveys.html [accessed 22 March 2011].

Small Business Service (SBS), United Kingdom (undated). *A Government Action Plan for Small Business: The Evidence Base*. Small Business Service. [Online] Available at: http://www.bis.gov.uk/files/file39768.pdf [accessed 9 August 2011].

Smith, A. and Spenlehauer, V. 1994. Policy evaluation meets harsh reality: instrument of integration or preserver of disintegration? *Evaluation and Program Planning*, 17(3), 277–287.

Toulemonde, J. 1995. Should evaluation be freed from its causal links? *Evaluation and Programme Planning*, 18(2), 179–190.

UK Trade and Investment (UKTI) 2010 *UKTI PIMS: Position at Q2 for Year 2010/11*. [Online] Available at: http://www.ukti.gov.uk/uktihome/aboutukti/ ourperformance/performanceimpactandmonitoringsurvey/quarterlysurveys. html [accessed 23 March 2011].

White, H. 2010 A contribution to current debates in impact evaluation. *Evaluation*, 16(2), 153–164.

W.K. Kellogg Foundation 2004. *Logic Model Development Guide*. Michigan: W.K. Kellogg Foundation. [Online] Available at: http://www.wkkf.org/ knowledge-center/resources/2010/Logic-Model-Development-Guide.aspx [accessed 22 March 2011].

18

Evaluating Policy Initiatives: The Case of Enterprise Insight's Local Youth Enterprise Campaigns

Ron Botham

Chapter Summary

To stimulate new business formation, governments around the world have sought to increase the supply of future entrepreneurs. In the UK, Enterprise Insight was established in 2004 to create a more entrepreneurial culture amongst young people. To achieve this, it developed and ran several national programmes and in 2006 it launched local initiatives (known as hubs) to run intensive local campaigns in areas with below average business birth rates and an above average proportion of economically excluded young people. This chapter describes the implementation of the hub initiatives and analyses the results of a study to estimate their impact on young people's entrepreneurial attitudes and the creation of a more entrepreneurial culture. The hubs were found to have had positive effects. However, these largely offset what would otherwise have been a trend towards less positive entrepreneurial attitudes. It then highlights the difficulties caused for impact evaluation by continuous policy change and, even with control areas, allowing for the effects of other policies. Finally, it suggests that initiatives to increase the business birth rate via cultural change require long-term commitment and a clear definition of enterprise.

Introduction

Over recent years governments around the world have sought to encourage entrepreneurship and increase the business birth rate (Bakkeries, Schouwstra and Snijders 2009, Leitae and Baptista 2009, BERR and HM Treasury 2008, HM Treasury

2004, Small Business Service 2004, European Commission 2003, Stevenson and Lundström 2001, OECD 1998, 2001). However, it has been argued that traditional methods of increasing entrepreneurship have failed and experimentation is required to develop new mechanisms with greater emphasis on societal attitudes, norms and role models (Bridge 2010). In the UK, Enterprise Insight (which subsequently became known as Enterprise UK) was one such experiment. It was set up in 2004 with the aim of creating a more entrepreneurial culture amongst 14–30 year olds and specifically to increase the proportion considering setting up their own business or social enterprise (Enterprise Insight 2006).

Enterprise Insight had a government grant of £5 million per annum to develop and run a national campaign to inform and inspire entrepreneurial interest amongst young people and to 'recruit' other organisations to participate in the campaign. In addition to influencing young people directly, it also planned to do so indirectly by generating greater support for youth enterprise amongst those who influence them, such as parents, teachers, employers and the media. To achieve this cultural change, its main mechanisms were Enterprise Week (which subsequently became Global Enterprise Week), the Make Your Mark (enterprise) Challenge, a series of other enterprise challenges (such as Make Your Mark with a Tenner), the promotion of enterprise education, the provision of information and the 'placement' of positive youth entrepreneurship stories in the media. It ran Enterprise Week in November each year, during which it encouraged organisations to hold and publicise events about youth enterprise. As a campaigning and awareness-raising organisation, it did not provide direct assistance to young people actually starting their own business.

In 2006 a decision was taken to set up five local initiatives, known as hubs, to run intensive campaigns in tightly defined geographic areas to demonstrate what the approach could achieve and persuade other localities to adopt similar campaigns. (Within tightly defined areas it was believed that impacts would be more visible and more easily identified.) The hubs were to stimulate participation in Enterprise Insight's national programmes and develop specific local dimensions to the campaign. For example, the hubs were to utilise local entrepreneurial role models and media, mobilise local young people to participate in the campaign, and move youth enterprise up the local policy agenda. Each hub was to have a team of four including one individual responsible for increasing participation in Enterprise Insight national programmes (for example, persuading organisations to run events during Enterprise Week and schools to participate in the Make Your Mark Challenge), a press officer and an individual (the hub leader) with responsibility for persuading other players to take youth enterprise more seriously. The budget (including staff and other costs) for the five hubs was initially planned to be approximately £1 million per year.

The hubs were selected as places with low business birth rates, above average proportions of socially and economically excluded young people and reasonably receptive local players (such as local authorities, chambers of commerce and the enterprise education community). The eventual selection was for hubs in the local authorities of Redcar and Cleveland, Coventry, Liverpool, Wakefield and Waveney (that is, the town of Lowestoft). Following discussions with local organisations, two hub models emerged. In Liverpool and Wakefield, the hubs were 'stand alone' each with four Enterprise Insight staff. In Coventry and Waveney the hubs were embedded in an existing organisation (the Coventry Chamber of Commerce and Enterprise Lowestoft) with service contracts to deliver Enterprise Insight activities.[1]

With the launch of the hubs, a study (Botham and Sutherland 2010) was set up to evaluate their impacts and how these varied between individual hubs, hub models and specific hub activities. By demonstrating impacts, Enterprise Insight hoped it could persuade other areas to adopt its campaigning 'model'. This chapter aims to estimate the effects of the hubs on young people's entrepreneurial attitudes and intentions, to identify some of the evaluation difficulties which arose as policy evolved during the study, and to draw out some lessons for both policy and its evaluation.

Study Methodology

The study adopted a before-and-after/control area methodology. 'Before' was defined as prior to the 2006 Enterprise Week and 'after' was post-2009 Enterprise Week. It was designed within the context of Enterprise Insight's 2006 plans for the national campaign and the hubs. From the outset, Enterprise Insight adopted a broad definition of 'youth enterprise' to include social and community enterprise and involvement in other forms of enterprising behaviour (such as clubs and charities). Reflecting the idea that employers increasingly (or at least should) require enterprising individuals, the definition was further broadened to incorporate the employability agenda. It was also the intention to increase employer involvement in the enterprise agenda, persuade them to recruit more enterprising young people and increase the number of 'enterprising workplaces'. The methodology was also designed to estimate hub impacts on those who influence young people and local youth enterprise policy.

---

1   As discussed subsequently, the Redcar and Cleveland hub was not included in the study because of a delayed launch. When it was eventually set up, it adopted neither of the two models.

Published data were used to select three control areas (Newcastle, Wolverhampton, Grimsby) which were similar to the hubs on criteria such as the business birth rate, self-employment, social and economic exclusion, the existence or otherwise of universities, urban density and existing policy initiatives. However, how similar the control areas were to the hubs on issues such as entrepreneurial attitudes, self-efficacy and intent was unknown at the commencement of the study. Nevertheless, the basic assumption was that trends in the control areas would have been replicated in the hub areas in their absence. In other words, the control areas provided a reliable estimate of the counterfactual (that is, what would have happened without the hubs). In the event, the before surveys found entrepreneurial attitudes to be very similar in both the hub and control areas.

It was anticipated that the effects of intervention would be long term, with limited immediate impact on the business birth rate. To get a feel for whether progress had been made towards the ultimate goal, a logic chain was developed which hypothesised that hub activities increased young people's awareness of entrepreneurship and their entrepreneurial self- efficacy, which in turn increased entrepreneurial intent and enterprising behaviour, and eventually resulted in increased business formation. These hypotheses were used to guide the design of before-and-after surveys consisting of:

- A household survey of 600 16–30 year olds in each hub and 350 in each control area. The large sample size was employed to enable reliable comparisons of the impact of individual hubs and specific activities.
- A household survey of 300 parents with offspring younger than 30 years old in each hub and control area. Enterprise Insight anticipated that it would both target and work with parents to influence indirectly young people's attitudes and career intentions. However, at the time it was not clear how this was to be implemented.
- A survey of 200 employers in each hub to examine impacts on, *inter alia*, their attitudes to entrepreneurs and entrepreneurship, support for an enterprise agenda, recruitment of enterprising young people, 'use' of young employees and the creation of a more enterprising work environment (that is, one which encourages and rewards individual initiative and participation).
- A survey (with 762 pre and 1245 post responses) via local schools of 14–16-year-old pupils and their teachers.
- An electronic survey of 550 local 'opinion formers'(with 101 responses), defined as local politicians and senior staff in local organisations such as local authorities, universities and the media.

These were complemented by 'mapping studies' for each hub based on local publications and an extensive interview programme to establish the nature and extent of local enterprise policies and initiatives. These surveys were to be repeated in late 2009 to enable comprehensive before-and-after comparisons.

However, following completion of the 2006 baseline surveys, policy began to evolve and change. Following debate with local interests, the Redcar and Cleveland hub was dropped (to re-emerge later as a hub for the wider geographic area of the Tees Valley) while others (especially Liverpool) took on a sub-regional role from the outset. The plans to influence parents and employers were never progressed. By 2008 the local emphasis had fallen out of favour. The Regional Development Agencies, which at the time had responsibility for strategic leadership, coordination and funding of economic development in their regions, wanted hubs to have a regional remit, while Enterprise Insight began to give greater emphasis to its national rather than local campaigns. Consequently, in 2008 without waiting for the study results, the hubs were given a 'strategic regional' remit by Enterprise Insight and their resources substantially reduced.

These developments had implications for the methodology and specifically the 'after' or 2009 surveys. The Redcar and Cleveland surveys along with the parents' survey were dropped. An analysis of how impacts varied between hubs and hub models was no longer to be a study objective. Consequently, large samples were less necessary. For example, the household samples were reduced from 600 to 300 in each hub and the scope of the questionnaires narrowed. Hence much of the data collected in 2006 had no role in the evaluation and proved to be wasted effort. At the same time, much data required to evaluate what the hubs actually did was not collected. With hubs adopting a sub-regional remit (and subsequently, a regional one), the study did not collect before data enabling it to identify the hubs' full impacts (that is, those occurring outside the local hub areas). Nevertheless, the data continues to provide a useful assessment of hub impacts, when taken in aggregate. This chapter relies mainly on data from the household survey of 16–30 year olds as the statistically most robust source, supplemented by Enterprise Insight monitoring data.

Participation in National Programmes

As illustrated in Table 18.1, the hubs successfully increased participation in Enterprise Insight national programmes. To allow for the differing size of the hub and control areas, the data for Enterprise Week events and the MYM Challenge are expressed as numbers per 100,000 inhabitants. On this basis, the number of events rose much more rapidly in the hubs than in the control areas (from 7.2 per 100,000 residents in 2005 to 38.4 in 2007, the first year in which the hubs were fully operational). In contrast, the number in the control areas rose from 4.7 to just 6.8. In 2007 there were over five times more (that is, 382) events than there would have been without the hubs (using the control areas to estimate the counterfactual). The number of organisations running events also increased substantially. The hubs were particularly effective in getting more employers to organise events, such as Ideas at Work Days. The number of young people registered for the MYM Challenge increased from 50.0 per 100,000 residents in 2005 to 217.2 in 2007, a much more substantial increase than in the control areas. It is estimated that in 2007, 1652 more individuals did the Challenge in the hub areas then would otherwise have been the case.

Similar conclusions are reached if the UK or English trends are used to calculate the counterfactual. However, as with most monitoring data, there are some limitations. While the hubs certainly increased activity, it is far from clear whether it is all additional. Some organisations simply moved events into Enterprise Week (which would have been held at some other time) or registered events that would have been held but not registered with Enterprise Insight. Nor is it known if all those registered to participate in the MYM Challenge actually did so. It is also clear from Table 18.1 that prior to their creation, there was already more activity in the hub areas. This reflects one of the selection criteria (namely, the existence of receptive local players). Consequently, some above-average increase in activity might anyway have been expected. With the adoption of a regional remit in 2008 the level of local activity began to decline.[2]

Effects on Young People

The obvious question is whether this increased activity translated into impacts on young people's entrepreneurial attitudes, self-efficacy, intent and behaviours. Table 18.2 is based on a selection of responses to the before-and-after household surveys. Young people were asked to what extent they agreed or disagreed that 'they would not try to set-up a business in case it failed'. The proportion agreeing with this statement (that is, expressing a 'fear of failure') actually rose in the hubs between 2006 and 2009 from 29 per cent to 31 per cent. Taken in isolation, it may seem that the hubs increased the 'fear of failure'. However, the proportion rose more substantially from 31 per cent to 44 per cent in the control areas. Based on Chi-squared tests there was no statistically significant difference between the hub and control area proportions in 2006.

---

2   However the standard regions in which the hubs were located achieved above-average levels of activity.

Table 18.1   Impact on uptake of enterprise insight national programmes

	2005	2006	2007	2008
Number of Enterprise Week Events (Per 100,000 Pop)				
Hubs	7.2	12.2	38.4	35.7
Controls	4.7	1.8	3.5	6.8
Estimated impact (number)			382	311
Number of Event Organisers (Actual Numbers)				
Hubs	25	53	131	145
Controls	12	8	13	18
Estimated impact			108	113
Mark Your Mark Challenge Participants (Per 100,000 Pop)				
Hubs	50.0	158.8	217.2	176.3
Controls	20.8	35.4	67.1	91.8
Estimated impact			1652	729

Source: Calculated from Enterprise Insight Enterprise Week and MYM Challenge registration data. Estimated impacts are: (i) the hub actual number minus the counterfactual estimated from the per capita number in the control areas; (ii) but with an allowance for the higher 2005 Enterprise Insight activity in the hubs.

By 2009, the lower 'fear of failure' in the hubs was statistically significant at the 99 per cent level. Assuming the control areas are a good estimate of the counterfactual (that is, without intervention, the proportion would have been 44 per cent in the hub areas), the hubs prevented the 'fear of failure' becoming a more severe constraint on entrepreneurship. It appears the intervention resulted in 32,900 fewer young people in 2009 expressing a 'fear of failure' in the hub areas (that is, 13 per cent of hub young people).

An alternative way of measuring the 'fear of failure' is the proportion of young people essentially saying they are definitely not put off entrepreneurship by the 'fear of failure' (that is, disagreeing strongly that 'they would not try to set-up their own business in case it failed'). The number of young people with no 'fear of failure' increased in the hubs (from 33 per cent to 37 per cent) but fell dramatically in the control areas (from 33 per cent to 19 per cent). These figures imply that because of the hubs there are an estimated 45,500 more young people in the hubs (18 per cent of the total) definitely not put off entrepreneurship by the 'fear of failure'. However, much of this positive impact was to offset what would otherwise have been a negative trend. Overall the hubs seem to have polarised (or perhaps clarified) views. The proportion of young people saying they were put off and definitely not put off by the 'fear of failure' both increased.

While the effects are less substantial, Table 18.2 shows similar patterns for self-efficacy (measured as the percentage agreeing with the proposition 'I have what it takes to set up my own business') and entrepreneurial intent (the proportion of respondents who had recently considered setting up their own business). With regard to entrepreneurial self-efficacy, the proportion increased marginally more rapidly in the hubs. While there was no statistically significant difference between the hub and control areas in 2006, by 2009 self-efficacy was somewhat higher (statistically significant at the 95 per cent level) in the hubs. Turning to entrepreneurial intent, it actually declined somewhat (from 36 per cent to 34 per cent) in the hubs. However, it fell dramatically (from 41 per cent to 27 per cent) in the control areas. Consequently, there were 15,200 more individuals in the hubs who had recently considered setting up their own business then there would otherwise have been. Again this positive impact prevented what otherwise would have been a much more substantial decline in entrepreneurial intent. Several other indicators, such as participation in some form of enterprise activity, education or training (not shown in Table 18.2), confirm these developments with small 'anti-entrepreneurial' trends in the hubs compared with much larger ones in the control areas.

It was anticipated that the hubs would reduce the proportion of young people with no interest in the entrepreneurial career option. However, there is no evidence that the hubs had any such effect. The proportion actually increased to just over 30 per cent in both the hubs and control areas. However, Table 18.2 shows there was a small impact on self-employment with the proportion increasing from 5.8 per cent to 8.9 per cent in the hubs (a statistically significant increase at the 99 per cent level) compared to a small decline in the control areas. In 2006, there was no statistically significant difference between hub and control areas; by 2009 self-employment was higher in the hubs (statistically significant at the 99 per cent level). The number of young people who said they were self-employed/running their own business was 8,850 higher than it would have been without the hubs.

Impact on Other Players

An important dimension of the hubs' remit was to influence and persuade others to get involved in the campaign. The mapping studies found that, after

Table 18.2 Effects on hub 16–30 year olds: comparison of before-and-after survey

	2006	2009
% Agreeing 'Would not try to set up in business in case it failed'		
Hubs	29	31**
Controls	31	44**
Estimated impact (number)		32900
% Strongly disagreeing 'Would not try to set-up business in case it failed'		
Hubs	33	37**
Controls	33	19**
Estimated impact (number)		45500
% Strongly agreeing 'I have what it takes to set-up my own business'		
Hubs	26	30*
Controls	25	26
Estimated impact (number)		10100
% Saying they had 'Recently thought about setting up their own business'		
Hubs	36*	34*
Controls	41	27
Estimated impact (number)		15200
% Saying 'They have no interest in setting up their own business'		
Hubs	24	30
Controls	23	31
Estimated impact (number)		2500
% Saying 'They are self-employed/running their own business (part or full time)'		
Hubs	5.8	8.9**
Controls	5.4	5.3**
Estimated impact (number)		8850

Notes: Using Chi-squared tests, hub and control area proportions of 16–30 year olds were compared in 2006 and 2009. *Denotes statistically significant differences at the 95 per cent level. **Denotes statistically significant differences at the 99 per cent level.

spending considerable time and effort winning local credibility and acceptance, the hubs successfully encouraged and assisted other organisations to develop and implement a range of projects. These included enterprise education and entrepreneurship support projects in schools, further education colleges and local authority departments such as Children's Services. However, beyond specific projects, the surveys found no evidence that they had generated widespread attitudinal or behavioural change. For example, employers' perspectives on entrepreneurs, the recruitment of 'failed' entrepreneurs, and their need for (and recruitment of) enterprising young people had not changed. Given they were not in the event targeted, this is not surprising. Nevertheless, there was a substantial increase in employer/education interaction. However, this related to employability (for example, provision of work experience) rather than the entrepreneurship agenda. Indeed, along with teachers and 'opinion formers', they became less supportive of expanding school enterprise education.

Based on the views of both employers and 'opinion formers', economic development moved to the top of the local policy agenda in the hubs and control areas. However, when asked about the means of achieving economic development, support for start-ups was lower than support for the attraction of inward investment and other business development options such as reducing business closures. Creating a more enterprising culture became a marginally higher priority but remained well down the list of priorities. Despite hub activity, there remained no strong 'lobby' or support for start-ups as a means of economic development.

Conclusion

The study was undertaken to evaluate the impact of an experimental approach to creating a more entrepreneurial youth culture. The methodology was reasonably consistent with Storey's (1998) recommended 'good practice' and towards the more sophisticated end of the Organisation for Economic Co-operation and Development's (OECD) (2008) range of entrepreneurship evaluation methodologies. It was designed to reflect planned activity and anticipated (or hoped for) impacts in such a way that a wide range of both subjective and objective baseline data were collected. To allow for the effects of other factors, control areas were carefully selected to provide estimates of a realistic counterfactual. Large sample sizes were used to enable reliable before-and-after comparisons and assessments of different hub models and policies. To link activity to longer-term impacts, a logic chain was specified to enable assessment of progress made towards the long-term goal of increasing entrepreneurship and (for an evaluation study) a reasonably long-term three-year perspective was adopted.

The importance of an appropriate evaluation methodology is perhaps well illustrated by the use of control areas. A before-and-after comparison of the hubs suggests they had minimal (or even negative) impacts. A comparison of hub and control area changes implies a substantial positive impact. However, the costs of such a methodology are high. Before committing to such cost and 'good practice', careful thought is required to ensure the methodology is appropriate for the circumstances (Greene 2009). This is particularly the case where policies, activities and, consequently, study aims are subject to change. In this study policy changes undermined some of the methodology's rationale and resulted in a substantial waste of resources. Much data was collected in the baseline surveys which proved unnecessary and was not replicated in the 'after' follow-up surveys. At the same time the adoption of a sub-regional and then regional remit meant much hub impact could not be identified because the required 'before' data for these geographically wider areas were not collected. To enable comparisons with national trends, some questions were designed to replicate national surveys. However, while the questions were identical, their differing contexts and positioning in the surveys made such comparisons unreliable. Comparisons then became impossible when the national surveys were discontinued. The best of evaluation intentions may prove impossible to realise in practice.

Beyond these practical problems, several methodological issues are worth stressing. While the research was relatively long term compared to most SME evaluation studies, it is still short term when measured against the time it takes for cultural change policies to affect entrepreneurship. Whether the observed attitudinal changes will be sustained or eventually convert into increased business formation are unknown. Despite careful selection, the control areas may not give reliable estimates of the counterfactual. Enterprise Insight activity was already relatively high in the hub areas prior to their formation and might have increased anyway. Furthermore, it is always possible to identify other potential causes of differing trends between hubs and control areas. For example, Local Enterprise Growth Initiatives were established in some of the hubs during 2006/7, but not in the control areas. These could have been responsible for some of the observed changes in the hubs (Amion Consulting 2010). Finally, it is not obvious how to convert 'cultural change' into recommended standard metrics (such as cost per additional job) to make the evaluation consistent and comparable with officially recognised methodology (BIS 2009a, 2009b, BERR 2008).

The hubs were based on the assumption that attitudes and culture can be changed to increase the supply of potential business founders. The methodological difficulties encountered during the study means the evidence is far from conclusive. Nevertheless, it appears that the hubs had a positive impact throughout the logic chain with increased awareness of entrepreneurship, a reduction in the fear of failure as a constraint on business formation, and increased entrepreneurial self-efficacy and intent. Finally, there was a positive impact on business formation and self-employment. With a relatively small resource it appears that local initiatives (especially within a wider national campaign) can have a positive impact on the supply of potential entrepreneurs in less entrepreneurial areas. In contrast, trends in the control areas illustrate the limited effects of national campaigns on socially excluded areas. A local presence is important. However, the hubs failed to reduce the proportion of young people with no interest in the entrepreneurship option. Perhaps some individuals are born non-entrepreneurs and are immune to this type of initiative. It should also be stressed that much of the hubs' positive effect was to offset what would otherwise have been a retreating enterprise culture (perhaps reflecting the financial crisis and recession which began in the UK in 2009).

The study findings suggest that intensive local campaigns publicising entrepreneurship as a social norm and a 'good thing to do' may be an effective means of increasing the business birth rate. However, as the experience and limitations of the study make clear, impact evaluation studies alone cannot provide the necessary supporting evidence or all the policy answers. A more fundamental understanding of what influences the entrepreneurial decision and the relationships between, for example, entrepreneurial attitudes, efficacy and intent is necessary (Fitzsimmons and Douglas 2010, Sequeira, Mueller and McGee 2007, Zhao, Seibert and Hills 2005, Kreuger, Reilly and Carsrud 2000, Boyd and Vozikis 1994). Policy experiments also need to be given time to work. As illustrated by the rapid demise of the hubs and the subsequent closure of Enterprise Insight in April 2011, this is far from easy. Serious long-term commitment is required before embarking on this type of initiative. Equally important, careful thought needs to be given to the definition of 'enterprise.' Enterprise Insight integrated the notions of both enterprise and employability into its campaign. These are overlapping but not identical agendas. By adopting a broad definition of enterprise, a wide range of organisations could 'sign-up' to the campaign, including some happy to support enterprise in the most generic sense but with little empathy for entrepreneurship. The review of Enterprise Week events, for example, found many were only tenuously related to entrepreneurship (Botham and Sutherland 2010). At least for the post-school age group, a more specific campaign focused on entrepreneurship (that is, business start-ups) should perhaps be seriously considered.

References

Amion Consulting. 2010. *National Evaluation of the Local Enterprise Growth Initiative Programme: Final Report*. Department of Communities and Local Government, United Kingdom. [Online] Available at www.communities. gov.uk Accessed 8th July 2012.

Bakkeries, M., Schouwstra, M. and Snijders, J. (eds) 2009. *Ten Years of Entrepreneurship Policy: A Global Overview*. Zoetermeer: EIM.

Botham, R. and Sutherland, V. 2010. *Enterprise Insight Impact Evaluation*. London. [Online] Available at www.rbotham.co.uk. Accessed 8th July 2012.

Boyd, N. and Vozikis, G. 1994. The influence of self-efficacy on the development of entrepreneurial intentions and actions. *Entrepreneurship Theory and Practice*, 18(4), 63–77.

Bridge, S. 2010. *Rethinking Enterprise Policy: Can Failure Trigger New Understanding?* London: Palgrave.

Department of Business, Enterprise and Regulatory Reform (BERR), United Kingdom 2008. *Guidance for RDAs in Appraisal, Delivery and Evaluation*. London: OffPAT.

Depatment of Business, Enterprise and Regulatory Reform and HM Treasury, United kingdom 2008. *Enterprise: Unlocking the UK's Talent*. London: HMSO.

Department of Business Innovation and Skills (BIS), United Kingdom 2009a. *Research to Improve the Assessment of Additionality*. Occasional Paper No. 1. London: BIS.

Department of Business Innovation and Skills (BIS), United Kingdom, 2009b. *RDA Evaluation; Practical Guidance in Implementing the Impact Evaluation Framework*. London: BIS.

European Commission 2003. *Green Paper: Entrepreneurship in Europe*. Brussels: European Commission.

Enterprise Insight, United Kingdom 2006. *Business Plan 2006*. London: Enterprise Insight.

Fitzsimmons, J.R. and Douglas, E.J. 2010. The interaction between feasibility and desirability in the formation of entrepreneurial intentions. *Journal of Business Venturing*, 24(4), 431–440.

Greene, F.J. 2009. Assessing the impact of policy interventions: the influence of evaluation methodology. *Environment and Planning C; Government and Policy*, 27(2), 216–229

HM Treasury, United Kingdom 2004. *Creating an enterprise culture*. Discussion Paper. London: HM Treasury.

Kreuger, N., Reilly, M. and Carsrud, A. 2000. Competing models of entrepreneurial intentions. *Journal of Business Venturing*, 15(5/6), 411–432.

Leitae, J. and Baptista, R. (eds) 2009. *Public Policies Fostering Entrepreneurship: A European Perspective.* (International Studies in Entrepreneurship): New York: Springer.

Organisation for Economic Co-operation and Development (OECD) 1998. *Fostering Entrepreneurship: The OECD Jobs Strategy.* Paris: OECD.

Organisation for Economic Co-operation and Development (OECD) 2001. *Putting the Young into Business: Policy Challenges for Youth Entrepreneurship.* Paris: OECD.

Organisation for Economic Co-operation and Development (OECD) 2008. *Framework for the Evaluation of SME and Entrepreneurial Policies and Programmes.* Paris: OECD.

Sequeira, J., Mueller, S. and McGee, J. 2007. The influence of social ties and self-efficacy in forming entrepreneurial intentions and motivating nascent behaviour. *Journal of Developmental Enrepreneurship,* 12(3), 275–293.

Small Business Service, 2004. *A Government Action Plan for Small Business: Making the UK the Best Place in the World to Set-up and Grow a Business – the Evidence Base.* Department of Trade and Industry. London: HMSO.

Stevenson, L. and Lundström A. 2001. *Patterns and Trends in Entrepreneurship Policies in Ten Economies. Vol 3 in the Entrepreneurship Policy for the Future Series.* Swedish Foundation for Small Business Research. Stockholm.

Storey, D.J. 1998. *Six Steps to Heaven: Evaluating the Impact of Public Policies to Support Small Business in Developed Economies.* Working Paper 59, Centre for Small and Medium Sized Enterprise, University of Warwick, Coventry, United Kingdom.

Zhao, H., Seibert, C. and Hills, C. 2005. The mediating role of self-efficacy in the development of entrepreneurial intentions. *Journal of Applied Psychology,* 90(2), 1265–1272.

19

Challenging Default Perspectives on Entrepreneurship and Small Businesses

Simon Bridge and Ken O'Neill

Chapter Summary

Policies for encouraging and supporting small businesses start-up and/or growth have been pursued for many years. However, much of what is variously (and sometimes imprecisely) described as enterprise, entrepreneurship and small business policy appears not to work, because overall rates of entrepreneurship or business growth have not risen, at least not in a way which is attributable to specific interventions.

The programmes used to deliver such policies are generally designed, delivered and/or supported or observed by people such as government policymakers, delivery agency staff and management consultants, or other 'professionals' including business academics. These people have generally approached entrepreneurship and small businesses from a professional rather than a practitioner route and often appear to share a 'professional' perspective on small businesses.

This chapter argues that, too often, such a perspective and the policy initiatives which have been informed by it are based on a set of unstated, untested and apparently questionable assumptions about what motivates entrepreneurs and how they behave in the context of their businesses. The impact of this has been the failure of policy, with a consequent waste of public monies and the disillusionment of entrepreneurs. Therefore, if effective policy is to be developed, these assumptions need to be challenged and revised.

Introduction

In the eighteenth century Cantillon introduced the word entrepreneur to economic discourse, and two centuries later Schumpeter highlighted the essential contribution of the entrepreneur to economic development. Nevertheless, it was not until about 30 years ago, after the publication of Birch's findings that small businesses were the key creators of new jobs (Birch 1979), that governments really became interested in them, and therefore in the entrepreneurs behind them.

Because entrepreneurs are supposed to create new small businesses which are expected to provide more jobs and other economic benefits, governments have since pursued 'enterprise' policies to encourage entrepreneurship and small businesses. However it is becoming clear that much of what is variously (and sometimes imprecisely) described as enterprise, entrepreneurship and/ or small business policy appears to have failed, because overall rates of entrepreneurship or business growth have not risen, at least not in a way which is attributable to specific interventions (Norrman and Bager-Sjögren 2010, Bennett 2008, Greene, Mole and Storey 2008, Huggins and Williams 2007, the Richard Review 2007 and Bannock 2005).

The field of enterprise policy is complex. It has many components, including research, formulation, objectives, appraisal, delivery methods, instruments, monitoring and evaluation. In turn these components depend on the input of many people, embracing not just politicians but also government officials, enterprise agency staff, management consultants, business academics – and entrepreneurs.

It might seem obvious that, if policies are failing, they should be ended and the cost of delivering them saved. However, once started, policies acquire a considerable momentum. Governments usually want to be seen to do something, so doing nothing is not attractive and no alternatives may appear to be available. Also, often, those responsible for policy have the comfort of knowing that they are following the example of what is presented as international best practice which, in turn, is supported by received wisdom about entrepreneurs and small businesses (Bridge 2010). Thus there is an incentive to ignore or discount warnings of failure.

Disentangling policy, and establishing the reasons for failure, is not an easy process. Nevertheless this chapter suggests that a start could be made by reassessing the received wisdom about entrepreneurship and small business which supports much policy. Through their contacts with people throughout the policy system, the authors have observed that most of them have acquired their understanding of enterprise indirectly, not from close involvement with owners or running their own businesses, but from sources such as professional courses and colleagues. As a result they have come to share with other business 'professionals', such as accountants and bank managers, a perspective on entrepreneurship and small businesses which seems to be derived from a set of assumptions which are often unstated, and which, consequently, usually go unchallenged.

However, if some of these assumptions are wrong, then the 'professional' perspective based on them may be inappropriate. This, in turn, will have an impact, not just on policy design and/or delivery, but also on any assessment of that policy and any diagnosis of its failure. Identifying and reassessing these assumptions would be a necessary first step for any substantive re-appraisal of policy in this area.

Enterprise policy is not the only field of knowledge afflicted by such shortcomings. For example, in the field of medical practice bleeding patients to cure them was once the received wisdom, but is now considered to be counter-productive. Nevertheless, before other cures could be developed and applied, it was necessary to re-educate the doctors. Without that, their diagnoses and prescriptions would not have changed and new methods would not have been sought.

Therefore the aim of this chapter is to present the case that policy initiatives have too often been based on a set of unproven and untested assumptions about what motivates entrepreneurs and how they behave in the context of their businesses. Because this has led to the failure of policy (with a consequent waste of public monies) and to the disillusionment of entrepreneurs, these assumptions need to be challenged and revised if new effective policy is to be developed.

Identifying and Examining the Assumptions

Identifying the assumptions which underlie received enterprise wisdom is difficult because, although they have long been held, they are rarely acknowledged. Lists of them cannot be assembled from official sources because they are taken, often sub-consciously, as given and not recorded. Based on the authors' own experience and observation, five of the more common examples are explored here:

ASSUMPTION: THE KEY COMPONENT IS THE BUSINESS

It is assumed that the principal components of the small businesses sector are the small businesses themselves, and so it is on the businesses that any analysis should focus.

It was in the mid-1990s that Scott and Rosa (1996) pointed out that much research in this area assumed that the firm was the fundamental unit of definition and analysis. They commented that, while the role of the entrepreneur as founder of the firm might be acknowledged, the practice of firm-level analysis was paramount and underlay other key assumptions. It is easy to see why there should be such a focus. As indicated above, Birch highlighted small businesses, rather than the entrepreneurs behind them, as the key creators of new jobs. Businesses are easier to measure and evaluate, they can be seen to start or to end, they have turnovers and employment levels which can be measured, and it is businesses which deliver things people want such as jobs and economic growth.

However, in common with Scott and Rosa, Gibb (1988: 14–15) had earlier highlighted the need, when dealing with small businesses, to understand their owner–managers:

> To many managers the business is the ego ... Attitudes of owner-managers may therefore not be as objective or impersonal as those of professional managers ... The business will embody the value system of the owner-manager reflecting his [sic] own personal objectives and those of his family. He may not therefore easily identify with the value systems of advisers, accountants, bank managers and professional managers of large companies.

If small businesses thus reflect the attitudes of their owner–managers, then the key component to consider in seeking to understand small business actions will be the person, not the business. As Gibb suggests, owner–managers often do not perceive a separation between themselves and their businesses, and will make business decisions for their own personal reasons rather that because of any 'business' logic. Thus, for instance, when a grant support programme offers grants to help business to grow, the businesses' owners may be motivated by different objectives than those intended by the initiators of such a programme. Some owners, for example, will see capital grants as a source of help in emulating peer businesses which are acquiring attractive new machines or as a means of increasing their asset worth in the short-term. Thus while grants will be applied for and better machines bought, any effect on business growth may be coincidental.

ASSUMPTION: BUSINESSES SEEK TO MAXIMISE THEIR PROFITS

It is assumed that any business exists to maximise the financial return to its owner(s).

The assumption that the sole, or at least the main, purpose of a business is to maximise the financial return to its owners implies that a business should focus its attention on its 'bottom line'. However Bridge, O'Neill and Martin (2009: 245), when examining what constitutes success or failure in a small business context, identified two models of success. Many business professionals, they suggest, look primarily at the business and have as their model of the successful business one that is achieving its highest potential in terms of growth, market share, productivity, profitability, return on capital invested or other measures of the performance of the business itself. However, they point out, many owner–managers of small businesses do not have the same model. Their main concern is whether the business is supplying the benefits they want from it. These benefits are often associated with a lifestyle and an income level to maintain it and, if that is achieved satisfactorily, they see no need to grow the business further.

Scase and Goffee (1987: 161) pointed out some time ago that, while 'politicians and opinion formers … often claim that people who start their own businesses are motivated solely by economic self-interest … We found in our study few 'entrepreneurial personalities' fuelled entirely by the quest for profit maximisation'. Beaver (2003: 2) has also commented that 'few owner–managers and entrepreneurs make financial gain their primary goal'.

Businesses, it has been suggested, are in reality driven by the decisions of people who 'are purpose maximisers, not just profit maximisers' (Pink 2010: 29) – which implies that, in order to understand their business intentions, it is necessary to ascertain what their purposes are. In other words, rather than being an end in itself, 'an enterprise is a goal-realisation device' (Hunter 2007).

What are their owners' goals and what, therefore, do owners want of their businesses? Often it seems they want sufficient profit to support what might be called a 'lifestyle' and, while they might desire more profit, they do not want to have to expend the further time and effort involved in increasing turnover and/or employment that might be necessary to get it. One comparison between businesses in Northern Ireland and similar businesses in Germany reported that in Northern Ireland public policy appeared 'to have reinforced market failure because the firms in Northern Ireland lacked the incentive to train more, to invest more in R and D [research and development], and to aim for higher quality products because they were already profitable enough … because of the subsidy to profits arising from grants' (Hitchens, Wagner and Birnie 1989: 19). Proving this *a priori*, however, is another matter as both grant applicants and grant givers know that their paperwork has to demonstrate the need for the grant in business growth terms.

Even when its owners want a business to make more profit, it seems that focusing primarily on profit can be bad for a business. For instance, Kay (2010:

8 and 1) has reported investigations which suggest that 'the most profitable businesses are not the most profit-oriented' and that 'visionary companies make more money than … purely profit driven companies'.

ASSUMPTION: BUSINESSES HAVE A GROWTH IMPERATIVE

It is assumed that, in order to maximise the financial return to its owner(s), a business will want to grow.

This assumption seems to be behind the comment in one small business guide that 'one of the things that most, if not all, businesses have in common is a desire to grow and expand' (Ulster Bank 2008: 5). While that quote might exemplify the prevailing professional view about growth as an inherent imperative for all businesses, the reality is that businesses are inanimate and of themselves do not want anything. It is their owners and/or managers who want something and, as suggested above, often that is not primarily business profitability and growth. Nevertheless, most small business policy initiatives seem to be based on the assumption that growth is the normal aspiration of a business which implies that, if a business is not growing, it must be due to one or more constraints such as a lack of finance, inadequate information or poor training. Therefore providing more finance, information, and/or training should enable the frustrated growth to proceed.

Similarly in horticulture it was thought that plants naturally tried to grow and that, if they did not, it was due to external constraints such as a lack of warmth and light, a drought, or a shortage of nutrients. Thus, growth was assumed to be the natural tendency for a plant. However recent research (Harberd 2007) suggests that growth is restrained by internal inhibitors (arising from parts of a plant's DNA) and therefore non-growth is actually normal. Growth may occur when the conditions are right for the plant to produce hormones which overcome the growth-restraining effects of the inhibitors, but just providing more sunlight, water and/or fertiliser may not be enough. It is further suggested that this lack of growth can be in a plant's longer-term interest if it prevents it from growing too fast for its conditions.

Might businesses also have internal growth inhibitors, with those inhibitors being located in the minds of their owners? If those owners don't want to grow their businesses, then incentives designed to help their businesses grow by relieving constraints will have little effect. Does this account in part for the commonly reported 'failure' of small businesses adequately to avail of the services of public support agencies and others?

ASSUMPTION: BUSINESSES DECISIONS ARE BASED ON LOGIC

It is assumed that a business will follow that course which a quantitative logical analysis suggests will offer the best balance of risk and reward.

Some commentators on entrepreneurship have specifically stated that 'the assumption [is] that individuals choose between wage-employment and business ownership by assessing and weighing the potential financial and non-pecuniary rewards and risks' (Wennekers, Uhlaner and Thurik 2002: 37) and that 'an individual's decision upon whether to become an entrepreneur will be based on a comparison of the expected reward to entrepreneurship and the reward for the best alternative use of his time' (Casson 2003: 195). Thus Bridge (2010) argues that, throughout the world, much entrepreneurship policy is based on this assumption of conscious, logical risk-benefit assessment. Therefore the methods used to encourage entrepreneurship involve the provision of finance, training, advice and/or premises because it is assumed that this help will sway logical decisions by making it easier and less risky to start a business and/or by increasing the perceived benefits.

The assumption that logic, even in the form of bounded rationality, is always applied in business decisions may be supported by feedback from owners/managers. Being human, they will try to rationalise the actions they take and to persuade others, and even themselves, that it was the logical thing to do. This, for instance, was recognised by Benjamin Franklin in what has been called Franklin's Gambit: 'so convenient a thing it is to be a reasonable creature, since it enables one to find or make a reason for everything one had in mind to do' (Franklin 1791: 88).

But in reality owner–managers of small businesses often have guiding motives other than profit maximisation (Stanworth and Curran 1973). They are people and people are very socially influenced, as behavioural economics now recognises (New Economics Foundation 2005), and they do things to conform to what they think is the social norm. For instance Turner (2008: 223) has pointed out that 'social influences can affect such outcomes as creativity, innovation, originality, and inventiveness' while Bridge (2010) suggests that many business start-up decisions are the result, not of logical analysis, but of family and/or peer culture. He concludes that, if the aim of policy is to encourage more people to start businesses, rather than just to help those who will probably start anyhow, then policy effectiveness is unlikely to improve until this reality is recognised.

ASSUMPTION: BUSINESS PLANS ARE ESSENTIAL AND MEANINGFUL

It is assumed that the logical analysis of the best business course to follow, and the steps needed to implement it, will be established by developing a business plan.

It seems almost to be a fixation of some business 'professionals', especially those trying to help start-ups, that, when founding or growing a business, the essential first step should be a business plan. Examples of this are a bank website which states that 'if you intend to start a business you need to write a business plan' (HSBC 2011) and a business text book which states that 'one of the most important steps in setting up any new business is to develop a business plan' (Burns 2011: 365). In other words it is assumed that when starting or growing a business, a business plan is not only an appropriate, but also a necessary, help and that it will correctly reflect the business's aims and plans.

However business plans were designed by professionals, not business owners, and they do not necessarily suit owners' purposes. Indeed, it would appear that for many start-up businesses the traditional business plan is not helpful. For them the future cannot be well forecast: there are too many unknowns which are often impossible to assess without running the business for a period. Therefore, in practice it is impossible for many people contemplating business starts-ups to make useful projections for key aspects of business until they have actually been operating for a representative period. Forcing such people to produce written plans according to the standard format may only introduce an unhelpful hurdle which might act as a significant deterrent to getting the business started. An alternative approach which is often more appropriate and is used by many entrepreneurs is the 'entrepreneurial method', based on effectuation principles and advocated by Sarasvathy and Venkataraman (2011), but it is rarely promoted officially.

Even when they are prepared, business plans do not even necessarily reflect the business owners' intentions because, especially in the case of grant applications, it is the authors' experience that business plans are tailored to justify the grant or otherwise meet the funder's expectations. The applying businesses, the people assessing the applications, and any accountants or other consultants hired to prepare the business plans all know that if the plans do not justify the applications, the applications will be rejected. It is thus in the interest of all those involved to have, and to believe in, plans which do justify the applications. The end result is that applications for finance will often be adapted to meet the criteria of the funders, regardless of the reality of the owners' ambitions.

A 'Default' Perspective

Only five assumptions are considered above. In practice there are significant others. Because they are long-held, documenting the origins of many assumptions is not easy. Collectively, and because they have been accepted for so long without being challenged, they have developed into a pervasive perspective about entrepreneurship and small businesses which has become what J. K. Galbraith called the 'conventional wisdom':

> *We associate truth with convenience [and] with what most closely accords with self-interest and personal well-being or promises best to avoid awkward effort or unwelcome dislocation of life ... Economic and social behaviour are complex, and to comprehend their character is mentally tiring. Therefore we adhere, as though to a raft, to those ideas which represent our understanding. (Galbraith 1958: 7)*

Does this perspective influence policy? If those formulating policy or those evaluating it share the same perception, they are not likely to highlight or question it, or the assumptions on which it is based. Since it is a poorly researched topic the evidence that policy is based on such assumptions tends to be anecdotal, as in the following examples based on the authors' findings:

CUTTING TAXES TO STIMULATE GREATER EFFORT

Policy assumptions: People seek to maximise their financial return and will respond logically to opportunities so to do. Reducing income tax will therefore provide an incentive to work more.

Result: For people in certain categories of (self-) employment (such as cab driving), whose target is a particular level of weekly income after tax, a lower rate of income tax means that fewer hours were needed to achieve this goal. Thus, for them, a cut in tax rates led to fewer hours being worked, not more; Scase and Goffee (1987: 53) even suggest that high taxes can paradoxically encourage the creation of enterprise.

CAPITAL GRANTS TO STIMULATE BUSINESS GROWTH

Policy assumptions: Businesses want to grow but are restricted by a lack of finance. Capital grants will therefore stimulate growth because they will contribute to the finance necessary for growth. (It is also generally also assumed that applications for such grants can be assessed on the basis of business plans submitted with them.)

Result: The availability of grants can have unintended and unwanted consequences. Capital grants for machines have encouraged their purchase by some business owners – not to increase capacity, productivity and competitiveness (as typically reflected in their business plans) but for different reasons. Such owners have taken advantage of grants simply because others have done so. They didn't want to feel that they were missing an opportunity or were less progressive than their peers and competitors. In such circumstances future unit costs can rise instead of fall. The new (more expensive) machine may often be more complex and have higher depreciation and maintenance costs (which would not be grant-aided). Thus a business can, as a direct result of the grants, have higher future production costs with no compensating increase in output.

In both these examples it is suggested that the policies concerned failed, at least in part, because they were based on incorrect assumptions. It might be argued that, if they are wrong, these assumptions will, over time, be corrected by better information provided by research. Indeed, as explained by Gibb, since the 1980s there has been 'an explosion of research into entrepreneurship and the small and medium enterprise'. But, he adds, nevertheless 'there has been a growth of ignorance' – an ignorance about entrepreneurship manifest, for instance, in the assumptions that guide policy (Gibb 2000: 13–14).

It is suggested here that these assumptions are part of that ignorance because many people will not consciously be aware of the link between the assumptions and the overall mind-set they have acquired. Thus their perspective has become detached from the reasoning that created it. The result is that, even if some assumptions are corrected, the perspective, and any thinking based on it, will still persist. Even if it is directly challenged, custom and practice means that any change to the perspective is likely to be resisted, as indicated by Paine in 'Common Sense':

> A long habit of not thinking something is WRONG, gives it a superficial appearance of being RIGHT, and raises at first a formidable outcry in defence of custom. (Paine 1776: 63)

This chapter contends that this perspective is what many people working in this area pick up from inadequate involvement with the business owner. It has become, nevertheless, the 'default' view of the small business sector, and of the businesses within it. It is a 'default' because it is like the standard setting on a computer which is downloaded with the software and which, while it can be overridden for particular applications, will still be reloaded when next operating in that area. Thus, although individuals may intellectually know that some of the assumptions are wrong, they continue to act in accordance with the overall perception to which the assumptions have contributed.

Attacking the perspective piecemeal is thus unlikely to work. It is like a persistent weed in a garden which will not be dispatched by just cutting down what is in view. Instead, for permanent removal, it is necessary to get to the roots and destroy them.

Conclusion

According to Galbraith (1958: 11), 'the enemy of the conventional wisdom is not ideas but the march of events'. The thinking behind this chapter was triggered by the emerging evidence that much entrepreneurship and small business policy is failing and that much of the money spent on them is therefore wasted. It is suggested that much of that policy is informed by a conventional wisdom of entrepreneurship and small businesses which is based on questionable assumptions.

Showing that policy initiatives are based on such wisdom and its underlying assumptions is difficult, as often neither the assumptions nor the policy rationale are recorded. But typical policy schemes for encouraging small business start-up and growth are consistent with this view. Frequently they appear to focus on the business, rather than the owner–manager; they appear to assume that businesses want to increase their profit; and they thus believe there is a growth imperative constrained by external factors such as a shortage of finance, of training or of information. They seem therefore to expect that there will be a logical response to schemes which seek to encourage growth by addressing those constraints, and often they seem to accept business plans as reliable statements of business intentions.

It is acknowledged that fully diagnosing the reasons for policy failure requires consideration of many aspects of policy including its formulation, management, communication, implementation and evaluation. Exploring all of that is beyond the scope of this chapter. Nevertheless the contention of this chapter is that much entrepreneurship and small business policy is designed and/or carried out by people who may, albeit unconsciously, share a perspective of enterprise based on false assumptions. Policy is also often evaluated by people who share the same perspective and, as a result, policy evaluations will often fail to pick up these errors. If evaluators have not queried the assumptions underlying the policy process, that cannot be taken as evidence that the assumptions are correct.

This does not mean that it is impossible to influence the dynamics of many businesses, but it does mean that just continuing present policy is unlikely to do it. Although policy may not be based directly on the assumptions explored here, it is likely to be affected by them, as they appear to contribute to a default perspective which influences the thinking of both policymakers and deliverers. If it is not corrected, this perspective is likely to continue to affect not just policy design and delivery, but also its review and evaluation. Addressing this throughout the system should therefore be a priority. It will not be the end of the process of correcting policy, but it would be a necessary start.

References

Bannock, G. 2005. *The Economics and Management of Small Business*. London: Routledge.

Beaver, G. 2003. Beliefs and principles: the compass in guiding strategy. *Strategic Change*, 12(1), 1–5.

Bennett, R. 2008. SME policy support on Britain since the 1990s: what have we learnt? *Environment and Planning C: Government and Policy*, 26(2), 375–397.

Birch, D. 1979. *The Job Generation Process*. Cambridge, MA: MIT Programme on Neighborhood and Regional Change.

Bridge, S. 2010. *Rethinking Enterprise Policy: Can Failure Trigger New Understanding?* Basingstoke: Palgrave Macmillan.

Bridge, S., O'Neill, K. and Martin, F. 2009. *Understanding Enterprise, Entrepreneurship and Small Business*. Basingstoke: Palgrave Macmillan.

Burns, P. 2011. *Entrepreneurship and Small Business*, 3rd edition. Basingstoke: Palgrave Macmillan.

Casson, M. 2003. *The Entrepreneur: An Economic Theory*. Cheltenham: Edward Elgar.

Franklin, B. 1791. *The Autobiography of Benjamin Franklin*. New Haven, CT: Yale University Press, reprinted 1964.

Galbraith, J.K. 1958. *The Affluent Society*, 4th edition. London: Penguin, reprinted 1991.

Gibb, A.A. 1988. *Towards the Building of Entrepreneurial Models of Support for Small Business*. 11th National Small Firms Policy and Research Conference, Cardiff.

Gibb, A.A. 2000. SME policy, academic research and the growth of ignorance. *International Small Business Journal*, 18(3), 13–35.

Greene, F.J., Mole, K.F. and Storey, D.J. 2008. *Three Decades of Enterprise Culture*. Basingstoke: Palgrave Macmillan.

Harberd, N. 2007. *Seed to Seed: The Secret Life of Plants*. London: Bloomsbury.

Hitchens, D.M.W.N., Wagner, K. and Birnie, J.E. 1989. *Northern Ireland Manufacturing Productivity Compared with West Germany: Statistical Summary of the Findings of a Matched Plant Comparison*. Belfast: Northern Ireland Economic Research Centre.

HSBC 2011. *Quick Start Business Plan*. [Online] Available at: www.tsbc.co.uk/sbo/hsbckn/viewLesson.aspx?lid=35&cid=1 [accessed: 16 August 2011].

Huggins, R. and Williams, N. 2007. *Enterprise and Public Policy: A Review of Labour Government Intervention in the United Kingdom*. University of Sheffield Management School Discussion Paper No 2007.03, August.

Hunter, L. 2007. Speaking at University of Ulster seminar on 'Developing a strategy and vision for social entrepreneurship', 10 September.

Kay, J. 2010. *Obliquity*. London: Profile Books.

New Economics Foundation 2005. *Behavioural Economics: Seven Principles For Policy Makers*. London: New Economics Foundation.

Norrman, C. and Bager-Sjögren, L. 2010. Entrepreneurship policy to support new innovative ventures: Is it effective? *International Small Business Journal*, 28(6), 602–619.

Paine, T. 1776. *Common Sense*. Edition edited by Isaac Kramnick London: Penguin, 1976.

Pink, D. 2010. Gainful employment, *RSA Journal*, Spring.

Richard Review on Small Business & Government, Interim Report 2007. [Online] Available at: www.conservatives.com/pdf/richardreport-interim-2007.pdf [accessed: 17 October 2009].

Sarasvathy, S.D. and Venkataraman, S. 2011. Entrepreneurship as method: open questions for an entrepreneurial future. *Entrepreneurship Theory and Practice*, 35(1), 113–135.

Scase, R. and Goffee, R. 1987. *The Real World of the Small Business Owner*. London: Croon Helm.

Scott, M. and Rosa, P. 1996. Has firm level analysis reached its limits? Time for a rethink, *International Small Business Journal*, 14(4), 81–99.

Stanworth, M.J.K. and Curran, J. 1973. *Management Motivation in the Smaller Business*. Epping: Gower Press.

Turner, M. 2008. Introduction – social influence and creativity: setting the stage for inventiveness. *Social Influence*, 3(4), 223–227.

Ulster Bank 2008. *Business Bite*, 2nd edition. Belfast: Ulster Bank.

Wennekers, S. Uhlaner, L.M. and Thurik, R. 2002. Entrepreneurship and its conditions: a macro perspective. *International Journal of Entrepreneurship Education*, 1(1), 25–67.

20

Pragmatic Approaches to Evaluating SME Policies and Programmes

Kim Houghton and Thomas Fell

Chapter Summary

Most countries, whether developed or developing, offer government-provided, or government-subsidised, policies and programmes to assist SMEs. Evaluation of policies and programmes can serve many purposes including: continuous improvement; demonstrating value for money; quantifying tangible outcomes; strengthening the case for continued funding; or helping recruitment of enthusiastic participants, partners or sponsors. Evaluation of the benefits of these policies and programmes is complicated by three common challenges: lack of clearly defined objectives; difficulties linking cause and effect; and problems deciding and resourcing the most suitable level of evaluation activities.

Reliable methods exist which can overcome these challenges and provide quality information that can be used to meet the diverse purposes of SME policy and programme evaluation. Sound understanding of six useful methods detailed in this chapter can help tailor the design of an evaluation to suit the purposes and resourcing available. These tools are: activity measures, satisfaction feedback, surveys, focus groups, interviews and case studies. Judicious use of these methods enables evaluations to be undertaken efficiently, while also ensuring comprehensive and robust results.

Introduction

SMEs are usually a significant part of a country's economy, and in most developed and developing countries taxpayer funds are used to provide assistance to support their growth and development (Hill 2002, Stevenson and Lundström 2001, Storey 2000). The variety of forms that this assistance may take is discussed elsewhere in this book, but while assistance may be politically popular, there are few examples of evaluations that rigorously assess whether or not the outcomes justify the expense. The diversity of policy instruments used to support SMEs, coupled with the common neglect to build clear objectives into programme design (Robson, Wijbenga and Parker 2009, Donaldson and Gooler 2003, Storey 2000, Curran 2000), makes the effective evaluation of public policies that target SMEs a challenging activity.

Ideally, the objectives of a policy will be set out clearly and with measurable targets, allowing an evaluator to follow a clear process for assessment. However, this is rarely if ever the case when dealing with programmes for SMEs (OECD 2004, Wren and Storey 2002, Curran 2000, Storey 2000). It is more likely that an evaluator will have to infer what to assess based on the stated objectives of the policy and the data and methods available, which most often will be retrospective and participatory (that is, based on surveys, consultation, interviews or focus groups), rather than based on controlled data collected before and after an evaluation.

This chapter discusses the issues faced in designing and implementing SME policy evaluations. It considers both challenges and solutions, and offers a practical framework, using the methods most often available to evaluators, for undertaking cost-effective, meaningful evaluations.

Why Evaluate SME Policies and Programmes?

Deficiencies or difficulties in evaluating SME policy do not mean there is no value in undertaking evaluations or having a requirement for an evaluation. Embedding evaluation activities into programme delivery is the critical ingredient in enabling a cycle of continuous improvement, where feedback from participants on experiences and outcomes is used to refine programme elements and further improve outcomes.

At the policy level, too, evaluation has many benefits. 'Evidence-based' policy is the best practice model in many jurisdictions, emphasising long-term monitoring and evaluation so that available money and effort are focused on the areas of greatest need (Hall and Jennings 2006). For government agencies, effective evaluation can help build the case for refunding a programme, and can have benefits for the organisations or stakeholders involved in programme implementation, such as providing the opportunity to 'sell' or 'celebrate' success stories. The ability to state a programme's benefits (or failings) in rigorous analytical terms can help encourage wider SME participation, will help build relationships with funding and delivery partners, and may also help to avoid politicisation.

SME Policy Evaluation: Challenges

This section considers three main difficulties associated with designing and implementing an effective evaluation: defining clear objectives, linking cause and effect, and deciding on a suitable level of sophistication.

CLEAR OBJECTIVES

Clearly stated objectives of a policy are fundamental to effective evaluation, as they set the targets against which progress should be measured. However, objectives are often stated in a way that makes it difficult to assess whether they have been achieved, or are not defined clearly at all (Barrett, Billington and Neeson 2004, Curran 2000). For example, the Organisation for Economic Co-operation and Development (OECD) (2004) explains that objectives are often specified in generic terms, such as a desire to promote an 'enterprise culture'. Taking this example, an evaluator could consider a wide range of measures that could be used to assess policy impact. These might include the number of new firms started, those started by young or disadvantaged people, those started by people who have not been in business before, the increase in the total number of firms, whether these firms grow and whether the firms survive. All could be considered measures of whether an 'enterprise culture' has been achieved, but assessing the overall effectiveness of the policy will be strongly influenced by the particular measures and targets used. The clearer the objectives, goals and targets, the more robust the evaluation assessment will be.

LINKING CAUSE AND EFFECT

Accounting for the myriad of influences upon the performance of an SME, other than that of programme participation or policy direction, is another challenging aspect of evaluation. These influences include the skill of the owner, the sector and location of the business, macro-economic conditions and the role of chance. In principle, only when proper account is taken of these exogenous factors can the impact of the programme be estimated (OECD 2004).

Additionality refers to net positive outcomes attributed reliably to a policy or programme (Curran 2000). Data from qualitative methods usually cannot prove additionality, as in principle it can only be measured using before-and-after research designs, and this has proved difficult in practice for SME policies and programmes (Donaldson and Gooler 2003, Curran 2000, Storey 2000). However, Vega, Chiasson and Brown (2011) note that, while important, additionality is not the only objective of evaluation of policies affecting small business.

ATTAINING THE RIGHT LEVEL OF SOPHISTICATION

Storey (2000) provides an analytical framework for classifying SME evaluation tools that has become widely used. The paper identifies 'six steps to heaven', beginning with the most simple and ending with the most sophisticated in terms of analytical rigour. The steps are also divided into what Storey considers to be 'monitoring' and 'evaluation'. Table 20.1 shows Storey's six steps.

Table 20.1   'Six Steps to Heaven'

Monitoring
Step 1 Take up of schemes
Step 2 Recipients' opinions
Step 3 Recipients' views of the difference made by assistance
Evaluation
Step 4 Comparison of the performance of typical and assisted firms
Step 5 Comparison with 'match' firms
Step 6 Taking account of selection bias

With regard to these steps, Storey (2000: 186) says:

> *The difference between monitoring and evaluation is that the latter are attempts, demonstrating analytical rigour, to determine the impact of the policy initiatives. Monitoring, on the other hand, merely either documents activity under the programme or reports participants' perception of the value of the scheme. In short, the difference between monitoring and evaluation is that monitoring relies exclusively upon the views of the recipients of the policy. Evaluation however seeks, by some means, to contrast these with non-recipients, in order to present a 'counter-factual'. The difference between actual changes and the 'counter-factual' is viewed as the impact of the policy.*

Ideally, it would seem, evaluation should always be carried out at the fourth, fifth and/or sixth level. The argument for the highest level of evaluation is that it ensures that two or more programmes can be compared because they have been evaluated in the same way. In addition, programmes that have not been compared to a control group, or in other words those that have not been evaluated against what Storey has called the 'counter-factual', are more likely to have their impacts overstated (OECD 2004).

Unfortunately, the more sophisticated levels of evaluation are usually also the most expensive and resource intensive; statistical expertise and monitoring of programme and non-programme participants are required. The most sophisticated approaches also assume that the policy design incorporates evaluation so that the correct data exists and/or will be collected during implementation, which is rarely the case (for example see Schaper 2008, Barrett et al. 2004). In addition, it is difficult to justify the same level of evaluation, and hence resource allocation, for small and large programmes. Finally, the most sophisticated approaches operate by comparing firms that participate in programmes or policies with those that do not, so they cannot be used to examine policies that apply to all firms in the economy simultaneously, such as tax incentives that are taken up by all SMEs (OECD 2004).

It can be seen that, in practice, the highest levels of evaluation are sometimes unattainable and even undesirable. While it is important to use these approaches where possible, often evaluations are retrospective, and are limited to the use of information readily available from the participants. The next section discusses how to get the most out of such information using a variety of tools.

Evaluation Using Participatory Methods

As a result of the challenges discussed above, an evaluator will often have to deal with some form of participatory method to obtain information. The term 'participatory' is used here in a similar sense to that used by Diez (2001), in that it describes evaluation methods that involve the participants of the programme and have an element of collaboration and learning. This approach, while having quantitative elements, relies heavily on qualitative methods. Even when appropriate quantitative measures are available, evaluators should consider the advantages of qualitative techniques to complement hard data. Curran and Blackburn (2001) have pointed out that qualitative methods have the ability to capture the heterogeneous, human element that is so important to the micro-level of small business growth and decision making.

This section provides an inventory of six participatory methods for SME policy evaluation and discusses some practical issues associated with using such methods. The methods are: activity measures, satisfaction feedback, surveys, focus groups, interviews, and case studies. Figure 20.1 illustrates how these methods can be applied across four stages of analysis.

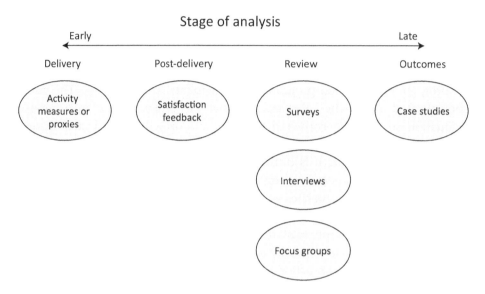

Figure 20.1   Participatory methods

ACTIVITY MEASURES

Information on the number of activities and number of participants is usually collected by the organisation delivering a programme. Information collected may include actions like website hits, calls to hotlines, or registered users of online programmes, as well as the number of participants in more personalised services. Gathering this information is central to any type of monitoring or evaluation, as it provides the foundation information from which to investigate aspects like the cost of delivery (an efficiency measure) or the outcomes achieved.

In some cases reliable measures of the variables actually needed are not available and proxy measures need to be used (for example, see Nishimura and Okamuro 2011). Some examples are shown in Table 20.2.

SATISFACTION FEEDBACK

For those programmes based on specific events, for example a workshop or an advice session, it is often useful for post-activity feedback to be gathered, preferably at the completion of the event. Completion of a survey immediately after participation (for collection by those delivering the event) improves

Table 20.2   Examples of outcomes and typical proxy measurement variables

Outcomes Desired	Proxies		
Greater innovation	Patents granted	R&D investment accounted for	R&D tax offsets claimed
Improved safety	Reported accidents	Documented safety procedures reviewed	Safety meetings and follow-up
Improved business strategy	Turnover/employment trends	New products/markets	Survival rates
Reduced business failure	Debt levels	Turnover/employment trends	Survival rates

response rates and is preferred to allowing participants to complete their evaluation forms later and post them back or lodge them online. Response rates will also generally be better when the post-event questionnaires are designed to have the least 'interruption potential'; that is to make them as short and easy to complete as possible, while still gathering the information needed (Brinkerhoff, Brethower, Hluchyj and Nowakowski 1983: 87).

Post-event evaluations can elicit information such as broad satisfaction with the event, knowledge gained, possible improvements and any follow-up expected. Evaluators can also consider Likert-style intensity scale questions that relate to the respondents' opinions on achievement of broader programme objectives (for example, see Nardi 2006: 74–77).

SURVEYS

Questionnaires are an efficient way of surveying large numbers of respondents in a short time period. Depending on circumstance and information needed, surveys may be self-administered, computer or web-based, conducted by face-to-face interview or over the telephone. Because survey research is more suitable to probability sampling than interviews or focus groups, it can usually be generalised to larger populations, making it a useful tool for policy or programme evaluation (Nardi 2006: 68). In the context of SME policy evaluation, surveys can be used as a follow-up to a given programme, asking questions about the processes and participant experiences, or as a way of testing whether broader outcomes have been achieved, or as a combination of both. Longitudinal surveys can also be useful for measuring the achievement of policy objectives over time (Nardi 2006: 121).

Survey questions can be 'open-ended' (participants answering questions in their own words) or 'closed-ended' (participants choosing from a number of options), with the latter being more efficient and easier to analyse, but with the disadvantage of limiting the depth of information available. The evaluator can use a mix of open and closed questions depending on the information needed, and open questions are typically coded into groups of similar answers during the analysis phase. Survey questions about outcomes will need to be as specific as possible in order to retrieve the right information. For example, a question that seeks to measure value creation should gauge increases in employment or turnover attributable to the programme that are over and above a base case or 'business as usual'. A 'counter-factual' question may also be useful, for example: 'Would you have made these changes without your involvement in the programme?' This will not yield as defensible a data set as a formal control group, but it will provide some indication of the way in which the programme has impacted on the firm.

With regard to sample size, a heterogeneous population will require a suitable sample to reflect its diversity. Random sampling is the best way to ensure that results can be generalised, and stratified random sampling, where respondents are randomly selected from predetermined categories within the population, provides the most efficient method of probability sampling for heterogeneous populations (Nardi 2006, Bartlett, Kotrlik and Higgins 2001). In the case of SMEs, which are often very diverse in their circumstances, such categories could include business size, industry and location. While a larger sample is in general more likely to be statistically valid than a small one, the evaluator should be aware of the statistical impact of increasing sample size, as the considerable time and cost of increasing the sample may not reflect similar gains in reliability. For example, Mole (2002) was satisfied with a response rate of 175 (25 per cent) out of 712 Personal Business Advisers in England, as this was a typical response rate to a self-administered survey (mailout or emailed surveys often have a response rate of around 20 per cent) and showed no location bias.

Good practice in survey design involves making a survey as efficient as possible – gathering the most useful information in the most efficient way. Many surveys end up being too long, cluttered with questions which might be 'nice to know' but which evaluators do not actually 'need to know'. Surveys which are too long place an extra burden on costs for the evaluating organisation, and on the respondents as well. Optimising the length of the survey can be achieved by careful piloting of the questionnaire to assess response rates.

A second aspect of efficiency is identifying the right sample size. The trade-off here is the cost of gathering responses against the statistical reliability of the findings: a large sample will improve the statistical reliability of the findings, but will usually be more expensive. Statistical tables show the relationships between sample size and reliability, with the main reliability measures being the confidence level desired (typically either 90 per cent, 95 per cent or 99 per cent) and the error margin acceptable at that confidence level (typically in the range +/- 1 per cent to +/- 5 per cent). For example, a random sample of 500 responses (normally distributed) will yield an error margin of +/- 4.3 per cent at the 95 per cent confidence level for an evenly distributed Yes/No question. Increasing the sample to 750 would reduce the error margin to +/- 3.5 per cent. The evaluator needs to weigh up the benefits of increased reliability (in this case reducing the error margin from 4.3 per cent to 3.5 per cent) against the cost of the larger sample. Smaller samples may be used for programmes used by small numbers of SMEs, and a sample of 300 respondents provides the same reliability as the previous example (+/-5 per cent at the 95 per cent confidence level) for a programme with 2,000 participants. The sample will need to be randomly drawn from the database of participants in each programme, and again key dimensions like business size, industry and location need to be benchmarked against the mix of these for all programme participants to ensure that the sample represents the population of SMEs that participated. Two examples of useful free online calculators which show the confidence and error margins for different sample sizes are available at www.raosoft.com and www.surveysystem.com.

FOCUS GROUPS

Focus groups usually consist of eight to 12 participants, with a skilled facilitator following a consistent set of questions across each group that is convened (for example, see Mole 2002). The groups need not be representative, and participants can be recruited with particular characteristics in mind. The focus group is not simply a brain storming session, but is focused on gathering in-depth information on a small number of issues (Krueger and Casey 2009, Morgan 1988). In a small business context, Blackburn and Stokes (2000: 44) have pointed to the potential of focus groups to contribute to understanding the 'motivations, rationales and experiences of small business owners'. A comprehensive guide to using focus groups (Krueger and Casey 2009) has been published by Sage Publications (www.sagepub.com), and other shorter guides are also available (for example, through the International Association for Public Participation, www.iap2.org).

Although focus groups can be used to explore survey questions in more depth, caution in interpreting the information is recommended as a focus group (by definition) will only represent a small subset of survey respondents. Rather than exploring survey questions, focus groups yield most value when they are used to test experiences, alternative scenarios and real or potential changes to programmes. Focus groups enable robust discussion (with present or future programme participants) of issues such as implementation methods, potential problems, perceived advantages and disadvantages, and options for improvement. Testing options for change through a focus group also means that programme leaders get to hear firsthand how users will receive suggested improvements, and this highly targeted feedback can greatly improve programme responsiveness (Gredler 1996: 83–100).

INTERVIEWS

Interviews can be an important part of understanding the effectiveness of a programme, but they should be used selectively and without expectations of statistical robustness; in fact they can complement and validate quantitative results (Mole 2002). Structured or semi-structured interviews can be used to seek out in-depth explanations of personal experience. For example, the evaluator can gain a valuable insight into what the programme feels like for the participants, what thoughts participants have about programme processes and outcomes, and what changes participants perceive in themselves as a result of the programme (Patton 1990). The richness of information provided by interviews means that they can also provide material for case studies (Kvale 1996: 98–105).

Interviews will generally be longer in duration than surveys, and they are usually more costly to complete; thus the number of interviews conducted need only be that which provides the necessary information (Kvale 1996: 98–105). Interviewees should be carefully selected for their suitability and to highlight particular aspects of the broader evaluation (for example, see Ahmad and Seet 2009, Mole 2002).

CASE STUDIES

A case study is a study of an individual entity's experience of a particular circumstance, which is enlightening for both for its 'uniqueness and commonality' (Stake 1995: xi–13). In the context of SME policy evaluation, case studies can present the findings from individual interviews and other selected data in a concise format; this provides a narrative that is easy for stakeholders (such as elected representatives, policymakers or other SME owners) to relate to. Case studies are widely used in promotional material and marketing campaigns.

Case studies are often presented using a common format and consistent structure, so they can illustrate different experiences against common characteristics. For example, each one of a series of case studies might report on the capabilities of the subject SMEs, followed by their use of support programmes, and rounding off with their own views of their future prospects and the role that the policy direction or programme might play. The common structure of each case study enables researchers to report on each of these aspects – giving cohesion across the set of case studies and enabling readers to see how SMEs in different circumstances responded to different stimuli. In designing the structure of the case studies, it is useful to consider the pattern of applications and outcomes that have emerged from other aspects of the evaluation.

Case studies can also provide unique insights into programme experiences. Bianchi and Winch (2009) document an approach to SME policy evaluation using case studies in which they examined the adverse effects of funding for rapid expansion of small businesses by comparing two case studies derived from direct experience, observation and interviews. The authors point out that:

> When compared with conventional approaches, such an analysis provides more, and different, insights for both entrepreneurs and other decision makers involved in drawing up and implementing policies for SME growth support. (Bianchi and Winch 2009: 170)

Putting the Evaluation Together

A good evaluation process will minimise the burden on respondents while gathering robust information at all necessary points. To achieve this, the information required can be targeted to different evaluation activities, putting the broad context questions into any baseline and follow-up surveys, and gathering specific information from participants through the more intensive interview, focus group and case study methods. During the data collection process, it is also important that the evaluator identifies and minimises any bias in their results (for discussion of research bias in relation to SMEs, see Curran 2000: 40).

Table 20.3 shows how tools might be selected to suit different evaluation purposes, with the grey shading linking suitable tools with purposes. For example, if the purpose of the evaluation is to support bids for further funding, it is useful to supplement the monitoring information with tangible evidence of

Table 20.3   Evaluation purposes and suitable tools

Evaluation purpose	Tools					
	Activity Measures	Satisfaction Feedback	Surveys	Focus Groups	Interviews	Case Studies
Monitoring & reporting						
Continuous improvement						
Re-funding						
Positive stories						
Relationship building						
Measuring outcomes						

outcomes from surveys and interviews. The emphasis on outcomes is generally not so important when an evaluation is seeking to either collate positive stories (for example, to encourage wider participation) or when the aim is to build relationships with delivery partners. It is important to emphasise here that evaluation is an iterative and dynamic exercise; there is no one approach, and the evaluator must take into account the best methods based on their own resources and research needs (Diez 2001, Brinkerhoff et al. 1983).

RECOGNISING THE LIMITS OF PARTICIPATIVE METHODS

Recognising the limitations and biases of the data provided by methods described above can help the evaluator avoid some pitfalls in interpretation. Linking cause and effect is perhaps the biggest challenge, reflected in the methodological issues of *additionality, deadweight* and *displacement* (Curran 2000). Additionality, discussed earlier, refers to net positive outcomes attributed reliably to a policy or programme. Deadweight refers to desired outcomes that would have resulted even if the policy or programme had not been initiated. Displacement occurs where, as a result of a policy or programme, other firms not involved are subjected to adverse consequences such as higher costs. Data from qualitative methods usually cannot prove additionality, as in principle additionality can only be measured using before-and-after research designs, and this has proved difficult in practice for SME policies and programmes (Wren and Storey 2002, Curran 2000, Storey 2000).

The problems of response bias, survivor bias and self-selection can also make evaluation using survey feedback difficult. Response bias occurs where one type of firm is more likely to complete feedback than another. For example, in many cases larger firms are more likely to respond to surveys than smaller firms, and firms in some industry sectors tend to respond more than firms in others. Survivor bias occurs in most programmes as firms which complete the programme are more likely to view the experience positively. Such biases can weaken the value of results where they attempt to disaggregate by firm size or industry. Self-selection occurs when a programme or policy favours firms with certain characteristics, making broader comparisons and generalisations difficult or impossible, or exaggerating the benefits of a programme compared to 'average' firms (Curran 2000, Wren and Storey 2002, OECD 2004).

Conclusion

This chapter has discussed the main challenges for SME policy and programme evaluations and reviewed some useful tools for conducting them. There are many challenges in evaluating SME policies, including lack of clarity in expectations and difficulties identifying causality, but there are tools that policymakers and programme administrators can use to address these challenges. This chapter has discussed a mix of evaluation tools, their strengths and weaknesses and how they can be combined to suit different purposes.

Evaluating SME policies and programmes can provide valuable insights into their outcomes, effectiveness and value. Often seen as an expensive burden on programme delivery, a well-designed approach to evaluation can be efficient, cost effective and useful to those involved in designing and delivering programmes. Judicious use of the right tools in the right context will help both policymakers and SMEs by reducing overall evaluation costs, and provide a sound basis for improving existing and subsequent programmes through the accumulation of documented experience and sharing best practice.

References

Ahmad, M.H. and Seet, P. 2009. Understanding business success through the lens of SME founder owners in Australia and Malaysia. *International Journal of Entrepreneurial Venturing*, 1(1), 72–87.

Barrett, R., Billington, L. and Neeson, R. 2004. Evaluating hands-on business assistance in the Latrobe Valley. *Australasian Journal of Regional Studies*, 10(2), 181–194.

Bartlett, J.E., Kotrlik, J.W. and Higgins, C.C. 2001. Organizational research: determining appropriate sample size in survey research. *Information Technology Learning and Performance Journal*, 19(1), 43–50.

Bianchi, C. and Winch, G.W. 2009. Supporting value creation in SMEs through capacity building and innovation initiatives: The danger of provoking unsustainable rapid growth. *International Journal of Entrepreneurial Venturing*, 1(2), 164–184.

Brinkerhoff, R.O., Brethower, D.M., Hluchyj, T. and Nowakowski, J.R. 1983. *Program Evaluation: A Practitioner's Guide for Trainers and Educators*. Boston: Kluwer-Nijhoff.

Blackburn, R. and Stokes, D. 2000. Breaking down the barriers: using focus groups to research small and medium sized enterprises. *International Small Business Journal*, 19(1), 44–67.

Curran, J. and Blackburn, R.A. 2001. *Researching the Small Enterprise*. London: Sage Publications.

Curran, J. 2000. What is small business policy in the UK for? Evaluation and assessing small business policies. *International Small Business Journal*, 18(3), 36–50.

Diez, M.A. 2001. The evaluation of regional innovation and cluster policies. *European Planning Studies*, 9(7), 907–923.

Donaldson, S. and Gooler, L.E. 2003. Theory-driven evaluation in action: lessons from a $20 million statewide work and health initiative. *Evaluation and Program Planning*, 26, 355–366.

Gredler, M.E. 1996. *Program Evaluation*. New Jersey: Prentice Hall.

Hall, J. and Jennings, E.T. 2006. *Using Best Practices to Inform Public Policy Decision Making*. Paper presented to the annual meeting of the American Political Science Association, Philadelphia, 31 August–3 September. Available at: http://citation.allacademic.com/meta/p_mla_apa_research_citation/1/5/1/9/2/pages151929/p151929-1.php [accessed 21 May 2011].

Hill, H. 2002. Old Policy Challenges for a New Administration: SMEs in Indonesia, in *The Role of SMEs in National Economies in East Asia*, edited by C. Harvie and B. Lee. Cheltenham: Edward Elgar, 158–175.

Krueger, R.A. and Casey, M.A. 2009. *Focus Groups: A Practical Guide for Applied Research*, 4th edition. Thousand Oaks, CA: Sage Publications.

Kvale, S. 1996. *An Introduction to Qualitative Research Interviewing*. Thousand Oaks, CA: Sage Publications.

Mole, K. 2002. Business advisers' impact on SMEs: an agency theory approach. *International Small Business Journal*, 20(2), 139–162.

Morgan, D.L. 1988. *Focus Groups as Qualitative Research*, Qualitative Research Methods Series 16, London: Sage.

Nardi, P.M. 2006. *Doing Survey Research: A Guide to Quantitative Methods*, 2nd edition. Boston, MA: Pearson Education.

Nishimura, J. and Okamuro, H. 2011. R&D productivity and the organization of cluster policy: an empirical evaluation of the Industrial Cluster Project in Japan. *The Journal of Technological Transfer*, 36(2), 117–144.

Organisation for Economic Co-operation and Development (OECD) 2004. *Evaluation of SME Policies and Programmes. Background report to the 2nd OECD conference of Ministers responsible for small and medium sized enterprises.* [Online] Available at: http://www.oecd.org/dataoecd/6/5/31919294.pdf [accessed 18 May 2011].

Patton, M.Q. 1990. *Qualitative Evaluation and Research Methods*. Thousand Oaks, CA: Sage Publications.

Robson, P.J.A., Wijbenga, F. and Parker, F.C. 2009. Entrepreneurship and policy: challenges and directions for future research. *International Small Business Journal*, 27(5), 531–535.

Schaper, M.T. 2008. Creating independent advocates for entrepreneurs within government: Some reflections on the small business commissioner model. *Journal of Enterprising Culture*, 16(3), 299–309.

Stake, R.E. 1995. *The Art of Case Study Research*, Thousand Oaks, CA: Sage Publications.

Stevenson, L. and Lundström, A. 2001. *Patterns and trends in Entrepreneurship/ SME Policy and Practice in Ten Economies*. Voume 3 of the Entrepreneurship for the Future Series, Sweden. [Online] Available at: http://www.donner enviedentreprendre.com/documentation/IMG/pdf/Volume_3_Chapitre_1.pdf [accessed 3 May 2011].

Storey, D.J. 2000. Six Steps to Heaven: Evaluating the Impact of Public Policies to Support Small Businesses in Developed Economies, in *Handbook of Entrepreneurship*, edited by H. Landström and D. L. Sexton. Oxford: Blackwells, 176–194.

Vega, A., Chiasson, M. and Brown, D. 2011. *SME Innovation Policy Evaluation: A Balanced Approach*. DRUID 2011 on Innovation, Strategy and Structure – Organisations, Institutions, Systems and Regions, Copenhagen, Denmark, June 15–17 2011. [Online] Available at: http://druid8.sit.aau.dk/druid/acc_papers/lx5dsdsd8gmkqlsta7sbjsc9a6h6.pdf [accessed 14 August 2011].

Wren, C. and Storey, D. 2002. Evaluating the effect of soft business support upon small firm performance. *Oxford Economic Papers*, 54(2), 334–365.

Index